THE MAN WHO MADE NEWS

James Gordon Bennett

Other books by Oliver Carlson

HEARST: LORD OF SAN SIMEON (1936)
(In collaboration with Ernest Sutherland Bates)

BRISBANE: A CANDID BIOGRAPHY (1937)

A MIRROR FOR CALIFORNIANS (1941)

THE MAN
WHO MADE NEWS

James Gordon Bennett

OLIVER CARLSON

DUELL, SLOAN AND PEARCE

NEW YORK

COPYRIGHT, 1942, BY
OLIVER CARLSON

first edition

PRINTED IN THE UNITED STATES OF AMERICA

To Bea

Contents

CONTENTS

Introduction

SUPPOSE, as you picked up your favorite morning or evening newspaper, you discovered that there were:

    no banner heads,

    no photographs,

    no graphs, charts, or cuts,

    no news dispatches from the far-flung corners of the world, by the great news-gathering agencies or by foreign correspondents,

    no interviews with famous or notorious characters,

    no reports on schools, societies, or conventions,

    no church news,

    no weather reports,

    no display advertisements,

    no columnists,

    no sports section,

    no society page,

    no financial section,

    no woman's page,

    and no comic strips or cartoons.

"Impossible!" you say, "for if all these were missing there would be no newspaper."

So it would seem.

And yet not one of these features was to be found in the newspapers read by George Washington, Thomas Jefferson, James Madison, or any of the founding fathers of this nation. In fact, only one or two of these modern newspaper essentials had begun to appear in the press before Andrew Jackson concluded his second term as President of the United States on March 3, 1837.

The press of our forefathers, up to a short century ago, was as far removed from the dailies which we read as is the lumbering Conestoga wagon of the 1840's from today's streamliner or multi-motored airplane.

The story of that amazing evolution in American (and world) journalism is, in large measure, the story of a tall, gaunt, cross-eyed, sardonic Scotsman named James Gordon Bennett.

When Bennett appeared upon our journalistic horizon in the early 1820's, newspapers were essentially the same as they had been in the days of Benjamin Franklin a half century earlier. But when Bennett died in 1872, almost every device, both mechanical and journalistic, which we are familiar with today had been invented or tried. He found the daily press dull, drab, barren, and catering to a limited audience. He left it newsy, sensational, fighting desperately to cut off seconds in its delivery of up-to-the-minute news to its readers. The press was no longer the exclusive organ of small mercantile or political cliques. Its new life hinged on mass circulation and mass support.

To Bennett, and to Bennett alone, America owes a deep debt of gratitude for having broken the chain of tradition which tied the daily press to the tail of political parties, cliques, or ambitious seekers for the spoils and power of public office.

After fifteen years of apprenticeship in the then current school of journalism, Bennett broke boldly with the past and set out to create a daily paper that would be, first and foremost, a *news*paper. This revolutionary act on his part brought down upon him the scorn and contempt of his fellow editors. It brought hatred from small-minded politicians. It brought censure, contumely, and reprisals from short-sighted business men, shady speculators, and the stand-patters of church and Society. But Bennett's action also brought him readers—more and ever more readers—who grabbed eagerly and anxiously for each new issue of his *New York Herald*. It made his paper the most powerful and widely read journal in the United States, and for a time, in the whole world. It made Bennett the ace journalist and editor of America for a period of more than thirty-five years.

In the face of competition from such giants of journalism as Bryant, Greeley, Raymond, Dana, and Park Benjamin, Bennett managed to keep in the lead, year after year. Henry J. Raymond, the founder of the *New York Times,* expressed the feelings of all his fellow editors when he remarked, "It would be worth my while, sir, to give a million dollars, if the Devil would come and tell me every evening, as he does Bennett, what the people of New York would like to read about next morning."

The story of James Gordon Bennett is an early nineteenth-century tale of "life begins at forty"—a tale as stirring as the times themselves. But most of all, it is the story of the man who transformed the daily organs of the printed word into organs of information instead of mere opinion. It was of this new press, as molded by Bennett, that Henry Ward Beecher spoke when he said that the modern newspaper was "a window through which men look out on all that is going on in the world. . . . It is an ever-unfolding encyclopaedia; an unbound book forever issuing and never finishing."

James Gordon Bennett was for over three decades the most generally hated and most universally read editor in America. But even his most bitter critics would have agreed upon one thing, namely: that he more than any other man deserved in full measure the title—THE MAN WHO MADE NEWS.

PART I

EUROPEAN HERITAGE

Prologue

ONE DAY, when he was twenty-four years old, James Gordon Bennett, strolling down the streets of Aberdeen, chanced to meet an acquaintance whom he had not seen for several months. After the usual exchange of greetings, Bennett asked his friend what he was doing.

"I am going to America, Bennett."

"To America?"

Bennett stood silent for a moment, then to his friend's amazement declared, "William, my dear fellow, I'll go with you. I want to see the place where Franklin was born."

He was as good as his word. Passage was booked. Letters were written to friends and family. He made his rounds saying farewell to old schoolmates and acquaintances. He packed his few belongings. He tramped up and down the cobblestone streets of Aberdeen, taking one last look at the city which had brought him to maturity.

The day of departure came all too quickly.

"The vessel was to sail in the evening. All morning, up to noon of that day, I spent on the banks of the Dee, where it unites with the ocean. It was a beautiful, clear day. There was the 'Brig of Balgounie' so celebrated in the Life of Byron, which every Sunday afternoon I used to cross and re-cross, lingering over the parapet, watching the eddies of the deep blue water, and gazing on the picturesque scenes above and below."

That evening the moon hung full in the heavens. A gentle breeze began lapping at the sails. Night was closing in on the Old World, as slowly and quietly the ship left the lights of Aberdeen behind and headed out to sea.

3

1. Banffshire Lad

T<small>HE</small> <small>LITTLE</small> world of James Bennett, and his younger brother Cosmo, for the first dozen years of their life at no time extended so much as fifteen miles in any direction from their father's farm house. James Gordon Bennett was born, September 1, 1795, in Old Town (later called New Mill) Keith, in Banffshire. The little hamlet seemingly lay as far off the beaten track of trade and commerce to Scotland's new and growing cities, as did Scotland itself to the hustling, bustling world of London and the Continent. Those northerly shires of Banff, Elgin, and Inverness were little more than names to the good folk of Edinburgh and Glasgow. Even to the citizens of Aberdeen, fifty-five miles to the south of Keith, the fertile glens, the well-stocked streams, and the forest or heather-covered mountains of Banffshire were then largely terra incognita.

Although the soil was good and the climate not too severe, the people of Banffshire were mostly very poor, very industrious, and very pious. James's father was one of the few independent farmers whose standard of life was considered well above the average. Nearly all the land in the region was owned by the Earl of Fife, whose great residence, Duff House, not far from Keith, was overshadowed only by the neighboring princely estate of the Gordons at Gordon Castle.

The Bennett home, which was large and spacious only in relation to the miserable huts of the mass of the shire's population, left an indelible imprint on the mind of the boy. Breakfast was always the same. Like every other meal, except for holidays, it was served in the kitchen. His mother, or one of the maids at the farm, would slowly stir the oatmeal and salt into the boiling water, while father and the children waited eagerly, horn or wooden spoon in hand, for the thick hot porridge.

Dinner was the big meal of the day, with family, relatives, and hired hands all seated at the same table, although a chalk line extending across it at the upper end divided the family proper from the menials. Another rule, always adhered to, was that only the head of the house was to wash his hands before taking his place at the table. Members of the family, relatives, and the "hinds" (hired hands) were all seated according to a definite pattern depending upon age, relationship, status of work performed or length of service.

After Bennett père had asked for blessings, the menfolk put on their hats (both summer and winter) and the serious business of eating got under way. "Broth was usually the first dish," remarks a social historian of the period, adding, "From a large family broth-pot, in form resembling the Roman camp-kettle, the liquor was transferred to a boyne or wooden tub, and from thence conveyed in timber cogs to those who dined. The cog was afterward laid aside unwashed, since the application of water was supposed to rend and ruin it; but each member of the household kept his own cog and spoon and bicker, which were severally inscribed with his selected mark, or the initials of his name."

To the hungry boy, dinner, especially during the holidays, was high adventure. He used to picture his father as the cool and stately commander of a ship, with mother as first mate. Seated at her husband's right, she directed the movements of the servants with the steaming dishes of meat and vegetables, the removal of empty plates, and by appropriate nudges would indicate to her husband the honored guests or relatives not receiving due attention.

The meal invariably closed with cheese and pudding. Once again father said grace, after which drinks were served, toasts given, songs sung, while tongues wagged and gossip spread. Meanwhile the snuff-mill made its regular rounds, leaving an ever-mounting pile of evidence, on floor and table, on shirt and waistcoat and skirt, of indulgence in a habit "at once absurd, pernicious, and wasteful."

A few years before James Bennett was born, the British government had rescinded its decrees forbidding the use of kilt or tartan, so once again men wore skirts as of old. And just as the kilt was the symbol of manhood, the kirch, a linen cap was the inevitable headgear of the married woman, and a ribbon called the snood symbolized the maiden. "But," remarked the Reverend Alexander Stewart, "if a damsel was so unfortunate as to lose pretensions to the name of maiden, without acquiring a right to that of matron, she was neither permitted to wear the emblem of virgin purity, the snood, nor advanced to the grave dignity of the coif or kirch."

The Bennetts were Catholics, and as such were held suspect by the community at large. To be sure, many of the harsh laws and edicts against the Catholics which had been laid down at an earlier date by both the Scottish and English governments, had been recently withdrawn or modified, but there still remained a heavy residue of fear and suspicion of all things and persons tainted with Catholicism. To be charged with having married a "Popish wife" or of being "irregularly married by a priest" brought in its wake a heavy toll of social ostracism. To maintain one's Catholic faith in the face of a population so overwhelmingly Presbyterian, required, often, both physical as well as moral courage.

The stern cold doctrines of Calvin were assimilated by John Knox about 1547. Knox returned to his native land in 1555 to begin his crusade against the ancient faith. Two years later he organized the Solemn League and Covenant as the instrument through which the Pope and his Church were to be driven out of Scotland. That there were both corruption and indolence among the priesthood was a well-known fact to most of the inhabitants of the country. They rallied in great numbers to the banner of John Knox, and when he, in his sermon at Perth in 1559, urged his restless adherents in a burst of fury and hatred to let loose their passions upon the institutions of Papacy, there followed a whirlwind of destruction, as his frenzied followers attacked, looted, and burned churches and monasteries.

The following year, in 1560, there came into being the Established Church of Scotland which gave to the people a form of worship and creed somber as the brown hills, cold as the northern winds, narrow as the mountain streams, and barren as a rock-bound shore. The milk of human kindness was sieved through a blotter of theological dogmas. All that actually did drip through was due to the basic goodness of the people themselves and those few basic principles of Christianity which have withstood nearly two thousand years of abuse, zealotry, or corruption.

It is of this narrow, sectarian theology that Buckle was speaking when, three-quarters of a century ago, he asserted: "Of the clergy and of the people generally, it must be admitted, that in Scotland there is more bigotry, more superstition, and a more thorough contempt for religion of others, than there is in France. . . . Whoever has traveled in Scotland with sufficient attention to observe the ideas and opinions of the people, and whoever will look into Scotch theology and read the history of the Scotch Kirk, and the proceedings of the Scotch Assemblies and Consistories, will see how little the country has benefited by its religion, and how wide an interval there is between its intolerant spirit and the natural tendencies of the Protestant Reformation."

As the covenanting spirit spread throughout the land, the older faith gave way before it. At the dawn of the eighteenth century, Catholicism was largely confined to the more remote Highlands of northern and western Scotland, where the people still spoke Gaelic and the clans were still all-powerful.

It was the people from the Highlands who rallied to the banner of Prince Charles in 1745. The defeat of his forces at Culloden brought in its wake the destruction of the clans. More than a thousand highlanders were deported to North America and the Catholic Church was put under the ban more rigorously than ever. The result, according to the *Catholic Encyclopaedia,* was that there remained, by 1780, not more than 25,000 Catholics in the whole of Scotland, "and of these not more than twenty possessed lands and property worth over one hundred pounds per year in income."

James Gordon Bennett's father and grandfather were of the handful of Scottish Catholics not reduced to the ragged edge of poverty. But they and their families, though on friendly terms with their neighbors, were nevertheless always suspect. And if the flame of religious intolerance burned constantly in the regions all about them, their own flame of devotion to the church of their ancestors burned even stronger.

Day after day, year after year, James and his younger brother were fed an unending diet of Catholic ritual and theology, augmented by harrowing tales of persecution, which linked the heroic period of Scottish history with Catholic supremacy. England was the villain of every tale. England, the boy was constantly reminded, had, with force, bribery, or deceit, destroyed the old order of things: the old clans, the old customs, the old language, and the old religion.

Seared deep into the soul of the boy by this early environment were scars of prejudice against all things British which no amount of study and travel in later years ever fully destroyed.

By the law of the land, James had to be educated in the public school of the parish. As early as 1496, a law contemplated making school attendance compulsory, at least on the eldest sons of "barrenes and freholders," from the age of six or nine, until "competentlie founded in Latin and jure." Seventy years later, a School Act provided that the "youth be instructed in gude manners." This was further enlarged upon by the order of the Privy Council in 1616 which stipulated that every child be educated in "religion, secular learning and civility." Scotland, despite its poverty, was determined to foster public education.

A close and intimate relationship existed between the Kirk and the school. By Act of Parliament schoolmasters were obliged to subscribe to the Confession of Faith and Formula. The Church itself maintained a constant vigil over both the schools and the teachers. It was forever sending special committees to check against possible "negligence, error or immorality," or calling before its local presbytery the schoolmasters to "take trial of their sufficiency and qualification."

The school at Keith, where James Bennett and his fellow pupils had to be at their benches at seven o'clock each morning, and from which they trudged homeward at six o'clock each afternoon, was neither better nor worse than those scattered throughout the smaller parishes of Scotland. The schoolroom itself was both dingy and noisome. For some strange reason it was almost invariably located at the edge of the parish burial ground, thus giving to the low-roofed, ill-ventilated room a perpetual odor of the surrounding graves.

During the long, cold, winter months, school began at sunrise and ended at sunset. Fuel had to be provided by the pupils who, from October to April, came laden with peat or coal or timber.

The curriculum of those days consisted primarily of the *ars grammatica*. This was the most constant and fundamental subject of instruction, which, like an all-purpose glove, so it was thought, fitted everyone, irrespective of circumstance, capacity, or inclination no matter what the age at which he was to leave school or the profession he was to follow. Latin and Greek—these were the basis of every school curriculum, to which was added a heavy dose of the doctrines of John Knox, and a smattering of English and other subjects.

"Learners," says the historian Rogers, "were expected to master the Latin syntax from rules presented in the Latin tongue. And while thus school books were composed in a language unknown to the beginners, few schoolmasters had yet attained the art of communicating knowledge otherwise than by force. To every pupil the teacher was consequently an object of actual terror. By wielding the rod mercilessly he maintained a detested pre-eminence. Claiming an abject submission to his authority, he repelled without reason, and enforced order without justice."

Many years later, Bennett wrote: "The first book I recollect anything of was the Scriptures. In the school in which I was taught to read, the Scriptures were the principal book. The history of the patriarchs, of the prophets, of the apostles, of the martyrs, of the Son of Man himself—is as familiar to me as the expression of my mother's face, and the light of my mother's eye. My imagination, my fancy, my taste, my morals were formed on the perusal of the Scriptures. The literature of the Greek and Roman classics—that even of England and of Scotland, was a study subsequent to that of the Scriptures. In the day, and in the country in which I was a boy, the Scriptures were the text book—the reading book—the Vade Mecum—the companion of Saturday night and of Sunday all day. I was educated a Catholic, in the midst of a Protestant community—yet both Catholic and Protestant breathed the moral atmosphere of the Scriptures. My parents, my schoolmaster, my associates—all venerated the book of heaven alike."

In fact, it was this heavy diet of the Bible, which he received as a schoolboy, that served him in good stead as a journalist, for he remarked: "My literary and moral tastes are all founded on the striking passages in the Scriptures; and I do verily believe, that to this early habit of reading the Bible at school, am I indebted for that force, brevity, spirit, and peculiarity which makes the style of the *Herald* so popular with the uncontaminated masses of a community who are yet imbued with the spirit and literature of the Bible."

Young Bennett was an apt pupil because he had good memory— an indispensable factor at a time when education consisted largely of learning how to repeat word for word and phrase for phrase what the textbook or the teacher ordained. During his first year at school he had to learn "the Latin names of everything on earth and in heaven." Then came the long weary grind in grammar, syntax, and etymology. For hours on end he and his classmates would recite the rules or the sentences to be memorized, while the cold-eyed, shirt-frayed, overworked, and underpaid schoolmaster goaded his hated underlings.

In due time James became familiar with the Latin poets: Virgil, Terence, Lucan, Horace, and Juvenal. He read Cicero's *Select Orations,* Ovid's *Metamorphoses,* and Caesar's *Commentaries.*

While all about him the world was moving and changing at a pace hitherto unheard of and history was being made, he was being steeped in the sayings and doings of a world that had vanished nearly two thousand years earlier. Thus, both at school, by virtue of its curriculum, and at home, by virtue of his father's continuous discussions of the "good old days," the boy had no chance to know about, or give thought to, the world in which he lived.

In later years Bennett regaled his American friends with tales of his early school days. These invariably dealt with the floggings administered to unruly or tired boys. Most commonplace weapon for the schoolteacher was the tawse—a strap made of soft pliable leather cut into thin strips at one end—which, when applied vigorously to the outstretched palm, was very painful. Corporal punishment was also frequently inflicted elsewhere.

A fellow townsman of Bennett told how, after being away for

many years, he returned to visit the school of his boyhood days. The schoolmaster failed to recognize his erstwhile pupil, saying, "You seem to know me very well, but I have no remembrance of ever having seen your face before."

"That is quite understandable," came the reply, "for you were much better acquainted, sir, with my other end."

School days also meant games, some of which are as familiar to the American boys of the 1940's as they were to the Scottish lads of 1800. Leap-frog was always popular, as was top-spinning, prisoner's base, and marbles. The boys also enjoyed shinty, cross-tig, and smuggle-the-geg. Swimming, too, was indulged in during the summer. But there seemed to be no skating, skiing, tobogganing, or sleigh-riding during the long winter months.

Even as a boy Bennett enjoyed walking. Whenever time and the weather permitted he would wander off across the fields, sweet with the odor of green grass and white clover; or follow the cheerful Isla, down past the Loggie Pot, where the older boys liked to swim. Near by was the small cove used by the flax dressers to bleach their linens. He loved the bubbling brae, and knew its every twist and turn for several miles. With the other boys he fished in the trouting ground at the head of the mill stream. At one long-remembered spot he and another schoolboy fought a furious battle to the excited cries of their schoolmates. At another, where the little Burn of Kimmartie, darting out from a tiny tree-filled ravine, mingled its waters with the Isla, he loved to sit dangling his feet in the clear cold water, sniffing the sweet breezes, and dreaming the dreams that pop up from nowhere and vanish as swiftly.

Ripening into his early teens, James, with a head full of notions about Scottish history, sought out every available landmark in the vicinity to gaze upon with awe and reverence. Banffshire, though small, could boast of many historic spots. There was Cullen, where a fierce encounter between the Scots and the Norse had taken place in 960 A.D. And at Mortlach was a sculptured stone said to commemorate the victory by Malcolm II over the Norse in 1010 A.D. A dozen miles to the south of Keith was the imposing ruin of Huntley (Strathbogie) Castle, where had lived and reigned for many generations the Earls of Huntley, most powerful chieftains

of northern Scotland. Not far from that old ruin were traces of
the northernmost point ever reached by the Romans when they
had occupied Britain.

At Elgin, just a few miles north of Keith, were the ruins of the
great Cathedral, long known as the Lanthorn of the North which
had been founded in 1224.

All about the shire were spots commemorative of the long and
bitter strife after the Reformation. From 1624 to 1645, Banffshire
had been an armed camp. The Roman Catholics, fighting under
the Marquis of Huntley, had worsted the Protestants under the Earl
of Argyle—but to no avail.

Bennett's father was determined that his sons should be trained
to carry forward the faith of the Catholic Church. James, the eldest,
when he reached the age of fifteen, was to be sent to Aberdeen,
there to study at a Catholic Seminary.

If the boy couldn't quite make the grade that would carry him
into the priesthood, there was always the opportunity of following
the profession suggested by the farmer, who, accompanied by his
young son, waited on a haughty schoolmaster to ask that the boy
be taken on as a pupil.

"What do you intend to make of the lad?" asked the teacher
loftily.

"Well," said the farmer, "if he gets Grace we'll mak him a
minister."

"Ah," said the teacher, "and if he gets no Grace, what then?"

"Then," said the farmer, looking firmly at the pedagogue, "he
maun juist become a schulemaister, like yersel."

2. *Young Man in an Old World*

WHEN other boys of fifteen were already settling down to married life (you could marry in Scotland at fourteen in those days) or to the routine of a farmer's life, James was leaving for Aberdeen to study under learned men. A great new world was about to open before him.

On the day of his departure, long before the sun was up, the whole Bennett family was busy packing, talking, laughing, crying. Father, who hadn't been to Aberdeen for ten years, was taking his son to the small Catholic seminary—Blair's College—where James was to study for the next four years.

The sixty-mile journey to Aberdeen, in 1810, took four days— four days during which the stern and pious father plied his son with advice and moral and religious texts.

Aberdeen with its 40,000 inhabitants seemed immense to the boy. New Mill, after all, had only 136 inhabitants, while the whole of Keith could muster only 800. The giant four-story buildings, the busy streets, the shop windows filled with a multitude of goods, the wharves piled high with boxes, barrels, and crates; the hundreds of fishermen's boats and the scores of larger ships in the harbor; the great fish market—these were but a few of the amazing things in this new and greater world. James gasped at them all in awe and admiration.

But the city, for all its enlightenment, shared with the small villages that all-pervading gloom which the Kirk imposed upon the whole people each Sabbath. Parks were closed. Amusements of every kind came to a standstill. The window blinds remained undrawn. The streets, normally so busy, were deserted except for the folk going to and from church. To be found going out for a stroll, or a swim, or to stop to discourse with friends upon the street on a Sunday, brought prompt public disapproval and put one in the category of "Sabbath-breakers."

Blair's College was small and insignificant as compared with the two larger and older colleges—King's and Marishal—which were soon joined as the University of Aberdeen. But for all its limitations, Blair opened up a new universe to the young Banffshire lad. His teachers were abler men than the schoolmaster at Keith. They did not follow the crude system of pedagogy or the narrow course of study prevalent in the grammar schools. In addition to courses in Greek and Latin, James studied French, History, Geography, Bookkeeping, Logic, Church History, and General Science.

He was an eager student, and the four years he spent at the small college, which looked down on the banks of the Dee from heather-clad hills, were happy ones. Of the school, Bennett wrote: "Our teachers mixed in all our sports—took part in every play—and would go down with us to the river, undress like the boys, plunge into the clear water, and swim away like ducks among the whole group. In music, dancing, playing, swimming, our teachers mingled with us just like brothers on a footing of perfect equality. It was only during the hours of study that the difference of pupil and preceptor was visible.

"Oh, those happy, happy days when I studied Virgil in the morning, played ball in the afternoon, and swam through the warm translucent waves, just as the sun receded from the eye, beneath the high dark mountains of another land."

The world of letters also became meaningful to Bennett at this time. Scotland had just become—largely through the medium of the *Edinburgh Review*—the center of British literary criticism. The *Review,* founded in 1803 by Sydney Smith and Francis Jeffrey, set a new standard for periodicals. It was liberal in politics—but not too liberal. Yet so outstanding did it become that it forced the whole English-speaking world to pay homage to Scottish criticism.

Sydney Smith, a contributor to the *Review* until 1827, was eminent both as a scholar and as a churchman. Perhaps the most apt description of Smith was that made in a letter by young Thomas Babington Macaulay who wrote that it was Smith's misfortune to have chosen a profession at once above and below him. "Zeal would have made him a prodigy; formality and bigotry would have made him a bishop; but he could neither rise to the duties of his order, nor stoop to its degradations."

Lord Francis Jeffrey, the guiding spirit of the *Review* for nearly thirty years, whose pronouncements opened and closed so many literary careers, amazed those who met him for the first time. He was full of jokes and light table-talk which seemed out of place in a learned editor of that day. In appearance he was anything but prepossessing; a short swarthy man with black wiry hair standing in ragged bristly clumps about his head, and with a delicate kind of sneer forever hovering about his lips. Like most other great editors in those days, his penmanship was atrocious and caused no end of trouble for his printers. Even his good friend and editorial associate, Sydney Smith, often failed to decipher his scribble and on one occasion wrote:

"My Dear Jeffrey:
"We are much obliged by your letter, and should be still more so were it legible. I have tried to read it from left to right, and Mrs. Sydney from right to left, and we neither of us can decipher a single word of it."

It was Jeffrey's scathing review of a thin volume of poems—*Hours of Idleness,* by Lord Byron, which filled that author with "rage and resistance and redress, but not dispondency and dispair." Instead of being deterred from further writing, Byron declared, "I was bent on falsifying their raven predictions, and determined to show them, croak as they would, that it was not the last time they should hear from me."

True to his word, Byron came back with his *English Bards and Scotch Reviewers,* which set the whole English literary world back on its heels and launched Byron on the road to fame.

Bennett and his college friends, while standing in the greatest awe of men like Jeffrey, were at the same time delighted to quote the more juicy sections of Byron's satire, and especially the following:

A man must serve his time to every trade
Save censure—critics all are ready made.

Take hackneyed jokes from Miller, got by rote,
With just enough of learning to misquote;
A mind well skilled to find or forge a fault;
A turn for punning, call it Attic salt;

To Jeffrey go, be silent and discreet,
His pay is just ten sterling pounds per sheet:
Fear not to lie, 'twill seem a sharper hit;
Shrink not from blasphemy, 'twill pass for wit;
Care not for feeling—pass your proper jest,
And stand a critic, hated yet caressed.

Lord Byron became quite a hero for Aberdeen's young intelligentsia. They formed a literary club—to which Bennett belonged—and held their meetings in the same small room of the Aberdeen grammar school that Byron had attended as a boy from 1795 to 1798.

It was at this literary club that Bennett first came to know well the poems of Robert Burns, the novels of Dr. Tobias Smollett—the father of Scottish fictionists—James Boswell's *Life of Samuel Johnson,* and Scott's *Lay of the Last Minstrel, Lady of the Lake, Marmion,* and the *Vision of Don Roderick.*

Meanwhile someone had placed in young Bennett's hands a copy of Thomas Paine's *Age of Reason,* as well as writings of Voltaire and Rousseau. The boy, who had long been revolted by the narrow and dogmatic attitude of the Church of Scotland, now began to see flaws and shortcomings in the Catholic Church as well.

It was a period of severe soul-searching for the eighteen-year-old-student. He found he could discuss this crucial matter frankly with only one or two intimate friends. He determined that he could not dedicate his life to the Church. Many months were to pass before James could summon enough courage to notify his father of this fact. Perplexed and confused, he would wander for hours along the banks of the Dee, there to "pour out my regrets into its gentle ripples, that I had not lived in the dark ages, when there was only one opinion and one religion to believe."

Doubts, once born and given wing, came back with greater frequency. Bennett tried prayer to drive away the doubts which were constantly assailing his mind, but to no avail. A crisis was at hand. The more he read, the more he thought, the more he argued—the more certain he became that, to quote his own words, "the progress of truth and knowledge had broken to pieces all the ridiculous superstitions of the church of Rome, without affecting a single moral principle which I had received in the course of my early instruction. With the sacred document in my hand, and all history spread out before me, I would not submit to bigotry, either Catholic or Protestant, even at that early age. I went to the sources of true religion, and drank of the pure stream, uncontaminated by priest or prelates, parsons or minister; and as long as we have these sacred volumes in full circulation here below, defiance may alike be set to the bigots of Catholicity or of Protestantism."

Thereafter, and to the end of his days, Bennett maintained a position of religious independence, good-naturedly tolerating the many new and unique creeds he encountered in the United States. On the other hand, he never missed a chance to draw a bead on the Church of his forefathers for its bigotry, intolerance, and interference with secular affairs.

"Religion—true religion," he wrote, "consists not in eating and drinking—not in high salaries—not in hanging around the apron strings of rich old women—not in presuming to judge the opinions of others beyond what their acts will justify. Neither does true religion—nor real Christianity consist in believing the dogmas of any church—or the *ipse dixit* of any man. The Bible is before me. Have I not a right to read that book—to draw out from it religious opinions—and to create a belief and a church of my own?"

Bennett's strong dislike of the Catholic Church was also in some measure based upon the fact that his younger brother Cosmo, to whom he was deeply attached, and whom their father had sent to the College of Angelites to train for the priesthood, died at the age of twenty-three from the rigors imposed upon him by the Church.

When James visited his family in 1838, his sister showed him letters which Cosmo had written to the family. To the family's astonishment, Bennett, upon reading the letters, exhibited uncontrolled grief and wrath. He stamped up and down the house red-eyed from weeping and mute with rage, while his sister frantically followed at his heels begging him to exert self-control. At last he paused and addressed her with cold calculated calm: "Do not be surprised at my conduct, sister. No one can understand the loss of my brother but myself. You loved him as a brother—mother as a son—but I always looked upon him as my confidential associate. . . . Our hearts, and thoughts and feelings had grown up together from nothingness to deep and abiding impulse. For the negligence that led to his death, my holy mother, the Church, must suffer some, and by my hands! See if she don't!"

James Gordon Bennett, usually so loquacious about himself, for some strange reason has left us very few clues as to what he did between the spring of 1814, when he left college, and the time he sailed for North America five years later.

We do know that during this period Bennett's first article was published. It appeared in a small Aberdeen periodical immediately after the Battle of Waterloo. And the subject of his writing was Napoleon Bonaparte—one of his heroes whose life and activities he had studied feverishly. Bennett, who read French well, frequently secured copies of French newspapers, and eagerly followed the newspaper reports of Napoleon's activities. If the young editor-to-be read the issues of the *Moniteur,* from the time Napoleon escaped from Elba to the day he reached Paris, he must have been amazed by its rapid change in attitude.

The first announcement read: "The monster has escaped from the place of his banishment; and he has run away from Elba!" Thereafter the *Moniteur's* daily reports on the situation appeared in the sequence indicated:

Second. "The Corsican dragoon (L'Orge) has landed at Cape Juan."

Third. "The tiger has shown himself at Gap. The troops are advancing on all sides to arrest his progress. He will conclude his miserable adventure by becoming a wanderer among the mountains; he cannot possibly escape."

Fourth. "The monster has really advanced as far as Grenoble, we know not to what treachery to ascribe it."

Fifth. "The tyrant is actually at Lyons. Fear and terror seize all at his appearance."

Sixth. "The usurper has ventured to approach the capital to within sixty hours' march."

Seventh. "Bonaparte is advancing by forced marches; but it is impossible he can reach Paris."

Eighth. "Napoleon will arrive under the walls of Paris tomorrow."

Ninth. "The Emperor Napoleon is at Fontainebleau."

Tenth. "Yesterday evening his Majesty the Emperor made his public entry, and arrived at the Tuilleries—nothing can exceed the universal joy!"

If young Bennett was not impressed with such reporting, at least, in the face of it, he clung tenaciously to his ever-growing respect for the career of journalism. Often he recalled a statement of the little Corsican which he ran across in those years: "A journalist! That means a grumbler, a censurer, a giver of advice, a regent to sovereigns, a tutor of nations! Four hostile newspapers are more to be dreaded than a hundred thousand bayonets."

During those last years in his native land, Bennett traveled extensively throughout Scotland. He visited every national shrine, every battlefield, every spot hallowed by a thousand years of war and conquest. At the same time he commenced the study of economics and philosophy. He read Thomas Reid's *Inquiry Into the Human Mind,* David Hume's *Treatise on Human Nature,* and Adam Smith's *Wealth of Nations.*

As Bennett became more deeply appreciative of the contribution to human knowledge made by his fellow countrymen, he was shocked to discover how many of them carried on their work in the face of overwhelming economic hardship.

He learned that James Tytler, one of the early editors of the *Encyclopaedia Britannica,* was unable to provide himself and family with even the bare necessities of life while engaged upon this important editorial work. He learned that the historian and critic, Robert Heron, died at the age of forty-three from a fever contracted while confined to a debtors' prison. He discovered that Smollett had died in want at the age of fifty; that the poet Robert Fergusson "breathed out his spirit on the straw-covered floor of an Edinburgh workhouse." And he learned that even Bobby Burns, in the delirium of his approaching death, was haunted by the dread that a merciless and hard-fisted merchant, to whom he owed a few pounds, would fulfill his threat to have him sent to a debtors' prison.

Bennett was so moved by Scott's *Rob Roy* that he determined to visit the region forthwith. It was his first visit to the bustling city of Glasgow on the Clyde, which had just replaced Edinburgh as the most populous city in Scotland.

"I remember," reminisced Bennett, "I remember to this very hour every nook and corner of that enchanting place so beautifully described by Walter Scott in *Rob Roy*.

"It was about the period when that novel was first published, and a spirit of enthusiasm carried me to the very spot to see the scenes so accurately described by the then mighty unknown.

"I also looked through the Saut-market, with all the adoration of youth for the creations of genius. I thought, in my youthful fancy, I saw Bailie Nicol Jarvie in every respectable-looking merchant that toddled down that singular street. One man in particular caught my youthful eye. I gazed upon him with delight.

"'Oh,' said I, half aloud, 'that is the Bailie outright.'

"'Laddie,' said he, 'are you mad—you look scart—what's the matter wi' ye?'

"I blushed, and begged his pardon.

"'I thought,' said I, 'you looked like a friend of mine!'

"From that place I went to the Broomielaw, I think it was called. There was Nelson's pillar, with the capital shoved to one side by a thunderbolt. It was on a lovely Saturday afternoon. The Clyde was transparent as a mirror, and here I first saw a steamboat, and could hardly believe my own eyes.

"On Sunday I had an invitation to hear the celebrated Dr. Chalmers, who then preached in Glasgow. I went to hear him. What a crowd! What eloquence! What piety! What deep, absorbing eloquence fell from the lips of that excellent man!

"On Monday I went to the wild ravine near the College, and spent a whole blessed, beautiful afternoon 'in that burn brae'— lounging on the green grass dreaming over the days that were passed—thinking of the sweet girls and lovely women I had seen the day before at kirk, and sometimes reflecting for a moment on the startling thoughts with which Dr. Chalmers had astonished his breathless auditory, and discoursed of the kingdom of his Redeemer.

"In the evening I went to the theater. I remember it as well as yesterday. It was a dull, empty, big, gloomy house. I got tired in a few half hours, and escaped to my lodgings, near the Trongate. I far preferred the kirk to the theater, and Dr. Chalmers sank deeper into my mind than any player there.

"On the fourth day of my visit to Glasgow, I left it with tears in my eyes, partly because I had not seen enough, and partly because I had seen a black-eyed girl too many."

Bennett was only one out of hundreds of thousands of people who were profoundly moved by the sermons of Thomas Chalmers. A magnificent speaker, a clear thinker, a widely read and courageous man, Dr. Chalmers labored hard to abate the appalling ignorance and immorality of his Glasgow parish; and in his sermons he tied religion to the advancing scientific thought of the day. Described by many as "the grand old Christian Giant—the John Knox of the Nineteenth Century," he finally broke with the church to which he had given so many years of his life, to lead 470 fellow ministers in founding the Free Church of Scotland. The *Dictionary of National Biography* (1887) said of Chalmers that "he let in daylight and fresh air on the evangelical enclosure of the church."

Bennett bought, read, and often quoted from Chalmers two books of sermons: *Astronomical Discourses* and *Commercial Discourses*. These books were widely circulated in the United States.

It was at about the time of his Glasgow visit that Bennett became seriously interested in North America. A new wave of emigrants (sometimes as many as a thousand a week) had begun to flow westward at the conclusion of the peace with France and the United States. Books on the strange land across the Atlantic became the vogue. Benjamin Franklin's *Autobiography* was published in Scotland in 1817. Bennett read it with great enthusiasm—and added the sage of Philadelphia to his personal Hall of Fame. He also read John Bristed's *America and Her Resources,* published in 1818.

Bennett read in Bristed's work that: "The people of the United States possess, in an eminent degree, the *physical* elements of na-

tional greatness and strength. Add to these, the general prevalence
of elementary instruction, which enables the great mass of the
people to develop their natural faculties and powers, and capacitates
them for undertaking any employment, success in which depends
upon shrewdness, intelligence, and skill; whence their singular
ingenuity in mechanical and manual operations, and their sound
understanding, enterprise and perseverance in the practical concerns
of life. And to crown it all, the *political sovereignty* of the nation
residing in the people, gives them a personal confidence, self-
possession and elevation of character, unknown and unattainable
in any other country, and under any other form of government;
and which renders them quick to perceive, and prompt to resent and
punish any insult offered to individual or national honour. . . ."

Two other widely read books published in 1818 left the young
Scotsman with a strong interest in America: John Mellish's *Advice
to Emigrants—from Travels through the United States of America*
and Morris Birkbeck's *Notes on a Journey in America.*

Without a profession and knowing full well that he could get
along with neither Catholics nor Presbyterians in Scotland, dislik-
ing the Irish and bitterly hating the English, James Gordon Bennett, "at the ripe old age of twenty-five," needed only the slightest
inducement to send him forth into the new world.

PART II
FIRST YEARS IN AMERICA

3. New World

Four weeks is a long time, especially if you have to spend it on a small and crowded ship. It seems an eternity if the voyage is rough and stormy and you suffer from seasickness. Bennett's nautical experience, up to the time he sailed for the New World, had been confined to rowing on the small rivers of Scotland, and an occasional sailing excursion with fellow students at Aberdeen. He derived no satisfaction from the circumstance that nearly all of his fellow passengers were equally upset by the stormy Atlantic. A thousand times during the voyage Bennett wished he had never taken the impulsive step that started him westward.

Halifax at last! Almost the whole of the town's twelve thousand inhabitants were down at the waterfront to greet the incoming vessel, not because of any person of special importance aboard, but to get the latest news, to thrill to the momentary contact with the Old World, to meet friends or relatives, to receive long-awaited goods, or from curiosity. It was a regular occurrence, whenever a British ship arrived, for the townsfolk to drop their work and make for the quay. Within a week after his arrival, Bennett was doing the same thing.

The young Scotsman had never looked upon Halifax as more than a jumping-off place for points farther south. He did not like the spirit of the town,—"servile," he called it, in its every effort to ape the fashions of England. Nor did he like the British soldiers parading the streets, a constant reminder of the colonial status of the country. To the romantic Scottish youth whose head was full of quotations from Ben Franklin and Tom Paine and who could not for long conceal his contempt for English authority, Halifax must have seemed a terrible place.

Nova Scotia as a whole was the most intensely "loyal" outpost of the British Empire. Halifax, its capital, was the fountainhead of this loyalty. It was a very real thing, this unbounded faith and affection for the Crown and Empire, as Bennett was soon to discover. To speak critically of the home government or its actions, past or present, was to put yourself under a cloud of suspicion. To refer to the young republic to the south and its people in anything but terms of scorn and contempt just wasn't done. To speak of the new country with admiration and enthusiasm was to invite both social and political ostracism.

Within a fortnight young Bennett understood how this strange state of affairs had come about.

The close of the Seven Years' War between France and England, in 1760, brought all of Canada under British rule. But even previous to this time, in 1755, the victors-to-be made sure of their possessions by a mass expulsion of the Acadian French from their fertile lands in the Maritime Provinces. These lands were then made available to British and American colonists who had proved their loyalty to the Empire. Halifax as the main port of entry into the Canadas was established by the British as early as 1749 to serve as both town and fort, where only those of unimpeachable devotion to the Crown were permitted to live.

When the American War for Independence broke out, the Maritime Provinces became the rallying point of those who stood firm against the revolting colonists. In 1776, Lord Howe withdrew from Boston and nearly a thousand Loyalists accompanied his army to Halifax. Each succeeding year of the war brought its quota of Loyalists fleeing northward from New York, New Jersey, Pennsylvania, and New England. Nova Scotia was filled with the most ardent pro-British elements, whose love of the Empire was only exceeded by their hatred for the rebellious Yankees.

At last came peace—peace and independence to the thirteen American colonies. But to many thousands of American Loyalists who had stayed on in their homes during the long conflict, it meant heartbreak, bitterness, and bankruptcy. Some resigned themselves to their fate and remained in the United States. But others, to the number of 35,000, sailed northward to Nova Scotia during 1782-83.

It was the greatest mass evacuation ever witnessed by the young republic.

The pre-Loyalist migration to the Maritime Provinces had been made up largely of hardy and adventurous folk, of frontiersmen, of tough peasants, of ex-soldiers and sailors. These were folk to whom hardship, toil, and coarse foods were the accepted things of life. But the Loyalist migration was totally different. These were the city dwellers, the clerks, tradesmen and government officials, used to soft living, good food, and little manual labor. They had had much to lose—and did—by their devotion to the Empire. To them, too, the problem of adjustment to life in Halifax or throughout the Maritime Provinces was both hard and bitter. All these factors made their hatred for everything American more pronounced. The British government recognized how important it was to give aid and comfort to these loyal subjects. It paid out more than three million pounds to assist them in getting re-established. It gave them the best lands taken from the Acadian French. It created hundreds and hundreds of unnecessary positions so that they might have a livelihood. And, as a final token of its esteem, the government announced that, as a mark of distinction to these devoted Loyalists and their descendants, it proposed they affix "U. E." to their names, "alluding to their great principle, the Unity of Empire."

Nova Scotia and Halifax prospered and grew. Farming, fishing, lumbering, and shipbuilding flourished. Commerce, too, mounted rapidly in importance, and Halifax became the main port of entry for goods needed by the United States. Thus, strangely enough, the very region whose political temper was most fervently British and anti-American found itself becoming ever more firmly tied to the "despicable" Yankees of New England in almost every field of economic endeavor.

During the War of 1812, Halifax boomed as never before. Privateers in great numbers operated from that port to prey upon the transatlantic or coastwise shipping of the Yankees; every prize brought into port was doubly cheered by the Loyalists. The young Republic was badly divided on the issue of the war. In fact, almost the whole of New England and much of New York were definitely opposed to it. But Nova Scotia rejoiced at the conflict. The Earl of

Dalhousie reported to London that he had been unable to detect even "the most distant doubt of Loyalty to this Province" or to the Crown.

Such was the historical setting of the city and the province in which young Bennett had set foot when he reached the New World. A fortnight's stay had taught him to hold his tongue if he wished to survive in this ultra-patriotic community—at least until the wheel of fortune would permit him to head south to the United States.

In the meantime, his slender purse was a daily reminder that work must be obtained. Jobs were plentiful at the time, and so, picking what seemed the least distasteful, he hired out as a school-master. Bennett had received no formal training in pedagogy nor had he ever given serious thought to the art of teaching. To him, as to thousands of other teachers, the job was an endurance con-test between pupil and teacher, with the former stubbornly resisting every effort of the latter to cram learning into his head.

Bennett had no objection to the long hours of work, nor even to the monotony of it, but he gagged at the thought of having to turn each lesson, be it Latin, Greek, spelling, or arithmetic, into a sermon on the goodness and greatness of the British Empire. As soon as he had saved a little money from his work, he resigned his position, packed his few possessions, and set forth for the land of Benjamin Franklin.

The coastwise schooner, Portland bound, which brought Bennett to the United States, suffered damages off the coast of northern Maine and put in at what is now Eastport, for repairs. Bennett went ashore. Completely unconcerned about continuing to Portland, Bennett eagerly canvassed the village for work. He was told that a schoolmaster was needed at the village of Addison, a few miles inland. To Addison he went. There, the village fathers immediately hired the lean and lanky Scotsman.

Addison had a population of three hundred, smaller even than that of Bennett's native Keith. Like thousands of other frontier communities, it was a crude, raw collection of humanity, pitting its labors against the encircling forests and the elements. There was little if any time for intellectual occupations. The farmers had no

interest in learning for learning's sake. They wanted their children
to be taught "just plain readin', writin' and 'rithmetic with no fancy
frills or do-dads." They had no time for ancient history—"Hell,
mister, we're a-makin' history over here right now!"

Yet, Addison, for all its crudities, while not the America that
Bennett had dreamed about, was still very much America. Its people
had a tremendous self-confidence. They looked forward and not
back. There was a tremendous political consciousness. In fact, every
farmhouse, the tavern, the general store, the church, and the school-
house were perpetual forums. The people of Maine wanted statehood for themselves. They wanted the right to send their own representatives to Washington, the right to elect their own legislature
and governor, to make their own laws and govern themselves. They
were tired of being tied to the apron strings of Massachusetts and
governed from Boston. They disliked having Maine called The Dis
trict, as though it were some faraway province peopled by savages.
The Maine folk had fought as bravely as any others during the long
years of the Revolution. The fires of freedom, so they kept telling
themselves and all who would listen, burned as fiercely in their
breasts as in those of other patriots. And, above all, they resented
the charge, so often made by Massachusetts politicians, that there
weren't enough people of wit and learning in Maine to govern it.

Ever since the United States became a nation Maine had clamored
for statehood. Time after time her citizens had sent petitions to
Washington and Boston on this matter. Time after time they had
voted for statehood—only to have the issue put off by more powerful political and economic interests.

Young Bennett gloried in the fervor of these self-assured Maine
folk. Here were true sons and daughters of liberty and equality.
It was hard for him to conceive of Boston as they did—a usurping
tyrant—for to him it was the very cradle of liberty. But it warmed
his heart to find the common people so convinced of their ability
for self-rule and so determined to get it.

In the fall of the year, less than sixty days after the new schoolteacher had settled down to teach the young Addisonians, elected
representatives of "The District" were converging upon Portland,

there to convene a constitutional convention and set up the machinery for state government.

The convention was frowned upon in many quarters. Condemnation was voiced by several representatives in Washington who argued strongly against Maine's petition for admission as a commonwealth into the Union. To hold a constitutional convention and set up the machinery for statehood before Congress had granted such permission, was, they argued, an undue assumption of powers. But others, speaking for Maine, declared this not to be the case, for did not the people of Maine, as part of the Commonwealth of Massachusetts, already enjoy statehood? After much debate, on January 3, 1820, the House of Representatives passed the bill granting full and complete statehood to Maine.

The more Bennett came to know the people of the young republic the better he liked them. The more determined he likewise became that one of his energy and ability could not afford to lose himself in a backwoods village. Boston—cradle of liberty, hub of freedom, and the self-confessed Athens of the New World—beckoned him. When Christmas came, Bennett resigned his position, pocketed the few dollars he had earned, made his way to Portland, and from there, immediately after New Year's Day, 1820, he sailed on to Boston.

Recalling his emotions that cold, clear, January day as the small vessel sailed into the harbor, Bennett wrote: "Boston appeared to me as a residence of a friend, an associate, an acquaintance. I had drunk in the history of the holy struggle for Independence, first made on Bunker's Hill. Dorchester Heights were, to my youthful imagination, almost as holy ground as Arthur's Seat or Salisbury Craig.

"Around the isles arose the waves of the mirrored bay. Beyond was Boston, her glittering spires rising high into the blue vault of heaven, like beacons to light a world to liberty."

Had the Bostonians of the day been less self-assured of their own and their city's greatness, they might have been amused at the actions of their latest acquisition from abroad. The eager young Scotsman, dressed in his Aberdeen best, and with a broad, thick brogue, felt there was not a moment to be lost in seeing, touching, or hearing about every nook and cranny of historical interest. The narrow winding streets echoed to his heavy boots both day and night as he walked about, head high, breathing the crisp cold air of freedom. Each shrine and monument, every hallowed spot, every historic roadway was visited again and again.

Years later he told how he had "lounged whole afternoons on the brows of Bunker's and of Breed's Hill. Here Warren fell! There the blood of liberty flowed! Here the enemy landed! There the spirits of the dead took their flight to Heaven! . . ." "Once," he admitted, "I passed a whole moon-light night within the old ruined fort on Dorchester Heights, which Washington formerly occupied."

One can feel in his words the spirit that must have animated Bennett at the time. Here was no hard, worldly wise, and cynical editor. Here was the young romanticist, re-creating in his own mind's eye the heroic period of a Boston forever gone, and which, for that matter, was much more matter-of-fact even during the hectic days of 1775 than Bennett could possibly imagine.

So long as there was a shilling left, the enthusiastic young man had no inclination to look for work. Boston was a never-ending thrill. "I felt the same glow in wandering over these scenes, as I did on the fields of Bannockburn in my more youthful days. It was Liberty and Freedom struggling against Pride and Tyranny in both cases."

He found release at last in the form of some very bad poetry. But bad as the poetry is, with its obvious attempt to follow in the footsteps of Lord Byron—it is important to us, for it is the earliest written material we have from his pen.

Inspired by the view of Boston and its famous State House, Bennett burst into this ode to freedom:

> *Of sweet domestic bliss the fires are burning bright—*
> *The despot dares not touch them. The lofty hall,*
> *Where freedom oft with legislation meets,*
> *To measure justice out, high over all*
> *Is seen; and here and there the busy streets,*
> *Peopled with myriads, arrest the passer-by—*
> *These are thy blessings, blue eyed Liberty!*

Another bit of verse concerns itself with sunset over the city, as the old cannon at Castle Island booms out its salute to the day that is done:

> *The numerous isles are bright;*
> *I've heard in softness, murmurs of the evening song*
> *Ushering in the twinkling stars of night:*
> *The deep-toned evening gun sends out a sudden flash—*
> *The billows trembling up the white shore dash.*

At last came the day when the young man's fancy had to turn to more prosaic matters. He had just about reached the bottom of his purse. It was time to look for work. But, alas, there was no work to be had. The positions for which he applied had either already been filled, or he was unable to meet the requirements. It was springtime in Boston, and Mr. James Gordon Bennett, late of Aberdeen, Scotland, wandered hungry and penniless up and down its crooked streets for two days. He was too proud to beg for food or money, though he did ask for work—any kind of work. The gods were against him. The gnawing pangs of hunger compelled him to ponder indignantly over the strange working of Providence which would permit a man who was both eager and willing to work, to starve for the want of it.

For the first time in his life he felt thoroughly dejected. For the moment he had no interest in matters historical. He wandered about aimlessly, eyes to the ground, kicking savagely at sticks and stones and piles of rubbish, asking himself over and over again that most perplexing question: "How shall I feed myself?" Then quite suddenly a glint of something stuck between two cobblestones! It was a coin! A York shilling! A few minutes later the pangs of hunger had been largely stayed. And, as luck would have it, he met next day a fellow countryman, who, impressed by the young man's knowledge and sincerity, gave him a position as clerk in his store.

The firm of Wells and Lilly was then one of Boston's leading publishers, printers, and booksellers. It was Mr. Wells, who had encountered the tall, black-haired, blue-eyed Scotsman, listened to his plea for a job, and taken him to the store.

Both Mr. Wells and Mr. Lilly were kind and intelligent men. From the start they took an interest in their new clerk, helped him to understand the printing and publishing business, guided his reading, and brought him into contact with the men and women who were Boston's leaders in commerce, literature, and politics.

It was through his association with the publishing firm, too, that he began, little by little, to understand Boston and New England— information which served him well as a journalist.

Exceeded in size only by New York, Philadelphia, and Baltimore, the Boston of 1820, with its 25,000 inhabitants, was more truly than any of the other three, the real capital for the adjacent regions. Boston was already old and venerable, with nearly two full centuries of history behind it. Furthermore, its own population, as well as that of all New England, was quite homogeneous, as compared with the conglomerate assortment of races and nationalities in and adjacent to the other great urban centers. Boston folk, with few exceptions, were of English origin, and there had been no noticeable addition to the New England colonies by emigration from abroad for more than a century.

Beyond his enthusiasm for the romantic aspects of Boston, young Bennett also found other elements which made it seem like home to him. There was the hard thin soil, with its outcroppings of rock. There were the short, turbulent rivers; the creeks; the abundant lakes and mountains; the same rugged coast line and the same thrifty God-fearing people.

Although Bennett had spent little time in Edinburgh, he sensed its affinity to Boston, and could easily have subscribed to the remarks of one of his fellow countrymen who wrote a few years later that in Boston one found "as in Edinburgh, the same wealth, similarly earned, the same regard for manners and decorum, the same respect for learning, the same religious point of view, alike in its antecedants and in its liberal modifications, the same scrupulous conscientiousness, the same punctiliousness and the same pride, even the same prudence."

Bostonians, as Bennett discovered, possessed a local patriotism which far transcended their faith in state or country. Nor was this fervid loyalty to the city of their birth something to be blatantly shouted from the housetops. That would have been bad taste. "All of them," remarks Van Wyck Brooks in *The Flowering of New England,* "lived and moved, walked and spoke as if their little town were a holy city and Rome, Paris and London were their suburbs."

But what Bennett did not see or realize was that the Boston of 1820 had little in common with the Boston of 1775. True, its first citizens were sons and daughters of those who had so daringly fought and bled during the Revolution, and mighty proud of this they were indeed. But they were equally determined that revolution and progressive political theory must remain a thing of the past. Social lines were, so far as they were concerned, already firmly fixed and must not be disturbed. Not only had New England shied away from the French Revolution as from a plague, it had been equally fearful of the dangerous doctrines of Thomas Jefferson, and to avoid contamination had drawn tightly about itself the garments of Federalist righteousness.

The very year, 1820, when James Gordon Bennett arrived in America, Daniel Webster, the political oracle of New England, in a speech before the Massachusetts Constitutional Convention, reiterated the basic political philosophy of the Bostonian blue-bloods. "It seems to me to be plain," he said, "that, in the absence of military force, political power naturally and necessarily goes into the hands which hold the property. In my judgment, therefore, a republican form of government rests, not more on political constitutions, than on those laws which regulate the descent and transmission of property. . . .

"The English Revolution of 1688 was a revolution in favor of property, as well as of other rights. It was brought about by men of property for their security; and our own immortal Revolution was undertaken, not to shake or plunder property, but to protect it."

Here was an interpretation of the long war for independence to which the first families willingly subscribed. Tabled, if not forgotten, were the stirring words about all men being created equal with the right to life, liberty and the pursuit of happiness. In short, as the late Vernon Parrington wrote, "Revolutions that were not made in Boston, by Boston gentlemen, were quite certain to be seditious; and Boston had definitely gone out of the revolution business. It wanted above all things to undo the mischief that had already been done, and take back into safe hands the political power which in the days of revolutionary enthusiasm had been seized by the agrarian democracy."

Oblivious to all this at the time, young Bennett applied himself diligently to learning the publishing business. He became familiar with the technical and financial aspects of the trade; and his love of reading plus his excellent memory made him a better than average clerk. He was sober and industrious, too, with no fear of long hours. But despite these qualities, which his employers admired, there were some definite handicaps. In the first place, he was careless about his personal appearance, which even under the best of care was anything but prepossessing. Boston was, at the time, not only the hub of culture but also the hub of fashion. Storekeepers and clerks in all respectable establishments were almost fastidious as to both dress and deportment. Nor was the firm of Wells and Lilly any exception to this rule. But the young Scotsman saw no reason why he should abandon his Aberdeen wardrobe so long as the clothes were fit to be worn. Furthermore, he had never mastered the art of formal politeness. He asked too many questions. He offered too much advice. And, as he was to discover in later years, there was a dry, cynical humor to his remarks which frequently shocked his listeners. Last of all, customers of the bookstore complained to the owners that they had difficulty in understanding the new clerk.

In the face of these handicaps, Mr. Wells and Mr. Lilly did their best to keep Bennett on as a clerk, but after many months of trial gave up. Instead they assigned him to the position of proofreader. They had been somewhat fearful that their young protégé would look upon this as a demotion, but he was thoroughly pleased with the change. No longer did he have to worry about his appearance nor did he have to weigh his words. Furthermore, he felt more at home with the printers than with the clerks.

In the meantime, he continued his quest for information and for historical spots till he knew them all—better perhaps than most natives. Except for the Reverend Chalmers, whose sermons so stirred him in Glasgow, he had never seen any of the great men of Scotland. But here, in Boston, he rubbed elbows with the great every day. To be sure, he was never invited to their homes, but he knew where they lived and how they lived. For Boston was, in terms of our modern cities, a small and crowded town. In area it had expanded little since the day of its founding. East Boston was, in 1820, a barren and almost treeless island, its total population the single family which inhabited its one solitary farmhouse. The Back Bay region, so famous in later years, had not yet been filled in. Cambridge seemed a long way out from Boston. Even Boston Common, which for generations has been looked upon as the very heart of the city, was then on the edge of town. Except for a few benches provided in one secluded spot where men were permitted to smoke (for smoking was forbidden on the streets of the city) the Common was still largely given over to grazing ground for sheep and cattle. The Common was surrounded by an old wooden fence, to prevent the animals from straying through the streets.

The dead hand of its Puritan past still lay heavy upon the community in many ways. Observance of the Sabbath, for instance, which began at midnight Saturday, was as strictly observed as in Scotland. Stores and shops were tightly closed. No hired vehicle was allowed to leave or enter the city. Chains were frequently placed across the streets in the neighborhood of churches to prevent traffic. A state law of 1792, confirmed in 1816, forbade Sabbath labor of every kind, decreed that no one should travel, no ship leave the harbor, no one lounge in the tavern, and that any person in good health, who, without good reason, failed to worship God in public for three months, must be fined.

Every form of amusement was strictly forbidden, even bathing. This led a local weekly newspaper, *The Centennial,* to protest:

> *In Superstition's days, 'tis said,*
> *Hens laid two eggs on Monday*
> *Because a hen would lose her head*
> *That laid an egg on Sunday.*

Now our wise rulers and the law
Say none shall wash on Sunday;
So Boston folk must dirty go,
And wash them twice on Monday.

Boston itself was being rebuilt. Thanks to Charles Bulfinch and other architects, the city had developed a unique style that bespoke its dignity, its primness, its self-assurance, and its wealth.

Boston believed strongly in education. The most widely read book in the whole country was Noah Webster's *Spelling Book* of which some five million copies had been published by 1820. The note sounded by this Yankee lexicographer in his introduction to the speller was just what the people wanted. He wrote, "For America in her infancy to adopt the present maxims of the Old World would be to stamp the wrinkle of decrepit old age upon the bloom of youth, and to plant decay in a vigorous constitution." Bennett was fascinated by such forthrightness, and never tired of quoting it.

Next to the speller, the most important textbook for the children was the *New England Primer,* first published in 1813, subtitled "An Easy and Pleasant Guide to the Art of Reading."

The Reverend Joseph Emmerson set the tongues of all New England wagging when he opened his Girls Seminary at Byfield in 1818. After all, what was this world coming to when girls were taught the same studies as boys! A writer in the *Analectic Magazine* as early as April, 1817, had sensed this dangerous trend, and voiced the public view at the time. "If the system of female education goes on in the course it has now taken, the daughters of our fair countrywomen may make good musicians, good dancers, good frolicers—but we are afraid that they will never make good wives."

In 1821 Boston opened its—and America's—first high school. And again the tongues wagged. Some feared too much education would make the nation soft and effete. There were others, such as the writer in the *Western Review* of 1820, who called for a halt to dangerous newfangled educational theories; he warned: "Should the time ever come that Latin and Greek should be banished from our Universities; and the study of Cicero and Demosthenes, of Homer and Virgil should be considered as unnecessary for the formation of a scholar, we should regard mankind as fast sinking into absolute barbarism, and the gloom of mental darkness as likely to increase until it should become universal."

Such forebodings, however, were not much in evidence to Bennett. Quite to the contrary, he sensed a strong and quickened interest in all things educational. Schools were on the increase. Libraries were being built—and used. Boston had opened its Library of Law in 1806, to be followed the next year by the Boston Athenaeum and the Theological Library. And Harvard, having shaken off the theological dust of its founders, was in the throes of a renaissance which was to make it the intellectual spearhead for the whole country. New standards of exacting scholarship were established. Professors became as eager as their students in their search for new ideas, in ferreting out information, in developing an interest in the history and institutions of the United States and the whole New World.

Whenever opportunity permitted, Bennett attended the public lectures of Story, Ware, Ticknor, Elliot, Everett; of the great preachers such as Buckminster, Parker, and Channing; and of public figures such as John Quincy Adams, Dr. Bowditch, and the great Daniel Webster. He was fortunate in having come to Boston at a time when talent and ability stood in such high favor.

Unitarianism, which had replaced the narrow Calvinism of an earlier Boston, was all to Bennett's liking. He chuckled at the thought of how the liberalism of the French Revolution, so thoroughly banned and damned by New England, had nevertheless slipped quietly and unobtrusively into the homes of Boston's first families by the door of theology. It had taken its erstwhile enemies into its fold without their recognizing what was happening. Here was a case in which, as Parrington has pointed out, the "dangerous and seditious" doctrines of French Jacobinism, when presented under a new name, and arrayed in garments cut after the best Yankee fashion, "presently walked the streets of Boston and spoke from its most respectable pulpits under the guise of Unitarianism."

New horizons were constantly opening up before his eyes and mind. He was amazed to learn the tenuous nature of the bond between the several states and the federal government; how Boston and the whole of Massachusetts had been openly and bitterly against the War of 1812, with local Federalist papers gloating over the fact that wealthy Boston had given a niggardly $75,000 to the government war loan. He learned that Daniel Webster had been elected to Congress as an anti-war man in 1812. And he was told how the Massachusetts Senate had adopted a bitterly worded resolution denouncing the action and attitude of the federal government, which, it charged, was waging a war without just cause, with conquest and ambition as its true motives.

Down at the busy wharves, where Bennett would ply the sailors, stevedores, and teamsters with questions, he gained a picture of the paralyzing effects of the British and French blockades and counter-blockades during the Napoleonic wars; how Jefferson's embargo had made matters worse; and how the War of 1812 had left the wharves empty and the ships idle. They told him, too, how wagon trains had replaced the ships for coastwise trade, with every road leading out of Boston, New York, or Philadelphia choked with Mud Clippers, as the wagon-trains were called. They told him how the newspapers, which had once devoted so much of their space to the all-important subject of ship news, transferred attention to the new mode of transportation, though nautical terms survived. Every wagon-team became a "fleet of fast-sailing wagons," every teamster a "captain." The news itself was now printed under headings such as "Jeffersonian Commerce," "Horse-Marine Intelligence," or "Horse and Ox Marine News." One of the most popular songs of the day was a parody on Campbell's "Ye Mariners of England."

> *Ye Wagoners of Freedom,*
> *Whose chargers chew the cud,*
> *Whose wheels have braved, a dozen years,*
> *The gravel and the mud . . .*
>
> *Columbia needs no wooden walls,*
> *No ships where billows swell;*
> *Her march is like a terrapin's,*
> *Her home is in her shell . . .*

With the coming of peace came also a post-war boom. The waterfront sprang to life. Ports were jammed with ships and the warehouses were emptied almost before they were filled. All America was clamoring for goods so long denied it. Prices went up and up. If you couldn't pay cash you bought on credit. Uncle Sam's children were multiplying rapidly and were pushing westward in three great parallel streams. The first, or northern stream, spilled over from New England and New York along the south shore of Lake Erie into Indiana, Ohio, Michigan, and Illinois. The middle stream followed the broad and fertile Ohio Valley all the way to the Mississippi River. The southern stream, blocked for three long decades by inability to cross the lands of the Creek and the Cherokee Indians in Georgia, had detoured around them by pouring down the valleys of the Cumberland and the Tennessee.

All this young Bennett learned—and much more—facts startling, unbelievable, and often contradictory. Boston, during his entire stay, had every outward appearance of prosperity; and yet there were many voices crying out that poverty and distress were ruining the land. Prisons overflowed with debtors; stores and factories were closed and workingmen idle. Some blamed these conditions on speculation, on the banks, on the excessive importation of foreign goods, on the depressed value of real estate, or on the heavy migration westward.

Bennett heard Daniel Webster, then an ardent free-trader, denounce the high-tariff group at Faneuil Hall that summer of 1820. Manufacturing establishments, said the great Daniel, were desirable only when they grew up naturally, without being fostered or protected by taxes levied against a whole people for the benefit of a small and special class. Boston's merchants and bankers and shippers applauded long and loud. The mill owners were silent.

The young Scotsman was amazed at the reports that pauperism was rampant in all the larger cities, that Philadelphia was declared a veritable "emporium of beggars," that every seventh person in New York was living on charity, with prostitution, gambling, gaming, and drunkenness debauching and degrading young and old alike. The prisons were hothouses for vice instead of institutions of reform, or so reported a Senate Committee on Penitentiary Systems in Pennsylvania. "Culprits come out more depraved and desperate than when they went in," read the report. "The young

are advanced in the path of guilt; the old, hardened in their base-
ness; morals are destroyed, conscience blunted and the ranks of
the criminal classes steadily recruited."

Even Boston, with all its enlightenment, with its humanitarian
religion, with its wealth, had its drunkards and thieves, its pimps
and prostitutes, its beggars, paupers, and unemployed. Between
January 1, 1820, and April 1, 1822, the debtors' prisons of Boston
alone housed 3,492. Of these a full 2,000 had been thrown into jail
for debts of less than twenty dollars each. The unfortunates included 430 women. The historian McMaster asserts that for a
twelve-dollar debt, one woman with a child still at her breast was
dragged to jail, where she remained for twenty days. The infant
became "insane" and the mother seriously ill.

In 1820 James Monroe was re-elected to the presidency of the
United States by the most overwhelming vote of confidence ever
given any president except George Washington himself. In fact,
on the basis of the actual election returns, Monroe had gained the
electoral vote of every state. When the electors gathered to cast
their ballots a New Hampshire representative cast his vote for John
Quincy Adams, explaining that he felt no other man should share
with the Father of His Country the honor of a unanimous election
to the presidency.

The Era of Good Feeling was coming into its own. And yet,
political unanimity, Bennett thought, should mean above all things
that the previous administration of Monroe must have been one
of great wisdom coupled with great advances both economic and
social. Instead, there had just been made public a report by the
Committee on Manufacturing of the House of Representatives,
which summarized its findings in this scathing fashion:

"It is a matter of little consolation that, after being thirty years
in operation, the Government has not brought the country into a
more prosperous condition.

"The debt has been increased twenty millions. The revenues are
insufficient to meet expenditures. The national domain is impaired
and twenty million dollars of its proceeds gone. . . .

"In a time of profound peace, the country is embarrassed with
debts; real estate is shrinking in value; the markets for manufac-

tures and the yield of the farm are declining; commerce is struggling not to retain the carrying trade of other lands, but of our own. Not one national interest is thriving. . . .

"History affords no other example of a people impoverished while in the full enjoyment of health, peace, and plenty."

But as if to challenge this gloomy picture, Bennett read a letter from a Yorkshireman on his way to the broad acres of Ohio with his family. "This be a main queer country, for I have asked the labouring folks all along the road how many meals they eat in a day, and they all said three, and sometimes four, if they wanted them. We have but two at home, sir, and they are scanty enough. And only think, sir, many of these people ask me to eat and drink with them. We can't do it so in Yorkshire, sir, for we have not enough for ourselves."

The vastness of the country, the newness of so much of it, and the fact that conditions, customs, and the way men made their living differed so widely from section to section, interested Bennett mightily. Boston, though fascinating as ever, had been explored so completely that the joy of discovery was largely gone. Such at least were the young man's thoughts. He was restless. He had mastered his trade as a proofreader, and he longed to widen his knowledge of the whole country. After all, he was footloose and fancy free. Once he could decide just where he wanted to go and what he wanted to do, he would, he was sure, leave Boston with the same speed with which he had left Aberdeen.

In the meantime he had become intensely interested in the long and bitter controversy between English and American periodicals. The firm by which he was employed as proofreader carried in stock almost every important British and American magazine, current as well as back issues. Of the more than two-score magazines born during the administrations of Washington and Adams, few survived into the nineteenth century. And though each and all were out for the improvement of the morals and culture of the American people, and, of course, would print nothing that could "call a blush to the cheek of innocence," they were almost universally badly printed and were even more badly edited.

The new century saw still more magazines born. Boston's An-

thology Club—composed of "gentlemen of literary interests"—
launched their *Monthly Anthology and Magazine of Polite Literature* in 1803. Boston also had its *Columbian Phoenix* and *Boston
Review*. *The Polyanthus,* which made its appearance in 1805, announced its purpose: "To please the learned and enlighten the
ignorant; to allure the idle from folly and confirm the timid in
virtue."

Flowery language was considered essential—as essential as the
paste pot and shears which every editor used unsparingly on books,
newspapers, pamphlets, or magazines in his quest for material. He
might announce, as did the editor of the *Emerald* (successor to
The Boston Magazine), that the pages of the new periodical would
"be polished by the labors of the learned, and occasionally glitter
with the gaiety of wit," thus making it altogether worthy of its
new name, "worthy to shine among the gems which sparkle on
the regalia of literature." In actuality, as the researches of Frank
Luther Mott have shown, "When an editor hoisted the black flag
of the magazine, he assumed the privilege of levying tribute upon
all other craft that sailed the literary seas. . . . Nor was it any
crime, or even a misdemeanor: it was expected. It was not even
necessary, thought many editors, to give credit to the original
source."

James Gordon Bennett had one advantage over many of his
American contemporaries; he had long been familiar with the
great British and Scottish periodical literature. He had read Addison, Steele, Swift, Pope, and Congreve in the issues of *The Tatler*
and *The Spectator*. He had enjoyed the biting phrases of Samuel
Johnson's *Rambler*. He was familiar with reprints as well as with
current issues of Cave's *Gentleman's Magazine*. And, quite naturally, he had been a devoted reader of the big three of British
periodicals—the *Edinburgh,* the *Quarterly*, and the *London Reviews*.

Bennett admired the high standard of British magazines to the
fullest degree. But he had an even greater admiration for the young
republic to which he had come. He saw it had many shortcomings,
that it loved to brag and boast. But it made him furious to find

native-born sons of the United States viewing their homeland as intellectually barren and sterile—a land,

> *Where Fancy sickens and where Genius dies,*
> *Where few and feeble are the Muses' strains,*
> *And no fine frenzy riots in the veins.*

British conceit, Bennett knew, had always been above par. It had always looked upon the Americans as a queer breed—whose long contact with the wilderness and the Indians had rubbed thin, and in some cases rubbed out, the veneer of English culture. Why, oh, why, he asked himself, was it necessary for Americans to add more fuel to this conceit? And this question, too, must have been asked by many Americans as well.

The British press and periodicals, almost without exception, had ever since 1800 been picturing their over-ocean cousins as "a whittling, spitting, guessing, reckoning, gambling, slave-beating, dram-drinking people, and a parody on the race whose language they speak."

Many American magazines reprinted these caustic comments—some even admitting that there was more than a grain of truth to the charges. A few, and only a few, stood up against the withering blasts from overseas. Meanwhile, from 1814 to 1823, the British continued to point the finger of scorn at the young republic. The distinguished *London Quarterly Review* of January, 1814, in a lengthy analysis of the United States and its people, arrived at the following conclusions: To be a public figure in America you must be a "man of the people"; and a man of the people was one who smoked cigars, frequented grogshops, and was forever engaged in loud and violent abuse of the opposing faction. Extension of suffrage, according to the *Review,* had produced a debased and ignorant body of representatives; while the separation of church and state had led to the establishment of a host of illegitimate sects. The people were irreligious, which meant they must be immoral. Try as it would to find some saving grace for the Americans, it sadly confessed the best it could say was that they were a people "of little taste, limited manners, still less literature, and no genius at all."

The *British Review* of May, 1819, declared that, in its considered judgment, "the mass of the North Americans are too proud to learn and too ignorant to teach, and, having established by Act of Congress that they are already the most enlightened people in the world, they bid fair to retain their barbarism from mere regard to consistency."

The staid *Quarterly Review* took up the refrain, charging that "America, if not priest-ridden like Spain, is in a worse state—she is lawyer-ridden."

The *Edinburgh Review,* that peer of all reviews, whose opinions one never questioned, asked loftily: "In the four quarters of the globe, who reads an American book? Or goes to an American play? Or looks at an American picture or statue? What does the world yet owe to American physicians or surgeons? What new substances have their chemists discovered, or what old ones have they analysed? What have they done in mathematics? Who drinks out of American glasses? Or eats from American plates? Or wears American coats or gowns? Or sleeps on American blankets?"

But it remained for Sydney Smith—preacher, teacher, writer and reviewer—to deliver the most devastating attack upon the government, people, and culture of the New World. Writing in the *Edinburgh Review* in 1819, he asked: "Why should the Americans write books when a six weeks' passage brings them in their own tongue our sense, science, and genius in bales and hogsheads?"

Dipping his pen ever deeper into his inkhorn of deprecation, Smith wrote on, "If nations rank according to their wisdom and their virtue, what right has the American, a scourger and murderer of slaves, to compare himself with the least and lowest of European nations?"

Then, to fend off in advance the attacks which he knew were sure to follow from across the Atlantic, pointing to the long and unsavory record of the British, he concluded: "Let the world judge which is more liable to censure, we who, in the midst of our rottenness, have torn off the manacles of slaves all over the world, or they who, with their idle purity and useless perfection, have remained mute and careless while groans echoed and whips cracked round the very walls of their spotless Congress!"

Bennett was furious. Furious at the British, to be sure, but even more furious at the cold-blooded Bostonians, who in their new-found smugness and self-assurance didn't feel it necessary to take up the cudgels on behalf of their country. Many of those, with whom he spoke, told Bennett that the severity of the British criticism was quite justified. But, of course, they usually added, it must be obvious that these charges didn't apply to Boston.

Then, just as he had foreseen, one day the proofreader got up from his table, walked to the inner office where the proprietors had their desks. Mr. Wells looked up:

"Bennett—what's the trouble?"

"I'm leaving, Mr. Wells. . . . I'll stay till you get another proof-reader, if you wish . . . but I'm leaving."

"Anything wrong, my boy?"

"Nothing, sir . . . you've all been very kind to me, sir."

"In that case, don't you think you'd better reconsider? We've plans for you, Bennett—Mr. Lilly and I."

"Thank you, sir . . . but I can't do that. My mind is made up."

"And where are you going? What do you plan to do, Mr. Bennett?"

"Well, sir, I can't say."

"Can't say?"

"To tell the truth, sir, I don't know."

4. Bennett Chooses Journalism

"THIS must be the real America," mused the young man as he sauntered down the crowded thoroughfare known as Broadway. The faces he saw were of many types—pugnacious, freckled, red-headed Irish; square-headed, blue-eyed Dutchmen; swarthy Latins; eagle-beaked Jews; ruddy Englishmen; aristocratic-looking southerners; lean and leather-faced frontiersmen; tobacco-chewing New Englanders; pasty-faced dandies; gawking yokels and gimlet-eyed sharpers. Never before had he seen such an intermingling of peoples. Augmenting and confirming the visual record of this melting pot of nations and peoples was the record of the ear, as snatches of French, German, and Spanish mingled with the soft tones of the southerner, the brogue of the Irish, and the nasal twang of the Yankee.

The cut and pattern of the clothes worn by the passing parade told a tale of fashion in transition. Some of the older men still clung to their powdered wigs, knee breeches, buckled shoes, and capes. Others wore their hair cut long; the more modern parted theirs on the side. A few of the fops wore curls to enhance their manly charms. Young men wore fancy baggy pantaloons, tucked Cossack fashion into Hessian boots; older men wore trousers. Vests of fancy cut and in gay colors were much in vogue. Coats were often of the square-skirted kind; though others, "of blue or green cloth, with large gilt or pearl buttons, a high rolling collar, and long narrow tails reaching down to the calves," were in the best of taste. Shirts were of ruffled linen, but collars had grown taller and taller, till they reached to a man's ears, adding much to the general dignity, as well as discomfort, of the well-dressed man. Footwear ranged from beautiful hand-tooled leather boots, and shoes, soft and pliable as a glove, down to the hard brogans of the common man. The clop-clop of wooden shoes and the patter of barefoot men and boys were as commonplace as the silent tread of the moccasined frontiersman.

Bennett was right—New York was the real America—the America to which adventurous and oppressed of all the world were drawn as by some mighty magnet. Largest and fastest-growing of all the cities in the New World, its population in 1822 was 130,000 —more than three times that of Boston.

For all its age, its colonial and revolutionary traditions, New York had no time to think of its past. Its eyes were set on today and tomorrow—not on yesterday. Lacking, too, at this time, was a reverence for culture. The dominant note was a lusty material- ism, which left no stone unturned to make sure that Manhattan became the financial and commercial capital of the Western World. Thirty years earlier, when George Washington had come to New York, to assume the presidency, its population had been 29,000. Then its tempo had been slow and peaceful, its population more homogeneous, its ambitions more modest.

Somehow, had come the metamorphosis, with new blood, new vigor, a new outlook, and a new sense of values. Father Knicker- bocker cast aside his three-cornered hat and cane, shaved his face, and set out to do things in a new way. It was all very exciting. "What's happened to us?" "Where are we going?", asked some. "Who cares?" roared the crowd. "It's fun, isn't it! Fun and ex- citement!" Under such circumstance, as Parrington said, the changes were enough to muddle a head stronger than Rip Van Winkle's. "The quiet ways of colonial times were gone, and in their stead was a restless activity that had no leisure for its pipe and mug in the sleepy tavern. Business and politics could not wait on men who like Wouter Van Twiller pickled their dreams in tobacco smoke."

The day of the patroon, with his great landed estate and his feudal outlook, had come to an end. To replace him came ambi- tious men who built and managed shops and factories, warehouses, ships, banks, canals. They were gamblers, speculators, organizers, entrepreneurs, capitalists—call them what you will.

It did not take very long for Bennett to decide that New York was more to his liking than the home of the Brahmins. His ardor and reverence for the landmarks of the Revolution were on the wane; and though he did visit most of the historic spots in New York, he never bothered to express his feelings in verse. In Boston, Bennett had never been able to break through the polite but frigid barrier which stood between the New Englander and any outsider. In New York, he found himself accepted as just another of those newcomers who were a part and parcel of the young republic. Then, too, the New Englander, with his long and heavy theological heritage, was too much akin to the people of Scotland. Bennett had had his fill of soul-seeking, dogmatic theology and metaphysical speculation. New York, he found, was not eternally concerned about its conscience, cared little for the subtleties of creed, and wasted neither talk nor sleep worrying over the fires of Hell, or the joys of Paradise. New York was earth-minded, success-minded, and money-minded; and, to judge by appearances, was eminently content with such a philosophy.

New York harbor was a constantly changing forest of masts and sails and spars; the city itself in the throes of a hectic and seemingly never-ending period of expansion. Broadway wound its way up the island almost four miles. Wall Street, once distinguished as the home of the landed aristocracy, was on the way to an even greater renown as the hub of America's commercial and banking aristocracy.

The eyes of Boston had been forever fixed upon its ships sailing the seven seas. Only on occasion did it cast its glance toward the hinterland—and then with a scowl, for it did not want to see the peopling of the interior. But New York, on the other hand, while in no sense neglecting the trade routes across the Atlantic, was far more concerned with the roads and canals leading to the fertile lands of Ohio, Indiana, Michigan, and Illinois. The Erie Canal, which so many had labeled Clinton's Folly a short year or two ago, though still incomplete, was already helping to make New York the logical terminal point for the movement of goods both to and from the rapidly growing West.

Bennett saw these things and was content—content though he

found no job which he deemed worthy of himself and his abilities. Sooner or later, he told himself, the right job would come his way. Till then, he resolved to apply himself in learning to know the city and its people. He read the papers at the coffee houses; he chatted with merchants, sailors, farmers, and speculators; and all the while he tried to make up his mind as to which particular field of enterprise he should devote his time and talents.

The choice, when he did make it, came unexpectedly. For that matter, he really had little to do with the choice at all. James Gordon Bennett became a journalist by virtue of a chance acquaintance at a waterfront coffee house with the owner of a southern newspaper.

Aaron Smith Willington, just returned from a trip to England, spent a fortnight in New York before returning to Charleston, South Carolina. He was in the market for new type, new presses, paper, ink, and an editorial assistant. New York was bitterly cold that winter of 1822-23, so Willington spent more time in the coffee shops drinking hot rum than he did in search of the needed supplies. Bennett, who had been doing odd jobs, overheard Willington ask the proprietor of the coffee house if he knew anyone familiar with printers' supplies whom he could employ to do the purchasing for him. Bennett introduced himself, mentioned his work as proofreader and clerk with Wells and Lilly, and offered his services. Willington, who had been born and raised in Massachusetts and was acquainted with both the men, hired Bennett forthwith.

Day after day, Bennett made the rounds of the New York firms, checking prices, placing orders, while Willington toasted his toes at the tavern hearth and warmed his innards with hot rum. The Charleston editor became impressed with the drive and ability of the scrawny Scotsman. If he only knew how to write, thought Willington, he'd be a good man for the *Charleston Courier*.

"You're a single man, aren't you, Mr. Bennett?"

"That I am, sir," came the reply. "The ladies don't seem to care for me."

"Is there anything which holds you to New York? I mean— friends, relatives, or some prospective job?"

"Nothing, sir."

"You've a good head, Bennett. You do your work well, and you know a deal about printing and publishing. Have you ever done any writing? Have you ever thought of journalism as a career?"

"Printers get better pay and so do proofreaders," came the reply.

"Pay! That's not the most important thing in the world! A journalist, Mr. Bennett, is the most potent personage of our day and age. Think of it, you as a journalist! Your thoughts, your ideas, become on the morrow the thoughts and ideas of hundreds, perhaps thousands, of people. You walk the streets hearing them utter your thoughts as their own. You sit in the taverns, while all about you people weigh and discuss, denounce or praise, what you have written. It's fascinating—let me tell you, it's fascinating."

Willington's enthusiasm struck a responsive chord in Bennett. His eyes sparkled. His wide mouth stretched wider still into an approving grin. He nodded his head.

"Excellent, Mr. Bennett, excellent. I see you understand. In that case, pack your bags and meet me here tomorrow night. You're going to be a journalist, Mr. Bennett—a journalist on one of the oldest and best newspapers in this country—and your salary will be five dollars per week."

The ten months which Bennett spent in the employ of Willington on the *Charleston Courier* were monumental to him in more ways than one. Not only did he experience the thrill of seeing his words in print, but he arrived at the definite conclusion that his life's work would be in the field of journalism. In addition to this, his stay in Charleston caused him to look forever afterwards with feelings of friendliness and sympathy upon the southern cause.

Charleston, in 1823, was the undisputed intellectual capital of the South. More than that it was perhaps the most delightful spot in the whole country. Lacking both the austerity of Boston and the hustle and confusion of New York, the capital of South Carolina was gay, yet gentle and refined. The mild climate, the profusion of flowers, the stately trees, the dignified homes and mansions, the cleanliness of the streets, the grace and beauty of the women, the refined manners of the men, and the cheerful obedience of the slaves—all these made an indelible impression upon the twenty-eight-year-old novice journalist.

Charleston was as sure of its own high purposes and fine breeding as Boston itself. And though it had given freely of its sons during the long years of the War for Independence, and proclaimed itself a leading champion of the United States Constitution, it maintained a hard-and-fast caste system with equal firmness. Its aristocracy had yielded little, if at all, to the strong winds of the Revolution or the democratic doctrines of Thomas Jefferson. Feeling so eminently secure in place and position, these Charlestonians had not feared the slogans of the French Revolution—as had the New Englanders. In fact, they thought them very fine and worth-while for all of mankind, though, of course, there was no need to apply them to their own situation, for they were convinced that they already possessed the best of all possible political, economic, and social orders.

Spokesman for the South in the nation's Capitol was John C. Calhoun, beloved son of South Carolina, and champion of a white democracy firmly resting upon a base of black chattel slaves.

With twelve eventful years in Congress behind him when Bennett reached Charleston, Calhoun had just attained that national stature which was to make him a potential candidate for the presidency for the next quarter century. Lacking the winning grace and mellow voice of Henry Clay and the cathedral-like qualities of Daniel Webster, Calhoun—gaunt, ascetic, coldly logical, and plain-spoken—did more than hold his own with them in the congressional debates. He was their peer in intellectual attainments and was the only man of his period from the South who contributed decisively to American political doctrine. That he was more instrumental than any other public figure in setting the course for the South destined to be led into war and destruction is now pretty generally admitted. But at that time his blind and devoted followers saw in him their only salvation against the steady inroads of the commercial and industrial North.

Harriet Martineau, who once happened to be in Charleston when Calhoun and his family arrived from Washington, jotted down in her notebook that "there was something very striking in the welcome he received, like that of a chief returned to the bosom of his clan. He stalked about like a monarch of this little domain, and there was certainly an air of mysterious understanding between him and his followers."

Calhoun was, in truth, the uncrowned king of South Carolina, as Bennett discovered almost before his feet touched the soil of the Palmetto State. It was Calhoun who laid the theoretical and political groundwork for nullification. And it was Calhoun who, with faultless logic and a down-to-earth realism, pulled the props from under the political philosophy of Thomas Jefferson. Thus, speaking in the name of democracy, as Parrington put it, "He attacked the foundations on which the democratic movement in America had rested, substituting for its libertarian and equalitarian doctrines, conceptions wholly alien and antagonistic to western democracy."

It is only in the light of understanding Calhoun's basic philosophy of politics, and the overwhelming grip he had upon Charleston and the whole of South Carolina, that we can get a clue to James Gordon Bennett's position on slavery, states' rights, and nullification in the years preceding the Civil War. For Bennett, too, came to accept Calhoun's theories as his own. The comparatively short stay in Charleston gave him a definite bent which he might not otherwise have had.

The limited view which young Bennett had of the South and the institution of slavery was all on the favorable side. He saw kindness and consideration—not the harsh life on the cotton plantations. He saw culture—not crudity; fine homes, not unpainted shacks; contentment and a life of comparative ease, not the chain gang, the whip, and the chiggers.

In his eagerness to make good as a journalist, Bennett learned many things and learned them well—but he never did see the blot which was slowly and surely spreading over the fair face of the South.

Not so with John Randolph of Roanoke. Sick, solitary, and half mad at his lonely home, and himself at once the end-product and the symbol of this dying social order, Randolph saw clearly what was happening. Said he, "We hug our lousy cloak around us, take another chaw of tabbacker, float the room with nastiness, or ruin the grate or fire-arms, where they happen not to be rusty, and try conclusions upon constitutional points."

The *Charleston Courier,* whose most ambitious and newest member in the early spring of 1823 was James Gordon Bennett, was more than just a good paper. It was, at that time, one of the three or four most important and influential newspapers in the whole republic, whose news and editorials were widely reprinted.

Like its worthy predecessor, the *South Carolina Weekly Gazette,* the *Courier* could say:

I'm not High-Church, nor Low-Church, nor Tory, nor Whig,
No flattering young Coxcomb, nor formal old Prig.
Not eternally talking, nor silently quaint,
No profligate sinner, no pragmatical Saint.

I'm not vain of my judgment, nor pinn'd on a Sleeve,
Nor implicitly any Thing can I believe.
To sift Truth from all Rubbish, I do what I can,
And, God knows, if I err—I'm a fallible man.

Founded in 1803 by Loring Andrews and Aaron Smith Willington—a couple of Massachusetts men turned Carolinians—the *Charleston Daily Courier* was from its inception far better edited than most of its contemporaries, of North or South. The tone of the paper was always on a high plane. Its news, though scanty to begin with, was intelligently prepared; its articles on trade and politics were better than average, and its editorials continued for a great many years to follow the lead of its very first editorial, which was entitled "Intolerance." That editorial concluded:

"To moderate, not to inflame—to mediate and heal, not exasperate —to fill up the hideous gulph which now yawns across the commonwealth, dividing one portion of the people from the other, shall be the object of our strenuous efforts as it is of our most anxious wishes. Were the former as potent, as the latter is sincere, there would soon be in this country but one heart, one hand, one sentiment, and one voice—and that voice would proclaim to the world: America is and ever shall be a Confederated Republic."

Willington, who became sole owner of the *Courier* in 1813, scooped every newspaper in the country on word of the Peace of Ghent, by rowing out beyond the bar at Charleston Harbor to board an incoming vessel and get the latest news from Europe. Editors everywhere congratulated him on his achievement, but none took the trouble to follow his example in getting the latest information from across the water.

Willington, however, made it a point to send a boat out (usually rowed by two stalwart slaves) whenever an incoming vessel was sighted off the bar. A member of the newspaper staff was regularly assigned to this task—and was known about town as the *Courier's* "boarding officer."

The latest addition to the staff, whom Willington had brought south with him, discovered that—unlike the rowdy and restless men, able but half-educated, who made up the working crew of most newspapers at the time—the *Courier* was staffed by men of scholarship and brilliance.

Under Willington served William Crafts, the actual editor-in-charge, of whom it was said that "no limit could have been assigned to his reputation, felicity and usefulness, had his application been equal to his genius." In other words, he was lazy—the one charge never used in the whole dictionary of abuse later heaped upon Bennett. Crafts, too, like Willington, was originally from New England—a transplanted Bostonian who carried the torch of Harvard into the South.

William Gilmore Simms, novelist, essayist, and acute observer of the social scene of the South, was a member of the *Courier's* staff, as were Thomas Bee, Henry T. Farmer, Reverend Samuel Gilman, William Henry Timrod, and that vigorous pamphleteer, James Carrol Courtney.

With such an array of talent—the cream of Charleston's intelligentsia—the *Courier* well deserved the title of the most distinguished newspaper in the United States. Bennett was indeed fortunate in having begun his career as journalist on such a paper, with such a battery of able men as his co-workers, and in such a friendly, genial, and cultured town as Charleston.

The dancing craze had reached Charleston about 1820, and to the consternation of the older folk, the venerable St. Cecelia Society, which, since 1770, had been conducting musical festivals both vocal and instrumental, found itself compelled in 1822 to give up the concerts and substitute dancing assemblies instead. Time after time, members of the *Courier* staff did their best to induce Bennett to attend these dances, but he stubbornly refused to do so. Not only then, but for many years thereafter, Bennett found it difficult to participate in the social life of his colleagues. He knew that his figure was ungainly, his face ugly, his speech harsh and queer-sounding, his manners brusque, and his tongue sharp. Knowing these facts, instead of trying to correct or modify them, he scoffed at those who wasted their time with such tomfoolery as dancing, flirting, drinking, or playing cards. He turned all his energies into his work, driving himself furiously till exhaustion brought almost instant sleep. That cynicism, that scoffing attitude, which was for many years to keep him from success, and which later on was to make his pen the most successful and vitriolic in America—all this he built up, perhaps quite unconsciously, as his psychological defense because of these shortcomings.

And thus it was that Bennett, during his period of apprenticeship in journalism at the *Charleston Courier,* never became intimate with other members of the staff or anyone else in the city. Instead, he familiarized himself with the history and background of the city and the state. He wandered about the countryside. He watched the Indians, with squaws and children trailing behind—ragged and filthy remnants of strong and warlike tribes—shuffle about the streets selling pottery or earning a few pence by showing their skill with bow and arrow.

He peeped in upon the famous Two Bit Club, and was himself asked to join that of St. Andrew, to which every worthy son of Scotland belonged. He listened in the coffee shops to the brilliant conversations of the other leading intellectuals of Charleston who were not connected with the *Courier*—Stephen Elliot, Hugh Legare, Edmund Morford, Thomas Grimké, and J. D. B. DuBow, whose *Review* was soon to gain national fame.

He learned with amazement and horror that during the previous year (1822) Charleston had nipped in the bud a slave insurrection carefully planned by the blacks of the region. One of the ringleaders of this Negro rebellion had been Rollo, a slave belonging to Governor Bennett, who confessed that on Sunday night, June 16, "a force would cross from James Island and land on South Bay, march up and seize the Arsenal and Guard House." Another group of the insurrectionists was to seize the other Arsenal, while a third contingent was to gather near the flour mill of Governor Bennett, then, at a given signal, "sweep the town with fire and sword, not permitting a single white soul to escape."

The authorities had moved swiftly and quietly. More than 130 Negroes were arrested. Trials were held. Thirty-five of the ringleaders were executed and thirty-four more sentenced to jail or transportation outside the state; the remainder were acquitted.

Bennett's work on the *Courier* was largely that of translating into English from Spanish or French the latest news from the Havana papers which were picked up from the incoming ships. At that time, fast packet ships sailed regularly from Cadiz, Spain, to Havana. Hence, news from Spain, France, Portugal, and Italy very frequently first reached the American public by way of the *Charleston Courier,* rather than via London, Liverpool, and Havre to New York or Boston.

Latin America, too, was in the throes of rebellion at this time; and so Bennett, by virtue of his position as translator for the *Courier,* was forced to familiarize himself with the customs, politics, and economics of the South American countries and the West Indies. This was exceedingly helpful in later days. For nearly thirty years in the *New York Herald* he wrote penetrating articles and editorials on developments in Latin America; they are still worth reading and show him to have been far better equipped to discuss Latin America than any of his journalist contemporaries.

We do not know what prompted Bennett to leave his position in Charleston. He, himself, never left any record of it that has been found, nor did Willington or his co-editors.

Richard Yeadon, who became editor of the *Courier* in 1832, and who for nearly thirty years steered its course in opposition to Calhoun with his theories of states' rights and nullification, used to boast that James Gordon Bennett had obtained his very first lessons in journalism on the *Courier*—that it was, in fact, his newspaper cradle.

But proud as Yeadon might be to think that Bennett had taken his first steps in the field of journalism on the staff of the *Courier,* he later looked upon Bennett as an unmitigated scoundrel and wrote of him and his paper in 1858: "This scurrilous journal has made a gross, vulgar, and unprovoked attack on one of the editors of the *Courier,* so utterly at war with propriety and decency, as to require no other notice, than an expression of unmitigated contempt for the author, whose notorious venality, destitution of moral sense, and insensibility to shame, have long since caused him to be put on the social ban, and to be *tabooed* by the press of New York, where he is generally regarded as a moral leper, whose touch is pollution, and whose disease is so deeply seated that not Arbana and Pharpar, the rivers of Damascus, nor Jordan and all the waters of Israel, can wash him clean."

Willington's protégé had certainly made good as a journalist!

5. Grub Streets of America

TRAVELING by steamer from Charleston to Philadelphia, and then overland by stage coach, James Gordon Bennett reached New York within a week, surprised to find how much it had grown during his year's absence. Though the streets were filled with mud and snow, the sky black with the smoke of a thousand chimneys, and the ears of pedestrians battered by the rumble and creak of drays, carts, and wagons over which could be heard the shouts of the teamsters, Bennett was glad, genuinely glad, to be back in the city he would henceforth call "home."

"Bless my heart! you talk like a southerner," teased his land-lady.

"Yep, he's the spittin' image of John Calhoun," put in her husband, "and carries hisself more erect and jaunty-like than when he was here afore."

Bennett was quite a hero at the McCracken's boarding house, returning, as he had, from a strange and distant land. New Yorkers, then as now, were too concerned with the affairs of their own little island to become familiar with the rest of the country.

With the smell of printer's ink in his nose and the taste of the quill-pen in his mouth, Bennett was willing to write pro or con about any person, subject, or issue. The important thing was to get a job. He was entering his profession as a hack—the lowest species in the writing profession, who lets not his left hand know what the other is writing. He was taking his place in the Fourth Estate on the Grub Streets of America.

Grub Street was never Easy Street, but even if James Gordon Bennett had realized its more foreboding character, that fact would in no sense have dampened his spirits.

61

Assured that he had at last found his true vocation, and exhilarated by his journalistic endeavors at Charleston, Bennett returned to New York confident that he was already well along the highway to success. New York, he reasoned, was the logical place for an ambitious writer, for not only was it the largest and fastest-growing city in the whole country, it was also the undisputed newspaper capital of the New World. It had fathered no less than 127 papers, as against ninety-eight for Philadelphia and seventy-one for Boston. But if the journalistic birth rate was high, so too was the mortality rate, for fifty-five of the 127 did not live a full year—and only twenty-three had been able to function for a full decade.

The New York to which Bennett returned in the early spring of 1824 had as many daily papers as the New York of 1942. Its population, growing by leaps and bounds, was rapidly approaching 150,000. He had heard it reported on good authority that three of these dailies—the *Mercantile Advertiser,* the *New York Evening Post,* and the *Daily Gazette,* had attained daily circulation in excess of 2,000 copies, while that of the others varied from 800 to 1,750 copies per day. There were rumors that the *Evening Post* was netting a profit of $25,000 per year—a truly fabulous sum!

Furthermore, political struggles were again mounting in fury. The "era of good feeling" was already ended, a full year before James Monroe retired from the presidential chair. Political activity, Bennett had already come to realize, meant work for newspapermen. Parties, cliques, and factions bought or subsidized existing papers or established new organs to carry their message to the electorate. Besides, there was the rapid growth of trade and industry, which meant that commercial firms, banks, shippers of goods, and industrialists would advertise more freely in the daily press, thus augmenting heavily its source of income. Facing such a world, it is easy to understand why Bennett could have such confidence in himself and his newfound profession. Nor did he let himself forget that he need not grab at the first position offered—for he had nearly a hundred dollars to tide him over till the appropriate employment was found.

As soon as he had arranged for board and room at three dollars per week, the young journalist planned his line of attack. First of

all, he must familiarize himself with each of the daily papers. Then
he would strike up acquaintance with members of the staff, with
the printers, and, if possible, with the editors. Following this, he
would offer his services to that paper which seemed to provide the
greatest opportunities for advancement. Such a program, he reflected, was both sound and sensible. His own experience, energy,
and enthusiasm, combined with it, must of necessity spell success.

In the year 1824 you did not hail a passing newsboy or stop at a
corner newsstand, drug store, or tobacco shop to get the latest edition of your favorite paper. Drug stores sold only drugs and tobacco
shops only pipes and tobacco. Newsstands and newsboys, as we
know them, had not yet come into being. And besides, newspapers
printed but one edition daily. If you wanted a paper, you either
subscribed to it for a year (the usual price was ten dollars), read
it at your favorite coffee shop or club, or went to the office of the
paper (or the printer) and bought a copy.

The newspapers of 1824 were not meant for general consumption, and any editor so brash as to have his paper hawked in the
streets like fresh greens, would have been disowned by the newspaper fraternity and his subscribers alike. So far as their *news* value
was concerned, beyond the accurate reporting of the arrival and
departure of ships and the nature of their cargo, and the belated
reporting of speeches by political leaders, labors of the Congress,
and the actions of the President and the governors—all else was
largely opinion.

The press of 1824 was still predominantly political. Its editorials
were always slanted in favor of those interests which underwrote
its deficits by outright subsidy or through the medium of advertising. The press was used by some to avenge private wrongs done
to themselves or their families. By others, it was used to harass
or destroy business or political rivals. Editors, in turn, learned how
to use their papers as organs of blackmail, holding the threat of
public scandal over the heads of their victims. If among the rumor,
gossip, vilification, and praise, there was any news, it was scarcely
as a conscious achievement, but rather as an unsought-for by-
product.

The daily paper of 1824 was usually a six-column affair of four pages. The type was small, often bad, and was unrelieved by headlines or illustrations. The successful papers were filled with scores of small advertisements, which occupied from one half to three-quarters of each page, including the front page. Advertisers usually paid thirty dollars per year to the paper, which entitled them to as much space and as many notices as they desired in the paper for a whole year. These advertisements were generally as dull and uninspiring as the rest of the paper; but what was even worse, they were frequently allowed to remain for weeks and months after they had accomplished their object. Whole columns, sometimes whole pages, of long-dead announcements and notices continued to stare the reader in the face, day after day.

The quickened life of the city and the nation was apparent no matter which way one turned. Schools were multiplying; illiteracy was being reduced among both native born and immigrant. Lowly clerks, laborers, and farmers were clamoring for the right of suffrage—and getting it. Women, too, were asking questions about matters not directly related to church, child, or kitchen. Nathan Hale, editor of the *Boston Daily Advertiser* and a nephew of the Revolutionary War hero, was one of the few journalists who sensed this stirring, this "insatiable appetite which exists in all classes of the people of this country for *news.*" "It is a thirst so universal," remarked Hale, "that it has given rise to a general and habitual form of salutation on the meeting of friends and strangers: *What's the news?*"

But Nathan Hale failed to recognize the significance of this newly acquired national trait of the American people and to make his paper meet this challenge. Instead, he grumbled and fumed at it, asserting that "this diseased state of the public taste" placed new and heavy obstacles in the way of the editor.

To Hale's statement almost every editor in the country would have echoed "Amen," for the editors of that day were rarely well educated or cultured men, aware of their responsibility in the molding of public opinion. As a rule they possessed a certain facility in the use of the written word. They could denounce or ridicule, but seldom analyze or explain. They were highly partisan in outlook and hasty in judgment, and were more concerned with blasting an opponent than in supplying the reader with facts.

Coleman, the Federalist editor of the *Evening Post,* had been highly commended for his rhymed assault upon two Jeffersonian editors, James Cheetham of the *American Citizen* and William Duane of the *Aurora:*

> *Lie on, Duane, lie on for pay,*
> *And Cheetham, lie thou too,*
> *More 'gainst truth you cannot say*
> *Than truth can say 'gainst you.*

Charges and counter-charges of bribery and corruption were the regular stock-in-trade of the editors during the early decades of the nineteenth century. These led inevitably to physical assault of editor upon editor, till the reading public took it for granted that the men who wrote their editorials must be prepared to give or take thrashings as part of their journalistic duties.

The condition of the American press in 1824 was still essentially that which it had been in 1807 when Thomas Jefferson asserted: "It is a melancholy truth, that a suppression of the press could not more completely deprive the nation of its benefits, than is done by its abandoned prostitution to falsehood. Nothing can now be believed which is seen in a newspaper. Truth itself becomes suspicious by being put into that polluted vehicle. The real extent of this state of misinformation is known only to those who are in situations to confront facts within their knowledge with the lies of the day."

Having made a careful study of every daily paper in New York, young Bennett set out to offer his services to the editors. The *American,* an evening paper, supported by Tammany and edited by Charles King (later president of Columbia College), appealed to Bennett. It was new (founded in 1819) and aggressive. Editor King had difficulty in understanding Bennett nor did he think the ungainly and ugly foreigner a suitable staff member for the *American.* Bennett's first venture toward New York journalism was repulsed.

He next tried for a position on the *Commercial Advertiser.*

Founded by the great lexicographer Noah Webster in 1793 as a Federalist organ, the *Advertiser* had become the spokesman for the vested interests of the city. Its policy, as stated by Webster, was that of "The Friend of Government, of Freedom, of Virtue, and Every Species of Improvement." The *Advertiser* was probably the first isolationist paper in the United States. Its editor cautioned his fellow citizens "against all foreign intrigues, because I am aware of the fatal dissensions they would introduce into our councils, and because I hold it proper for us to attach ourselves to no foreign nation whatever, and be in truth and spirit, *Americans.*"

Webster had given up his post to Zachariah Lewis, who in turn had been replaced by Col. W. L. Stone in 1820. The Colonel was as unimpressed by Bennett as his colleague, Charles King. The best Stone promised was that he would "consider" any material Bennett wrote.

At the *Evening Post,* where caustic William Coleman had been the skipper since it was founded in 1801 (founded, it was said, by Alexander Hamilton to further the fortunes of his Party), there was no opening for Bennett, either. But two years later, in the summer of 1826, Coleman added to his staff a thirty-year-old New Englander. This young man, an indifferent and unenthusiastic attorney, had already gained a nation-wide reputation as a poet. His name was William Cullen Bryant.

Unlike James Gordon Bennett, the celebrated author of *Thanatopsis* entered upon his career in journalism with considerable misgiving. Yet he brought to his new profession high intelligence, great integrity, and a fluent and forceful pen. He alone, of all Bennett's contemporaries, was still to be found at his editor's desk at the *Evening Post* when Bennett passed away in 1872, for William Cullen Bryant, who was so hesitant about the position offered to him by Coleman, remained on as editor, and later as publisher, of the *Post* for fifty-two years.

Bennett, meanwhile, continued his round of the newspapers only to find that there were no openings available for him. Most of the papers, he learned, were deeply in debt. Their editors were mostly poor, arrogant, and lazy. The editorial staff, which seldom exceeded four men, was equally lazy and arrogant, but inevitably much poorer than the editors. Their rate of pay varied from five to eight dollars per week. They were as a rule heavy drinkers, and none of them looked kindly upon the sober, earnest, uncouth foreigner who plied them with questions about their jobs and the papers they worked for.

As the days grew longer, Bennett's purse grew shorter. But he continued to make the rounds of the daily and weekly papers certain that, sooner or later, he would get a job as a newspaperman. His spare time was spent in reading every daily paper he could lay his hands on, in getting acquainted with local politics, and in lengthy discussions with acquaintances about economic and political problems of the nation. It may have been one of these newfound friends who suggested to Bennett, that he expound his theories to a wider circle of listeners.

During the summer of 1824, Bennett blossomed out as a lecturer on political economy at the old Dutch Church in Ann Street. For more than a fortnight, a tall, thin, shabbily dressed Scotsman did his best to win an audience in the vestry of the old Dutch Church. Ministers and laymen alike were hostile to the experiment. Bennett, himself, soon realized that lecturing was not his strong point. He gave it up to continue his search for employment as a journalist.

It is quite probable that he found odd jobs as a proofreader during those long months of bitter disappointment. And we do know that at last, in desperation, he decided to go back to the disagreeable job of schoolteacher, for in October, he had printed the following notice, copies of which he posted in many parts of the city:

Permanent Commercial School

The subscriber, encouraged by several gentlemen, intends opening in Ann, near Nassau street, an English classical and mathematical school, for the instruction of young gentlemen intended for mercantile pursuits. Instruction will be given in the following branches:

Reading, elocution, penmanship, and arithmetic; algebra, astronomy, history, and geography; moral philosophy, commercial law, and political economy; English grammar and composition; and also, if required, the French and Spanish languages, by natives of these countries.

Book-keeping and merchant's accounts will be taught in the most approved and scientific forms.

The school will be conducted, in all the principal branches, according to the inductive method of instruction, and particularly so in arithmetic, geography, and English grammar.

It will commence about the first of November.

References—J. S. Bartlett, M.D., Albion office; Messrs. Smith and Hyslop, Pearl street; Mr. Henry T. Magarey, Broadway; Mr. P. Whitin, jr., Maiden Lane.

J. GORDON BENNETT.

N.B.—Application may be made to J.G.B., at 148 Fulton street.

The pretentious plans were presented to the public, but the school itself did not materialize. Fortunately for Bennett, he did at last succeed in getting temporary employment in his chosen field.

The first man in New York to hire him was a stolid, unimaginative printer, Thomas Snowden, by name, to whom the New York General Republican Committee had just turned over control of the *National Advocate*. The man who had been editing that paper, Mordecai M. Noah, had turned in his resignation.

Mordecai M. Noah was to play a considerable part in Bennett's life, first as editor over him on the *Enquirer,* later as co-worker with him on the *Courier and Enquirer,* and then for many years as rival editor and publisher.

Of the many colorful characters which Jewry has given to the New World, few have been more picturesque than Mordecai Manuel Noah. Dramatist, diplomat, and demagogue; journalist, judge, and self-proclaimed leader of world Jewry—such was the man who was to cross the path of Bennett for many years to come. Noah was born in Philadelphia in 1785. Handsome, keen of mind, and quick of tongue, he dabbled in politics before he was old enough to vote, and by 1808 was a leader among Philadelphia's young Democrats. By appropriate wire-pulling Noah wangled himself the job as United States Consul to the Barbary States from President Madison, which position he held from 1813 to 1815.

Back in New York after his foreign adventures, Noah was initiated into Tammany politics by his uncle Naphtali Phillips, who was already a power in that organization. The *National Advocate* had been founded in 1813 by the Tammany crowd, as their exclusive organ. Its editor, Henry Wheaton, was appointed to the State bench in 1816. Meanwhile, ownership of the *National Advocate* had passed into the hands of Phillips, who placed his young nephew, Mordecai M. Noah, at the helm.

The ambitious editor set out to become both the mouthpiece as well as the penman for Tammany. For eight years he was its front man, writing, speaking, drawing up declarations, odes, and resolutions for the organization. Isaac Goldberg, his biographer, asserted that Noah wanted not only to make a good living for himself, but he wanted also "the power to advance himself in the local, state and national politics. His eye swept the panorama, as it were, alighting now on the shrievalty, now on the contract for the State printing, again upon a foreign post that would make him once again the proud—and redeemed—representative of his people."

When he was not making speeches, writing editorials, or pulling wires to advance himself politically, Mordecai M. Noah was either busy as a playwright or romancing on how to create a new kingdom for the Jews of the world. Several of his plays were highly successful, a fact which led Fitz-Greene Halleck to versify about him:

> *To these authentic facts each bucktail swore;*
> *But Clinton's friends averred, in contradiction,*
> *They were but fables, told by Mr. Noah,*
> *Who had a privilege to deal in fiction,*
> *Because he's written travels, and a melo-*
> *Drama; and was, withal, a pleasant fellow.*

John Quincy Adams, then Secretary of State to President Monroe, noted in his diary during the summer of 1820 that an emissary of Noah had called upon him. "He [Noah] has great projects for colonizing Jews in this country, and wants to be sent as chargé d'affaires to Vienna for the promotion of them. He is an incorrect, and very ignorant, but sprightly writer, and as a partisan editor of a newspaper has considerable power. He argues with great earnestness his merits in supporting the administration, as a title to the President's favor. He is, like all editors of newspapers in this country who have any talent, an author to be let. There is not one of them whose friendship is worth having, nor one whose enmity is not formidable. They are a sort of assassins who sit with loaded blunder-busses at the corner of streets and fire them off for hire or for sport at any passenger they select. They are principally foreigners; but Noah is a native. He is salaried at a low rate by the anti-Clintonian Tammanies at New York to keep up a constant fire against his administration; and Noah pretends that this is serving the General Government, because Clinton is a standing presidential candidate and carries on an insidious war against Mr. Monroe."

Nothing came of this attempt by Noah. But in the meantime, he was busily engaged in maneuvering himself into position as the strong man of the Tammany Society and at the same time perfecting plans for a giant Jewish colony on Grant Island in the Niagara River.

By 1822 Noah had sufficient power to gain for himself the lucrative position of sheriff. But this position, contended his biographer, crystallized the Jewish influence in Tammany so that "the latent anti-Semitism in the municipal life came naturally to a head."

Many Christians were horrified at the thought of a Jewish sheriff. And they pointed out the eternal disgrace of having a Christian hanged by a Jew. Noah, never at a loss for a pointed comeback, replied that it was a pretty bad sample of Christianity who would need hanging at anyone's hands!

Certain it was that Noah gained few friends but many enemies during the year and a half he served as sheriff. The position was to be open for election in 1824, so Noah devoted the columns of the *Advocate* to blasting his foes and telling the electorate of his own many fine accomplishments. Tammany split wide open on the issue—and when the votes were counted, Noah had lost the contest. It was at this point that he resigned his position as editor of the *National Advocate,* that Snowden temporarily took over, and that James Gordon Bennett obtained temporary employment on that paper.

Tammany was not anxious to lose the service of Noah, so he was brought back to the editorship. Meanwhile, the paper was heavily in debt, and Naphtali Phillips could no longer meet its deficits. Noah and his friends finally managed to get a wealthy shipbuilder, Henry Eckford, to agree to put up enough money to keep the paper afloat, and it was agreed that Noah's salary would be cut to one thousand dollars per year.

No sooner had the scheme been consummated than a bitter struggle broke out between Noah and Eckford. Noah was ousted from the *National Advocate,* but since he held the lease on the property he refused to let Eckford and Snowden get at the presses, type, and paper on hand. These then enjoined him from using the name of the paper. During the next few months New York was deluged with *Advocates.* For a short time both Noah and Eckford-Snowden used the name *National Advocate* for their respective papers. Then, when Noah was prohibited by court order from using that name, he called his paper *Noah's New York National Advocate.* But within a year his opponents had obtained another court order forbidding him from using the name *Advocate* altogether. He then adopted the name *New York Enquirer.*

In the midst of all this battle, Noah took time off to launch one of the most fantastic schemes of the age. In the summer of 1825, there was sent out to the Jews of all the world a proclamation written and signed by "Mordecai Manuel Noah, citizen of the United States, late consul of said States for the city and kingdom of Tunis, high sheriff of New York, counsellor at law, and, by the grace of God, Governor and Judge of Israel."

The Hebrews were told that he was their king; that he was reviving the Jewish nation; that a census of world Jewry was to be undertaken at once; and all rabbis and elders were ordered to respect his proclamation and see that it was carried out.

The new homeland—upon a forest-covered eight-mile-long island midway between the United States and Canada—was given the name of Ararat. The engraved cornerstone for Noah's kingdom, for many years the property of the Buffalo Historical Museum, is all that remains of that dream. Upon it are these words:

ARARAT

A City of Refuge for the Jews
Founded by MORDECAI MANUEL NOAH
in the month of Tizri, Sept. 1825
and
in the Fiftieth Year of American Independence

During all this time, James Gordon Bennett had been getting more work from Snowden as well as from the *Commercial Advertiser*. His name was becoming known to the newspaper fraternity, not so much because of fine writing or originality, but because of his dogged perseverance, his sustained and indefatigable industry. No task was too arduous. No job was too humble. And the editors learned that he would work at any hour of the day or night. He was punctual and exact in his work. He had no vices. He neither smoked, drank, nor gambled. "I eat and drink to live," he declared a few years later, "not live to eat and drink. Social glasses of wine are my aversion; public dinners are my abomination; all species of gormandizing, my utter scorn and contempt. When I am hungry, I eat; when thirsty, drink. Wine or viands taken for society, or to stimulate conversation, tend only to dissipation, indolence, poverty, contempt, and death."

Neither editors nor politicians welcomed such a man into their homes or clubs, but they were glad to use his enormous capacity for labor—and it was to this that he owed his first upward steps on the ladder of success.

For a few short weeks in 1825, Bennett took over the ownership of a small weekly publication, the *New York Courier*. This was the first Sunday paper in America. It had been founded earlier that year by a poor but intelligent newspaperman named John Tyron. Bennett had written various items for Tyron; but when the editor found the public was not yet prepared for a Sunday paper, he gladly turned it over to Bennett for a few dollars and some promissory notes. It took Bennett less than a month to discover that he could not make the paper go, so he turned it back to Tyron, who published a few more issues before he let it die. Many years elapsed before the next Sunday paper made its appearance, the *Sunday Morning News,* which lasted for several years.

The election of 1824 had greatly excited Bennett. Already an active, though lowly Tammany man, he had his first baptism in national politics. Like so many of the common people, he was attracted to the colorful candidate from Tennessee, General Andrew Jackson, and was quite at odds with those compromisers who shouted: "Give us

JOHN QUINCY ADAMS
Who can write
And ANDREW JACKSON
Who can fight.

In the four-cornered fight, Jackson won the largest popular vote—153,544 against 108,740 for Adams, 47,136 for Henry Clay and 46,618 for W. C. Crawford. John C. Calhoun was elected Vice-President by an overwhelming majority.

The electoral vote indicated that no candidate had a majority. Therefore in accordance with the Constitution of the United States, the House of Representatives had to select the president from one of the three leading contestants. This meant that Henry Clay, who had the smallest electoral vote, was eliminated. On the other hand, Clay was the most powerful person in the House, and it was obvious that he would be the deciding factor in determining who should be the next president. Clay had already put himself on record against the "military chieftain" several times.

All through the winter of 1824-25 popular indignation mounted higher as it became more than ever obvious that Clay would not bow to the will of the people. When Congress convened on the second Wednesday of February, 1825, Clay threw his support to John Quincy Adams, who was elected.

Bennett, the newcomer to the strange ways of a political democracy, was for the time inclined to agree with the paper which declared: "The sale of the presidency to Mr. Adams has disheartened many worthy persons and made them doubt the capacity of the people for self-government." But he refused to go along with the indignant Jacksonian editor who announced in black-faced type:

EXPIRED AT WASHINGTON

on the 9th of February, of POISON administered by the assassin hands of John Quincy Adams, the usurper, and Henry Clay —— the Virtue, Liberty and Independence of the United States.

6. First Washington Correspondent

HAVING lost the battle of the *Advocates,* Mordecai M. Noah late in 1826 changed his paper's name to the *New York Morning Enquirer.* Symbolic either of its owner's name or high moral purpose was a woodcut of the Ark, floating gently on quiet waters, above which was a dove bearing a leaf on a twig. This woodcut—the only illustration in the entire paper—was conspicuously centered on the top of the front page. The editor's name appeared in heavy blackface type at the left of the paper, more conspicuous by far than any item in the paper itself. Noah believed in advertising himself to the limit. At no time, however, did the name of any of his co-editors ever appear in the *Enquirer.*

The paper itself was neither better nor worse than its competitors. Its front page was usually a solid mass of small advertisements. Reading matter, made up of essays, bits of verse, editorials, items of news culled from European papers, information on incoming and outgoing vessels, and political harangues—these made up, at best, one full page of material. The rest of the paper was merely more advertisements. Politically, the *Enquirer* was pro-Jackson.

It was politics—politics plus the need for work—which brought Bennett over to Noah. Beyond that they had little in common. Noah acknowledged the journalistic ability of the scrawny, squint-eyed Scotsman, and on more than one occasion had felt the barbed sting of his pen. Bennett, whose ego blossomed under the fire of attack and criticism, viewed the Jewish editor with good-natured contempt. He felt that Noah was a better dramatist than journalist, and a better actor than dramatist.

The *National Advocate* meanwhile had shifted over to the camp of President Adams, a course which Bennett refused to follow. So,

74

undaunted by his former attacks upon Noah, Bennett paid him a visit and offered his services to the *Enquirer*. Noah did not make an immediate commitment. He did, however, agree to buy specific articles from time to time. Meanwhile, the two men would get to know each other better. Noah was no fool. He wasn't going to buy a pig in a poke. Bennett, he decided, was too volatile a substance to be taken into the inner sanctum without careful examination.

Bennett, for all his frugality and hard work, had only a few dollars between himself and starvation. He agreed to the terms, and began forthwith to write articles for Noah. Noah rejected most of them. Those he did accept were largely rewritten. In this way he hoped to tame and humble his would-be assistant.

To keep alive, Bennett tried his hand at versification again and also wrote many short stories and essays for the New York and Philadelphia papers and magazines. He journeyed to Washington in December, 1826, where he remained for nearly a month. During this time he must have written a great many political articles, and he may well have done work for some of the Tammany men, whom he knew well—but we are certain of only one article from his pen at that time. Written on December 30, 1826, and published in the *Enquirer* on January 5, it told of the sensation created in the House of Representatives by the Vice-President's communication to that body respecting charges made against him of profiteering on contracts when he was Secretary of War.

The letter was a straightforward piece of reporting but in no sense unusual. The only glimpse of the Bennett to-be was contained in his comments on the remarks of Congressman Rivers, who represented Thomas Jefferson's old district in Virginia. In contrast to so many other congressmen whose speeches were "stuffed with political common-places, rhetorical flourishes and thread-bare quotations," that of Rivers was "brief, condensed, clear, elegant, forcible in argument . . . and very sound in its republican doctrine."

Back in New York again after his first trip to the nation's capital, Bennett was busier than ever in his determination to become a successful journalist. His head was forever popping with ideas, which the editors of the day, with invariable monotony, told him were wild, visionary, and impractical. He called them "blockheads" and "fools" which in no way helped in the sale of articles. Many of the editors were lazy—mentally as well as physically—content to follow the conventional pattern of the newspaper world. They did not dream of trying to shape a paper that would have a broad mass appeal. They were in no hurry for news—and their definition of what constituted news was woefully narrow. Articles and editorials were considered good only if they moralized; well-written only if they were dull and ponderous, abounding in poetical allusions and Latin phrases. Beyond this, of course, every paper was the spokesman for a particular political party or clique. Hence, every item that appeared in print had to be carefully weighed in terms of its particular value at enhancing the prestige of one's political friends or blasting the reputation of one's political enemies.

James Gordon Bennett was as yet in full agreement with the editors that a newspaper must, of necessity, be a staunch political partisan. He himself was wedded to the doctrines of Andrew Jackson, to such a degree that he could not and would not work for any paper that supported John Quincy Adams.

Partisan though he was, Bennett knew full well that man does not live by politics alone; and with this in mind he again approached Mordecai Noah in the spring of 1827, asking that he be permitted to write light and humorous sketches for the *Enquirer*. After much hemming and hawing, the paunchy editor agreed to permit the columns of the *Enquirer* to be used as a journalistic guinea pig.

The readers of the staid and stodgy *New York Enquirer* were undoubtedly shocked when, on Friday, April 27, 1827, they read an article entitled, "Shaking Hands," which was obviously out of place in the journal. The article was an indication of Bennett's sense of humor, and showed as well that he was no longer a novice writer.

Foreigners who come amongst us [began the article] frequently complain of our national propensity to *shake hands*. On the slightest introduction, an American seizes the stranger's hands and shakes it with a violence that sometimes threatens dislocation. It is evidence, no doubt, of great kindliness of feeling, and is meant to be a compliment, not a curse. It is, at best, a troublesome civility and may be abandoned without any imputation on our courtesy or our sincerity. But what are we to substitute in its place?

Bennett then proceeded to discuss the many forms of salutation existing in countries and regions, real or imaginary. The Greenlanders, he claimed, never saluted each other because that would lower them in their own eyes. On the other hand:

The whole of *Caraminia* testify their joy on meeting a friend by opening a vein and presenting it to him to suck the blood. This vampire fashion has not much to recommend it, except with very plethoric people. . . . The *Ethiopian* takes his friend's garment and binds it around himself in such a way as to leave the former naked. This is a better system because you get a cloak or waistcoat whenever you meet a friend. Yet, it has its disadvantages, for you lose the same things if your friend meets you. In *New Guinea,* they place leaves on the head of the person saluted. This is very rural and picturesque, but it would not always be practicable on Broadway or Hudson Street—in a high wind particularly. It is, however, an appropriate mode of saluting a poet and we (that is, *ourselves*) mean to adopt it toward our friends B***** and H*****. The *Laplanders* press their noses strongly against that of the individual they are saluting. In cold weather we should remonstrate against any such salutation. In saluting an impertinent enemy it is, however, a very agreeable and impressive thing to press his *nose* strongly.

Bennett continued his banter with respect to many other strange types of salutation.

The *Phillipinos* put their hands upon their cheeks, and bending forward, poke out one leg behind them, in the style of those ingenious devices which head the advertisements for runaway slaves in the Southern papers. . . . The Chinese . . . have a kind of ritual or academy of compliments, where the number of reverences and genuflections, and the words suitable to each, are regularly laid down. Ambassadors repeat these ceremonies 40 days before appearing in Court. Now, though we like their tea, their silk and their cotton stuffs, yet we have a special abhorrence of *Kotou,* nor would we submit to it in order to be made Mandarin of the highest Order of Buttons, or shiek of the province of *Whang-Foki-Hi-Hum.*

In the *Straits of Sunda,* the foot of the person saluted is raised and passed gently along the right leg and over the body. The Japanese takes off one shoe; the people of Arracan take off their sandals if they meet in the street; in the house they take off their *inexpressibles.* This last may be an *honorable* way of evincing respect, but it would not do in our cold climate, with the thermometer 15 degrees below zero; it would be 'a custom more honored in the *breach* than in the observance.' . . .

At *Cairo* the question is, "How do you perspire?" because a dry skin is looked on as an indication of deadly fever. . . . In the Southern provinces of *China,* the salutation is, *y a fan?* Have you ate your rice? etc., etc.

In *Africa,* a young betrothed damsel puts a little water in a calabash, and kneeling by the side of her lover, invites him to wash his hands in it; the girl, then weeping with pleasure, drinks the water. This is looked on as the greatest proof of fidelity and attachment that can be manifested by a lover.

We are bachelors, as all the world knows, and, of course, are exceedingly anxious to quit that state of "single blessedness" but we would wither forever on the "virgin thorn" rather than sentence any "young betrothed damsel" to such sacrilegious observance, particularly after having handled a hundred mail papers. However, the practice of the African brides is not quite so singular as that which the early travelers tell us prevail amongst some of the Tartar tribes. We will follow the example of Gibbon, and "veil it in the obscurity of a learned language." The bride, says the traveler, *ad hospitem quem maximo honore officeri valuerit mittit poculum urinae suae plenum quod necesse sit ut bibat; aliter fecisse haud levi injuriae ducitur.* This is worse than swallowing the contents of the wash-basin, but love and fashion reconcile us to many strange things.

We are forgetting all this time that our object was to choose some new mode of salutation for ourselves. Our specimens are numerous, and the reader may choose which he pleases. None of them, however, appear worth being introduced into general use. We shall continue our researches and the public may possibly soon hear their result. In the meantime, the old custom of *shaking hands* must remain in *status quo.*

Mordecai M. Noah was flabbergasted at the number of extra copies of the *Enquirer* sold as a result of the article. There were many who were amazed to learn of the strange customs in far-off lands. Others realized at once that here was a new and fresh note in journalism. Merchants and brokers roared loudly over their rum or coffee as they discussed the impertinent article.

Bennett, noting the response with pleasure, lost no time in presenting the readers of Mr. Noah's paper with another article. Once again the town rocked with laughter—and, incidentally, circulation grew.

This time the subject under discussion, as it appeared in the April 26 issue, was entitled "Intemperance."

The *Times* says that New York is a very *moral city*. Now the *Times* is a very moral newspaper and we would gladly bow to its authority— if we could. But there is a vast mass of fact which refutes the assertions of our contemporary in the most awfully conclusive way.

A Mr. Lewis Dwight, for example, has printed in the *Boston Recorder* a melancholy catalogue of victims of intemperance in our city. With a prudence, as commendable as it is rare, he has forborne to give their *names,* and contents himself with the initial letters merely. He runs through the whole alphabet. It is quite surprising to see how amazingly addicted to strong drink the English alphabet is. S. R.R. TDW. K.D. PE. &c, &c., stagger through Mr. Dwight's catalogue in a state of confirmed intoxication. B is so very tipsy that he cannot CD, and M is sadly perplexed about his P's and Q's. Z is in a L of a condition. But the greatest reprobate of all is A himself. Mr. Dwight says: "A has been dreadfully intemperate for thirteen years. His father, who is now dead, was the same, and brought up his son in his own habits!!!"

Shocking, indeed! Well may the poet write—"Just as the twig is bent, the tree's inclined." Little *a* is, if possible, worse than his father, great *A*. "He has been twice a lunatic; three times brought to the gates of death by fits; ten times committed to the watch house; and repeatedly brought home drunk to his mother,* who is a widow, all in consequence of intemperance! Young profligate that he is! How then can our friend of the *Times* call New York *"a moral city"* when the very alphabet is a common tippler.

The increase in circulation of the *Enquirer* resulting from these and other articles by Bennett was in part offset by the indignant protests of those who felt Mr. Noah was injuring and lowering both himself and the whole editorial profession by permitting such "froth" and "trash" to be published. So, being withal a somewhat cautious man, he ceased their publication. Bennett fumed to no avail. He was permitted to write for the *Enquirer* only on such subjects as might henceforth be assigned to him—and these articles were carefully blue-penciled to make them as dull and drab as everything else in the paper.

Chief assistant to Noah on the *Enquirer* from its inception was

---

* We presume the widow is Mrs. E, inasmuch as we know that A & E occasionally lived in a state of diphthongal cohabitation. She is a respectable old lady, and lives quite at her E's.

W. G. Graham, whose essays on "Good Society" appeared regularly in its columns. These essays, well written, lofty in tone, and loaded with moral platitudes, were well received by the Good Society of New York, and Mr. Graham was looked upon as a bright and shining example of good taste, good judgment, and good behavior in a somewhat dubious profession. Mr. Noah, too, was highly elated at having such an assistant, rather than one as cynical as the cadaverous Bennett.

Mr. Graham frequently wrote against the danger of card-playing and gambling. Early in November he had outdone himself by his ridicule of the barbarous custom of dueling. A few days later the New York papers announced that Mr. Graham had died in New Jersey. The body had been hastily buried. Public clamor for an investigation as to the young man's death mounted rapidly. The body was disinterred; a coroner's inquest held, which announced that Graham had died of wounds at the hands of a person, or persons, unknown. Meanwhile, it had become public knowledge that he had died of wounds obtained in a duel with a young Philadelphian, with whom he had quarreled over a game of cards!

Graham's death left Noah without an assistant. Reluctantly he engaged Bennett to fill the position. The two men did not get along well at all, so when Bennett suggested that he be sent to Washington to report the doings of Congress and to keep an eye on the Adams administration, Noah readily assented to the proposition.

The year 1827 was drawing to a close when Bennett made his second entry into the capital. Washington was no longer a small town—it had 19,000 inhabitants and nearly 3,000 buildings. During the year just ending this number had been augmented by sixty-two new brick structures as well as sixty-three wooden ones, "some of them two and three stories high." Streets were alternately puddles of mud or clouds of dust. Government buildings were so widely scattered that they reminded Bennett of angels' visits, "few and far between." Washington Society was already firmly entrenched, with its inner cliques and factions, each with its heroes and villains. And the wives and daughters of newly arrived congressmen and senators, whether from frugal New England, the great plains of Illinois and Missouri, or the red clay of Alabama and Mississippi, underwent a miraculous transformation from simple wholesome folk to mannequins.

But for all its Society and its formality, Washington was still small enough to be neighborly. Clerks and cabinet members drank at the same taverns, swapped stories, and cursed the weather. The President himself could regularly be seen by early risers in the summer, as he walked to or from the Potomac, where he had his morning dip. Nor did it take the Washington correspondent for the *New York Enquirer* very long to discover the best sources both for the "straight" as well as the "inside" news on the capital.

Restless, eager, never-tiring, Bennett haunted the galleries of the House and Senate, visited with the congressmen in their offices, talked to administration leaders and heads of departments, spent long hours pouring over bills and government reports, read voluminously at the Congressional Library, and made the round of Washington's parties and balls.

It was, no doubt, his own sharp sense of curiosity which made him such an admirable reporter of what was taking place at the political heart of the young republic. And because he was so partisan in his politics, he applied himself more thoroughly to an understanding of the men and issues than was otherwise considered necessary.

For a period of more than four years, James Gordon Bennett covered Washington, Albany, New York, and Saratoga Springs as a reporter. He became an intimate of many of the leading figures of the period, and knew, and in turn was known by, every politician of national scope. His articles were widely read both in New York and in Washington, and many were reprinted by other pro-Jackson papers throughout the country. Every historian of American journalism admits that Bennett was not only the first, but likewise one of the most influential, of Washington correspondents. But strangely enough, neither they nor historians of the period seem to have bothered to avail themselves of the fascinating and at times acute reporting by James Gordon Bennett in the *New York Enquirer* and later in the *Courier and Enquirer*.

Let us, therefore, open up the torn and dusty files of these old

papers, so that we may perceive how far in advance of other journalists Bennett was even at that early date. And at the same time
we can enjoy his excellent word-pictures of politics and personages
of the time when a heavy-booted democracy was riding hell-bent
for victory straight to the White House; when common people
everywhere, like young Abe Lincoln of Illinois, were putting into
bad verse their political aims and aspirations:

> *Let auld acquaintance be forgot,*
> *And never brought to mind;*
> *May Jackson be our president,*
> *And Adams left behind.*

The first evidence of Bennett's trip to Washington is a rather
lengthy letter, unsigned, of January 2, 1828, which appeared in the
Enquirer on Tuesday, January 8, describing the New Year's Day
party at the White House. The style, of course, is typical of the
man. An earlier biographer of Bennett claimed that it was not until
Bennett had spent considerable time at the capital that he began to
develop a distinct and lively style. It is obvious that such a charge
could be made only by one who had failed to read the letters which
Bennett sent to Noah. The reader must be his own judge as to
whether or not Bennett set a new fashion in Washington reporting,
lively and scintillating from the start, with a style as chatty and
brilliant as that of any later-day correspondent.

In this first letter, Bennett describes the immense crowds pouring
in to the President's New Year's Day party. "Friends and foes,
high and low, the polished and the vulgar," stalked about through
the numerous apartments of the White House—"trying to catch the
refreshments which are scudding round on the heads of the servants, and then go home and tell what they heard, saw and did."

President Adams, we are informed, "was punished for more than
a couple of hours. He stood in the center of the center room and
most pathetically shook hands the whole time." In the ladies' corner,
"it was all chat, flutter and graceful *conges,*" while in the adjacent
hall, a band held forth "to keep the nerves of the company in a
proper degree of agitation. The corps diplomatique appeared, each
in their own national costume. All the fashionable, of course, now

resident in the city, filled up the company. Many sober citizens from the neighboring countryside showed themselves off in their native homespun. They looked upon the gay creatures before them, arranged in all the brilliancy of color, as so many splendid visions of romance."

For several paragraphs the new Washington correspondent describes the mad rush of the people back and forth at the party and he concludes by asking, "Don't you think that both sexes return to a state of nature at large parties? They are absolutely ferocious. Their politeness, on such an occasion, is precisely of the same quality which Mephistopholes sports so generally in the company of Faustus."

Having enjoyed himself sufficiently, Bennett recalled that he was after all an ardent Jacksonian and a hater of all who stood in the way of Old Hickory, so he added a final paragraph, which had nothing to do with what preceded it.

The Adams party are afraid of losing the advantage of riding the Tariff hobby. The animal is sliding from beneath them. They try to catch his tail, as the witch did that of Tam O'Shanter's mare, but their vociferations, etc., will not avail them. It will be found that the Jackson party are the truest friends of the country, and that they will encourage every interest, but favor none.

A few days later appeared the second letter from Bennett to the *Enquirer*. This was written on January 11 and appears in the issue of January 15. The discussion concerned primarily the jockeying of forces in Congress on the issue which was soon to split the nation into two warring camps.

The House of Representatives has been engaged for some time on a subject, trivial in itself, but involving warm feelings—the paying for a slave killed in the service of the United States at New Orleans. This brings up the question whether slaves are property under our Constitution; and everything touching on slavery fires all the gunpowder feelings of all sides, which are always so ready to catch and explode.

On the twenty-second of January, Bennett devoted over 2,000 words to a description of the huge dinner given in honor of General Andrew Jackson in Washington on January 8. Jackson, of course, was the most popular figure in the country, with voters everywhere flocking to his banner. Bennett remarked how people, in general, enjoy public gatherings, especially when they can find a man who symbolizes their sentiments and emotions strongly and effectively. Jackson, of course, was such a man although, in Bennett's opinion, the President completely lacked this ability. "Has Mr. Adams ever done an act capable of exciting a strong feeling of enthusiasm? His very name would freeze a pair of the most juicy Potomac ducks, even those lately presented to the mayor of the city."

Shrewdly aware of the fact that many readers of the *Enquirer* would enjoy a close-up view of the social life of Washington in 1828, Bennett approached the subject with studied casualness:

I don't think I ever said a word to you about the fair we had here a few weeks ago. I must not forget that mad frolic, for such I must call it. It was *outre* altogether. All the fashion in the city participated in that piece of monstrous benevolence. It's *locale* was at a place baptized Carusi's Assembly Rooms.

To speak in the language of the topographers who have lately been sinning in Old Virginia, it is banked on the west by a bed of pulverized *brescia,* with a due proportion of water (vulgarly called *mud* six inches deep), on the South by a similar bed and a creek called the Tyber. . . . The room was finished with a range of stalls, on which were all the toys of the milliners, the hair-dressers, and toy-sellers that Washington could furnish. Behind these stood the fair divinities, and in front, the buyers. The floor of the apartment was liberally sprinkled with sand which ascended to the nostrils and kept that region all alive.

The first day was a most delicious squeeze. . . . It was most delightful to see the pretty little wretches selling dolls most wickedly to the bachelors, and the bachelors, looking most woefully up in their faces, like an old fox at a bunch of grapes elevated on the architrave of an ionic column.

Letters of enthusiastic commendation poured in upon Mordecai Noah. His Washington correspondent was bringing scores of new subscribers to the *Enquirer* every week—a truly remarkable tribute to the drawing power of Bennett's articles. And, since people clamored for more, Bennett willingly gave them what they wanted and laid bare the social life of Washington in greater detail.

The tide of fashion is rolling onward with splendour. Music, cards, dancing, visiting and hearing sermons occupy the whole time of the gay world. Secretary Barbour's Saturday nights are ravishing. Only transport yourself to his hospitable mansion and gaze round on the brilliancy and beauty which attracts you. Or, if you please, imagine Secretary Clay's Wednesday nights which are more ravishing still. There sparkles a beautiful creature around her group in all the buoyancy of youth and beauty. Were you to meet her in a cottage *ornée* of lower Virginia, with a grape tree at one end and a honeysuckle at the other, you would fall down and adore her as the divinity of the place. Do you see that lady at the Northeast corner of the second cotillon? She dresses elaborately. Every pin has its place, every hair its locality. The caputography of her head would puzzle a corps of engineers—her smiles rise, brighten, decay and disappear with as much preconcert as a drama. She is half *belle,* half *bleu.* Some show their skill in dancing; others drawl through the cotillon with the greatest *nonchalance.* Dresses are found of all kinds, the French, the English, the Anglo-French, the classical, the picturesque and the no-style. Did you ever see something half-way between Egyptian mummery and *en-bon-point,* arrayed in a style that would make a fellow imagine a rainbow had been hauled down from the clouds and made up into a dress by some outlandish French milliner? If you have not, come to Washington!

This is not all. Gaiety is mixed with listlessness, and the brightest beauty with the greatest pieces of homeliness. Here is one counting the lustres; there is one comparing the candles; and a little way off, a group criticizing the dancers. In another, a member of Congress saunters about picking out all the long noses he can find and comparing the sizes and complexions with the precision of a Tycho Brake. Here is a dandy from Baltimore trying to match eyes and measure heights and distances; and there is a girl from the West endeavoring to appear with most rueful ease, in a *Cantelo* tightened to suffocation. Some run after waiters and others run from them; the politicians chat, the office-seekers cringe, the foreign diplomats look fierce, and the ladies look sad, gay and exhausted by turns.

The forces behind President Adams were desperately trying to find some means of turning the tide of sentiment away from the lean Tennessee warrior. But every lance turned against Jackson merely added to his popularity. In Congress no occasion was ever lost to throw firebrands at the Jacksonians. Essential bills for the conduct of government were delayed or emasculated by the administration forces, who hoped that in this way they could hurt their opponents.

The *Enquirer's* Washington correspondent never missed any

chance to keep his readers informed of the "dastardly and devious" methods used by the Adams men. "They are," he reported as early as January 20, 1828, "most amicably engaged to create as much quarrelling as possible. One branch of their system is to introduce flaming denunciations against military men into any debate, be it what it may. Everything in the shape of swords, epaulets, feathers and great guns is to dance through their speeches."

Bennett reported how the Administration even resorted to denouncing aliens and naturalized foreigners, thus stirring up "the ghost, not of Morgan, but of the departed Alien Law of 1798." Nor did he fail to give his readers vivid pen pictures of those responsible for such acts. One of the best is his description of Congressman Wright of Ohio, floor leader in the House for the Administration, whom he declared to be "gifted with a horrible fluency of well-conditioned phrases and ill-savored commonplaces." President Adams, his press and supporters, in their effort to build the prestige of Wright, kept referring to him as a great man. Said Bennett, "He is indeed a *great* man, for he is unembarrassed with the slightest obstruction of modesty; never fearful of tiring the House, because he is always sure to please himself; never rising above the pitch of very mean understandings and quite insensible to the rebuke of higher ones. . . . On he goes, forever creaking and croaking like an ungreased cartwheel."

Indications of the impending defeat of Adams grew with each passing week. The Jacksonians were as jubilant as the Administration men despondent. And Bennett, who at no time in his whole career showed compassion for his enemies, rubbed salt into the wounds of the men whose political careers were on the verge of a total eclipse. On May 5, he wrote:

The first of May dawned upon the inmates of the presidential mansion with a glimmering of hope. Who can resist the genial breathings of spring? Even Clay himself, with the disease of vaulting ambition preying upon his heart, could not sit idly when the sun mounted over the hills that embosom the eastern branch.

On that delightful morning the Cabinet and the administration leaders went out a Maying, but they found little comfort in the excursion. So many and numerous are the signs against their hopes, that the administration have become as superstitious as the most ignorant nations of the old world. They take comfort now in anagrams, omens, and the flights of birds.

Bennett's letters frequently concerned themselves with suggestions for future actions by the government. One of these was a recommendation for the establishment of a mail line to the Orient and the Pacific Coast by way of the Isthmus of Panama. He argued that by such action the West Coast, Japan, and China would be brought at least five months nearer on every round trip, as compared with the lengthy and dangerous voyage around the Straits of Magellan. Many of his letters also dealt with the developments of Latin America.

By the time he had been in Washington for a few months, Bennett had developed a definite style of reporting. There was a definite rhythm to his sentences, a basic unity to his paragraphs, and a happy use of metaphor. In addition, he had learned the trick of injecting something of himself into the context of his letters, much in the nature of our modern columnists. Nor did he follow a set pattern in reporting the Washington scene. One day it would be straight reporting of events. On another it would be anecdotal, or perhaps sharply analytical. And again it might moralize and philosophize. Readers never knew what to expect, and for fear of missing something particularly rare or juicy, scanned each issue of the *Enquirer* to be sure that they hadn't overlooked his letter.

On one occasion, after a lengthy discussion of Washington affairs, he breaks off abruptly:

Enough of politics for the present. It is often a dull, dry and somewhat deceiving subject; yet it is full of fascination to minds of a certain cast. With it is mixed up human passion and feelings. *It is the moral ocean of a nation.* It ebbs and flows like its prototype, heaving some fortunate individuals on the top of its billows, and overwhelming others in the gulf of forgetfulness; but from these tumblings and tossings arises the purity of the whole mass of national feelings.

On another occasion, following a highly technical discussion of a proposed tariff measure, he bursts into a blaze of ecstasy as he visions the benefits to be derived from the reduction of duties on wine and tea.

The imagination warms, and the brain absolutely turns round and grows giddy at the thought of it. What visions open of oceans of champaigne, and LaFitte, and Burgundy, of every delicious growth and exquisite flavor; of Moselle and old Hock, of Sherry and Alicant, of old Port and dry Lisbon, of Muscadine, Lacryma Christi, and Monte Pulciano—all at half price, to say nothing of the wines of Greece, Cyprus and the Cape of Good Hope.

Moreover, the reduction of the duties on tea is likewise a good measure. There are sound reasons of public policy in support of it, some of which Mr. Rush has touched upon, and others which he has omitted. But for my own part I am not ashamed to say that I like it for private reasons,—because I am as inveterate, and hardened, and shameless a tea drinker as Leigh Hunt, or old Sam Johnson, and therefore fully sympathize with those good people in every quarter of our country, who, as the great English moralist says, with a declamatory grandeur suited to the deep interest he felt in his subject—"dilute their meals with the infusion of this fascinating plant—whose kettle is never allowed time to cool—who with tea welcome the morning—with tea amuse the evening, and with tea solace the midnight."

Friends in after years claimed that Bennett had become squint-eyed from his long labors in the poor light of the Library of Congress. That close peering, hour after hour, at the small print or hardly readable script of documents and manuscripts, may have seriously affected his eyesight is undoubtedly true. But the squint belonged to Bennett's physiognomy long before he ever entered the portals of the halls of Congress or its library.

Feeling like a journalistic St. George, Bennett smote fast and furiously at the dragon of the opposition with his quill pen. He was out to smother each bit of unverified gossip and slander, to nail each unproved or untrue assertion of the Adams men to the mast of political fear; and to prove that Andy Jackson and his cohorts were the real patriots. To do this job required time, patience, and hard work. Bennett had infinite patience in digging up clues. He always had plenty of time, too, for he maintained too much sleep was harmful. And hard work agreed with him.

The anti-Jackson forces launched a combined whispering and press campaign, charging that Old Hickory was illiterate, unable to read, write or spell. It is quite probable that the old general paid little attention to such a charge, but Bennett was furious.

To answer these charges he made, first of all, a careful study of a great many of Jackson's letters and reports. He then gave careful attention to the autographs and letters of many of the leading men of the day as well as great men of the past. "Who," he asks, "would dare to say that Edmund Burke could not spell? Yet I can prove it by 'construction' and following literally the exact form of his letters. In Prior's *Life of Burke,* published in 1824, there are two *fac-simile* receipts in Burke's autograph to Dodsley, in which there are five words in forty misspelled." He tells of many errors in spelling by Pope, Addison, and others—but yet who would charge them with illiteracy! "I could prove in the same way," continues the scholar, "that Canova, the celebrated Italian artist, and Sir Christopher Wren, the great English architect, could not spell their own names. Look at Napoleon's handwriting, and it would appear that he could not spell a single word!"

Warming to the chase, Bennett describes how Elbridge Gerry committed unpardonable errors in spelling; Edward Everett "studs capitals throughout his autograph"; Jefferson never used a capital letter except at the beginning of each paragraph; how at least three words in every line of a seventeen-line autograph by DeWitt Clinton could be construed into misspelling, while "by the same rule, every fourth word in Secretary Southard's autograph is most miserably misspelled."

During that summer of 1828 Bennett followed the politicians to Saratoga Springs, and reported on their doings. By a careful comparison of gossip, hints, tips, and conversations, he was able to give the readers of the *Enquirer* an amazingly accurate picture of political trends as well as what was taking place in various parts of the country. He also regaled his readers with reports on the lighter side of life as enjoyed by bankers, lawyers, and politicians at the Springs. In one seven-mile walk, said Bennett, he saw wonders enough to fill two quartos, including "five rattlesnakes, two Indians, a Faro and two Roulette tables, a score of white pated urchins, a whole regiment of militia Generals, Colonels, and Captains, an idiot, two wild cats, and an editor."

By September he was back in Washington writing lengthy reports on the libels of the politicians against Jackson, discussing the tariff and United States Bank, the threatened war between Russia and Turkey, and a host of other topics, social, economic, and literary.

Bennett's dissertations on problems of political economy were as sprightly and unusual as his letters on the personalities of the capital.

Economy in life is a most excellent thing [began one of these letters]. It is the golden rule which leads to comfort, repose, independence, respectability, and happiness. Yet there is one idea abroad in the world which ought to be corrected. Cheapness, as Daniel Webster would say, cheapness, wholly and nothing but cheapness, does not form economy. This is the cheap age—but is it the economical? In every corner of the street there is a cheap shop, but is there an economical one? Boots, shoes, coats, pantaloons, hats and so forth, may be found in any part of the city at half price. Buy them, put them on, and wear them. What then do we find? Why they last less than half time.

Good, substantial wearables, edibles, or drinkables, that cost very fair, moderate prices—not cheap, not under price, not less than cost—are always cheapest in the end.

Not content with having made his point, Bennett felt that he must needs turn this argument to political account as well, so after again elaborating upon that fact that the present was an age of cheap goods, cheap shops, cheap everything, which meant that it was in reality a spendthrift and luxurious age, he asks:

Do you want proof? Look at the Adams party. They print cheap tracts, circulate cheap pamphlets, get up cheap coffin-hand bills, scrape together cheap barbecues, and all to put down Jackson; and *yet it is the most luxurious and expensive administration that this country ever had.*

So that we, who see our national debt mounting by billions of dollars per year, may comprehend the extent of national extravagance during John Quincy Adams' administration, let me recall that the total income of the federal government for the four-year period ending January 1, 1828, amounted to $98,000,000. Total expenditures were $95,500,000; and the total public debt of the nation at the beginning of 1829 amounted to $58,000,000.

The election of 1828 was a landslide for Jackson, who received 178 electoral votes to 83 for President Adams. John C. Calhoun was elected Vice-President by an equally large majority. The country went mad with joy. No longer would speculators, bankers, brokers, and shady politicians run the country! Once again, as in the days of good Tom Jefferson, the common people had taken over control of their government. Or so they thought. And in upon Washington, shortly after the new year dawned, came hordes of big-bearded, heavy-handed, rough-clothed, loudspoken men, anxious and willing to aid Old Hickory in purifying the new administration from the parasites of the old. There came, too, swarms of selfish men, shrewd men, crafty men, determined to get their pick of good jobs, fat fees, easy commissions, as just reward for their labors in the vineyard of Jacksonian democracy.

Washington's "good society" turned up its nose at the newcomers, wrapping itself more tightly in its self-righteousness, fearful lest it be spattered by the mud of the boots or the coarse and uncultivated language of the Jacksonians.

Bennett, of course, was overjoyed at the victory, to which he had in no small degree contributed. Gloating at the sad plight of the Adams men, who had waged such a bitter and vindictive campaign against Old Hickory, Bennett declared the impotency of their attacks upon Jackson reminded him of the great two-fisted girl who bawled out to her parent, "Mother, my toe itches!"

"Well, scratch it then!"

"I have, but it won't *stay* scratched."

"Mr. Clay, Mr. Clay," cries out a two-fisted uncle Tobey, "Jackson's a-coming—Jackson's a-coming!"

"Well, then," says Clay, "anti-tariff him in the *Journal*."

"I have; but he won't stay anti-tariffed."

"Mr. Clay, Mr. Clay," bawls out Alderman Binns, "the old farmer's a-coming, a-coming."

"Well, then," says Harry, "coffin-hand bill him!"

"I have," says Binns, "but he won't stay coffin-hand billed."

"Mr. Adams, Mr. Adams," says John H. Pleasants, "the hero's coming, actually coming."

"Well, then," says Mr. Adams, "Burr him and traitor him."

"I have, but he won't stay Burred or traitored."

"Mr. Clay, Mr. Clay," says Charles Hammond, "Jackson is coming."

"Well," says Clay, "prove him an adulterer and a Negro-trader."

"I have," says Charles, "but he won't stay an adulterer or a Negro-trader."

"Mr. Adams, Mr. Adams," bawls out the full Adams slandering chorus, "we have called Jackson a murderer, an adulterer, a traitor, an ignoramus, a fool, a crook-back, a pretender, and so forth; but he won't *stay* any of these names."

"He won't?" says Mr. Clay. "Why, then, I shan't *stay* at Washington, that's all!"

Andrew Jackson was an old man, full of pride, aches, and the scars of many a battle, when he took his oath as President; and there were many (including Jackson himself) who doubted whether he would last out his term of office. Bennett was one of the doubters. So, already before the hero of New Orleans had been sworn in as Chief Executive, the canny Scot was casting about for potential presidential timber for the next election. Martin Van Buren looked good to Bennett, so he began to play him up in his columns in the spring of 1829 as the logical successor to Jackson. Van Buren, recognizing Bennett's abilities and also being thankful at having such an able booster, opened the way for Bennett to get a more intimate picture of what went on behind the scenes in the new administration.

When the day came for Andrew Jackson to be inaugurated President, Bennett outdid himself in his fulsome and flattering description of the event. The climax of the lengthy article indicates the patriotic and partisan fervor of a young man, who only eight years earlier had landed in Boston, penniless and alone.

The Chief Justice of the United States then administered the oath of office; and thus, in the sight of Heaven and the surrounding multitude, was Andrew Jackson declared the chief of the only free and pure republic upon earth. The welkin rang with music and the feeling plaudits of the populace; beauty smiled and waved her kerchief—the first spring birds carolled their notes of joy, and nature poured her various offerings to the Giver of all good. The very marble of the pediment seemed to glow with life—justice, with a firmer grasp, secured her scales—"Hope,

enchanted, smiled," and the Genius of our country breathed a living defiance to the world. What a lesson for the monarchies of Europe! The
mummery of a coronation, with all its pomp and pageantry, sinks into
merited insignificance, before the simple and sublime spectacle of twelve
millions of freemen, imparting this Executive Trust to the MAN OF THEIR
CHOICE.

Among the office-seekers and advice-givers who had deluged
Washington were many of the editors of the papers which had sup-
ported Jackson, among them being Blair, Kendall, Isaac Hill and
Bennett's boss, Mordecai Noah. It was called "the irruption of the
Goths." Major Noah told Bennett about the plans of the editors—
twenty-one in all—to sally forth in a body to see the president-elect.
Isaac Hill wanted Noah, who had had long experience in all mat-
ters pertaining to political wire-pulling, to lead the troop.

"No," said Noah, "I'm too fat and in too good condition. If Old
Hickory sees me, he will think that editors require no office. Our
deputation must be headed by our worst looking—the lean, the halt,
the blind." Whereupon Noah nominated Blair, Hill, and Kendall
to lead and act as spokesmen for the delegation.

The merger of Mr. Noah's *New York Enquirer* and Mr. James
Watson Webb's *Morning Courier* became a fact on Monday, May
25, 1829. On that day the new combined *Journal* presented itself
to the readers of New York with an editorial which began:

We this day present to the public the first number of the *Morning
Courier* and *New York Enquirer* and feel it incumbent upon us to say
a few words in relation to the future course of the paper.

Our principal aim will be to make it a commercial and reading paper,
equal in all respects to its numerous and ably conducted contemporaries.
We say that this will be our *principal* aim, because experience has taught
us that it is absolutely necessary to make our paper commercially important, in order that we may continue to render those services to the Republican Party which it has heretofore received from two papers now
united.

The editorial went on to expound its support of Gen. Jackson
and his policies. It also mentioned the fact that the combined circulation of the new paper was 4,000 daily.

Later writers on journalism have, almost without exception, stated that the new paper was at its beginning the joint enterprise of Noah and Webb. This obviously was not the case, for a signed article by Mordecai Noah which followed the above editorial declared that he had disposed of "All my right, title and interest in the *Enquirer* to James Watson Webb, Esq., proprietor of the *Morning Courier,* and Daniel E. Tylee, an old and esteemed citizen; and I shall continue to afford the paper all the aid which my editorial labor and experience will enable me to do."

Bennett, according to letters written years later, claimed to have been instrumental in bringing about the merger of the two sheets. His name, however, at no time during the year appeared in the newspaper. But he continued his work as correspondent from Washington for the *Courier and Enquirer* for nearly three years' time. Although his name was never mentioned as such, the articles were usually labeled "FROM WASHINGTON—Extract from [or Correspondence from] one of the Editors of this paper."

A short one-paragraph item, dated May 30, may very well be from the pen of Bennett. It reads: "Solomon Southwicks' last paper does not contain one indecent or blasphemous sentence and there are only four that are scurrilous. Wonders will never cease!"

From the nation's capital on June 2, 1829, the Washington correspondent for the *Courier and Enquirer* reported:

The weather has been excessively warm for some days past and with a solitary exception, its enervating effects have been apparent in the conduct and proceedings of the opposition.

The exception referred to, is the United States Librarian who was very politely informed a few days since, that the system of reform which has thus far been pursued with great singleness of purpose and will secure General Jackson the gratitude of posterity, rendered it necessary for him to vacate his office in favor of ——. It did not enter into the thoughts of the most pugnacious that the organs of combativeness were so developed in the pericranium of the Librarian as to induce an open declaration of war against the United States, consequently, when the little gentleman refused to vacate, and set to nought the combined power of the President and his Cabinet, they were literally taken by surprise and found themselves placed in a predicament as rare as it was awkward.

Webb's new paper had a rapid growth, and much of the credit for this should have gone to the Washington Correspondent, but blustering Webb, like his predecessor Noah, never gave Bennett recognition by name at any time for what he had done. In fact, both of these men let it be known that they themselves had either written or indicated the lines along which the articles were to be written. They also—in later years—because of their hatred for Bennett, were willing to give anyone except the real author credit for the brilliant and provocative letters from Washington. But his style was too distinct; and besides, Washington was filled with men who knew, and oftentimes saw in advance, the letters which Bennett forwarded to his paper in New York.

Previous to my arrival here [wrote Bennett on June 9], I heard it frequently said that the President was in the habit of visiting daily the different offices and examining into the manner that the auditors and clerks perform their duties. I supposed it quite possible that he had done so in some few cases, but certainly was not prepared to find that it was a daily constant and habitual practice. Such, however, is the case, and not a day passes without his devoting some time to this important and necessary duty.

The consequence is that the idle clerks—and there were many of them—instead of spending their time at Billiard Tables, or lounging about the offices, are now busily occupied in attending to those duties for which they received from the Government a liberal support. Accounts which formerly required months to settle and large *doceurs* to clerks for labor out of office hours, are now disposed of in a few days, without those *doceurs* and the loss of time and expenditure of money, which has heretofore been the necessary consequence of having unsettled accounts with the Government.

The present Cabinet is emphatically one of business and from six o'clock in the morning till ten at night the President and Secretaries are busily engaged in the discharge of their all important duties. This incessant and untiring application is now, however, drawing to a close and they anticipate some little relief in the course of a few weeks. Abuses and defalcations have been discovered where least anticipated, and when Congress convenes a committee of that body will lay a statement before the public as will astonish even those who have for years been urging the necessity of reform.

Turning to the charge that was being made in every anti-Jackson paper throughout the country, of mass dismissals from government posts, Bennett reported on June 15:

Were we to credit what the opposition prints, the conclusion would be almost irresistible that the greater part of the Postmasters in the United States have been removed from office.

With a view to a correct understanding of this subject, I have just visited the Postmaster General's office and find that the whole number of changes since the 4th of March are something less than three hundred; of which ninety-seven were using their offices as *rendezvous* for political meetings, loaning their names and influence in traducing the present Chief Magistrate and his late pious and amiable consort, and neglecting their duties to become active partisan politicians. Two, and only two, have as yet been removed against whom there was no other charge than their being opposed to the present administration. In both these instances, the offices were lucrative, the incumbents wealthy, and the persons appointed Republicans of '98 who had rendered important services to the country.

Continuing his discussion of the situation, he pointed out that there were at the time 8,000 postmasters in the country, most of whom were both safe and secure. In his opinion, what was needed was still more removals rather than less. Then, as if replying to the charge that such actions as Jackson had taken had never even been contemplated by Mr. Adams, Bennett explained:

It is said Mr. Adams made no removals on political grounds but it is also said, and with truth, that he abstained from doing so because he was fearful of adding to the number of his enemies and thereby losing his election. General Jackson acts from different motives. He did not seek for the office which the people have conferred upon him, nor does he wish to retain it beyond the term for which he already has been elected, unless it becomes necessary to do so in order to prevent those men getting the control of public affairs who have already proved themselves unworthy of the trust.

A few days later, on the nineteenth, the *Courier's* correspondent informed its readers that:

The President daily improves in health and spirits and his present appearance gives assurance of years of vigorous and intellectual action. He walked to church yesterday, carrying in his hand that beautiful and appropriate present from a patriotic fisherman, the cane made from a piece of hickory supposed to belong to the submarine defense of West Point during the Revolutionary War.

Bennett's reporting of the Washington scene was doing great damage to the forces opposing Jackson, for he was checking up on their charges as carefully as ever, and he never missed a trick. The *United States Telegraph,* to whom long lean years seemed the only prospect after the lush days of Adams, charged that the *Courier and Enquirer* was printing letters from Washington "in which the idle tittle-tattle of the streets are retailed for truth." The *Courier,* in a lengthy blustering editorial by Webb, replied that it considered such action and statements by the *Telegraph* as "unworthy of more than a passing notice."

On July 17 Bennett wrote that because of illness he had been unable to send in any letters for more than a week.

In my last communication [writes Bennett, on July 22], I promised additional explanations of the progress of reform, which now begins to have some other meaning with people than a mere cabalistic phrase. I have taken pains to learn particulars that I might be able to vindicate the administration, to bring which into power, I had contributed with all my ability; and I can assure you the salutary reform will, for the best reasons in the world, continue notwithstanding the groans of a few, displaced for the faultlessness, or worthlessness, and of desperate politicians who vainly imagine that every groan will be converted into a vote for them at the polls.

That you may fully comprehend the value of fidelity and vigilance in high public office, permit me to remark that in the Department lately superintended by Mr. Rush, there have been discovered no discrepancy while in those of State, War and Navy Departments, depredation upon depredation have been piled like mountain upon mountain. Now mark the cause of this difference! Mr. Rush remains steadily at his post, faithfully guarding the public interest; while the President, Secretary of War, and Secretary of Navy were traveling over the country promoting parades, shows, barbecues and all sort of pageantries in which they might have a chance to display to the best advantage their splendid capacities for eating, drinking, toasting, speaking and hoodwinking some sycophants and as many fools. In the meantime, the *confidentials* were left to take care of the trusts committed to their hands; and like bad children, without a head to control, they despoiled the household. The wonder is that they did not at last set fire to the departments, if not to make one grand *bonfire* to conceal their iniquities. Indeed, the contract and consequence are so striking that public justice will award to Mr. Rush an equivalent measure of applause, while it will doom the faithless to an equal measure of popular indignation.

The battle for fulfilling the promises of Jacksonian democracy was under way. James Gordon Bennett, no longer an unknown, but a journalist whose words were read and repeated in both New York and Washington, stayed on as watch-dog for the public and the party to which he belonged, reporting and interpreting the news of the nation's capital.

7. Knee-Deep in Politics

WITH the Jacksonian revolution in American political life came a new growth in American journalism. New names and new faces, such as those of James Gordon Bennett, William Cullen Bryant, and Mordecai M. Noah, were augmented by those of James Watson Webb, Thurlow Weed, Horace Greeley, Gerard Hallock, David Hale, Benjamin Day, and Moses Beach.

The first innovation of note took place in 1827 when the *Morning Courier* and the *New York Journal of Commerce* were launched. Much larger in size than any of their predecessors, they set the pace for the nation's new and higher-priced "blanket sheets," as Bennett dubbed these unwieldy papers. For a full decade their editors vied in a contest of size, forgetful that content and style were also important.

Editorially, too, the new papers were innovators. More completely than any of their older competitors, they let it be known that they were out to serve the interests of the city's business men. Said the *Courier,* in a frank editorial, "Commercial patronage is the best, safest, and most unchanging of any, and less affected by prejudice, whim or petulance than any other." And it added, significantly, "Merchants are ever ready to bestow their confidence and their support on those who exhibit zeal, industry, and vigilance in their service and devotedness in their interests."

The *Journal of Commerce* announced that it too was "devoted principally to commerce and manufactures," but it also stressed a moral and religious tone. Its founder, Arthur Tappan, a wealthy merchant, announced that the *Journal of Commerce* would "meddle as little as possible with popular elections, and the angry altercations they excite," and added that it would not transact business on the Sabbath or accept advertisements for theaters, lotteries, patent medicines, and alcoholic beverages.

Tappan's high-minded venture cost him more than $30,000 in less than six months, so he turned the paper over to his brother who, in turn, sold it to David Hale and Gerard Hallock. Under these gentlemen, the *Journal of Commerce* was made a highly successful venture.

The *Morning Courier,* established in May, 1827, was within six months turned over to James Watson Webb, a brother-in-law of its founder, and the man who remained its editor and publisher till it merged with the *World* in 1861. Webb, the son of one of George Washington's aides-de-camp, was a handsome, adventurous, arrogant, bumptious, and magnificently self-assured young man of twenty-five years, when he took over the reins of the *Morning Courier.*

As a boy of seventeen, young Webb went to John Calhoun, then Secretary of War, with letters of introduction and asked to be commissioned as an officer in the United States Army. Calhoun, amazed at the boy's audacity, told him that to become an officer he would have to graduate from West Point. Webb replied that he already had a first-class military training given him by his father who had served under General Washington. Calhoun became so impressed with Webb's plea, that he broke precedent and granted him a lieutenant's commission in the Army.

Webb served his country with distinction for nearly eight years. Then, as he many years later observed, "We left the army, a mere boy, to take charge of a political press at the commencement of the political campaign which terminated in the election of Andrew Jackson to the presidency in 1828." He possessed, so he said, "not a solitary qualification for the position" except "the one leading characteristic of the army, a determination on all occasions to speak not only the truth, but the whole truth." This characteristic, he later boasted, caused him to be "the best-abused personage connected with the American press."

Webb's best friends asserted that he invariably considered his own conclusions on any subject to be well-nigh infallible. He was constantly embroiled in controversy. When the Civil War broke out he wrote to President Lincoln suggesting he be made a major-general. Lincoln, upon appropriate advice, offered him the slightly lower rank of brigadier-general. Webb returned the commission to Lincoln, with the words "Respectfully declined—J. W. Webb" written across it.

Webb's hot temper brought him into conflict with Duff Green, the Jacksonian editor of the *United States Telegraph* and official printer for both houses of Congress. The fight between the two, began early in 1829, when Webb, on the advice of Bennett, suggested Van Buren as the logical candidate to succeed Old Hickory, while Duff Green carried the banner for Vice-President Calhoun. The war of words grew in intensity till at last Webb hurried south to punish "the St. Louis upstart." They met in the rotunda of the Capitol, where Webb lay in wait for Green; and, despite the fact that Green drew "a pistol, about eight inches long" to defend himself, he was severely castigated by Webb, who called Green a "poor, contemptible, cowardly puppy."

Thurlow Weed was another young man whose name was beginning to loom large in both political and journalistic circles. Born in upstate New York, 1797, Weed's career as a newspaperman began at the same time as Bennett's. He became the owner of the *Rochester Telegraph,* a weekly, in 1825, and made that paper a daily in 1826. Already a lobbyist and political manipulator of local renown, he was one of the first to make political capital out of the anti-Masonic feeling after William Morgan, who had published the secrets of the Masonic Order, was abducted and murdered. Building upon the fear of secret societies, Thurlow Weed gained national notoriety. By 1830 when he took over the editorship of the *Albany Evening Journal,* he was one of the most powerful and astute political bosses in the country.

In the summer of 1825, Weed made his first visit to Washington. Determined to see as much as possible of the nation's capital, he arose at daybreak and strolled down toward the banks of the Potomac. He was not prepared, when he started out, to witness a sight not commonly seen by many Americans of his day: "A gentleman in nankeen pantaloons and a blue pea-jacket walked rapidly from the White House towards the river. This was John Quincy Adams, the President of the United States. I moved off to a respectful distance. The President began to disrobe before he reached a tree on the brink of the river, where he deposited his clothes, and then plunged in head first, and struck out fifteen or twenty rods, swimming rapidly and turning occasionally upon his back, seeming as much at his ease in that element as upon terra firma. Coming out, he rubbed himself thoroughly with napkins, which he had brought for that purpose in his hand. The sun had not yet risen when he had dressed himself and was returning to the presidential mansion."

Bennett and Weed met in 1826, and were on relatively good terms for more than a year. Bennett, who had been opposed to the anti-Masonic politics of Weed from the start, finally uncovered what he believed to be evidence that Weed, acting as a tool for President Adams, was distributing funds to swing the anti-Masonic vote to Adams. In one of his letters from Washington to the *Courier,* dated March 26, 1828, Bennett wrote:

I have already given you a few slight sketches of the uses to which the coalition have attempted to turn the Morgan excitement in the western counties of your State. But this is not all the iniquity of this business. I have heard through a channel on which I can rely, and it can be proved by respectable evidence, if gentlemen would permit their names to be used, that during the present session a check or checks for a sum of money, between two thousand and three thousand dollars, were carried out of this city for the purpose of furnishing aid directly or indirectly to keep up the Morgan excitement in the West, to spread it as far and wide in the State as possible, and by these means to give the administration of Mr. Adams a few Anti-Masonic votes at the next election. Put these questions to Mr. Weed. Ask him if he has not heard of such a check? ask him if he has not fingered it? ask him if it never reposed for a day and a night, or days and nights, in his pocket? I sincerely hope that he will say "No" to all those interrogatories, and that his conscience will echo back the monosyllable without trembling.

Weed was furious and published long denials. Thereafter the two men remained bitter enemies, and did not speak to each other till Weed, at the request of President Lincoln, called on Bennett in 1861.

Most potent of all the newcomers to journalism at this period was the New Hampshire lad, Horace Greeley. Fifteen years younger than Bennett, he did not reach New York City until August, 1831, a ragged youth of twenty, with five years of experience as a printer behind him.

Pasty-faced as well as baby-faced, with large, unblinking, Dresden-doll eyes, young Greeley appeared like a bleached-out country bumpkin to the worldly wise New Yorkers. The shrill voice, the awkward gait, the ungainly manners of the young man all tended to confirm these first impressions.

In the face of such physical handicaps and the fact that he had only ten dollars and didn't know anyone in the city, Greeley made himself felt and known much more quickly than any of his contemporaries. Within a year he helped found a printing firm which prospered almost from the start. Luckily Greeley's partner, Story, secured a considerable quantity of lottery printing, which was highly profitable. Included in this work, was that of publishing a small tri-weekly paper, *The Constitutionalist,* which was the official organ of the great lottery dealers. Each issue carried the advertisement of the printers who respectfully solicited the patronage of the public to their business, "especially Lottery Printing." In 1834, Greeley founded a weekly, *The New Yorker,* which was quite successful. Soon thereafter he tied in his political fortunes with Thurlow Weed and William Seward, editing the *Jeffersonian* in 1838 and the *Log Cabin* in 1840. Shortly after his thirtieth birthday, in April, 1841, Horace Greeley launched his daily, the *New York Tribune.*

With new faces came new life to the New York press. In 1827 the morning papers pooled $2,500 to cover the cost of hiring a boat to meet the incoming ships from Europe. The following year Webb's *Courier,* possibly at the suggestion of Bennett, withdrew its funds and launched its own boat, which was able to score continual beats on the others. The *Journal of Commerce* then built a faster boat, which resulted in its expulsion from the Association. At last there had developed a spirited rivalry between the newspapers as each sought to be first with the foreign news. By 1831 there were six news schooners in use, and the yearly cost for maintaining them amounted to more than $25,000. The swift-sailing craft would often go as far as a hundred miles beyond Sandy Hook to lie in wait for the incoming ships.

A direct result of this rivalry was the appearance of "flash news" briefs on the front pages of the papers. "Extras," too, made their first appearance, bearing the latest tidings from across the water, sometimes not more than twenty-five days old.

Webb and Bennett had become suspicious that some of their fast news was being cribbed by other papers, especially by their chief competitor, the *Journal of Commerce,* so they determined upon a scheme to expose it.

Frederic Hudson, in his *History of American Journalism,* told how the *Courier and Enquirer* one morning carried a postscript announcing the arrival of its news-schooner, with latest reports from the incoming "Ajax." The "news" was printed in a separate column. Only a handful of the papers were set up and printed with this "news" and these were then distributed at the doors of sub-scribers, adjacent to the other newspapers. Watchers soon discovered that one of these copies was "borrowed." All the rest were immediately picked up and replaced by regular copies of the paper.

Later that morning the *Journal of Commerce* was the only paper in the city to give its readers the "news" from the "Ajax." The rejoicing at the *Journal of Commerce* for its scoop soon turned to mortification as word spread about the city that there was no "Ajax" arriving from Europe. The paper with the high moral tone had been caught red-handed stealing its news from the *Courier and Enquirer.*

Reform movements of a hundred varieties blossomed out during the early 1830's. Some demanded an end to auctions and lotteries; others that the manufacture or sale of liquor be prohibited. The Agrarian Party was organized to help the farmers. Labor unions sprang up to give aid and comfort to the mechanics and wage-earners. The Equal Rights Movement demanded that women be given equal status with men before the law. Stump speakers, urging their latest and most favorite nostrums, held forth on street corners, at county fairs, in schoolhouses and churches; while spit-and-argue clubs held perpetual meetings before the cracker barrels of every crossroads store.

Bennett was delighted with these manifestations of popular opinion. Not that he agreed with them—for he didn't. But they gave him ample human-interest material about which to write his articles. His own attitude was that "the ultraism of the age is the great enemy of all reform." The intelligent and genuine reformer, insisted Bennett, "proceeds slowly, cautiously, temperately. Prejudices are not best overcome by violence. The popular mind is not to be taken by storm." That many reforms were needed and long overdue, he readily conceded, but added that *time* was the essence in enlightening and convincing the great mass of mankind.

During the late spring and summer of 1830, Bennett functioned as a roving reporter for the *Courier and Enquirer*. From upstate New York as well as from Massachusetts, Rhode Island, Connecticut, and New Hampshire, he submitted colorful bits of description of the people and the countryside.

In August, Bennett gained considerable notoriety for himself by his manner of reporting a sensational murder trial at Salem. Early in April, a rich, retired sea captain, Joseph White, was found murdered in his bed. Two brothers, Richard and George Crowninshield, were accused of committing the crime at the behest of Captain White's prospective heirs.

The whole of New England was stirred by the murder. Interest was further stimulated when it became known that Daniel Webster would assist the state in its prosecution of the case. The *Courier and Enquirer* announced that its associate editor would cover the case, and on July 21 Bennett sent in his first report, to the effect that legal wrangling had delayed the case till early August.

When the trial opened on August 3, a dozen reporters—the most ever to cover any murder up to that time—were on hand. The haughty and pompous Attorney General for the Commonwealth of Massachusetts, Perez Morton, lectured the reporters and laid down a series of restrictive regulations which he announced they must follow.

Such action was meat for Bennett's pen. Three days later, the judge, Webster, Morton, and the whole of Salem were astonished to read Bennett's caustic indictment of the Attorney General:

He knows more of the technicalities of the law [declared Bennett] than he does of the tactics of a well conducted Press. It is an old, worm-eaten, Gothic dogma of the Courts, to consider the publicity given to every event by the Press, as destructive to the interests of law and justice. This superstition arose towards the close of the Middle Ages, and was in its full vigor during the last century in Europe, when the contest arose, not only between the Press and the Princes of the world, but also, between the Press and the craft of the law. Is it possible that the publication of facts, or even rumors, can have any tendency to defeat the general operations of justice? If this were true, the more utterly ignorant a man is, the fitter he is to sit as a juror.

There seems to be a set of people in this world [he continued with righteous indignation] who, whether they are in the court, at the bar, or in the Senate, have a particular *penchant* for degrading and belittling the Press; and who embrace every opportunity to cast aspersions upon its character and usefulness. The honesty, the purity, the integrity of legal practice and decisions throughout this country, are more indebted to the American Press, than to the whole tribe of lawyers and judges, who issue their decrees. *The Press* is *the living Jury of the Nation.*

This was too much for the learned judges and the Attorney General. Who were they to be lectured by a miserable scribbler? And a foreigner at that! They'd teach him, and the rest of the Press, that law was law in Salem! So Bennett and all other members of the Press were forbidden to take notes of the proceedings for immediate publication.

Bennett, not content to let matters rest, at once reported to his paper:

This morning the court carried their threats against the Press a little further than before. They probably repented of the condescension they had shown yesterday. They this morning gave notice, that, if any person was *detected* (Shade of Franklin! what a word to make use of relative to reports of a public trial!) in taking notes of the evidence in the Court House, for the purpose of sending them out of the State for publication, previous to the conclusion of the trial, he would be proceeded against by the court as for a contempt.

For the edification of our Massachusetts neighbors, it will not be amiss to state, that in New York State they order these things better. By a reference to the Revised Statutes of New York, part third, chapter third, regarding the general provisions relative to Courts, it is expressly enacted that the publication of testimony, while a trial is still pending, shall not be restrained.

Thereafter, public interest in the case shifted away from the oratory of Webster and Morton to the larger question raised by Bennett: Have the people, through the Press, a right to get a full report of what transpires in a murder trial? Bennett's courageous stand did much to force that issue into the open. One by one, the states, including Massachusetts, were compelled to open the doors of the courtrooms to the Press.

President Jackson, meanwhile, had been slowly formulating his program of reform. The evil which he believed most dangerous to the welfare of the nation, was the power of the banking interests. And of all these, none was so powerful as the United States Bank, whose charter was due for extension, rejection, or modification by Congress.

Andy Jackson was not alone in believing that the waters of prosperity, which in theory belonged to all the people, were being siphoned off into the private reservoirs of the Philadelphia, New York, and Boston bankers and industrialists. This had to be remedied. The banks, he knew full well, would fight to retain the power already theirs, but the old warrior was never one to shrink from a fight. In restrained language he reported to Congress that "the great desideratum of modern times is an efficient check upon the power of the banks, preventing that excessive issue of paper whence arise those fluctuations in the standard of value which render uncertain the rewards of labor." But to friends and political associates he confessed that, desirous as he was to retire from public life to the comfort and repose of his Hermitage, he dared not permit himself to do so "until I can strangle this hydra of corruption, the Bank. . . ."

The position of Jackson on the bank issue was identical with that of James Gordon Bennett, who was already a close student of economic theory. Bennett had no difficulty in persuading Webb to let him write a series of articles on the highly controversial matter.

His first article appeared in the *Courier and Enquirer* on February 5, 1831. Thereafter, they appeared daily for the next two months.

Bennett argued that reforms of the federal banking system, along the lines of those already instituted in New York State, were imperative. In the light of evidence already made public, the United States Bank, with its many branches throughout the country, "deserves to be most rigorously examined," wrote Bennett, even if it confined itself to its brokerage business. But, he added, "when the great influence of such a corporation is turned to political uses, or is exercised to destroy one party, and build up another, or is directed to control the government and constitution of the country, then it is full time for the people and the State to look carefully into the whole matter and satisfy themselves that all is right."

Citing names, dates, and places, Bennett went on to tell his readers about the political manipulations of the Bank at Utica, at Buffalo, and elsewhere:

Let the mind, untinctured by prejudice—unawed by power—unbought by favors, look at the startling fact with steady attention, and unblanched gaze. What have we? An organized corps of presidents, cashiers, directors, clerks, tellers, lenders and borrowers, spread throughout the United States—moving simultaneously upon every given point—lending out money for hire, and distributing opinions for action—furnishing capital and thoughts at one and the same moment—buying men and votes as cattle in the market—giving a tone to public opinion—making and unmaking Presidents at will—controlling the free will of the people, and corrupting their servants—circulating simultaneously political theories, destructive of the constitution, and paper money injurious to every State Bank—curtailing and expanding, at will, discounts and exchanges—withering by a subtle poison the liberty of the Press—and, in fact, erecting within the States of the Union a new general government—an *Imperium in imperio,* unknown to the Constitution, defying its power, laughing at its restrictions, scorning its principles, and pointing to its golden vaults, as the weapon that will execute its behests, whenever it shall be necessary to carry them into action.

At a time when they were being widely discussed and frequently republished by other Jacksonian organs, the articles suddenly vanished from the *Courier and Enquirer.* Much to Bennett's disgust he was ordered to cease his attacks upon the bank and to concentrate upon other matters. Bennett would have understood the reason for his new assignment had he known of certain financial transactions which took place during the month of April, and which involved the sale of Daniel Tylee's share of the paper to

Mordecai Noah. Actually, the purchaser was not Noah but one Silas E. Burroughs, whose chief desire was to shift the position of the *Courier and Enquirer* away from Jackson. Even Webb, the editor, did not realize at the time what was taking place.

Bennett still remained on the editorial staff of the paper, but he was sent out on a roving commission again to cover conventions, murders, and a host of other topics. It was during this period that, in a review of the newly established *Boston Morning Post*, Bennett first formulated his concept of journalism:

An editor [he wrote] must always be with the people, think with them, feel with them, and he need fear nothing. He will always be right, always strong, always popular, always free. The world has been humbugged long enough by spouters and talkers and conventioners and legislators, *et id genus omne*. This is the editorial age, and the most intellectual of all ages.

Back in Washington during the spring and summer of 1832, Bennett found himself knee-deep in politics. His articles were well liked by the Jacksonians, and they made it a point to pass on to him special bits of inside information. Many, too, cultivated his acquaintance because they saw in him a vehicle to further their own immediate political ends. In turn, there can be no doubt that Bennett was flattered by the attention paid to him. It is altogether likely that he entertained notions (so common to newspapermen) that he could become a mighty power behind the scenes, making and unmaking those who strut the political stage.

He became friendly with Martin Van Buren, and that wily Dutchman used Bennett to start the campaign to make himself running mate to Jackson in the 1832 election. Bennett finally convinced Webb of the wisdom in backing Van Buren, and soon thereafter the *Courier and Enquirer* linked Van Buren's name with that of Jackson, as its choice.

Another politician who was about to use the journalist to his own advantage was Senator William L. Marcy, who let Bennett do the preliminaries of securing for Marcy the Democratic gubernatorial nomination of New York State. The reporter was fascinated by the part he was playing in American political life. Webb had by this time shifted a long way from the Jacksonian position on the Bank issue; Bennett was still vehemently in favor of Old Hickory's reform; but Marcy, the shrewd politician, remained noncommittal. Years later Bennett told how he had worked the wires in Washington while Webb fired the editorial guns in New York. "Senator Marcy and I," he wrote, "used to laugh and chuckle most amusedly on the movements by which, through the *Courier and Enquirer,* we accomplished ultimately his nomination, check-mated his personal foes at Albany and elected him, triumphantly, governor of the State for the first time."

Before the elections took place in November, James Watson Webb had hauled down the banner of Andy Jackson and gone over to the camp of Henry Clay. It became publicly known that the Bank crowd had gained dominance over the *Courier and Enquirer.* Senator Marcy, with his election as Governor assured, helped undermine Bennett among the Democratic politicians; and Bennett parted company with Webb, Noah, and the *Courier and Enquirer.*

A striking tribute to Bennett's journalistic abilities at the time was made by one of his severest critics, James Parton, who wrote:

During the great days of *The Courier and Inquirer,* from 1829 to 1832, when it was incomparably the best newspaper on the continent, James Gordon Bennett was its most efficient hand. It lost him in 1832, when the paper abandoned General Jackson and took up Nicholas Biddle; and in losing him lost its chance of retaining the supremacy among American newspapers to this day. . . .

Bennett, in the course of time, had a chance been given him, would have made the *Courier and Enquirer* powerful enough to cast off all party ties; and this he would have done merely by improving it as a vehicle of news. But he was kept down upon one of those ridiculous, tantalizing, corrupting salaries, which are a little more than a single man's needs, but not enough for him to marry on. This salary was increased by the proprietors giving him a small share in the small profits of the prinitng-office; so that, after fourteen years of hard labor and Scotch economy, he found himself, on leaving the great paper, a capitalist to the extent of a few hundred dollars.

Webb's last-minute flop to the anti-Jackson camp caused such a commotion that a congressional committee looked into the matter and unearthed the fact that loans totaling nearly $53,000 had been made to Webb by the United States Bank during the preceding year. Not content with the switch he made, Webb comforted himself with bitter attacks upon his former associate editor.

Bennett, for once, did not make a counter-attack. He did issue a lengthy statement explaining his own position and the Bank articles he had written, but in his opinion the blame for the change in policy of the paper was less the fault of Webb than it was of Noah. "The *Courier and Enquirer*," he wrote, "was in some financial difficulty at the period the loan was made by the Bank, and Mr. Noah, when he saw the breeches' pocket of Mr. Biddle open, entered it immediately, and presented the chief exemplar of inconsistency and tergiversation."

Freed from his bonds to Webb and Noah, and an intimate friend of many political bigwigs, Bennett felt he ought to strike out for himself. It was just before an election. The time seemed particularly appropriate.

The paper Bennett launched, twelve by seventeen inches, was only half as large as the big blanket sheets, and its subscription price was eight instead of the usual ten dollars per year. In announcing his new paper, the *Globe,* he informed his prospective readers that he was "in the field, sword in hand, with unfurled banner, resolved to aid the great cause of Jackson and Democracy." After the election, however, he intended to publish in the *Globe* such a wide variety of material as to make it the welcome visitor of both the tea table and the counting room.

Knowing that the public would be suspicious of the small size of his new venture, he declared:

For years past the public has *been cloyed with immense sheets—bunglingly made up—without concert of action or individuality of character—the reservoirs of crude thoughts from different persons* who were continually knocking their heads against each other, without knocking anything remarkably good out of them. I have avoided this inconvenience. I shall give my readers the cream of foreign and domestic events. My sheet is moderate in size, but neat and manageable, printed on fine paper and with beautiful type. When an overflow of patronage shall demand more room, as it soon will, I may enlarge a little, but I shall avoid, as I would a pestilence, those enormous sheets—the pine

barrens of intelligence and taste, which have been undoubtedly sent
into the world as a punishment for its growing wickedness.

Having hopefully committed the *Globe* to the none too tender
mercies of New York's newspaper readers, Bennett found that once
the election was over his customers were lost. The *Globe,* like his
earlier venture with the *Sunday Courier,* never had a chance. Bennett's slender purse, his lack of credit, and his inability to get the
backing from party leaders brought about its quick demise.

Gone for the moment were the dreams of master-minding New
York politics. Bennett was broke. To keep body and soul together
while he laid his plans for the next major step in his career, he
settled down to hack-writing again. He wrote short stories, poems,
essays, descriptive articles, and undertook any assignment given him
by the small weekly papers of the city.

Word came to him that he could buy an interest in a small Philadelphia daily, the *Pennsylvanian,* and take over its editorship.
Much as he disliked leaving New York, Bennett decided that here
was the big chance he had been waiting for, so in the early spring
of 1833, he left for Philadelphia.

Evidently Bennett had forgotten that Mr. Biddle and the United
States Bank were located in the city of brotherly love. Evidently
he thought that Wall Street was ready to forgive and forget those
damning articles he had written in the *Courier and Enquirer* about
banks and speculators. Evidently he believed Martin Van Buren,
Jesse Hoyt, and the many other leading Jacksonians whom he had
helped, would, in turn, help him to make of the *Pennsylvanian* a
powerful organ for Democracy in Philadelphia.

Whether he thought so or not, the fact remained that Wall Street
and the Biddles left no stone unturned to wreck Bennett's new
venture. And as for his old friends, the politicians, they were once
more solidly entrenched for another four years, and saw no reason
why they should extend themselves for a down-at-the-heels journalist. Furthermore, the politicians now had no desire to push their
old feud with the bankers, but Bennett, roused to new fury, fired
salvo after salvo at Wall Street and its cohorts in Philadelphia,
Boston, and Baltimore.

By mid-June the financial situation of the *Pennsylvanian* was so precarious that Bennett felt called upon to write his old political pal, Jesse Hoyt, for assistance:

Philadelphia, June 12, 1833

DEAR HOYT: You will see by the papers what we are about here.

My object is to make the party come out for a National Convention. It can be done by prudence, skill, and address.

In relation to what I talked to you in New York, I have an earnest word to say.

I really wish that my friends there would try to aid me in the matter I formerly mentioned.

Morrison I fear will do nothing.

John Mumford has been aided to the extent of $40,000. With a fourth of that sum I would have done twice as much—soberly and with some decency, too.

I should be sorry to be compelled to believe that my friends in New York should bestow their friendship more effectually upon a —— fellow than me, who certainly have some pretensions to decency.

I am sorry to speak harshly of anybody, but really I think there is something like ingratitude in the way I have been treated.

I want no favor that I cannot repay.

I want no aid that is not perfectly safe.

I should like to hear from you, if there is any likelihood of my success.

Yours, &c.,

J. GORDON BENNETT

Two days later, Mr. Hoyt replied:

MY DEAR SIR: I received your letter. You will see by the *Standard* of this morning that you are under a misapprehension in relation to what has been done here. I do not know what will be the result of that business. If I had the means I should not hesitate to do all for you that is required, but I do not find any here among all our friends, that are willing to put their shoulders to the wheel. All are anxious for honors and emolument from party, but are not willing to give the equivalent for it. I do not believe that anything can be done for our paper here, or for yours either. Those who are the best able will not contribute a farthing. I conversed with several of that description today.

The enthusiasm with which the President has been received exceeds all calculation.

Yours truly,

J. HOYT.

No loan was forthcoming. The situation grew more desperate. Once again Bennett wrote his friend:

Philadelphia, July 27, 1833

Dear Hoyt: I have written to Van Buren today about the old affair. I must have a loan of $2,500 for a couple of years, from some quarter. I can't get on without it—and if the common friends of our cause— those I have been working for for eight years—cannot do it, I must look for it somewhere else. My business here is doing very well—and the money would be perfectly safe in two years. You see already the effect produced in Pennsylvania—you can have the State. But if our friends won't lay aside their heartlessness, why, we'll go to the devil— that is all.

There is no man who will go further with friends than I will—who will sacrifice more—who will work harder. You know it very well.

I must be perfectly independent of the little sections in this city, who would hurry me into their small courses at the risk of the main object.

Kendall leaves Washington tomorrow on his tour of Bank Inspection. Let me hear from you.

Yours, &c.,

James Gordon Bennett

Hoyt replied. He had tried, he said, to get funds, but there appeared to be no chance till in November. Meanwhile he urged his friend to persevere, assuring him if he did so long enough, "you will not have to request favors."

By this time, Bennett began to suspect that he was being given the run-around by his old friends, and in a lengthy letter unburdened himself fully to Hoyt:

Philadelphia, Aug. 3, 1833

Dear Hoyt: I am extremely sorry at the result of your efforts. The effect is inevitable; I must break down in the very midst of one of the most important contests which Van Buren's cause ever got into in this State. I do not see how I can avoid it. With every advantage in my favor—with every preparation made—everything in the finest trim to check-mate and corner all the opposition to Van Buren, and to force them to come out in his favor—as I know they must do soon—I must give way to the counsels of those who have most hostile feelings to the cause—and on what ground? Because neither Mr. Van Buren nor his friends will move a finger in my aid. I must say this is heartless in the extreme. I do not wish to use any other language than what will convey mildly the anguish, the disappointment, the despair, I may say, which broods over me. If I had been unknown—if I had been blest in being a blockhead—I might not have got into my present posture—nor would I have expected any aid from your quarter. But after nearly ten years spent in New York, working night and day for the cause of Mr. Van Buren and his friends; surrounded, too, as I have been, with those who were continually talking against him, and poisoning me to his prejudice, the treatment which I have received from him and his friends during this last year, and up to this moment, is as superlatively heartless—and if I could use any other word more expressive of my sentiments I would —as it is possible to conceive or imagine. By many of those whom I have supported for years, I have been suspected, slandered, and reviled as if I had been in bitter hostility to Mr. Van Buren for years, instead of supporting him through every weather, and even sacrificing myself that I might retain the same feelings towards him, for I assure you I might have continued my connection with the *C. and E.* last year, very much to my advantage—retained my share in the printing office of that establishment, if I had not differed with Mr. Webb on the points that you know so well of. I sold out, however, to Hoskin—saved a small pittance from the wreck of the *Globe*—came here and invested it in the *Pennsylvanian,* which is now entirely under my control, provided I could find a friend anywhere between heaven and earth to help me along, and enable me to carry out my fixed purpose in favor of Van Buren and his friends. But that friend God has not yet made, though several of the opposite character the other gentleman has put his brand upon, and fondly says, "this is mine."

I except you, dear Hoyt—I am sure you would help the cause if you could. I find no fault with you, although what fault you find with me about the deposits is nonsense, and only a clamor raised in Wall street by a few of the jealous blockheads hostile to me, who have not brains to see that in this city we can use the deposit question very efficiently in the October election. I do not blame even the jealous blockheads or any others in New York—I blame only one, and that is the Vice President himself. He has treated me in this matter as if I had been a boy— a child—cold, heartless, careless, and God knows what not.

By a word to any of his friends in Albany, he could do the friend- ship I want as easily as rise and drink a glass of Saratoga water at the Springs. He chooses to sit still—to sacrifice those who have supported him in every weather—and even hardly dares to treat me as one gen- tleman would treat another.

I scarcely know what course I shall pursue, or what I shall do. I am beset on all sides with importunities to cut him—to abandon him. What can I do? What shall I do? I know not. You will excuse this letter, you can easily appreciate the situation of a man confident of success if supported properly—but nothing before him but the abandonment of his deliberate purposes, or a shameful surrender of honor and purpose, and principle, and all.

Yours truly,

J. G. BENNETT

I do not know whether it is worth the while to write to Van Buren or not—nor do I care if you were to send him this letter.

In his reply, Hoyt not only refused to help Bennett, but intimated that the leaders of the party had already become convinced that Bennett was preparing the way to do an about-face as Webb had done in 1832. In the meantime all the other party papers, with the *Washington Globe* taking the lead, opened up their guns upon their old friend and associate.

In his final letter to Hoyt, just before the *Pennsylvanian* gave up its ghost, Bennett wrote:

Philadelphia, Aug. 16, 1833

DEAR HOYT: Your letter amuses me. The only point of consequence is that conveying the refusal. This is the best evidence of the deadly hostility which you all have entertained towards me. It explains, too, the course of the *Standard* and *Post,* in their aggressions upon me ever since I came to Philadelphia. The cause for such a feeling in the breasts of those I have only served and aided at my own cost and my own sacrifice, puzzles me beyond example. I can account for it in no other way than by the simple fact that I happened to have been born in another country. I must put up with it as well as I can. As to your doubts and surmises about my future course, rest perfectly easy—I shall never abandon my party or my friends. I'll go to the bottom sooner. The assaults of the *Post* and the *Standard,* I shall put down like the grass that grows. I shall carry the war into Africa, and "curst be he who cries hold, enough." Neither Mr. Van Buren and the *Argus* nor any of their true friends will or can have any fellow feeling with the men—the stockjobbers—who for the last two years have been trying to destroy my character and reputation. I know Mr. Van Buren better—and I will stand up in his defence, as long as he feels friendly to me. I will go among my personal friends who are unshackled as to politics, or banks, and who will leave me free to act as a man of honor and principle. So, my dear Hoyt, do not lose your sleep on my account. . . . I fear nothing in the shape of man, devil, or newspaper—I can row my own boat, and if the *Post* and *Standard* don't get out of my way, they must sink— that is all. If I adhere to the same principles and run hereafter as I have done heretofore, and which I mean to do, recollect it is not so much that "I love my persecutors" as that I regard my own honor and reputation. Your lighting up poor Webb as a fat tallow candle at one end, and holding him out as a beacon light to frighten me, only makes me smile. Webb is a gentleman in private life, a good-hearted fellow, honorable in all his private transactions as I have found him, but in politics and newspapers a perfect child—a boy. You will never find the *Pennsylvanian* going the career of the *C. and E*. That suspicion answers as a good excuse to those who have resolved beforehand to do me all the injury they can, but it will answer for nothing else. I am, dear Hoyt,

Yours truly,

J. G. BENNETT

Penniless, an outcast from his own party, and for the third time a failure as a newspaper publisher, James Gordon Bennett returned once more to New York convinced that politics and journalism did not mix. Looking back upon that period, from his vantage point of success a good many years later, he remarked:

When I first entered Tammany Hall, I entered it as an enthusiast studying human nature, as a young man would enter a new country, full of interest, and deriving advantage from every movement and every sight. I kept a diary during the whole period of my connection with that party, and the sentiments therein recorded, just as they occurred to me, still remain, and are the very sentiments which I entertain at this moment. I found out the hollow-heartedness and humbuggery of these political associations and political men; but yet I was so fascinated with the hairbreadth escapes and adventures that I could not disconnect myself from it until the revulsion took place between me and my partners in Philadelphia. After that period I regained my liberty and independence completely; and a fortunate thing it was for my prosperity that Van Buren and his men did behave so meanly and so contemptibly towards me in the year of 1833. I then returned to New York, started the *Herald* with the knowledge I had of men and matters throughout the country, and have been successful ever since.

PART III
THE *NEW YORK HERALD*

8. An Editor, an Idea, and Five Hundred Dollars

"THIS IS it," said the tall, gray-haired man, leading the way down half a dozen rickety steps. "Follow me."

He opened the creaking door, peered into the inner darkness, lit a tallow candle, sniffed the damp and musty air, wheeled about quite suddenly to face the incredulous-looking middle-aged Englishman at his heels.

"This is it, George. What do you think of my new office?"

Still blinking to accustom himself to the darkness after the bright sunshine of a May morning, George Houston looked about at the low, dark, damp cellar for a moment, then at his friend.

"Surely you're not serious, Jimmie! You're up to one of your tricks, eh? Why, this ill-smelling hole would scarce be fit for a fish-market, much less a newspaper office."

"You are wrong. I *am* serious. This is going to be my office, my headquarters, my editorial sanctum—in short, from within the confines of these dank and dirty walls will emanate and radiate that wit and wisdom which God has given me, to entertain and enlighten the public, to confute my enemies, and to make the name of James Gordon Bennett the most famous in newspaper history."

"A brave speech, Jimmie, but I think you're daft. Have you any money? They've stopped giving away paper and printers' ink, you know. And who will print your paper?"

"Daft, eh! We'll see who's daft. I have five hundred dollars—or at least I did have that much yesterday, till I signed a contract with Anderson and Smith, who will print my paper and be partners in my venture."

121

"Anderson and Smith! How in the world did you talk them into such a deal? Why, they're already printing both the *Sun* and the *Transcript!* They'll be having a deal of trouble with both of them, as soon as your paper appears. For your sake I hope you have a good contract with the printers."

Bennett grinned broadly. "It's ironclad. And you just wait, Houston, till I've had a chance to get under way, and I'll be bringing you over here to work for me."

"By the way," said the Englishman, as he turned to leave, "what will be the name of your new paper? And when will it appear?"

"I'm calling it the *Herald,* and the first issue will appear May 6. Watch out there, Houston," he called to his departing friend, "watch out so you don't trip over my office furniture."

Houston looked about in amazement. He saw no office furniture whatsoever, only a long pine board and two empty cracker barrels on the narrow sidewalk. "Hm," muttered Houston to himself, "Bennett's in a gala mood today, with all his jokes. Furniture indeed!"

James Gordon Bennett, veteran journalist and political hack, was turning forty as he made his fourth desperate attempt to become a newspaper publisher. Forty then was what fifty-five is now, when man has reached the western slope of his high plateau of adulthood and sees before him that downward slope which leads to old age, and death. Not so with Bennett. He was thin as a rail but hard as nails. His hair was already well streaked with gray, but his head was erect, his eye clear, his head buzzing with ideas, and the blood pulsated through his lean frame with the ardor of youth. To protect himself against the charge of being old in years, he had become very vague as to the date of his birth, and when pressed on the subject used to remark that he "guessed" he was born in 1800— thus lopping off five years.

While he rolled the barrels down the steps, to set up his office, he reflected over the events of the past weeks; how he had returned from his Philadelphia venture in journalism, disgusted with the city of brotherly love and with politicians; how he had applied for a position on the new sensational penny-paper, the *Sun;* how Mr. Day, the principal owner, had wanted to hire him only to be talked out of doing so by his junior partner and police reporter,

George Wisner, who was, no doubt, fearful of such high-powered competition; how he then determined to take another fling at newspaper publishing himself; how he had proposed partnership in this new venture to that curious-looking but able and ambitious young printer, Horace Greeley, who declined; and how at last he had gone to Anderson and Smith, who were already printing New York's two fast-growing penny-papers, the *Sun* and the *Transcript;* how by fast talk, computations on potential profits, and (to close the deal) flashing his five hundred dollars in their faces, he had signed them up as his partners.

Bennett never for a moment doubted his own abilities. Furthermore, his long apprenticeship in journalism had taught him a thousand things. In the first place, he made a firm resolve that never again would he publish a paper that was beholden to any political party or clique. His paper must be independent of the favors of office-seekers or job-holders—and by this independence he would force them to come seeking his help instead of the other way round. The paper he would publish must stand on its merits. It must win readers on the strength of its ability to entertain and enlighten. It must get information which people wanted, get it more quickly, more accurately than did any other paper. By so doing it would likewise be independent of the merchants, brokers, shippers—for if people would buy and read his paper for its news and views, then the advertising fraternity, whether they liked it or not, must of necessity advertise in his paper.

Thus it was that the *New York Herald* came into being—born of an editor, an idea, and five hundred dollars! Born in a cellar in the dim light of flickering candles, with James Gordon Bennett functioning in the triple capacity of father, mother, and midwife.

Having put up every cent he had to meet the costs of typesetting and printing, Bennett could not afford even a single assistant to begin with. He was his own staff, chief editorial writer, business manager, reporter, advertising solicitor, proofreader, and porter. His working day was co-terminal with his waking day. He arose at five every morning in his dingy tenement bedroom in a rear building on Nassau Street. Losing only a few minutes while he washed, dressed, and gulped down his tea and biscuit, he plunged into work in his room. By the time he dashed around the corner to open up his office at eight o'clock, nearly three hours' work had been accomplished. From eight until one o'clock he remained at his office, writing advertisements, preparing copy, and selling papers. Then, after a cheap and hasty lunch, he would visit the Stock Exchange, the coffee houses, the city hall, piers, shops, and the police courts, in search of news. Between four and six he was back at his pine-plank counter in the cellar. Evening would find him busily engaged in editing the material for the next day's edition or writing up last-minute news items. Then he went on to the printers, where he read proofs of the *Herald* till it was put on the presses at eleven o'clock. Such was the daily round of the busiest editor in New York.

One of Bennett's friends, the well-known bookseller, William Gowans, has left us an interesting picture of his first meeting with the editor of the *Herald*.

The proprietor, editor and vendor was seated at his improvised desk busily engaged in writing, and appeared to pay little or no attention to me when I entered. On making known my object in coming in, he requested me to put my money down on the counter and help myself to a paper; all the time he continued his writing operations.

The office was an oblong, underground room; its furniture consisted of a counter, which served also as a desk, constructed from two flour barrels, standing apart from each other about four feet, with a single plank covering both. On a chair placed in the center, sat the editor busy at his vocation, with an inkstand at his right hand, while on the end of the plank nearest the door was a pile of papers for sale.

Five months after the first issue of the *Herald* had seen the light of day, and when it and Bennett had become everyday topics of conversation in New York, Bennett brought on as his first employee, George Houston, who remained with him for many years. In announcing this doubling of the editorial force of the *Herald,* Bennett told his readers that heretofore he had done everything himself. "I have written my own editorials (for I employ at $5.00 per week no Peter Simples). I have written my own police reports.—I have written my own Wall Street reports.—I have written my own squibs, crackers and *jeux d'esprit.*—I have been my own clerk and accountant—posted my own books, made out my own bills and generally attended to all business details in the office."

The first issue of the *New York Herald*—in reality a specimen copy, for regular publication did not begin till five days later— appeared on May 6, 1835. It was a small paper, of four pages, which, though larger than the *Sun,* was nevertheless not more than a quarter the size of the big "blanket sheets" of the *Journal of Commerce, Courier and Enquirer, Post, American, Commercial Advertiser, Times,* and *Evening Star.*

The plans and purposes of the *Herald,* as announced in that first issue, declared:

Pledges and promises, in these enlightened times, are not exactly so current in the world as Safety Fund Notes, or even the U. S. Bank bills. We have had an experience of nearly fifteen years in conducting newspapers. On that score we cannot surely fail in knowing at least how to build up a reputation and establishment of our own. In *debuts* of this kind many talk of principle—political principle—party principle, as a sort of steel-trap, to catch the public. We mean to be perfectly understood on this point, and therefore openly disclaim all steel-traps, all principle, as it is called—all party—all politics. Our only guide shall be good, sound, practical common sense, applicable to the business and bosoms of men engaged in everyday life. *We shall support no party—be the organ of no faction or coterie, and care nothing for any election or any candidate from President down to a Constable.* [My italics.—O. C.]

We shall endeavor to record facts on every public and proper subject, stripped of verbiage and coloring, with comments when suitable, just, independent, fearless, and good-tempered. If the *Herald* wants the mere expansion which many journals possess, we shall try to make it up in industry, good taste, brevity, variety, point, piquancy, and cheapness. *It is equally intended for the great masses of the community—the merchant, mechanic, working people—the private family as well as the public hotel—the journeyman and his employer—the clerk and his principal.* [My italics.—O. C.] There are in this city at least 150,000 persons who glance over one or more newspapers every day. Only 42,000 daily sheets are issued to supply them. We have plenty of room, therefore, without jostling neighbors, rivals, or friends, to pick up at least *twenty or thirty thousand* for the *Herald* and leave something for others who come after us. . . .

Bennett had laid all his cards on the table. He had taken a stand —a stand in principle—against the existing form of daily papers, which were primarily journals of opinion, or, as in the case of the new penny press, retailers of gossip, and hawkers of the wit and wisdom of novelists, poets, and essayists by the generous use of scissors and paste pot. Bennett wanted—and was determined to create—a *news*paper. That concept in itself was one of the most revolutionary in the whole history of journalism—and it paved the way for making of the American and English press the most effective disseminator of straight news that the world has known. It also paved the way for better citizenship, for broadening the base of democratic government, by making this news equally available, and as Bennett said, "equally intended, for the great masses of the community."

This, too, was revolutionary. Nor can it in any sense be invalidated by the fact that Bennett himself, as well as many who followed after him, were to dip deep in the muck of public and private filth in their mad scramble for circulation.

There was very little *news* in the first issue of the *Herald*. But it was well written, well edited, and it contained material of sufficient variety to interest business man, mechanic, book-lover, housewife, and politician.

The four-column paper announced that the *New York Herald* was

Published Daily By

JAMES GORDON BENNETT & CO.

Office No. 20 Wall street, basement story

The front page was given over almost entirely to a lengthy "Biographical Sketch of Mathias the Prophet," a well-known, half-mad evangelistic crusader against the evils of alcohol. Next came a short and delightful essay on "Books," which concluded:

Wherever a book happens, there falls a spark which nothing but death can put out. Every man looks into a book as he looks into his glass to adjust his opinions and smooth down some rough spot on the face of his character. A book is a sort of little philosopher, whom we can force to chat whenever we choose, and draw from him an oracle without a fee; whom, as we bring fresh and warm from the bookshop, we tuck under our arm as if a wife or bosom-crony, and, retreating with it into some snug corner, hold agreeable and uninterrupted gossip.

An anecdote about Garrick, the actor, was there to tempt theatrical folk, followed by "Fashions for April" (it was already May) to tempt the ladies. "We have reason to believe," wrote Bennett, "that open pelisses, composed of summer silks, and edged with two or three pipings of different and striking colors, will be much in request toward the end of the month. They will be worn over muslin robes, either embroidered or trimmed with flounces. . . ."

The second page opened with the declaration of principle and purpose as quoted earlier. Then came a column and a half of "Late and Important from Europe," with information of what had been taking place across the Atlantic during February and March.

Williams' *New York Register,* which had just been published, was made the subject of a facetious review, with the editor jauntily proclaiming, "We shall enumerate some of the most striking facts furnished by Williams, throwing in a few of our own collections in the noble science of statistics, just by way of sauce for the pudding."

New York is truly "an Empire State." In 1830 we had nearly two millions of people in the State, and 202,957 in the city,—now probably two and a half millions in the State and 260,000 in the city and suburbs, including Brooklyn. . . . We have in the [city] directory a total of 31,510 names, of which 1,592 are cartmen, 2,704 grocers, 3,751 merchants, and over 4,000 widows, many of them "fat, fair and forty" and having no objections to marry.

We have 36 daily papers, 16 of which in the city issue 17,000 large sheets a day and 25,000 small; the best large daily morning sheet being the *Courier & Enquirer,* and the best small one the *Morning Herald.* . . . We have had heretofore only 8 broken banks, with a capital of 3 millions, to cheat the mechanics, but in time we may break hereafter a score or two, and thus far outstrip Penn, O, & Ky, in the art of rifling the poor. We have 6 or 7 colleges, all poor and proud, except Columbia, which is rich and lazy, educating only 100 students a year, and yet complaining of hard work. We have 8 or 10 Theological seminaries for making clergymen, 90 out of every hundred of which would make very good tillers of the ground. We have over 50 female academies for finishing the education of young ladies, where one half of the number are "finished," as we once heard John Randolph of Roanoke say in the House of Representatives, in his flageolet-sounding voice—"finished, Mr. Speaker, yes, sir, finished for all useful purposes." We have in State Prison 1,492 rogues, but God only knows how many *out* of prison, preying upon the community in the shape of gamblers, blacklegs, speculators and politicians. We have 6,457 paupers in the poorhouse, and double that number going there as fast as intemperance and indolence can carry them. We have about 500 dandies, who dress well, wear gold chains, spend their fathers' earnings and then their tailors' and hotel-keepers' and close their career with a pistol or a glass of laudanum. We have 249 people of fashion, who had an unquestionable grandfather and grandmother, and 750 *Parvenues,* who, like Melchizedick, king of Salem, have neither father nor mother. We buy and sell of each other in Wall Street, 300 millions of stocks a year, and by the operation only ruin 100 families to make the fortunes of 5 or 10 overgrown ones. . . . Here's an "empire state" for ye!

Half a column entitled "Theatrical Chit Chat" announces that Forrest is in Italy, Hackett has recently returned from the West, Miss Phillips is at Boston, Celeste "has got into fashionable society at the Opera House, having abandoned the Bowery where she made twice as much money and had ten times as much applause."

The column ends on a pessimistic note: "Theatrical criticism is at a low ebb. The lively *Star* has abandoned the field—the steady *American* ditto—the *Commercial* never entered—the *Times* is nauseating (*vide passum,* the mawkish trash on Miss Phillips)—the *Transcript* is incompetent—the *Jeffersonian* more incompetent—and the *Sun* most incompetent. Let's have a change."

Page three begins with an article entitled "The Mechanics," which deplores all the noise made, the abundance of promises made, and ephemeral legislation invoked—but which still leaves this hardworking group "where they ever were, at the mercy of caprice, custom, pride and fashion."

"What," asks Bennett, "does the journeyman mechanic stand most in need of?" and he answers in italics, *"Plenty of work and good wages."* Later in the article he reminds his readers that: "We were one of the first editors in this city to advocate the cause of the mechanics during the last ten years. The lien law—the suppression of small notes—the reform of banks—the abolition of imprisonment for debt, etc., etc., have all exercised our mind. But the journeyman mechanics are just where they were ten or twenty years ago. The evil is still untouched—the right remedy is still undiscovered."

"Police Reports," which heads column two, announces that "ignorance, insipidity and inanity reign triumphant" in that department of most of the papers, and cites numerous cases from the *New York Sun* and others.

"We shall exclude all such folly from our columns," wrote Bennett, loftily, with tongue in cheek, "and only trouble our readers with that species of reading when there is something interesting or useful to relate. . . . As we are generous and gentle, with this we shall stop, deeming it also somewhat irreverent toward a beneficent Providence to enquire too narrowly what are those motives, inscrutable to mortal ken, which dispose Him in his Infinite Wisdom, to drop down blockheads here and there to edit newspapers, like weeds in a garden, ere the rose has put forth its bud, or the hyacinth opened its blossom to the morning."

Several items of Washington news were placed under the heading "Court Circular." The paper also contained two poems, a short story, "The Broken Hearted," and numerous anecdotes and typical Bennett quips, as: "A Prim Lady;—She looks as if she were fed through a quill, and when she opens her mouth to yawn you would fancy she was going to whistle!"

There were several columns of advertising in this first issue. One announced that Sears' Chart of the World was available for twenty-five cents; another urged readers of the *Herald* to buy the monthly *Ladies' Companion;* and Horace Greeley—who hadn't wanted to go into partnership with Bennett—had the largest advertisement of all, announcing the good things to be found in his *New Yorker* magazine.

Those who bought the lively little sheet liked it. But they were few in number. Business men preferred the older papers; the politicians were chary of Bennett, and besides had their own organs to subsidize; mechanics and poorer folk were content to read the *Sun* and the *Transcript*. The overwhelming mass of the people hadn't heard of either Bennett or his new paper, the *Herald*.

The printers, Anderson and Smith, decided before a week had passed that the new venture would lose, rather than make, money. They wanted to get out from under their contract, the more so because Day of the *Sun,* whose 20,000 copies was by far the biggest printing job in the city, was threatening to take his printing elsewhere unless they stopped printing that "scurvy and blasphemous sheet of Bennett's."

In the meantime, Bennett himself, working furiously to attract attention and advertisers as his $500 melted rapidly away, felt doubly bitter at Day for having refused him, America's ace journalist, a job on the *Sun*. Every issue of the *Herald* carried one or more short but bitter attacks on the *Sun*. He'd show them!

Then one day, the fifteenth of May, the *Sun* retorted in kind. The reply was couched in the form of an advertisement.

> WANTED—prodigiously to be noticed by two or three journals whose circulation and influence will bring the existence of an obscure and unknown publisher to the knowledge of the public. Price—not particular, as Jeremy Diddler's bank is under the control of the advertiser. Apply immediately at No. 20 (basement story) Wall street.

Like the proverbial Irishman, there was nothing Bennett loved better than a good fight. He rubbed his chin with glee to think he had forced Day to notice him. But more than that, Day's spurious ad gave Bennett a lead on how to get his paper talked about—and read. Why yes!—of course!—why hadn't he thought of that before! His paper was small and unknown, and he himself, for all his long years as a journalist, had seldom seen his name in print, so how could the large newspaper-reading public know his name? Day had given him the answer.

The tactic to be pursued was one of running a continuous barrage of attacks upon the editors and papers which were well known. If he did this long enough they must, out of sheer necessity, defend themselves, attack him in turn, name him and his paper in theirs. Thus—thus—would he make them carry the name of the *Herald* and of James Gordon Bennett to their readers. Thus would they advertise him. The hotter the attack, the more would people talk—and if only enough talked, many would buy his paper, if only out of curiosity. Once that had been achieved, once he had the public talking about him and buying his paper, Bennett was convinced that his superior abilities as writer and editor would hold many of these newfound readers.

Here was another basic discovery for Bennett. He lost no time in converting it into practical application. The idea has been discovered anew for generations—and it always works. Barnum—Lincoln—Hearst—and Huey Long are only a few of the many who gained fame, fortune, or political power in this way.

The very next day Bennett replied to Day in sizzling terms.

The *Sun,* with its brace of blockheads for editors and lead of dirty and indecent police reporters, insinuates—for it dares not open its jaws plumply—that we are "obscure, unknown to the public, etc."

Here's a pretty objection to come from the garbage of society—a set of poor creatures whose light is going down faster than it ever went up; whose paper is too indecent, too immoral for any respectable person to touch, or any family to take in. Obscurity indeed! Why, we were associated in conducting some of the ablest and most respectable papers in the country, when several of their fellows were kicked out of the small gambling houses about the Five Points for indecent conduct and improper behavior.

The battle was on. Day, Webb, Noah, Brooks, Weed, Greeley, Raymond, and every other editor would henceforth be forced to be forever on the lookout in the columns of the *Herald* for the bitter invective and telling sarcasm of Bennett's pen. The public was startled—but grew to look forward to each new bit of editorial vituperation to spice its appetite for scandal.

Like a gadfly the *Herald* continued to harass poor Day. He was charged with using unscrupulous methods, as well as with "inundating the town with indecent and filthy police reports of drunkards, blacks, and negresses." Day and Wisner lost both sleep and weight trying to stop Bennett's attacks. Deport! Arrest! Stop this alien fraud and mountebank! shouted the *Sun*. Bennett's only chance of dying an upright man, wrote Day, "will be that of hanging perpendicularly from a rope."

Bennett enjoyed it hugely. But he didn't let it stop him from trying to find new innovations whereby he could gain readers and advertisers for the *Herald*. "I mean to make myself the greatest newspaper man in America—or a cipher," he declared to a friend. "It's all or nothing."

Of the many editors in New York, none but Bennett had applied himself seriously to the study of economics, and especially of money, banking, and the stock market. Where others regurgitated half-digested notions on finance and stock-jobbing for their readers, the editor of the *Herald* gave them opinions based upon a close study of Adam Smith, and the classical economists, augmented by personal observations of the leaders in American trade, industry, and finance. It was his firm and fixed opinion that wealth—real wealth —was the result of man's application of mental and physical labor to the natural resources of the earth. To him the men who grew rich and powerful through rigging the stock market, issuing worthless certificates, speculating, or through bribing and corrupting public officials—to him, all such were parasites, draining the juices of life from the common people.

Wall Street had already become the heart and center of America's financial interests, where shrewd and calloused men were garnering millions. The operations of Wall Street were a complete mystery to the average man as well as to most merchants, industrialists, and farmers. Only the insiders had a picture of what was taking place. The big newspapers were, almost without exception, always referred to as "the Wall Street papers." They catered to, and in turn were helped by, the Wall Street interests. Many of the editors, so Bennett charged, were themselves heavy speculators, and would oftentimes rig special stories in their papers to cause a rise or fall in the prices of those stocks in which they had a personal interest.

James Gordon Bennett decided that the public should be given a straightforward account of what took place in Wall Street. This would be a public service. At the same time it would serve to make his paper read by both Wall Street and the larger community of those who invest in stocks and bonds.

On Monday, May 11, 1835, the *Herald* contained its first report on Wall Street. Here was another innovation in American journalism. Today there isn't a daily in the country which doesn't carry stock-market reports. And every major paper has its own staff of writers on finance, commerce, trade, and industry.

For many years, Bennett went daily to Wall Street to get a first-hand picture of what was taking place there. He likewise gathered every report, every pamphlet, every book, and all available statistics on the money market, trade, agriculture, industry, the tariff, and so forth.

For the first month the articles—all published under the heading "Money Market"—appeared irregularly. Thereafter they were a daily feature. The first article reads:

Stocks are somewhat shaken since the late arrivals. The winding up of three or four U. S. Branch Banks makes dealers pause as to the future operations of the money market. On Saturday railroads started two or three per cent.

New York, Philadelphia, Baltimore, Boston, are all on the *qui vive* about stocks. Speculation in this article was never so flourishing. The rise is greatest in fancy stocks or new banks, such as the Morris Canal— Baltimore Canton Company—Kentucky Northern Bank—and especially certain railroads.

What is the cause of these movements? How long will they last? Who will be losers? Who the winners?

This uncommon rise in the stock market is not produced by accident. A secret confederacy of our large capitalists in the commercial cities, availing themselves of the political and commercial events of the times, could easily produce the speculation that has astonished the world during the last three months.

It is a universal law of trade that if an article is made scarce it will rise, if plenty it will fall. A dozen large capitalists, controlling twenty or thirty principal banks in the chief cities, can make money plenty or scarce just as they choose. When money is scarce stocks of all kinds fall. The confederates buy in at low prices; loan money to merchants also at 2 or 3 per cent per month. This is one operation. The next movement is to set on foot the machinery to raise stocks, which can be effected by permitting the banks to loan money liberally to the merchants at large. Stocks then will begin to rise slowly at first, but faster and faster as the speculators lead the way. When the confederates have got rid of all their fancy stocks at high prices to merchants, small dealers, or anybody not in the secret, then they begin secretly to prepare for the fall. This is done by a general and simultaneous curtailment of discounts by the Banks, which soon knocks down stocks, ruins thousands, and raises the value of money to 2 or 3 per cent per month, thus furnishing always, either falling or riding, the knowing ones an opportunity to make at least 30 per cent on their capital all the year round.

This is truth, and we seriously advise young merchants and dealers to be careful. Who can tell but at this very moment two dozen large moneyed men in our commercial cities have not already appointed the very week, day, even the hour, when a new movement will commence, which will knock down stocks 20 to 40 per cent a month? When the April weather is particularly sweet and soft, look out for a storm the next day.

The very next day appeared the first public listing of stocks—thirty-two in all—plus the prices asked and given on that day.

Wall Street was furious at Bennett. So, too, of course, were most of the other papers. But, as the public soon showed its interest, and as politicians, out-of-town bankers, and industrialists began to order the *Herald,* the other papers, slowly and reluctantly, fell into line.

On May 28, the editor of the *Herald,* perhaps a bit fearful of the counter-attacks being made upon him by the banking fraternity, suggested a truce:

Bankers and Editors! Editors and Bankers!—they form two distinct classes—two separate *cliques* in the community. The one set controls all the moneyed operations—the other the mental operations. They both most heartily and most hotly despise each other for the possession or the want of exactly opposite qualities. "A mere editor," says the banker, "a poor devil, with more ideas in his head than dollars in his pocket." "A scurvy banker," says the editor, "a man without ideas—no intellectuality—rough manners—purse-proud insolence—a mere arithmetical machine for striking the sums total for the statesman or financier to guide his ambition or his avarice."

A truce to all these bad feelings! Every class of society in the modern system of civilization is necessary, useful, and ought to be indulgent towards each, during their perilous journey through this vale of tears.

We mean to act on this principle.

Frederic Hudson, in his *History of American Journalism,* reported an interesting anecdote to illustrate the wide influence of the *Herald's* money articles:

Mr. Thomas Clarke, who was afterwards Treasurer of the first Morse Telegraph Company between Boston and New York, one day saw an advertisement for the back files of the *New York Herald.* He had purchased and saved the paper daily from its first number. His attic was "full of them, and in his wife's way at every house-cleaning." He called upon the advertiser and said he had the desired article. This was in 1845 or '46. "What do you ask for them?" asked the advertiser. "I don't exactly know, but I should say sixpence a copy would be about right," replied Mr. Clarke. "Send them down, and I will give you a check for the amount," said the advertiser. Clarke was astounded. He went home, counted the papers, had them carted to the gentleman's office, and received about $200 cash. "Now," said Mr. Clarke to the purchaser, "I would like to know what you want of those papers at two or three times their original cost?" "We have purchased them," answered the advertiser, "for a Hamburg banker. He sent over to us to buy a complete file of the *Herald* for its money articles, and we are glad to have secured them so easily."

In 1844, when the *Herald* and its editor were already the most widely known and most generally hated in the United States, a former employee of the *Herald* by the name of Kettell gained considerable notoriety for himself by asserting that he, and not Bennett, was the real author of its now famous articles on Money and Finance. The opposition press as cheerfully played up Kettell as it denounced Bennett.

The editor of the *Herald* then published not only his own version of how and when he had begun writing the money articles, but he also reported that Kettell, who had first joined Bennett's staff in February, 1838, as a collector of ship news and a reporter on local markets, was assigned by Bennett to write certain articles, along specified lines, when the editor and his wife went to Europe. Numerous letters were printed to vindicate Bennett.

Many years later, in February, 1869, when the reins of the *Herald* were being turned over to James Gordon Bennett, Jr., the old man reverted to a discussion of his attitude on speculation and the origin of the articles which had been the subject of so much controversy, both here and abroad. By 1869 every paper devoted much space to money, banking, and speculation. But Bennett felt that many of these were dishonest. He, himself, let it be said here, at no time during his long career ever took advantage of his inside information on financial manipulations to make money. He might be unscrupulous in other ways, but he refused to speculate, for he felt that by so doing he could no longer give an honest and unbiased report of Wall Street.

There is [wrote the septuagenarian editor] particularly one instrumentality in some cases, we fear, accessory to the swindling of the sharpers. This is the financial column. The financial editors of the several journals are much howled over on the street, and the opinion prevails that in order to set this or that stock all right in public estimation it is only necessary to hand a certain number of shares to the gentlemen whose duty it is to write for the various papers respectively a true history of the daily occurrences in that financial center. It is assumed, either on general principals or on special experiences, that these gentlemen, caring more for their own interests than for the interests of the public, will not hesitate to deceive the readers they are employed to enlighten in order that they may pocket part of the money thus extorted from they know not whom. In such hands the financial report becomes a dangerous machine; but it must not be in such hands, for it is capable of being a great benefit to the public. *The daily financial report was begun by us when we started the Herald. We made it personally.* Getting through that part of our varied labors that could be done at an early hour, we went to Wall Street, saw for ourselves what was in progress there, and returned with our report sketched out in fragmentary fly leaves of letters or other handy scraps of paper. We told the truth, for we were in the interest of the public; and the truth of that locality was not complementary in those days any more than it would be now. War was made upon us right and left by the men whose little games were spoiled whenever the public came to know what they were at; and, strangest of all things for a war originating in that quarter, it was a "moral war." We lived through it, however.

Compelled to delegate our labor in the preparation of a financial report, we have always meant and still mean to keep that report as honest as it was in its origin; to constitute it a legitimate and exact record of what is honestly done in Wall Street, and an exposure—a laying bare to the eyes of the public of what is dishonestly done there. We will compound none of the villainies with the fellows who trade on public credulity to abuse public confidence. *One journal shall tell what Wall Street really is and what is done there.*

The *Herald* was forever poking its nose into places which the other papers overlooked or feared to enter. Local politicians were called to task for neglect of duty, such as Alderman Barnes who was asked to look into the filthy state of Laurens Street. "The Five Points is a flower garden to it." There was considerable industrial unrest in the city, with mechanics on strike for higher wages and better conditions. A Workingmen's Party was being organized. The press and politicians were jittery. The Wall Street papers clamored for suppression of the unruly; the *Evening Post* took sides staunchly for the working men, urging a general strike, if necessary, to redress their grievances. Major Noah's *Evening Star,* as Bennett remarked, "has some droll ideas of political economy. It calls the wages of labor a tax paid by the rich. It dubs a mechanic a tax collector. If a poor man works hard and wishes to be compensated for it, the *Star* calls it Agrarianism. Really, the next move of the *Star* will be to advise the extinction of all the poor and laboring classes!"

The *Herald* lashed out furiously at the *Evening Post,* which it charged was urging the mechanics

. . . to lay aside all work, all labor, to organize themselves into idle masses, and to keep the spirit up by all sorts of inflammatory appeals to passion, prejudice and self-interest.

This is invariably the advice of these pests of society, the rascally politicians. We make no distinction—for both parties are alike in political morals or rather immorals. Instead of endeavoring to bring about a fair and equitable adjustment between the employers and the employed, the politicians endeavor to widen the breech—scatter inflammatory appeals, first against one set, then against the other.

During the winter season, when the mechanics suffer from want of work, want of fuel, want of every comfort, where is the sympathy of the knavish politician then? Gone to the winds! But in the summer season,— the season of work and industry, the time to lay up comfortable stores for a cold winter,—these knaves get wonderfully patriotic, talk of the poor mechanics, and do their best to set all classes of society in hostility to each other.

Why? Because they want their votes in the fall. By keeping the employers and the working people in a state of estrangement, hostility, and excitement, these fellows never fail to make politicians of these poor people, to the great injury of their wives, children, and families, and to the total ruin of thousands. Is there no remedy?

Determined to press his attacks on the larger papers whenever the opportunity presented itself, Bennett next turned his pen against Webb. In a lead editorial he described how his former boss had written a long, "ill-tempered, narrow-minded, sophomoric attack upon the Polish patriots, who, in order to escape the dungeons of Austria, seek liberty and independence in this free land."

Webb, to bolster his position, had cited the policies of the Roman Empire as a precedent for such action. Bennett, who was a close student of Roman history, proceeded to show that Webb didn't know what he was talking about. If he wanted to be bigoted and narrow-minded in outlook, that was his own business, but he had no right to distort history in justification of his position. Why, argued Bennett, the very greatness of Rome, which the *Courier and Enquirer* praised so highly, was due to a policy of broadminded, tolerant, political *inclusiveness.*

The Hebrews, the Persians, the Egyptians, the Greeks, the Carthagenians, and, we might say, every ancient tribe or nation, conducted their government on the narrow principle recommended by the writer of the *Courier*—and how long did they continue a great and magnificent people? In most of these nations the right of citizenship was confined to the accident of birth, the contingency of locality. The great Roman Republic was the first and only nation in ancient history that, discarding the same rules by which we would select a horse or an ass, conducted their government so as to admit intellect, talent, genius, power under whatever sun or whatever clime it came into existence. What was the consequence? Universal empire—eternal glory—a name that will never die—a spirit of legislation that still exists—an example that still invigorates the world—a civilization that yet flings its remains over half the world.

When the *Sun* and *Transcript* clashed, the *Herald,* which was forever waging war against both of them, took on the role of peacemaker.

"Come, come, Gentlemen," coaxed the canny Scot, "cease that nonsense. We little fellows in green coats and short hair must unite, get up a boat establishment, launch a fleet, swell out the dimensions of our breeches, and knock up two-thirds of the stupid $10 a year dailies. We can, if we will."

Advertisements were coming in, and the subscription list to the *Herald* was growing. Bennett determined to do some extra puffing of his paper to gain still more circulation and income, so he ran little news items like the following:

"ONE REASON FOR STOPPING AN ADVERTISEMENT.—A mechanic requested us the other day to tell him how much his advertisement, which had been in the *Herald* a week, would cost according to the original order—a quarter [of a year]. The amount was told.

" 'Well,' says he, 'I will pay you for the whole now and you will please stop it hereafter.'

" 'Stop it! Why not continue it in the *Herald* as long as you have paid?'

" 'I would have no objection; but really it is very inconvenient.'

" 'Inconvenient! how, pray?'

" 'Why, it brings me more work than I can manage.'

" 'Well, that's a droll reason to stop an advertisement.'

" 'It may be, but it's true. . . . I might have advertised in the *Sun, Transcript,* or even in the *Courier and Enquirer* till doomsday without any service. In the first two papers it would never have reached the downtown people—the merchants—the real men of business. In the last paper it would never have been seen in the crowd.'

" 'Well, that is strange.'

" 'It is true, however, so you will stop it immediately, in order that I may receive no more work than I can manage, for I get no rest from the crowd of customers.' "

"MEDICAL: 'I have something here very good I want to show you.'

"This was said to us the other day by a respectable-looking man with a box in his hand.

" 'I will be glad to see anything very good.'

" 'It is an infallible cure for corns.'

" 'Well, my dear sir, but I never had corns.'

" 'It will do for the gout.'

" 'I never had the gout.'

" 'It will do for rheumatism.'

" 'I never had rheumatism, God bless you.'

" 'The devil—you are too healthy!' and so he walked out.

"Some few minutes later another respectable gentleman walked in.

" 'I hope you are sick, my dear sir.'

" 'Indeed, no; but to oblige a friend I might be sick a few hours —not longer.'

"I have got a bottle here of Houston's real medicated syrup, excellent for dyspepsia.'

" 'But I never had dyspepsia.'

" 'It is good for diseases of the stomach and bowels.'

" 'I never had any trouble with these parts unless it was to line them well.'

" 'Well, it will do for a cordial for a person not sick. Take this bottle and taste it.'

" 'I wish it was good old Madeira wine—that is a medicine I would like.'

"The gentleman walked away, and our readers will see an account of the article in the advertisement."

It was at this time, too, that the *Herald* opened up its attack upon the Catholic Church—an attack that was to continue with but few interruptions for a great many years.

New York, in 1835, was already filling up with Irish immigrants, to the great disgust of many natives. In fact, Tammany had really been organized for the purpose of keeping the dynamic sons of Erin from getting a political toehold in New York. But the flow of the Irish continued from over the sea. The Protestant forces in the city became worried, lest this cohesive religious group of Irish, in collaboration with other Catholics, might not turn the first city of the New World into a dependency of Rome.

Bennett, of course, had long waged war, in his own small way, upon the church of his fathers. When he saw the rise of anti-Catholic sentiment, he determined to follow a line of action which, in his opinion, would win him support from both the anti-Catholics and the Irish. His method was to attack the Church and its prelates as agents of a foreign power, to play up the Irish as fine people, and then to urge the separation of the American Catholic Church from that of Rome—the American church to have its own independent hierarchy.

The *Star,* the *Courier and Enquirer,* and other papers had laid down an editorial barrage against the Irish. Bennett called them stupid for making such attacks. "We like the Irish boys and will defend them."

The heat of the controversy stirred up so much resentment that there were many serious riots in the city. The *Herald* placed the blame for these riots upon Bishop Dubois, whose conduct, it declared, had been "that of the veriest slave to the Vatican, and an ignorant tyrant towards his educated and respected Irish clergymen."

Seeking further to drive a wedge between the Bishop and the

Irish, Bennett wrote a few days later that "to anyone who is acquainted with the character of the Irish people, it is apparent that
to the weaknesses of human nature they join innumerable traits of
heroism, magnanimity, virtue and excellence. . . . We have found
the Irish people of this city tyrannized over and borne down by a
Roman bishop and a Bourbon knot of ignorant, uneducated priests
acting under the exclusive authority of the Church of Rome."

During the night of August 12, 1835, a fire broke out on Fulton
Street. Spreading like a prairie fire through the wooden buildings
of lower New York, it left a path of desolation and havoc in its
wake. Five lives were lost, more than $2,000,000 in property was
destroyed, and a thousand persons were thrown out of work, for
the district was filled with offices, warehouses, stores, shops, and
printing establishments.

Among the buildings totally destroyed was that at 34 Ann Street,
where the *Transcript,* the *Jeffersonian,* the *New Yorker* and the
Herald were printed. Anderson and Smith were ruined. Both died
shortly thereafter. Bennett's copy, paper, and other materials also
went up in smoke. He, too, was ruined—ruined just as he saw success ahead of him.

Undaunted by the disaster, Bennett set out at once to raise capital with which to continue his paper, and the very next day, the
thirteenth, there appeared the following advertisement in the *Sun.*

> A CARD—James Gordon Bennett begs leave to inform the
> public that the press, type and materials of the *Herald* estab-
> lishment having been destroyed in the great fire on Wednesday
> morning in Ann Street, the publication of the *Herald* will be
> resumed in a few days, as soon as materials can be procured."

On the twenty-seventh another advertisement in the *Sun* announced that the *Herald* would appear again on the thirty-first of
August.

Rising from the ashes of the old, the new paper was better and
more audacious than the old. Furthermore, Bennett was now sole
owner—the printers having dropped out. Bennett had learned many
things during the few weeks since the *Herald* had been borne. He

felt sure of himself and his future. He knew that the world was really his oyster, if he steered clear of the old clichés, the old traditions of journalism, and trusted solely to his own good judgment.

"We are again in the field, larger, livelier, better, prettier, saucier and more independent than ever," announced the new *Herald*. It told how its already phenomenal growth augured well for the future, and that it intended to reach the amazing daily circulation of *twenty-five thousand* before it stopped its upward climb. "It can be done, and if industry, attention, resolution, and perseverance can accomplish the feat under the encouraging smiles of a kind public, the *Herald* shall do it."

Announcing that the *Herald* would avoid the dirt of party politics, Bennett said it would nevertheless freely and candidly express itself on every public issue and public man. It meant also "to procure intelligent correspondents in London, Paris and Washington, and measures are already adopted for that purpose. *In every species of news the Herald will be one of the earliest of the early.*"

And the *Herald* did grow. Bennett moved out of his cellar to another on Broadway, a little bigger and brighter than the first.

In mid-October he moved again, this time to a still larger basement at 148 Nassau Street. It was a place, Bennett told his readers, quite truly remarkable—a very religious and theological neighborhood, with the Bible Society on his left, the Tract Society on his right, and, directly across the street, Dr. Spring's venerable brick church. "I regret to state," he added, "that a few doors on my left is Mr. Tappan's Anti-Slavery concern; and, what is worse, a few doors on the right, just across Spruce Street is the office of a thing generally called the *Sun* newspaper. . . . I mean to take a few spots out of the *Sun* as fast as I can, and as to the Anti-Slavery people, I think and pledge myself thus far to the South—that with the aid of the Bible Society and the Tract Society, the Missionary Society and Dr. Spring, we shall be able to emasculate the whole of them in nine or twelve months at farthest."

9. *The Ellen Jewett Murder Mystery*

Browse through the seared and yellowing newspapers of New York for the first third of the nineteenth century and you will be struck by the fact that news of crime—robbery, murder, sex triangles—is virtually non-existent. As a cold matter of record, the police and criminal courts of that day were as busy as they are now; and there is good reason to suspect that the proportion of crimes committed in proportion to population was greater than now.

The reason for omitting information on acts of crime was a sense of values on the part of the editors, far removed from that of today. The London *Morning Herald* pioneered in police-court news in the 1820's. By its humorous or pathetic treatment of the happenings at Bow Street, it won a large new circle of readers. This at last came to the attention of Mr. James Watson Webb, publisher of the *Morning Courier,* who attempted feeble imitations of his London compatriot.

Insignificant as these items were, they were frowned upon by the other metropolitan papers, which strongly condemned the practice.

"It is a fashion," editorialized the *Statesman,* "which does not meet with our approbation, on the score of either propriety or taste. To say nothing of the absolute indecency of some of the cases which are allowed occasionally to creep into print, we deem it of little benefit to the cause of morals thus to familiarize the community, and especially the younger parts of it, with the details of misdemeanor and crime."

William Cullen Bryant of the *Post* and many other editors concurred wholeheartedly with the *Statesman.*

The *Sun* and the *Transcript* in 1834 and 1835, first of the penny

143

press, followed up and improved upon the police-court news of the *Courier.* The *Transcript,* whose police reports were written by a witty young Englishman, William Atree, at once incurred the displeasure of its rival. It was accused by the *Sun* of dishing up as news a rewrite of the articles originally appearing in the London *Herald.* The *Transcript* retorted that it employed two full-time men for this work, who attended the police courts from three o'clock each morning till eight o'clock each night.

But even so, the total volume of police news rarely exceeded more than half a column. Bennett, who, as we have related in the previous chapter, scornfully remarked he would have nothing to do with such stupidities, soon thereafter advertised for a police reporter, and began to follow the lead of the *Sun* and *Transcript* in giving some coverage to the courts. This continued for almost a year.

As late as March 10, 1836, he was still following their lead. On that day he devoted only one short paragraph to an important criminal case.

IMPORTANT & INTERESTING TRIAL

The trial of Captain Harvey, for the murder of Good, one of the men employed on board his vessel, comes on this day in the Circuit Court. The trial must prove very interesting, as the charges preferred against him are of the most atrocious nature. He has engaged the most eminent counsel that could be procured—gentlemen equally celebrated for their legal acquirements and splendid eloquence, Hugh Maxwell and Ogden Hoffman, Esq'rs.

One looks in vain through earlier issues for details of the crime, how and where it took place, or information about the murderer, Captain Harvey, or the murdered man. The reading public had to depend upon gossip rather than the newspapers to get the information it wanted on this bit of crime.

Bennett, with that uncanny news sense which was to keep him ahead of all other newspaper men for so many years, must at this time have come to a realization that people were eager to get more detailed information on the tragedies of their fellow humans. At any rate, on the very next day, and for the following two days, he gave front-page space to the trial—devoting nearly two full columns on the first day, and the major part of a column on the next two days.

There was nothing sensational in the reporting—in fact, it followed too closely the matter-of-fact procedure of the courtroom itself. But the story of the case was related—in itself an innovation; and there can be no doubt but that there was an appreciable jump in circulation for the *Herald,* as well as a mounting volume of advertisements.

Dr. Brandreth's V.U. (Vegetable Universal) Pills, with lengthy testimonials as to their efficacy, were advertised on every page. Others announced: THE VARIOUS WEAKNESSES PECULIAR TO THE FAIR SEX *come* IMMEDIATELY *under the powers of* EVAN'S TONIC COMOMITE PILLS; or—TRY THEM: *And You Will Be Sure To Recommend Your Friends To Buy Them*—DR. GOODMAN'S AMERICAN ANTIGONORRHEAL PILLS. Dr. Boyd—late of Ireland—offered his services "in the treatment of a certain disease," while Hopper's Pharmacy at 364 Broadway announced: "LEECHES! LEECHES! A Lot of Very Superior Leeches just received."

A front-page editorial on March 15, entitled "Benefits of Advertising in the *Herald,*" reported that Mr. Hopper, whose leeches and other items had been announced to the public through the *Herald,* had experienced a truly tremendous rush of business. The causes for this, wrote Mr. Bennett, "are easily explained. From its peculiar business character—its regular Wall Street reports—its life and variety—it has a more general circulation among business men than any large paper in Wall Street. Our *city circulation* at this moment amounts to more than that of the *Courier & Enquirer* and the *Evening Star* combined."

"Our circulation is now of such an extent and character," boasted the *Herald's* editor, "that we care nothing about increasing it. We would not lift a finger to add another reader to the *Herald.* Yet, we take pleasure in increasing its circulation, merely to increase the pleasure of readers and extend true intellectual happiness as far as possible. . . ."

Less than a month after these words were written, James Gordon Bennett was to be engaged in the biggest, most sensational piece of journalism ever seen in America up to that time—and his circulation was to mount so rapidly that the overworked printers and presses could not keep up with the demand. By this venture, the editor of the *Herald* firmly established himself as the ace journalist of the day and placed himself firmly on the road to wealth and power.

But more than this—and somehow these facts have been overlooked by others who have written about him—Bennett, in 1836—and long before either Joseph Pulitzer or William Randolph Hearst had been born—created that sensational type of journalism which feeds upon sex, crime, and scandal. James Gordon Bennett was the real father of "yellow journalism." Lacking only were the smash headlines and the lurid drawings and photographs of a later day.

Not only did Bennett create a new type of journalism—he forced the other papers, willingly or otherwise, to follow in his footsteps. He established a new set of values for newspaperdom everywhere. Henceforth, crime, scandal, and the seamy side of life were to be sought for by enterprising reporters. And the public—scandalized and shocked as it was at first by such an exposure of man's lust and passion—the public, while in the very process of condemning the editors who published such "filth," rushed in to buy the latest issues of the *Herald,* or the *Sun,* or the *Transcript,* fresh off the presses.

There is another innovation to journalism that Bennett established in the spring of 1836—an innovation forgotten in the hectic atmosphere of those days, and not to be revived again till more than twenty years had elapsed. This innovation—which seems such a commonplace to all of us today—was the *interview*.

The first direct interview in American journalism appeared in the *New York Herald* of Saturday, April 16, 1836.

On Sunday, April 10, 1836, the life of New York differed little from that of any other Sabbath in the early spring. By horse-car, hansom cab, carriage, or afoot, the good folk of Manhattan went to church, to the Battery, or headed for the fields, woods, and ponds far to the north of the city.

On Monday morning, as clerks, brokers, merchants, and mechanics headed for their respective places of business, many, as

usual, bought copies of Mr. Bennett's sprightly and impudent
Herald.

The leading article announced:

MOST ATROCIOUS MURDER

Our city was disgraced on Sunday, by one of the most foul and premeditated murders, that ever fell to our lot to record. The following
are circumstances as ascertained on the spot.

Richard P. Robinson, the alleged perpetrator of this most horrid deed,
had for some time been in the habit of keeping (as it is termed) a
girl named Ellen Jewett, who has for a long period resided at No. 41
Thomas-street, in the house kept by Rosina Townsend.

Having, as he suspected, some cause for jealousy, he went to the house
on Saturday night as appears, with the intention of murdering her, for
he carried a hatchet with him. On going up into her room, quite late at
night, he mentioned his suspicions, and expressed a determination to
quit her, and demanded his watch and miniature together with some
letters which were in her possession. She refused to give them up, and
he then drew from beneath his cloak the hatchet and inflicted upon her
head three blows, either of which must have proved fatal, as the bone
was cleft to the extent of three inches in each place.

She died without a struggle; and the cold blooded villain deliberately
threw off his cloak, cast the lifeless body upon the bed *and set fire to
that*. He then ran down the stairs unperceived by any person, went out
of the back door, and escaped in that manner.

In a short time Mrs. Townsend was aroused by the smell of smoke—
she rushed up stairs and saw the bed on fire and the mangled body of
the unfortunate girl upon it. She ran down, raised the alarm, and the
watchmen rushing to the spot, rescued the body and preserved the house
from being consumed.

Robinson's cloak was in the room, and at once they suspected the
murderer. Mr. Noble, the assistant Captain of the Watch, instantly went
and aroused Mr. Brink. They received such information as the horror-
stricken inmates could afford them, and proceeded on their search. On
Sunday morning, at seven o'clock, Robinson was arrested in bed at his
boarding house, No. 42 Dey-street, and brought at once to the house
where had been committed the foul deed.

On seeing the body he exhibited no signs of emotion, but gazed
around and on his victim coldly and calmly.

The Coroner was summoned, a Jury formed, and on a patient examination of the testimony, they returned a verdict, that "she came to her
death by blows upon her head inflicted with a hatchet, by Richard P.
Robinson."

Robinson is a native of one of the Eastern States, aged 19 and remarkably handsome, and has been for some time past, in the employ of Joseph Hoxie, 101 Maiden-lane. *But his conduct upon this occasion, must stamp him as a villain of too black a die for mortal. Of this there can be no doubt,* for he took the hatchet with him, with which the murder was committed, and the deed done, he attempted to destroy all evidence of his guilt, by firing the house, and thus induce the public to believe that she had perished in the flames. He was very well and highly connected, and the sad news that must soon reach his parents' ears may be fatal to them.

Ellen Jewett, was a finely formed, and most beautiful girl—a girl about twenty years of age, and endowed by nature and education, with talents and accomplishments which should have saved her from her ignoble situation.

On his examination before the Coroner's Jury, Robinson denied himself and his name, and asserted that he had not been in the house that night; but a woman was brought from his boarding house, who swore positively to his cloak. The fact of his having carried the hatchet with him, is substantiated, by there being a piece of twine attached to his button hole, which tallied precisely with a piece attached to the handle of the hatchet. On leaving the house yesterday, he leaped lightly into the carriage which was to carry him to Bridewell, his countenance clear, calm, and unruffled, and on being put into his cell, his last request was for some segars to smoke. The remains of the poor unfortunate victim will be interred this day.

Here, indeed, were the elements of a tragedy to arouse great curiosity and emotion!

A beautiful prostitute! A rich, handsome young man! And a most cruel type of murder, augmented by an attempt to burn the body and the bawdy-house in which the crime was committed! Here was mystery, tragedy, and the basis for ample moralizing, while lifting the curtains upon the life of a fallen woman.

Bennett, sensing at once that this was just what he needed to build his circulation, threw what little caution he had to the winds, and gave all his time and effort in an attempt to solve the mystery, whet the appetite of his readers for more, and tell the whole story of Ellen Jewett.

The little basement office of the *Herald* was the scene of anxious and eager buyers. In the meantime, Bennett decided upon a course of action, which no other editor dared consider. He went to the bawdy-house—the scene of the crime—to see for himself what had taken place and to talk to the inmates. His story of that visit, told on the front page of the eleventh, set the whole of New York rocking back on its heels. It just wasn't done! One hostile critic compared his action with that "of a vampire returning to a newly found graveyard—like the carrion bird to the rotten carcass—like any vile thing to its congenial element." But Bennett cared little for such attacks—for he saw the lines of eager, news-hungry men and women clamoring for the *Herald*—and he also saw that the other papers, try as they would, were being compelled to deal with the case. His story on the second day reports:

Visit to the Scene

Yesterday afternoon, about 4 o'clock, the sun broke out for a moment in splendor. I started on a visit to the scene at 41 Thomas-street. On passing through Chapel-street, I came to the corner of Thomas-street, which runs west from behind the Hospital yard to Hudson-street. A large crowd of young men stood around the door, No. 41, and several groups along the street in various directions. The excitement among the young men throughout the city was beginning to spread in all directions.

The house is a large four story elegant double one, painted yellow, and on the left hand side as you go to Hudson-street. It is said to be one of the most splendid establishments devoted to infamous intercourse that the city can show. I knocked at the door. A Police officer opened it, stealthily. I told him who I was. "Mr. B. you can enter," said he, with great politeness. The crowds rushed from behind seeking also an entrance.

"No more comes in," said the Police officer.

"Why do you let that man in?" asked one of the crowd.

"He is an editor—he is on public duty."

I entered—I pressed forward to the sitting room or parlor. There I found another Police officer in charge of that apartment. The old lady of the house, Mrs. Townsend, was sitting on a sofa, talking to several young men, in a great state of excitement. She was describing what Ellen had said—how she discovered the fire—how she made an alarm—how she called for the watch. The room was elegantly furnished with mirrors, splendid paintings, sofas, ottomans, and every variety of costly furniture. The Police officer when he saw me said—"Mr. B. would you like to see the *place?*"

"I would," replied I.

He immediately rose—I followed him. We mounted an elegant stair case, dark and gloomy, being in the centre of a large double house. On reaching the second story, the Police officer took a key from his pocket, and opened the door. What a sight burst upon me! There stood an elegant double mahogany bed, all covered with burnt pieces of linen, blankets, pillows, black as cinders. I looked around for the object of my curiosity. On the carpet, I saw a piece of linen sheet covering something as if carelessly flung over it.

"Here," said the Police officer, "here is the poor creature."

He half uncovered the ghastly corpse. I could scarcely look at it for a second or two. Slowly I began to discover the lineaments of the corpse as one would the beauties of a statue of marble. It was the most remarkable sight I ever beheld—I never have, and never expect to see such another. "My God," exclaimed I, "how like a statue! I can scarcely conceive that form to be a corpse." Not a vein was to be seen. The body looked as white, as full, as polished as the purest Parian marble. The perfect figure, the exquisite limbs, the fine face, the full arms, the beautiful bust, all, all surpassed in every respect the Venus de Medici according to the casts generally given of her.

"See," said the Police officer, "she has assumed that appearance within an hour."

It was the first process of dust returning to dust. The countenance was calm and passionless. Not the slightest appearance of emotion was there. One arm lay over her bosom—the other was inverted and hanging over her head. The left side down to the waist, where the fire had touched, was bronzed like an antique statue. For a few moments I was lost in admiration at this extraordinary sight—a beautiful female corpse, that surpassed the finest statue of antiquity. I was recalled to her horrid destiny by seeing the dreadful bloody gashes on the right temple, which must have caused instantaneous dissolution.

I then looked round the room. It was elegant, but wild and extravagant in its ornaments. On the drawers was a small library, composed of light novels, poetry and monthly periodicals. There hung on the wall a beautiful print of Lord Byron as the presiding genius of the place. The books were Byron, Scott, Bulwer's works and the Knickerbocker.

A work table in a state of disorder, stood near by. It was covered with fragments,—pen, ink, paper, crayons, pamphlets, &c. &c. Above the mantel piece hung several theatrical fancy sketches.

I returned to take a last look at the corpse. What a melancholy sight for beauty, wit, and talent, for it is said she possessed all, to come to such a fatal end!

I came down stairs—the house looked dark and gloomy, all the windows being half shut; but it was throughout splendidly furnished.

Such is the scene as it was seen yesterday afternoon.

This extraordinary murder has caused a sensation in this city never before felt or known. I understand that a large number of fashionable young men, clerks and others were caught in the various apartments by the Police, when the cry of fire was given. *It was Saturday night.* The murdered girl was one of the most beautiful of her degraded *caste*. She was a perfect Millwood. She has seduced by her beauty and blandishments more young men than any known in the Police Records. She was a remarkable character, and has come to a remarkable end. The house is in danger from the mob. Let the authorities look to it. A morbid excitement pervades the city. It is said that she threatened to expose Robinson, when she lived, having discovered that he was paying attention to a respectable young lady. This threat drove him to madness. On Saturday she walked up and down Broadway half the day, nodding to her acquaintances among the dissipated young men.

In what a horrible condition is a portion of the young men of this devoted city?

His description, colored no doubt—especially that of the corpse—created a sensation. And his report on the books read by the murdered girl whipped up a frenzied sympathy for her among the church-folk and the numerous Female Societies. It also drew to the *Herald* a new segment of readers, who heretofore would as soon hold hands with the Devil himself as be seen reading "that scurrilous, infidel sheet, the *Herald.*"

The issue of April 12 contains at the top of the page a note to the public, apologizing for the irregular delivery of the paper on both the eleventh and twelfth, this being due to a breakdown of the steam engine which is used to drive the printing presses. "The constant call for the *Herald* yesterday," continues the note, "was beyond anything ever seen in New York. Single papers sold at a *shilling* each in Wall Street. . . . We could have sold 30,000 copies yesterday if we could have got them worked."

Once again, all other news was subordinated to the tragedy of Ellen Jewett. Bennett was quite content to feed the flames of popular indignation and curiosity with information which he and his staff labored day and night to amass.

"The excitement yesterday morning throughout the city," begins the article of the twelfth, "was extraordinary. Everybody exclaimed 'What a horrible affair!' 'What a terrible catastrophe!' "

"News was received from Texas, highly disastrous to the colonists, but the private tragedy of Ellen Jewett almost absorbed all public attention."

"Her private history," wrote Bennett, "is most remarkable—her character equally so."

"She is a native of Augusta in the state of Maine, and her real name is Dorcas Dorrance, but in the city she has generally passed under the name of Ellen Jewett—in Boston as Helen Mar."

The article then tells of her life as an orphan, who was taken into the home of Judge Western of Augusta, where she was raised, with his own daughters, as one of the family. It tells of her studious habits, good manners, and keen intelligence, and how she was sent to a Female Academy at Coney, Maine, to perfect her education.

In the summer of 1829, when Dorcas was sixteen years of age, she vacationed at a small town north of Augusta where, says Bennett, "she became acquainted with a young man by the name of H—— Sp——, a fine youth, elegant and educated, since said to be a cashier in one of the banks in Augusta. After her short acquaintance with him, all was gone that constitutes the honor and ornament of the female character."

She returned after a short season to Augusta. Her situation soon became known in the Judge's family. A quarrel ensued. She left her protectors, after having in a moment of passion lost all the rules of virtue and morality.

After having recovered from her first lapse from the path of virtue she retreated to Portland, took the name of Maria Benson, and became a regular Aspasia among the young men, lawyers, merchants, etc. . . .

Her life in Portland was rather experimental. She was quite young, and retained some traces of modesty. Falling into difficulty there, she took an opportunity one morning, and came to Boston. Here she assumed the name of Helen Mar, from a popular character in a . . . novel. She lived in Boston about a year and a half, and left that city in company with a distinguished man for NY. . . .

In this city she took the name of Ellen Jewett, and has lived at several houses round town. During the last winter she resided with a Kentuckian in a disguise for several weeks at one of our fashionable hotels. Her way of life in New York has corresponded with the terrible state of society in this city. At such fashionable houses, young men, married and single and all, meet together in the evening, spend their time and their money, exhaust their treasures and their sensibilities, and break down every moral tie that hitherto has kept the elements of social intercourse together.

The house at No. 41 Thomas street is occupied by Rosina Townsend, but this is not her real name. She is recently from Cincinnati, and is one of the most dashing in her infamous line of life.

Ellen Jewett was well known to every pedestrian in Broadway. Last summer she was famous for parading Wall-street in an elegant green dress, and generally with a letter in her hand. She used to look at the brokers with great boldness of demeanor—had a peculiar walk, something in the style of an Englishwoman. From those who have known her, we have been informed that she was a fascinating woman in conversation, full of intellect and refinement, but at the same time possessed of a very devil, and a species of mortal antipathy to the male race. Her great passion was to seduce young men, and particularly those who most resisted her charms. She seems to have declared war against the sex. "Oh!" she would say, "how I despise you all, you are a heartless, unprincipled set, you have ruined me, I'll ruin you, I delight in your ruin."

During her residence here, she carried on an extensive country correspondence with every part of the Union. We learn from the post office that during last summer she usually received from three to eight letters a day. Her postage bill exceeded that of several brokers in Wall-street. Her private correspondence is of a most remarkable character, resembling that of the famous Abelard and Eloisa. We are promised a choice selection from this correspondence, which are characterized by great talent, power, pathos and brilliancy.

There followed a lengthy description of the murder—a rehash of what had already appeared on Monday—both for the benefit of new readers as well as to rekindle the emotions of the old. Bennett did a bit of deduction on his own in the concluding paragraph of the article.

"The deed must have been done in the most profound silence, as a girl who sleeps in the next room, separated only by a single partition, did not hear a word or groan, and during the night she herself got up and fastened a shutter which was slamming with the wind. Mrs. Townsend stated, that when she carried the Champagne up, ordered by Ellen, Robinson was in bed, but Ellen, although attired in her *robe de nuit,* had not yet retired. The deed, therefore, must have been committed between the hours of 12 and 3."

Wednesday's issue (as well as those of the next few days) again apologized for the inability to get out enough papers, for the steam engine was still causing trouble. However, the editor was glad to announce that "for seven hours the people rolled in and rolled out of our office, buying the *Herald* as fast as they could be struck off. Probably *five thousand persons* rushed upon us in a few short hours."

New York was clamoring for more of the intimate details of the victim. Bennett was only too willing to gratify their desires, so once again he took his readers with him on:

Another Visit to the Scene

What a scene of desolation her room presented after the removal of the lovely remains of the unfortunate! Every thing was in confusion. Fragments of books, dresses, bonnets, paper were strewed around. Beneath an old boot that formerly adorned her beautiful ankle, was found a copy of Lalla Rookh, which had been read and re-read, till it looked like a school book, which had gone through a whole family of young ones: In an old bonnet that once flaunted its feathers over that alabaster brow which the murderer's axe has despoiled, we found a copy of Halleck's poems, every leaf cut and apparently well read. Beneath a fragment of fine velvet, constituting a portion of her winter dress, was discovered Byron's Don Juan and Beppo, in all the elegance of binding that London could afford.

What an air of elegance and intellectual refinement, without the slightest approach to principle and morals, dispersed itself round the apartment!

On turning over one of the linen sheets we found a most elegant octavo volume, in splendid London binding. What could it be? Who would imagine what it was? We turned over the leaves—looked at the title page. It was a recent splendid work of Lady Blessington's entitled the "Flowers of Loveliness," and treating on the resemblances of females and flowers to each other.

What a crowd of recollections this singular circumstance brings up to mind!

Lady Blessington! one of the frailest, yet most beautiful—one of the most unprincipled, yet most enchanting women now living in the world!

Lady Blessington and her two sisters, were the daughters of a vintner, who kept a small tavern near or in the city of Cork, Ireland. They were young, beautiful, and served his customers at the counter with glasses of whiskey at a six-pence each drink. Possessed of talents without principle, they started in the career of ambition. They picked up general knowledge as well as they could—they rose step by step, till one of the Miss Power's became Lady Blessington—another Lady Canterbury—and a third, Lady Something-else.

The recent publication of this woman was thus found in the boudoir of the poor unfortunate Ellen Jewett.

In another part of the room we found several receipts for the Albion newspaper, the *Mirror,* the *Lady's Companion;* all having been paid in advance, one year, and very recently, too. She was a patroness of our light city literature, and esteemed highly the *Knickerbocker* and *Monthly.*

Her Literary Correspondence

This is one of the most interesting remains of the "unfortunate." Her epistolary correspondence possesses interest of the deepest character. Police Justice Lownds has in his possession about fifty or sixty letters found in her trunk, several written by herself, and others written to her, by persons who admired or pretended to admire her talents and beauty.

Not a fulsome expression nor an unchaste word is from her in any of these letters. They contain apt quotations from the Italian, French, and English poets, on love and friendship, satirizing playfully the little incidents of her life. Her hand writing is uncommonly beautiful—a neat running hand possessing something of the character of Bristow's style, but far superior to her master, if he ever taught her. Every letter is written on beautiful embossed paper, green, blue, yellow, and gold edged, as accident might throw in her way. Some of the letters, from the hand writing—disclosures, incidents, and other circumstances are known to be from certain respectable persons in this city—and even married men, at least they are married now. The letters also bear various signatures, such as, "Wandering Willie"—"Roderick Random"—"Frank Rivers," &c. &c. All the letters addressed to Robinson, begin "Dear Frank," and close with, "To Dear Frank Rivers."

The correspondence like her life is a drama, a juggle, a mingling up of the various persons, passages and events. Every one of her correspondents took a name and a character, and supported it as well as he could. She also assumed various characters in her various correspondence, and sustained it with the same good keeping as if it had been a drama.

Among the letters, or on her work table, was found a beautiful Album or Scrap Book, containing choice quotations in prose and poetry, some of which had been, and is in her correspondence—others kept for future application. This pretty little book is also in possession of Justice Lownds.

Among the various letters on love and friendship in the escritoire, there was one, of so remarkable and characteristic a nature, as to identify at once the writer, who was well known last summer to have been engaged in certain prints of this city, now going into "the sear and yellow leaf." The one we allude to, is signed "Wandering Willie." The supposed writer has distinguised himself in the South recently, fighting against the Indians, and after a defeat, in rescuing a young lady from the watery grave. The manner he became acquainted with Ellen Jewett, was in an affair which took place at the Police Office, and was reported by him in an article, which appeared in one of the papers he was connected with at the time, June, 1834.

"Dearest Ellen.—Most lovely and enchanting creature! I shall never forget the moment I saw your fair form in the Police Office. You are fit to be a princess—a very queen. What a prize the villain had who seduced you at the Boarding School! How I should like to have been in his place! Yet you are as sweet a companion now as ever. Oh! lovely creature, what a form! what a figure! what a fine bust! Your lineaments * * * * * * rich lips, * * * full bust, * * * Your mind too, is of the first order. I want to come and see you, and talk to you—I adore to read Byron with you. Did you see the account I gave of you in my paper? How I have served up the immaculate rascal! Oh! such richness as you have in your bosom, sweet Helen. I could almost go the world over in your service—sleep away a whole life on your bosom. *Ma foi*, but I could. What is the reason, Helen, that after a woman falls from virtue she never gets up? I don't know, however, that I am much better than you. When shall I come and see you? Do lovely Helen, say?

> *Had I never loved so blindly,*
> *Had I never loved so kindly,*
> *Never meet or never parted,*
> *I had ne'er been broken hearted.*

There's a quotation for you.

I am, your's forever,
Wandering Willie

The lengthy article closes, effectively, on a high moral plane, and also raises, for the first time, doubts as to Robinson's guilt.

Ellen was by far the most popular girl, and the star boarder, among the dozen or more who lived with Rosina Townsend.

She was the pride of that infamous house, called the City Hotel on Thomas street, and knowingly let out for such purposes by one of our most respectable and pious citizens. She concentrated all attention—she was the flower of that garden of death—she was the Venus of that Paphos of destruction—she was the beautiful ruling spirit of that place of perdition—she gave a refined character to all its amusements—she gave grace to its licentiousness—elegance to its debauchery—and spirit and intelligence to its ignorance and vulgarity. . . .

It is rapidly becoming a doubtful point, notwithstanding the startling circumstances, whether the poor unfortunate girl was destroyed by the young man, now in the custody of the public authorities. It is asked, Is it possible for a youth, hitherto unimpeached and unimpeachable in his character, to have engendered and perpetrated so diabolical an act as the death of Ellen Jewett was? Is it the character of crime to jump at once from the heights of virtue to the depths of vice?

The various circumstances, showing the probable guilt of Robinson—can they be explained? Can they not be shown to be naturally growing out of other persons' guilt—of a deep laid conspiracy of female rivals—of the vengeance of female wickedness—of the burnings of female revenge? The cloak—the hatchet, the twine, the whitewash on his pantaloons, the traces of blood, all the circumstances accumulating to cover the youth with guilt, may yet be explained on the trial, a trial which, in deep interest, heart-rending pathos, remarkable features, and startling developments, will surpass any trial that ever took place in New York. . . .

We do not wish to interfere with the dark but stern current of Justice—but the death of Ellen Jewett is the natural result of a state of society and morals which ought to be reformed altogether in unhappy New York. That horrible tragedy is the legitimate fruit of laxity in our old men—want of principle in many of the married—and unregulated passion in the young. It as naturally springs from our general guilt and corruption as the pestilence does from water of death stagnating under an August sun. If the cold-blooded murderer of Ellen Jewett shall ever be fully and legitimately discovered, it may as likely be among her own rivals, and her own sex, as among the young men who frequented such infamous places. The deliberate setting fire to the house has more the character of female vengeance in it than that of the heedless passion of a youth of 19.

Day after day the *Herald* continued its front-page stories of Ellen Jewett, Rosina Townsend, and young Robinson. And day after day grew the excitement over the case, forcing Boston, Philadelphia, Baltimore, and Washington papers to reprint or rewrite the sensational news which the *Herald,* the *Sun,* and the *Transcript* were now playing for all it was worth. Hard-headed business men could talk of nothing else. Shoppers lingered over the counters to discuss the merits of the case with each other or with the clerks. The coffee shops buzzed with rumors, tips, and just plain gossip. Clergymen found material for a season's sermons in the tragedy—and the pews were always well filled when they moralized on the lives of Ellen Jewett and Henry Robinson. There was a decided increase in visitors to New York, anxious to get a close-up of the most celebrated murder case in American history. Even the houses of prostitution—

with the spotlight of publicity turned upon them for the first time —instead of being emptied, were jammed to capacity night after night. Rosina Townsend's place of business, alone, suffered a slump. The girls deserted her. Police stood about the premises day and night to prevent the mobs of curiosity-seekers from looting the place. When Rosina, a fortnight after the murder, decided to sell out, lock, stock, and barrel, her place was jammed by young bloods and many "ladies of fashion," eager to see, feel, and buy the ornaments, furniture, and tools of trade of the former inmates. The *Herald,* which reported these activities with tongue-in-cheek, also claimed that Ellen Jewett's bedstead was cut to bits and given away as souvenirs.

Each issue of the *Herald* told of the increasing difficulty to find a press capable of turning out the papers with sufficient rapidity. On the fifteenth of April, it carried an announcement addressed:

> "To ADVERTISERS.—The rapid increase of the *Herald* outstrips all calculation. We this day begin to strike off nearly 15,000 copies per day."

By this time, Bennett had become convinced that there were a number of obvious flaws in the evidence that placed the blame for the murder upon young Henry Robinson. Once more he visited the house of ill fame, making a minute inspection of the premises as well as conversing at length with Mrs. Townsend.

In the main parlor of this house of ill fame Bennett found what he thought might be an important clue to the whole case. On one of the walls, near a corner, was a large painting, vividly portraying a beautiful female "in disorder, and on her knees, before two savages, one of them lifting a tomahawk to give her a blow on the head."

"What a remarkable type," mused Bennett, "or hint—or foregone conclusion of the awful tragedy perpetrated upstairs."

Continuing this line of thought he asked his readers, "If a rival in the same line of life wanted to make away with such a troublesome competitor, would not the picture, perpetually hanging there— visible at all hours—suggest to female vengeance or female design the very act that was perpetrated?"

The journalist-sleuth turned his attention to the keeper of the house, who reluctantly answered his questions. He likewise unearthed a story about another visitor to Rosina's hotel the night of the murder.

There is a story of a certain married man, a merchant down town, who, caught in that night's brawl (!) begged the watchman to let him out.
"No, I won't."
"I'll give you a hundred dollars if you will."
"I can't."
"I'll give you five thousand dollars."
"I can't, I can't," said the watchman.
The opinions respecting his guilt vary.

More certain than ever that the press and the authorities were on the wrong track, he observed:

We say still, there is a mystery and a juggle about this whole affair. There is something that we cannot fathom. The verdict of guilty has already been heard sighing through the viewless atmosphere surrounding the Police Office, like a ghost or a demon breathing the events of futurity. The air they breathe is imbued with the conclusion. The murder of Ellen Jewett is a horrible tragedy; yet there are greater horrors going before, and coming after.

On the sixteenth, the *Herald* contained a lengthy verbatim report by Bennett of his conversation with Rosina Townsend. He prefaced his article by saying that he had taken another gentleman with him, and that both of them were willing to swear that the report, as published by him, was absolutely authentic. After a bit of general discussion Bennett asked Rosina to tell him exactly what had taken place on the night the crime was committed.

About the hour of 9 o'clock [said Rosina] on Saturday, I was called to the front door by a knock, and on enquiring "Who's there?" the reply was, "Frank Rivers." I opened the door and let him in, and he passed me with his face muffled up in his cloak, upstairs.
I went into the parlor and told Helen, Frank was there. Helen left the parlor and went out saying, "My dear Frank, I am glad to see you." They both went to Helen's room—nothing more was heard of either until about 11 o'clock, when Helen came partly down the stairs and called to me, and requested me to bring her a bottle of champagne.

I then went for the champagne, but on looking into the closet I found that there was not a bottle there.—I told Helen this and requested her, as she was in her loose dress, to return to her room, and I would bring her up a bottle, as I should be under the necessity of going into the cellar and opening a basket. I went downstairs and got a bottle, knocked off the rosin, and took it upstairs to Helen's door. I knocked at the door, and Helen said, "Come in." I opened the door and went in.—I saw Frank lying on the bed.

Question: What was he doing?

Answer: He was lying on his left side, with his head resting on his arm in the bed, the sheet thrown over him, and something in his other hand.

Q: What was that?

A: I can't say.

Q: Was it a book?

A: I think it was—either a book or a paper.—I saw his face.

Q: What did he say?

A: Nothing. Helen said to me, "Rosina, as you have not been well today, will you take a glass of champagne with us?" I replied, "No, I am much obliged to you, I had rather not."—I then left the room, as some of the other girls called me from below.—I neither heard nor saw anything more from that time.—The house was locked up for the night at 12 o'clock P.M.—I returned to rest.—About 3 o'clock A.M. I heard a noise at the front door, and found, on enquiring, that it was a young man who was in the habit of visiting one of the girls in the house.—I got up and let him in—after I had let him in I smelt smoke, and on going into the parlor I found the back door open, and Helen's lamp standing on the marble side table, by the door. I went directly to Helen's room, and found the door shut—I opened it, and on so doing, the smoke rushed out and nearly suffocated me.—I then raised the alarm of fire.—The watchman was called in, and he went into the room and found Helen lying on the bed and the bed on fire—she was burnt.—After the windows were opened and the smoke let out, the watchman discovered that Helen had been murdered, and then the bed set on fire.

Q: Had you ever seen Frank previous to the night after you let him in?

A: Yes—once—he was sitting in a room with me and some other girls—Helen was present, and on Frank's rising to leave the room, Helen remarked, "Rosina, don't you think my Frank very handsome?" I replied yes.

Q: How did you know that the lamp on the table belonged to Helen's room?

A: There are but two lamps alike in the house, the one used by Helen and the other by myself.

Q: Did you hear no other noise previous to the knocking of the young man you let in?

A: I think I heard a noise and said "Who's there," but received no answer.

Q: How did you know that the person you let in was Frank?

A: He gave his name.

Q: Did you see his face?

A: No . . . his cloak was held up over his face, I saw nothing but the eyes as he passed me—he had on a hat and cloak.

Q: Who first discovered the fire?

A: I did as I got up.

Q: On the morning of the transaction did you see Frank?

A: I did; he was in the back parlor, standing by an officer. I was called in and asked whether he was the person I had let in the night previous as Frank. I replied yes; to which he (Frank) said, "What! Me! You are mistaken!" I said yes, you are the person although last night you were dressed differently; you then had on a cloak and hat, now you have on an overcoat and cap.—He then sat on the sofa. Mrs. Berry was brought in and recognized him as Frank, as he had been in the habit of visiting Helen at her house in Duane street. She said, "You villain, Frank, how could you murder Helen?" He turned pale and leaned back on the sofa; that was the only time he lost confidence or changed color; he was then carried off to prison.

Q: Who gave the information where Frank resided?

A: I did. I knew his right name to be Robinson and that he boarded in Dey street; the officer went and arrested him there, as they said, in bed.

Thus ends the first formal interview ever to be published in any American paper.

Bennett, having presented this account to his readers, went on to analyze the situation in true detective-story style:

Now, on this extraordinary story, we have a few remarks to make. Admitting Rosina Townsend to be a woman of virtue and integrity, is it not perceived at once that there are material contradictions in her own story?

She admits she did not see anything but the eyes of Frank, and that was in the passageway, for he did not enter the parlor. She admits that she saw him lying in bed at some distance, but although she could not tell whether he had a book or paper in his hand, she has no hesitation in asserting that it was Frank Rivers. And further, this person she is so sure of, was only once seen before, by her.

Is it not extraordinary that she should know a man so easily without seeing his face—as it was covered by his cloak? Is it not equally so that she did not know what he read—a paper or book—yet she knew the person?

Again, the whole story—the very cue to the arrest—was given to the police by Rosina. She alone saw him come in—she alone saw him in bed—she alone discovered the lamp in the parlor—she alone first entered the girl's chamber—she alone raised the hue and cry—she alone told the police who it was that had committed the murder—she alone gave the police the number of his boarding house in Dey street—she alone is the only direct evidence in the whole investigation. No other person in the house saw Frank Rivers enter, or knew anything of the murder till Rosina entered the alarm. She is the author and finisher of the mystery.

Now, who is this woman on whom rests the principal evidence? The circumstance of the hatchet and all fall to the ground without the direct testimony of Rosina. A hundred hatchets and a thousand cloaks may look to these persons perfectly alike. It is the easiest thing in the world to make a mistake in these pieces and fragments. Who is Rosina Townsend? She is a common woman, who has lived several years in this city, kept the house in Thomas street, and is reputed to have been kept by an *attache* of that very Police who have this affair in their hands. She has an eye—a pair of them—and they are the eyes of the devil. We looked at them—we looked through them—we caught as we believed a glimpse of the very soul within. It is passion and malevolence. That hollow cheek—that deep-set eye—that perturbed spirit we did not like. When I cross-examined her, she could hardly look me in the face. She scowled, and averted her flashing eyes. In temper, I hear, she is a perfect devil. . . .

All the particulars related by Mrs. T. are of an extraordinary nature. There are several facts, however, we have heard, which are even more so. Mrs. T., I understand, had borrowed money of Ellen; and yet it is said, she intends to administer on her property. Ellen had many valuables about her—she had a large amount of jewelry—her wearing apparel was splendid, and worth probably $1,500. What has become of all this property? In whose possession is it? At this moment many of the girls have left Mrs. Townsend's, and she herself talks of selling out, clearing out, and blowing out.

Bennett's action threw confusion into the ranks of the other dailies, who consistently cried for immediate punishment of Robinson for the foul murder of Ellen Jewett. It likewise threw considerable confusion into the ranks of the police, whose case was being built up on the same premise. Benjamin Day, publisher of the *Sun,* working in obvious collusion with the police, now turned his guns on the nosey editor of the *Herald,* seemingly more concerned in smashing his lively competitor than in telling the story of the murder.

The unscrupulous and unsavory Bennett, charged the *Sun,* was too well known to be taken seriously in his attempt to place the blame for the murder other than where it rightfully belonged—on the blackened soul of Richard P. Robinson. Such actions on Bennett's part were obviously due to the fact that he had accepted a bribe from those interested in protecting Robinson. Besides, his attempt to place the blame upon Rosina Townsend, or one of her girls, was an obvious effort to obstruct justice and turn popular indignation upon these unfortunates.

Day published long extracts from private letters belonging to Robinson to prove that he was a wild, reckless, and immoral scoundrel who had seduced innocent girls.

These letters, replied Bennett, could only have come into Day's hands by thievery or collusion with the police. That the course of justice had been impeded, he freely admitted, but, he asked, by whom? And then went on to give reply: "By such infamous papers as the *Sun,* which, on mere *ex parte* evidence boldly declares that he [Robinson] is guilty. If Robinson had admitted on his bare word that he was the murderer, as the editors of the *Sun* have confessed, by affidavit, that they were accessory to breaking open the seals of a letter, and stealing the contents thereof—then might we, as they do, boldly declare Robinson to be the murderer of Ellen Jewett. We call Day and Beach indicted thieves—and we do so because there is their confession on oath in the records of the Police office."

The *Sun* came back at Bennett, calling him every kind of a liar. It claimed that Rosina Townsend, upon being shown the interview, published in the *Herald,* denied anything like it ever took place. "She averred unequivocally," gloated Day, "that the conversation was entirely confined to herself and Wilder [who had come with Bennett, and who claimed he was a friend of Ellen's] and to the subject of a monument [for her], and that Bennett uttered not a word during their stay at her house, but appeared to be wholly engrossed with an examination of a picture and attempts at flirtation with one of the girls still remaining." There was no doubt in her mind, she continued, "that he [Bennett] manufactured the whole of the nefarious publication which had been exhibited to her by the magistrates."

For a few days, public interest shifted from the case itself to the fierce battle between Day and Bennett. Circulation for both papers mounted as New Yorkers laid wagers on the outcome of the duel. The charge that Bennett had flirted with the inmates of Rosina Townsend's establishment—and as town gossip would have it— that he was far from an unknown person in those parts—stung the Scotsman to the quick. In the process of explaining his position, he lifted a small corner of the veil which covered his private life.

"I did not make any attempts at flirtation with any of her girls," protested the editor of the *Herald*. "During the whole interview there was not a girl in the house with us. I have, besides, long since given over all flirtation—and when I did flirt, I never did so with such girls. I always preferred young, pretty, virtuous, educated girls, at the Springs, Niagara Falls, Washington and elsewhere. . . . I have never seen or mixed with such company as Rosina Townsend's for many years, and I well remember the first and only time I ever entered a house of that kind was in Halifax, Nova Scotia, when the girls told me, 'You are too ugly a rascal to come among us; keep company only with the virtuous; you can talk; we doesn't them things; mere talk's nothing; we be Demoston's scholars, *all action.*' They also told my friend, 'Never bring that homely scoundrel to our house; the sight of him gives us the ague.'"

New York chuckled for weeks over this story. Everyone admitted that only James Gordon Bennett could tell such a story on himself and get away with it.

Respecting the other charges made by the *Sun,* he declared:

"I admit I examined the picture narrowly. . . . This painting struck me forcibly—it was such a perfect type of the tragedy upstairs. . . .

"As to the accuracy of the reported conversation, both myself and Mr. Wilder are ready to make an oath to it. It is exact to the word. I myself put the very questions there stated. It is probable that Rosina may have forgotten what she stated—she has been telling so many stories that it is likely enough she may be confused."

Determined by this time both to confute his critics and the police as well as to show up Rosina Townsend for what she was, his remaining articles, prior to the trial—and which made torrid reading for a New York ready for bigger and better scandals—were eminently successful.

What is the private history; what is the private character; what are the stains on the life of this Rosina Townsend? For some years she has occupied a brilliant position in the Aspasian society of New York. Her splendid establishment in Thomas street has been the pride of the gay reprobates from one end of the Union to the other. She unites under the same flashing eye, the manners of a lady, the elegance of a Lais, the passion of a Fury, and the cunning of a Serpent. In Greece and in Rome they had their celebrated woman in a certain line of life; their Lais, their Aspasias, their goddesses, that united beauty, business, ambition and luxuriousness in the same person, and under the same roof. The profusion and extravagance of the celebrated Aspasia, ministered to by Pericles, the greatest ornament of Athens, was not greater than what was nightly seen, during the summer season, at the Hotel in Thomas street. With some talent and more taste, Rosina Townsend stands at the head of her *caste*. Her house was the centre of attraction. Eight young females of surpassing beauty, and three or four, ugly and horrible as sin, just by way of contrast, drew crowds of travellers, clerks, brokers, gentlemen, blackguards, fools, philosophers, night after night, to those splendid rooms, hung round with elegant paintings, and tastefully decorated with numerous ottomans, scarlet curtains, and other emblems of refinement and elegance. * * * * * * Behind the pile of elegant yellow buildings was a garden decorated with elegant arbors, picturesque retreats, covered in the summer season with beautiful garlands, evergreens, flowers, and all the beauties of the vegetable world. Under the bright shining moon, climbing up the dark blue heaven, during the soft summer months these arbors would be filled with syrens and champagne, pine apples, and pretty *fille de joie,* talking, chattering, singing, and throwing out all the blandishments their talents could muster."

Bennett's parting shot before the trial began was the following bit of verse:

ROSINA

Rosina's parts for all mankind,
Were open, rare, and unconfined,
Like some free port of trade;
Merchants unloaded here their freights,
And agents from each foreign state,
Here first their entry made.

The whole country had become interested in the Jewett case. When the trial began, on June 2, 1836, the streets surrounding the court were jam-packed with surging mobs fighting vainly to get a glimpse of the main actors in the drama. For the first time in American history, many out-of-town newspapers were represented by reporters at a murder trial. James Gordon Bennett, who had been forced to move his paper to larger quarters during the excitement he had helped stir up, was now the best known, most feared, most hated newspaperman in his adopted land.

At the trial, witnesses were produced who proved to the satisfaction of the court and jury that Robinson could not have been at Rosina Townsend's the night of the crime. Testimony also brought forth many contradictions to the statements of Rosina. She, in fact, became very confused and was forced to make a number of damaging statements which, as Bennett had already indicated, pointed the finger of accusation at her.

"The evidence on this trial—the trial itself—and the remarkable disclosure of the manners and morals of New York," wrote Bennett on June 8, "is one of those events that must make philosophy pause —religion stand aghast—morals weep in the dust, and female virtue droop her head in sorrow. A number of young men, clerks in fashionable stores, are dragged up to the witness stand, but where are the married men—where the rich merchants—where the devoted church members who were caught in their shirts and drawers on that awful night? . . . The publication and perusal of the evidence in this trial will kindle up fires that nothing can quench."

The next day came the acquittal of Robinson, making of him, for the moment, almost a popular hero after the months that his name had been dragged in the mud by the press of New York.

The *Herald,* having grown so tremendously in both advertising, circulation, and prestige as a result of blowing up of the case, was loath to let it drop. In fact, Bennett tried very hard to keep up the interest in it—and to push forward to additional trials.

"The triumphant acquittal of young Robinson having been placed on record—the return of that interesting youth to the bosom of his friends and of society having taken place, it becomes the duty of the police authorities to find the murderer . . . and the first step in this great duty is the instant arrest of every man, married or single, who was caught in the arms of love and licentiousness in that house of infamy, on the awful night of the night of April last."

But try as he would Bennett could not rouse the authorities to further action. The city had had a great emotional spree and was now ready to settle down again. Robinson vanished, reportedly having gone to Texas. Rosina too disappeared. The real murderer of Ellen Jewett was never apprehended.

10. *"Generally Read but Universally Denounced"*

FROM 1836 to 1841, the *New York Herald* was without a doubt the most sensational, salacious, and sardonic newspaper in the whole world. It pried into private lives. It held up to ridicule and scorn, not only its political and editorial adversaries, but everyone, regardless of place or position, whose name was well known. Blue-bloods and bankers, actors and abolitionists, clergy and cloister, demi-mondes and demagogues, politicians, quacks, reformers, specu-lators, thieves, and union organizers—all were publicly impaled in the columns of the *Herald*. No person, no sentiment, no subject was too sacred to be spared. Bennett, having discovered that people were willing to buy his paper for its sensationalism, determined to give the public full measure of what it craved.

If James Gordon Bennett's contribution to newspaperdom were to be judged by what he did during the late thirties, he would be remembered only as the man who had spawned sewer-journalism. Certainly, to his contemporaries, there was little at the time to indicate otherwise.

Yet there was method in Bennett's procedure. He had arrived at the altogether startling and revolutionary conclusion that the basic purpose of a daily paper was to gather and give to its readers *news,* reported as fully and accurately and printed as quickly as men and machines made possible. But to accomplish this purpose required a completely reorganized newspaper staff and one much larger than any yet established. It required men trained to think in terms of the news values which Bennett proposed to give to journalism. It required money—much more money than had ever before been expended by any daily paper. And that money, Bennett determined, should not come from a political clique or any vested interest. It should come from an ever-growing army of subscribers. Reader interest would bring mass circulation. The life of the newspaper would thus be secure.

Sensationalism, as the Ellen Jewett case had demonstrated, was the road to new readers. It was also the road to an increased income from advertisements. It made Bennett's name and that of his paper household words in greater New York. Sooner or later, reasoned Bennett, these people would buy the *Herald* for its news value alone.

So with sensationalism the predetermined means to success, the canny editor left no door unopened which might add to his rapidly growing list of readers. Among the earliest of these new devices which he perfected was that of publicizing the attacks made upon himself by his opponents.

During the summer of 1835, James Watson Webb, his former associate, accosted Bennett on the steps of the Astor House, and threatened him with bodily violence unless the *Herald* ceased its scurrilous attacks upon the good name of Webb. Bennett replied to Webb in the *Herald* the next day with a "Declaration of Independence." He intended to preserve his rights to speak about men and issues as he chose; and so far as Webb was concerned, Bennett was through with him forever! Within a month, however, the *Herald* began sniping at Webb and his paper again. Newspapermen began to bet on how long it would be before Webb trounced his opponent physically.

Webb, with great difficulty, restrained himself from overt action for six months. But when the *Herald* printed an article charging that Webb had been paid by Wall Street speculators for helping to rig the stock market, and Bennett supplemented the article with a most malicious editorial, Webb lost his self-control. The following day he attacked Bennett, knocked him down, and beat him with a walking stick.

The *Herald* of January 20 sold nine thousand copies! People who never before had heard of the paper, were standing in line waiting to get their copy. The reason was that Bennett had made Webb's attack upon himself the feature article of the day. Never had an editor disgraced himself in such fashion. People were pop-eyed with excitement, and could scarcely believe the account of the attack, as written by Bennett.

Instead of hiding his shame, or threatening revenge, Bennett treated the whole episode with a jaunty air. First he apologized to his readers for his unusual want of life that day, due to the sudden and cowardly attack made upon him by Webb. He described how his assailant, coming up from behind, had "cut a slash in my head about one and a half inches in length, and through the integuments of the skull. The fellow, no doubt, wanted to let out the never-failing supply of good humor and wit, which has created such a reputation for the *Herald,* and appropriate the contents to supply the emptiness of his own thick skull."

The *Herald's* readers were assured that Webb had failed either to injure the skull or rifle Bennett of his ideas, which, he announced, would soon flow as freely as ever, as Webb would learn to his cost.

There were many who sympathized with Webb. *The Journal of Commerce,* for example, asserted Bennett should be horse-whipped every day. But there were many more who felt Webb had lost stature by his action.

Four months later, on May 9, Webb again assaulted the editor of the *Herald.* Again, Bennett wrote up the attack in such a way as to make Webb look ridiculous. Again the presses worked over-time to meet the heavy demand for copies.

Having described at length how the unprovoked attack was made, Bennett concluded:

"My damage is a scratch, about three-quarters of an inch in length, on the third finger of the left hand, which I received from the iron railing I was forced against, and three buttons torn from my vest, which any tailor will reinstate for a sixpence. His loss is a rent from top to bottom of a very beautiful black coat, which cost the ruffian $40, and a blow in the face, which may have knocked down his throat some of his infernal teeth for anything I know. Balance in my favor, $39.94."

Then, in righteous indignation, he added: "As to intimidating me, or changing my course, the thing cannot be done. Neither Webb nor any other man shall, or can, intimidate me. I tell the honest truth in my paper, and leave the consequences to God. Could I leave them in better hands? I may be attacked, I may be assailed, I may be killed, I may be murdered, but I never will succumb. I never will abandon the cause of truth, morals, and virtue."

Not a single paper came to Bennett's defense. He was a pariah in their midst. He should be driven out of the city! He was a disgrace to New York! He was a blackmailer, a scoundrel, a villain as crooked as his nose!

At this point Bennett came forward to sing his own praises. "All these attacks, falsehoods, lies, fabrications," he announced, "are but as the idle wind. They do not ruffle my temper in the least. Conscious of virtue, integrity, and the purest principles, I can easily smile at the assassins, and defy their daggers."

The attacks upon him, he claimed, were due to jealousy, fear, and the inability of the other editors to meet his new brand of competition. "We do not, as the Wall-street lazy editors do, come down to our office about ten or twelve o'clock—pull out a Spanish segar—take up a scissors—puff and cut—cut and puff for a couple of hours—and then adjourn to Delmonico's to eat, drink, gormandize and blow up our contemporaries. . . ."

Day after day, the *Herald* lashed at its opponents with unremitting fury, meanwhile proclaiming itself and its editor as paragons of virtue. "Get out of my way, ye driveling editors," shouted Bennett. On one day he would refer to himself as the Napoleon of the Press. On another, he would compare himself to the world's great moral reformers: Zoroaster, Moses, Socrates, Seneca, and Luther.

It is doubtful whether Bennett believed very seriously what he wrote about himself, but it made splendid copy, it sold his papers, and it kept people talking about him. Like modern advertisers, he kept telling the world how good he was, and what a great paper he edited, hoping that sheer repetition of this praise would in due time make a favorable impression.

Over and over again he pounded away at the idea that until the birth of the *Herald,* newspapers had been mere organs of dry detail, uninteresting facts, political nonsense, personal squabbles, obsolete rows, tedious ship news, and meager quotations from the markets. "I have changed all this," he blandly announced. "I have infused life, glowing eloquence, philosophy, taste, sentiment, wit, and humor into the daily newspaper. . . . Shakespeare is the great genius of the drama—Scott of the novel—Milton and Byron of the poem—and I mean to be the genius of the daily newspaper press."

Bennett was the recipient of three additional floggings during the year 1836. The first of these was administered by a Dr. Townsend, the second by a Wall Street broker, A. A. Clason, and the third by Thomas S. Hamblin, manager of the Bowery Theater. The first two were administered on Wall Street. Hamblin, however, marched into Bennett's private office at the *Herald* to pummel the editor. In the ensuing tumult, the till of the *Herald* was robbed of $300.

Hamblin had good reason for his anger. His theater had just burned down, and the other theatrical managers and some public-spirited citizens had arranged a Benefit Performance. Bennett, motivated chiefly by his personal opposition to some of the persons sponsoring the performance, launched a vicious campaign of slander and vilification against Hamblin to obstruct the benefit performance. Hamblin was accused in the *Herald* of being a violator of every sacred law, and a corrupter of the youth of New York. "This unchastened libertine, greater than the Great Unhung,—this GREAT HE ROSINA TOWNSEND in breeches, is recommended as an example to male and female—as a subject for public patronage."

Day after day the attacks continued, mounting in their fury. "This daring outrage must be broken up—and the impudent perpetrators forever driven into disgrace and obscurity."

Oh! ye avenging angels on High! [prayed Bennett], ye spirits covered with the fire of retribution, now looking abroad from the burnished threshold of high Heaven's outer gate upon this world below—do not yet pour out your vials of wrath upon this devoted, demoralized, beauteous city. If our holy judges and chiefs of the people throw their robes over the works of pollution and wickedness, do not punish the virtuous inhabitants for the errors, the forgetfulness, the weakness of their rulers. Give us as you gave to Sodom and Gomorrah, yet a little while, and we can produce you at least ten just men in this sink of immorality and sin. Give us time to search for them night and day—to advertise for them in every street, in every lane. Even the judges of this people are not so wicked as they appear to be. They have wheedled and deceived into the terrible lapse by those miserable loafers who call themselves editors of newspapers, and who are brought up to do such things by feasts on champagne and oysters, at the expense of the great He Rosina Townsend, himself. Let your vials of wrath be poured out on the heads of the instigators—if on any, on M. M. Noah, George P. Morris, and Peter S. Townsend, the plotters and fomenters, who lead the others astray. Do this, and you will do justice. Stay your hands, ye avenging spirits of Heaven—stay—stay—stay!

Bennett's new line of sensational news brought in a golden harvest. At the close of the year, he jubilantly announced that the measure of his success was surprising even to himself. Within a period of fifteen months, though twice burned out, and once robbed, and in the face of threats, beatings, and the combined attacks of the other papers, his establishment was now well equipped and paid for, and he anticipated within two years a revenue of not less than $30,000 per year from the *Herald*. "Yet I care not, I disregard, I value not money."

A second line of sensational journalism was built up by attacks upon and ridicule of the church, both Protestant and Catholic. This was always done in the guise of exposing the rotting fiber of the professional churchmen so that true religion could grow and flourish. There was at the time a much greater religious intolerance than exists today in this country. Each religious denomination was as uncritically certain of its own righteousness as it was hostile to all others. The misunderstandings between Catholic and Protestant were particularly acute; and each gloated over the reports of wrongdoing by the other. Bennett, while personally still most hostile to the Catholic church, missed no opportunity to ridicule the Protestants. While both sides, in turn, disliked the *Herald,* each bought it to keep up to date on what was being said about their opponents as well as themselves.

The theme of a hundred editorials during those years was that all public men were knaves—politicians, lawyers, brokers—with "the clergy probably the greatest knaves of all, for they encouraged all the others for the sake of their salaries." Bennett always stressed the fact that he, too, was a firm and enthusiastic believer in the Gospel of Jesus, but his belief was based "on a new principle" and came from the "impulse of a fresh spirit." He would have none of the "foolish, ignorant, witless, lazy, indolent, degenerate race," of present-day clergymen, who had "mystified, brutalized, and uncivilized the great truths of Jesus of Nazareth."

"A more corrupt, infidel, and rotten race of clergy than the clergy of the present age," wrote Bennett, "has not existed since the time of Caiaphas and Ananias, the high Priests and high scoundrels of Judea, in the time of Augustus Caesar."

Once he admitted that "possibly a few clergymen" might be sincere, but he issued a solemn warning to them that their reign was drawing to a close. "Through the medium of a daily newspaper press, conducted upon cash principles—(Our Saviour also did business on the cash system) the whole fabric of superstition, now existing, shall be crumbled to the earth."

On another occasion he referred to Moses as the man "who ran away from Egypt with all the second-hand clothes he could lay his hands upon, or pick up from the hedges of that civilized country. . . . I don't think much of Moses," he added. "A man who would take forty years to get a party of young women through a desert is only a loafer. . . . Moses himself, according to the best biblical critics, was the first white man who married a Negro woman, and thus gave a sanction to amalgamation and abolition."

There were many complaints that Bennett spoke in a too familiar fashion about the Virgin Mary. Bennett retorted that she was indeed an old and familiar friend of his. "Indeed, I care for nothing in this world or out of it, but the Holy Virgin and the blessed petticoat, to both of whom be all honor, glory, delight, and happiness, now and forever more. Amen."

And as if that were not enough, Bennett added to his series an article on the difficulties and confusion that were bound to occur on the morn of the Resurrection. "The squabbling will be curious," remarked the skeptic in mock-seriousness, "and the movement most astonishing. Bones will get so mixed up as to destroy all title to property, both here and here after. A young girl will get hold of the leg of one sweetheart, and the arm of another; and one skeleton may be thus compounded of the bones of a dozen different persons, so that he won't know what name to answer to when he hears the roll called over by the recording angel."

But of all the attacks, none were so vicious, none so numerous as those he made upon the church into which he had been born and raised. For years on end there was scarcely a day but what the Catholic Church was under fire from the *Herald*. Out of hundreds of examples, the following is typical:

As a Catholic, we call upon the Catholic Bishop and clergy of New York to come forth from the darkness, folly, and superstition of the tenth century. They live in the nineteenth. There can be no mistake about it,—they will be convinced of this fact if they look into the almanac. . . .

But though we want a thorough reform, we do not wish them to discard their greatest absurdities at the first breath. We know the difficulty of the task. Disciples, such as the Irish are, will stick with greater pertinacity to absurdities and nonsense than to reason and common sense. We have no objection to the doctrine of Transubstantiation being tolerated for a few years to come. We may for a while indulge ourselves in the delicious luxury of creating and eating our Divinity. A peculiar taste of this kind, like smoking tobacco or drinking whiskey, cannot be given up all at once. The ancient Egyptians, for many years after they had lost every trace of the intellectual character of their religion, yet worshipped and adored the ox, the bull, and the crocodile. They had not discovered the art, as we Catholics have done, of making a God out of bread, and of adoring and eating him at one and the same moment. This latter piece of sublimity or religious cookery (we don't know which) was reserved for the educated and talented clergy from the tenth up to the nineteenth century. Yet we do not advise the immediate disturbance of this venerable piece of rottenness and absurdity. It must be retained, as we would retain carefully the tooth of a saint or the jawbone of a martyr, till the natural progress of reason in the Irish mind shall be able, silently and imperceptibly, to drop it among the forgotten rubbish of his early loves, or his more youthful riots and rows.

There must be a thorough reformation and revolution in the American Catholic Church. Education must be more attended to. We never knew one priest who believed that he ate the Divinity when he took the Eucharist. If we must have a Pope, let us have a Pope of our own,— an American Pope, an intellectual, intelligent, and moral Pope,—not such a decrepit, licentious, stupid, Italian blockhead as the College of Cardinals at Rome condescends to give the Christian world of Europe.

In an ever-widening arc, Bennett spread the biting acid of his pen, till people wondered who or what would next be sizzled in the columns of the *Herald*. There were stories abroad at the time

that one could buy immunity from these attacks, that Bennett operated the *Herald* in part as a blackmail racket. Such stories were but
part of the weapons of counter-attack used by Bennett's enemies.
There seems to have been no direct evidence produced at any time
to substantiate them. Bennett was no fool. His campaign of sensationalism was a planned and calculated venture to bring attention
to himself and his paper, and to win a large reading public rapidly.
There were many attacks which fell flat, but as soon as Bennett
became aware of that fact, he would drop the issue to concentrate
on another.

"Why don't you go among your countrymen oftener?" a friend
asked Bennett one day.

"Do you mean the Scotch?" asked the editor.

"I do," replied the friend.

"Then I'll tell you the reason. They are a damned scaly set, from
top to bottom, and when I pass them in the street, I always take
the windward side, and avoid shaking hands as I would the itch.
. . . Ha! ha!—ho! ho! No, sir," continued Bennett, "my friends
are the natives. I'll stick to the natives—a fig for the Scotch!"

Shortly after this episode, two of his fellow countrymen sent him
a long and abusive letter (which he printed in full in the *Herald*)
urging him to mend his ways, if not for his own sake, then for
that of the land of his birth. In his answer (published alongside the
letter) he told his readers:

It is the fate of Scotland, as it is that of all other countries, to give
birth to its natural portion of barren, heartless, empty blockheads—yes,
as barren as the brow of Ben Lomond, without possessing as that picturesque mountain does, the slightest verdure over its bosom or the
softest touchings of nature on its breast. I am, indeed, a native of Scotland—but what of it? Do I possess any merit on that account? If I cannot stand in this community on an equal footing with not only every
Scotchman, but with every other human being, as to morals, just sentiments, talents, genius and education, I despise the ridiculous claim now
set up by a brace of fools—"I'm a Scotchman—I'm a Scotchman." No!
It is the man, not the accident of his nativity that should be weighed.

As might be expected, Bennett never missed a chance to lampoon
his former political associates. The manner in which he had been

booted about by those worthies, left a bitterness which rankled him
for years. Now that his paper had achieved the largest circulation
in New York, it gave him no little satisfaction to turn the *Herald's*
guns upon President Van Buren and his adjutants. "We have seen
them, with these very eyes, enter the house of assignation under the
sun's bright rays,—and we have seen them even turn the sacred
capitol itself into a common brothel. . . ."

Later, when President Van Buren came to New York, the
Herald offered this most unusual description of the parade staged
in his honor:

The following was the order of the procession as near as we could
gather it, from the confusion that followed their mighty march through
the city:

Beelzebub's high priest on horseback
Young imps of Satan two and two.
Band of music, playing "Go to the devil and shake yourself."
Loafers with clean but ragged shirts, two and two
  Pickpockets and Gamblers, on horseback.
Rioters, Rowdies, Rousers, Roarers and Rattlers on foot.
    Young Devils, three and three.
Decent democrats, with clean shirts, shoes and stockings
  Brimstone Stirrers in Indian file, yelling.
Band of music playing "The Devil to pay and no pitch hot."
Grand Banner—with the motto of "Buttenders,
  Hugepaws, Indomitables and Damnables.
Loafers with second hand shirts, borrowed for the occasion, four and
            four.
Triumphal car, with printing press attended by young and old devils,
            distributing paper currency.
Grand Banner—"printer's devils, and all other devils for ever."
  Loafers with no shirts, six abreast.
Banner—"Albany Basin Rattlers."
  Loafers without shirts or shoes, any how.
Band of music playing the "Rogue's March."
  Loafers without shoes, shirts or hats, any how.
Grand Banner—Rousers and Rattlers "till the resurrection morning."
  Beelzebub's body guard, well mounted.
    Young hell fires, five abreast.
Hunkers, bunkers, clinkers and stinkers, every how.
Loafers without boots or breeches, no how.
      More young devils.

> *More Brimstone stirrers,*
> *More Rattlers and Roarers.*
> A fellow on a jackass shouting "Blow the trumpet, Balaam."
> *More decent democrats.*
> *A bundle of rags on horseback.*
> A coffin containing the emblematical corpse of the United States Bank.
> Band of music playing "She's gone, the d——d old monster."
> Buttenders, nine and nine, some with breeches nad some without.
> A few more young devils sans culotts, sweeps, and savages of all kinds.
> *Tag, rag, and bobtail.*
> Band playing "Which is the properest day to drink."
> *Imps of Satan.*
> *A few more decent democrats.*
> *The riff-raff and the ruff scruff of creation,*
> The fag end of hell—Satan on a sable horse, superintending operations.

It was young William Randolph Hearst who made the startling journalistic discovery that every time his artists cut an inch off the length of the dress of the beautiful girls whom they drew for the *San Francisco Examiner* there took place a decided increase in newspaper sales. Thus leg-art was born, back at the dawn of the Gay Nineties.

It was James Gordon Bennett, back in 1836, who discovered that a three-letter word, if properly used and elaborated upon, would bring readers pouring in upon a newspaper. That word was SEX. Like the weather it was always at hand; and though banned as a subject of conversation among mixed groups, young people, or good society, the taboos placed upon it merely made the subject more fascinating.

The *Herald* set the pace for all later papers, by proclaiming that its only reason for calling attention to the otherwise unmentionable subject was to rouse moral and civic indignation against the evils arising therefrom. Or again, it could be a report on a sermon or a lecture; or perhaps a discussion on how the saints of old wrestled with temptation. Some there were who sincerely believed that James Gordon Bennett was the Devil himself, sowing mischief and obscenity.

"All nature," wrote Bennett on June 15, 1836, "all nature, animal and physical, seems to be in a state of insurrection. Wives are leaving their husbands—husbands are leaving their wives—clergymen kissing widows—widows enticing clergymen. The latter day is approaching to a certainty. Riots, murders, seductions, misdemeanors, and weather, ever changing, ever fretful—we must have some pestilence this summer beyond doubt."

Soon thereafter he reported: "At this moment there are twelve or twenty hotels . . . scattered throughout the city, where probably about two hundred and fifty beautiful and apparently accomplished young women are nightly engaged in fascinating the rich, enchanting the wealthy, seducing the single, learning fresh wickedness from the married, and sitting in the laps of the highest and lowest among us sipping champagne."

Short news items, such as the following, became an almost everyday feature in the *Herald:*

CHARGE OF RAPE

Peter Ritchie, a brother of James Ritchie, who is in the tombs for receiving goods, was brought up charged, on the oath of Charlotte Griffin, with pulling her on a bed, and thence taking certain liberties, et cetera. Peter said he did not mean any thing offensive to the lady; but seeing as how her husband and his brother were both in the tombs on a charge of felony, why he only wished to pay her certain little delicate attentions.—The Magistrate committed Peter to the tombs."

THE FAIR STRIKE

The pretty girls of Lowell are yet on the strike for higher wages. We advise them to kiss—not strike—and they would succeed. These strikes —these forcing methods—these compulsory processes are the worst in the world. Let them use gentle means—let them arm themselves with beauty, virtue, taste, and who can resist them?

One of Bennett's many nameless critics of that day charged that the editor employed a number of the needy *litterateurs* about town to write many of the fantastic tales, which in the guise of news, adorned the pages of the *Herald;* and that he paid for them "not in proportion to their length or merit, but according to their degree of lasciviousness."

"I don't mind lasciviousness," Bennett is reported as having said to one of his employees, "be as lascivious as ever you like, Attree, but damn it, don't be vulgar!"

When the celebrated Mrs. Gove began her series of lectures on anatomy to the ladies of New York, the *Herald* gave what were supposedly lengthy excerpts to its readers. Actually no men were allowed at these meetings and as the *Herald* employed no women reporters, the "excerpts" were largely the figment of James Gordon Bennett's imagination:

I now come to the most important part of all, the proof of the virginity in a female—there is no proof—no infallible test—I know of my own knowledge this to be the case—I had no such test—know not what is meant * * * I first married * * * When * * * consummation * * * these were generally thought to be sure signs, but it is not so. I know by dissections of female infants * * * could not by any means * * * the Jews thought * * * some have quoted the 22d Chapter of Deuteronomy to contradict what I can prove * * * from personal experience * * * verses 13 to 52. (We cannot give the passage from Deuteronomy, alluded to by Mrs. Gove; it is unfit for our columns.) Women are not so strong now as they were then, and therefore many are born without * * * the human race has degenerated in that respect as well as every other. Females of old, even of the higher orders worked hard—they wove and spun. Rebecca was the daughter of a wealthy man—and she went to the well with a large pitcher, more than we could carry empty, and filled it with two buckets of water at least. . . . She might have had a . . . but females now could not do . . . as she . . . Sarah the wife of Abram was 90 years old when . . . and therefore all this proves that the test adopted by the Jews to tell . . . part of their law to . . . young virgins . . . modern times . . . as may be seen by this print, &c, &c.

Here there was a general expression of wonder and delight, as Mrs. Gove proceeded to unfold and develop the beauty and mystery of the internal structure of the female form; in glowing terms she painted the superb springs of life, action, pleasure, and pain—how each spring was worked—how much tension each would bear—what oil (to speak mechanically) should be used to facilitate the movements of the machinery, and how the strained springs might be braced and renovated—how far we might go and no farther. Oh, had you seen the brightening of the eyes and the bending forward of the beautiful necks to catch every syllable of the speaker, you would have given the lovely listeners credit for enthusiasm, if for nothing else.

On another occasion, Bennett presented an imaginary conversation between himself and the Spirit of the Lord, at the Broadway Tabernacle, then the largest and most popular of all places of worship; and to which Tappan, the founder of the *Journal of Commerce,* had given much of his time and money.

I went to the Broadway Tabernacle on Sunday evening last [wrote Bennett] as a set off for having had the wickedness to go down to Brighton and see the fashionable cottages going up there. What a vast quantity of girls and gas lights Arthur Tappan has collected in that splendid house! Arthur has much better taste in this speculation than in his abolition business. Saint-making is a pleasanter business among pretty young girls, handsome widows, and pious matrons, than among black wenches, thick lips and wooly heads. Arthur has left the colored race to the improving labors of Col. R. M. Johnson and Fanny Wright.

The sermon on Sunday evening was preached by a young man of little mental capacity. While he was laboring to no purpose in the pulpit, the Spirit of the Lord said to me, "Bennett, why don't you get into the pulpit and give these poor suffering sinners around you some comfort—a warm bit of eloquence or a passionate piece of morality."

I looked around very quietly. The spirit arrayed in a garment dipped in an azure cloud was leaning over the next pew. His sweet countenance had something feminine in it, but there was a severity about the lips that caused respect.

"Why," replied I, with a smile and a slight squint, "my good spirit, don't be so impatient—give the parson a little time to collect his ideas— if he can't feel eloquent before these pretty young women, he never ought to be there."

"Don't be talking so much of the women," said the spirit with a severity of look, and shaking his auburn ringlets, which spread a delicious fragrance around, that made the girls feel happy.

"Why not?" said I, "ain't the pretty girls who come to the Tabernacle so many pretty angels!"

"Angels! they angels!"—said the Heavenly Being. "I know them better than you do. Do you observe that pretty girl in that pew, with the feathers?"

"Yes," said I.

"She was a boarder of Rosina Townsend's."

"The devil she was," said I.

"Don't swear, Mr. B.," said the celestial intelligence, waving one of his azure wings, and pointing up to the gallery behind the preacher,— "that woman in that corner is a fashionable pickpocket—that young girl was seduced last Monday by a married man—that blue eyed lady in pink is kept by a broker—that cherub in blue and gold is the *cherie amie* of a grocer—that fellow in blue is a gambler—that chap in black, a broker that cheated his creditors—that woman in pink broke her husband's heart—that beautiful girl in—"

"Oh! oh! oh!" said I, "the wickedness of the age!"

"Let us go," said the Angel, in a huff, "to Latourette's, he has more virtue and innocence after all—than Arthur Tappan."

"And so I will," said I, and out I went, and several good angels left the Tabernacle with me.

The publication of verse was a regular part of every daily paper. Many of the best productions made their first modest appearance in "The Poet's Corner" of a badly printed daily paper. In view of the fact that there was no copyright law, publishers had no hesitancy in cribbing from the latest books or magazines. Bennett was no exception to the rule. Much of the best English and American poetry of the period found its way at one time or another into the columns of the *Herald*. There were many who treasured and kept these gems in large scrapbooks. Here, at least, was one part of the *Herald* undefiled by ribald, lusty, sensational treatment. But even "The Poet's Corner" was not to remain uncontaminated for long. Those with an eye for smut were soon scanning its verses to find double meanings hidden therein. Perhaps Bennett hoped to improve the taste of the masses, by giving them Byron, Keats, Shelley, Coleridge, Bryant, and Longfellow, interspersed with salacious verse.

Resentment and indignation against the flagrant manner in which the *Herald* violated all accepted moral, social, ethical, and religious standards mounted rapidly. Go where you would during the late 1830's, the *Herald* and its proprietor were sure to be bitterly denounced. Bennett was the subject matter of a thousand sermons. Privately, he was hated by many of the business men who advertised in the *Herald* and was thoroughly detested by hundreds of respectable citizens who avidly read his journal. Old-time political associates never missed a chance to damn the editor. At last, even the snobocracy was forced to notice Bennett and took a hand in demanding that his paper be suppressed. Every other newspaper in New York enthusiastically approved such a move.

It was only a question of time before these many diverse elements would effect a union of their forces in an attempt to liquidate Bennett and his journal. The editor was well aware of the moves being made against him, but with supreme confidence in his own ability to thwart all enemies, he made no attempt to modify his policies. In 1837 a move was begun to boycott the *Herald* but it failed. Cheered by this fact, Bennett and his staff pushed their campaign of sensationalism still further.

Webb, declared Bennett, was insane. "It is highly probable that he lost his senses as rapidly as he ever lost his money in stock operations. As he has never paid up his defalcations, so neither is it to be expected that he will regain his senses. Yet henceforth I shall be obliged to carry weapons to defend my person, and if he gets killed in the street, the blood will be upon his own head."

The *Sun,* which was Bennett's main competitor, was called "a small, decrepit, dying penny paper, owned and controlled by a set of woolly-headed and thick-lipped Negroes" or "our highly respected, dirty, sneaking, drivelling, contemporary nigger paper" with Beach, its owner, listed as "a pale-faced nigger, from the banks of the Senegal."

James Brooks of the *Express* was referred to as "this impudent loafer of literature, this lazaroni of politics, this crawling office beggar."

The *Evening Post* was pictured as ready to fold up, "a victim to the empty pride and emptier pretensions of the beggarly respectability of the Wall street six-penny system." The whole six-penny press was accused of corruption and venality. It had become "so much the vehicle of mere stockjobbers and speculators that the public place no reliance in their statements—their morals—their principles—or anything they possess."

Turning next to an attack upon the newly rich, who were striving so hard to be looked upon as SOCIETY, Bennett lectured them on their loud talking at the table, impertinent staring at strangers, and brusque manner among ladies. Nor was it quite *"comme il faut* for gentlemen to blow their noses with their fingers, especially when in the street—a practice infinitely more common than refined." In his gratuitous capacity of nineteenth-century Emily Post, he advised against the common habit of using a knife to convey food to the mouth. The elite of New York were urged "to omit the disgusting foreign fashion of taking water into your mouth, rinsing and gar-

gling it around, and then spitting it back into the glass." He told
how he had seen a young lady "at a very fashionable house in one
of our great cities pull a dish of stewed oysters close to her, and
with a tablespoon fish out and eat the oysters one at a time, audibly
sipping up their liquor from the side dish." And he had seen a
young gentleman "lift his plate of soup in both hands, hold it to
his mouth and drink, or rather lap it up."

Bennett never tired of writing innumerable short paragraphs on
a thousand and one subjects. Sometimes they were serious; usually
they were sardonic; always they were calculated to draw a strong
reaction from his readers. On one occasion he declared: "Wanted—
A God.—We have nothing to admire in this country but General
Jackson, and he is no great gun, or God either. We have no Napoleon—no Chevalier Bayard—no Philip Sidney. Washington is too
good—too sacred for popular enchantment. We want a God like
one of our Greek deities—part divinity—part fool. Such an article
always enchants the populace."

Once again, in 1839, an attempt was made to unite all those who
wanted to put a stop to Bennett's attacks on men and morals. Once
again they failed. But at last, in the spring of 1840, the opposition
swung into action and this time it was firmly united. For a full
year, New York was treated to what was later called the Moral
War.

Don Seitz, in his biography of the James Gordon Bennetts, maintained that the combined assault upon the *Herald* was the result of
the prudery of the rest of the press. It was against this prudery
which Bennett fought for he "saw creeping over the country a reign
of formality and custom far more despotic than anything that could
be devised politically. *Against this he set his lance."* [My italics—
O. C.] This biographer asserted that because Bennett insisted upon
calling a leg a leg, and not a limb; because he spoke of such "unmentionable" things as pants, trousers, petticoats, using those plain
everyday names for them, that the newspapers of New York "regardless of party or principles, arrayed themselves for a combined
assault designed to demolish the impertinent intruder."

In the light of the many citations already made in this chapter from the writings of Bennett, the reader can draw his own conclusions as to what brought about the Moral War.

True it was that, as one writer of the period exclaimed, "Mock-modesty giggled and simpered everywhere, and frankness of expression and honesty of purpose were jostled from the walk by a sentimentality sickening in itself. . . ." True also was the fact that Bennett did lash at these pruderies with his racy and pungent editorials. "Petticoats—petticoats—petticoats," he exclaimed, "there—you fastidious fools—vent your mawishness on that!"

But certainly the heated battle against him was not fought over such trivia.

It was Park Benjamin of the *Evening Signal* who opened the campaign against the *Herald* and its editor, in late May, 1840. Immediately he was joined by Mordecai Noah and James Watson Webb, with their respective papers, the *Evening Star* and the *Courier and Enquirer*. The *Sun*, the *News*, the *Journal of Commerce*, and the *Express*, all of whose editors had long-standing accounts to settle, joined in the fray. Even the *Boston Advertiser* and the *Philadelphia North American* trained their editorial batteries upon Bennett; and, of course, every paper of any consequence in the country reported the whole affair in great detail, with a decided slant in favor of the attacking host.

Venting all their pent-up spleen upon their rival, the editors ransacked the dictionary for every mean and offensive word or phrase to be found. Never in all the history of man had there been such a blackguard, if one were to believe even a tenth of what was said of him. A few among the hundreds of choice epithets hurled at Bennett by Park Benjamin were: "Daring infidel, habitual liar, Prince of Darkness, profligate adventurer, venal wretch, contemptible libeler, and pestilential scoundrel."

Among those contributed by his former employer, Webb, were: "Infamous, grossly slanderous, unprincipled conductor, moral leprosy, disgusting obscenity, and lowest species of scurrility."

Mordecai Noah called Bennett "a turkey buzzard, rascal, rogue, cheat, common bandit, false, a humbug, and a polluter of the press."

By others he was called "a stigma of the city, a man of hypocrisy, ignorant and bloated with conceit, an immoral and blasphemous monstrosity, a double apostate, a traitor, a pest, a wretch, a forger, a poltroon."

Joining the press in the crusade were clergymen, teachers, society folk, brokers, bankers, and some merchants. Not content with rousing the entire community against Bennett to make him out a moral leper, they went further, and began a systematic boycott, not only against his paper, but against every business man or advertiser who dealt with the *Herald*. Self-appointed committees called upon every major advertiser and threatened reprisals against those who would not heed their warning to cancel all advertising in the *Herald*.

Philip Hone, ex-mayor, and long a pillar of Manhattan Society, noted in his diary of June 2, 1840:

The career of the infamous editor of the *Herald* seems at last to have met with a check, which his unblushing impudence will find some difficulty in recovering from. Some of his late remarks have been so profane and scandalous as to have drawn out the editors from the contemptuous silence which they have hitherto observed toward the scoundrel. . . . Bennett is absolutely excoriated by the *Signal,* and all the other papers, without regard to party, have joined the righteous crusade. This is the only thing to be done. The punishment of the law adds to the fellow's notoriety, and personal chastisement is pollution to him who undertakes it. *Write him down;* make respectable people withdraw their support from the vile sheet, so that it shall be considered disgraceful to read it, and the serpent will be rendered harmless; and this effect is likely to be produced by the united efforts of the respectable part of the public press.

Hotels and clubs were told they must throw out all copies of the *Herald;* and many did so, at least during the height of the battle. Theater managers were urged to cancel their advertisements. At least one of these, Hamblin of the Bowery, willingly acceded to the demand.

One of the smaller weeklies, the *New York Corsair,* early in July reported that a Mr. Thorne, manager of the Chatham Theater, had stopped in to transact some business with Mr. Snowden, printer of the *Courier and Enquirer*. Snowden had an almost complete monopoly on the printing of large theatrical show-bills. He used this position to keep prices high as well as to levy "a sort of black-mail by refusing to notice any theatrical establishment in the city whereof the managers had not given him all the printing."

In the course of the conversation between Snowden and Thorne, the latter was asked if he had given up advertising in the *Herald*.

"I have not," replied Mr. Thorne.

"Then," said Mr. Snowden, "you must do so at once."

"Must do so! By what compulsion must I?" inquired the manager.

"By my compulsion, and that of the public Press," answered Mr. Snowden, "for if you don't withdraw your advertisement in the *Herald,* the *Courier* wont notice the Chatham, and I wont print your show bills!"

"Well," said Mr. Thorne, "I presume you will give me a day of grace to consider?"

"Why, I don't mind," answered Mr. Snowden. And Mr. Thorne left. Said the *Corsair:*

Mr. Thorne might then be seen wending his way along Wall Street in what an immoral sixpenny paper might call "a devil of a pucker"— or else in a devil of a passion. His hands and arms were thrust almost up to the elbows in his breeches pockets; his hat was jammed over his eyes, and he kicked the paving-stones before him in such a fashion that it was very evident he was mediating the pleasure he would derive from kicking something else which would have a less awful effect on his corns. Nor is his paroxysm to be wondered at, for his republican spirit rebelled at the idea of being dictated to. At the same time, he knew he could not do without the show-bills, and labored under the impression that Snowden was the only man in the city who could print them. Suddenly, however, and just as he was in a fair way of exploding with internal combustion, he remembered having heard of Applegate's Mammoth Printing-press in Ann Street. So away he posted, and asked Mr. A. if he could print bills of such and such a size. "Certainly, sir, and four times the size, if necessary," replied the individual. "My dear boy," returned Thorne, heaving a long, long sigh, "you were born to be my deliverer." And then, having ascertained that his "deliverer" could do any sort of printing under the sun, and at prices that no one could grumble at, he made an arrangement with him for the printing of the Chatham bills from that day forward, through all time, and went his way rejoicing.

The next day Mr. Thorne went down to Mr. Snowden's. "Well, Mr. T.," said Mr. S., looking pretty big, as he mostly does, "have you made up your mind about that little matter?" "I have," said Mr. T. "And I suppose you intend to withdraw your advertisement from the *Herald?*" "No, I'm hanged if I do." "Then I won't do your printing for you." "Can't be helped—I must go elsewhere." This going elsewhere, how-ever, was just the thing of all others that Mr. Snowden didn't want, for he profited about thirty dollars a week by the job; so, after frowning a little, and fidgeting a great deal, and biting his upper lip, and look-ing as if he was wishing himself in the moon, he endeavored to calm down his agitated countenance into an air of excessive patronage, and said, "Well, had it been any one else, he should never have another type stuck for him in my office; but seeming that it's you that's in it, Mr. Thorne, I'll go on with the printing." "You must not do any such out-rage to your feelings on my account," returned Thorne, "especially as I have already made an arrangement with Applegate!" And, having thus delivered himself, he made himself scarce, for he didn't chance to have his smelling-bottle about him, and he perceived that poor Mr. Snowden was deeply affected, and might stand in want of some such delicate attentions.

There were many other cases, too, in which the moral-reform vigilantes met with defeat in their efforts. Edward K. Collins, a leading merchant and shipping magnate, was one of these. When the committee asked him to withdraw his advertisements from the *Herald,* he called in a clerk, asked how many were then being run daily in the paper. The clerk reported the number to be three. "Insert three more," ordered the merchant, looking squarely at the committee. "Good day, gentlemen."

Bennett quickly realized that his only chance of winning out against the mass attack was to play down the excitement; improve his paper, both mechanically and editorially; try to be as good-natured as possible in the face of the assaults; and assure his readers that he was in reality a man of the highest moral fiber.

To the charge that he had been a peddler in his youth, he re-torted, "I am, and have been a peddler. . . . This I admit. From my youth up I have been a peddler, not of tapes and laces, but of thoughts, feelings, lofty principles, and intellectual truths."

Nor was he an infidel. "Atheism," he declared, "is an absurdity. An atheist never existed."

He told his readers of his many charities. "In two years I have given away in generous and charitable acts $2,500 of well earned, hard earned current money." He reminded them that he had paid the highest wages to his employees (which was true); that he had been liberal to the poor, and "poured out [his] money like water to relieve the wants of either sex." But what had been his reward? This course of conduct had merely raised a host of bitter and malignant enemies "who consider my conduct a libel on them, and who, in consequence, take pains, night and day, to deny the truth of history, and to strip me of every attribute of humanity. . . . Every generous and liberal act of my life has been tortured into vice, villainy, and horrible atrocity."

At other times he resumed his cocky self-assured air, passing off the damaging statements as mere "piffle." He called the press arrayed against him the "Wall Street Holy Allies"—and on at least one occasion listed their combined circulation and compared it with that of the *Herald*. Theirs totaled 36,550; his, 51,000. Bennett, by boosting his own figure and cutting those of the opposition, left himself with a net advantage of over 14,000 in circulation.

Once he exclaimed, half in anger, half in jest, "These blockheads are determined to make me the greatest man of the age. Newspaper abuse made Mr. Van Buren chief magistrate of this republic—and newspaper abuse will make me the chief editor of this country. Well—be it so, I can't help it."

His wit and humor didn't fail him in the midst of the long struggle. On many occasions he would refer to the conflict and list the opposing forces in military terms:

The engineers, sappers, and miners which attend both camps may be estimated as follows:

HOLY ALLIES		HERALD	
Description	*Horsepower*	*Description*	*Horsepower*
Lies	10	Energy	20
Impudence	15	Sobriety	20
Ignorance	20	Moral Courage	25
Hatred	15	Intellect	20
Jealousy	15	Wit	20
Cash	..	Poetry	20
Credit	..	Virtue	20
Virtue	..	Cash	20
Horsepower	75	Horsepower	165

The war dragged on and on and at last wore itself out, with Bennett and his *Herald* still very much in the field. Though he claimed that the war had brought him new readers, later figures showed that he had suffered a considerable reverse. The circulation of the *Daily Herald* had dropped from 17,000 to 14,500 copies, and that of the *Weekly Herald* from 19,000 to 12,240. Advertising revenue, too, fell off while editorial expenses had mounted heavily. All that Bennett could chalk up to his credit was the fact that as the *Herald* was damned from coast to coast, it became more widely known than ever before.

As for the opposition press, while it failed to drive its chief competitor out of business, it did force him to tone down his paper. Never again did the *Herald* carry on the type of sensationalism which had characterized it from 1836 to the end of 1841. Though it remained breezy, flippant, and provocative, it was now to move forward along many new fronts and make its greatest contributions to modern journalism.

11. *The Editor Takes a Wife*

IT IS only in retrospect that we realize the fundamental greatness of James Gordon Bennett as a pioneer in journalism. The hue and cry and the smoke of battle in the great Moral War blinded all but the most acute observers to the long list of innovations which the *Herald* was making during that time. Like it or not, the other papers were forced to follow and imitate Bennett.

As early as December, 1835, he had taken the lead in publishing woodcuts to illustrate current events. The first of these, which appeared immediately after the heavy conflagration in downtown New York, was a two-column map of the district gutted by the fire. Another woodcut pictured the ruins of the magnificent and newly built Merchants Exchange. Six months later, Bennett published a special map of New York City showing the location of all places of business which advertised in the *Herald*. In January, 1838, when the Eastern states were excited about the so-called Canadian Rebellion, he not only gave full coverage to the attempted invasion of that country by hotheads from the United States, but he published what was undoubtedly the first war map to appear in any paper, a detailed layout of the strategic point of the rebels at Navy Island, just below Niagara Falls. The next year he ran one of the earliest of political cartoons—a humorous three-column cut of an election procession. When his old hero, Andrew Jackson, died in 1845, Bennett had a full-page woodcut showing the "Grand Funeral Procession." His rivals, knowing the exorbitant cost of such a job, accused him of having faked this cut from previously published illustrations of the coronation procession of Queen Victoria, and other commemorative ceremonies. In reply, Bennett published a letter from the noted engraver, Thomas B. Strong, who stated he

191

had made the woodcuts expressly for the *New York Herald*. And in December, 1846, the *Herald* issued an eight-page pictorial annual the first of its kind ever printed by any daily paper.

Another Bennett innovation, which was to save hundreds of thousands of dollars to publishers everywhere, was his "Cash in Advance" policy for all advertisements, which he began in June, 1836, with the announcement that "in consequence of the trouble, disputes, etc. growing out of our credit system, the advertisers in the *Herald* are informed that no advertisement will hereafter be inserted, unless paid for invariably in advance."

The business office of every paper was stacked with long overdue unpaid bills from advertisers. Many a good paper went to its grave for want of being able to collect its outstanding accounts. Webb's paper lost nearly half a million dollars during its forty years of existence, and Greeley lost over $10,000 on his weekly *New Yorker,* for at the time no man thought it dishonest to cheat a newspaper. Bennett, shrewd in business as well as journalism, had long recognized the need for a drastic change; and as soon as he was certain that he had acquired an assured clientele of daily readers, he instituted the policy of cash in advance.

Bennett also quickly broke with the established custom of a set yearly advertising rate for all business houses, of from thirty dollars to sixty dollars. His papers were so edited that readers actually read them. Each advertisement was carefully placed so that it would attract attention. Ship news was always an item of major importance in the *Herald,* with the result that it enjoyed a lucrative advertising business from all the passenger and freight lines. Frederic Hudson once told how Mr. Cunard, founder and manager of the steamship company which bears his name, in looking over the advertising accounts of his company with the various daily papers, discovered to his amazement that while they were paying the *Journal of Commerce* sixty dollars per year, they were paying the *Herald* $1,000.

"There must be some mistake in that bill," said Mr. Cunard, showing the statement to the manager of the *Herald's* advertising department.

"Not at all," replied the manager; "our bill is correct."

"How can that be?" asked Cunard. "Look at that," showing the

Journal of Commerce bill for sixty dollars. "Nine hundred and forty dollars' difference for the same advertisement, and no mistake! Impossible!" The angry steamship owner picked up his hat to leave.

"I'll tell you what we'll do," said the amiable and accommodating advertising man of the *Herald*. "We will advertise at the same rate that the *Journal of Commerce* charges you."

"That is what I thought," exclaimed the pleased executive.

"Stop a moment," continued the *Herald's* representative. "Our rates are to be the same as those of the *Journal*. The circulation of that paper is 4,500 copies, we'll call it 5,000. Ours is 100,000. Sixty dollars for 5,000 is $1,200 for 100,000 circulation, is it not? Then, where the *Journal* has three readers, the *Herald* has five. Again, cut your advertisement from one copy of the *Herald,* weigh it, multiply that by 100,000 and then by 365 daily publications, and the cost of the white paper alone on which it is printed will astound you. Then again . . ."

"Enough! Enough!" exclaimed the practical merchant. "I am satisfied."

The publication of news summaries on the front page was another of Bennett's ideas, first put into practice in December, 1836.

Texas was much in the news that year. The *Herald* was a staunch advocate of Texan independence, and ran many feature articles about that faraway region and what the brave Texans were doing.

Bennett and Sam Houston had become friends in Washington, years earlier. During the winter of 1833-34, Houston was in New York and met Bennett, then down on his luck.

"How are you, Bennett?" asked the general. "You are the man I want to see. I am going to Texas, and I want you to go with me. Start a paper there, and we'll build up a great republic. Will you go?"

Bennett demurred. The idea was appealing, but he did not want to leave New York. Many years later, when Dr. Anson Jones, last President of the Republic of Texas, called at the *Herald* to chat with Bennett, he reminded the publisher of this incident, but added with a sigh, "Texas was the place for Houston, and New York for Bennett. Texas would have been too small for Bennett!"

Increased revenue permitted Bennett to begin the organization of an efficient ship-news enterprise in 1837 to compete with those of the larger papers. Here, too, his skill, ingenuity, and daring soon gave him the advantage over his older and wealthier rivals. Not only were his pilot boats, the "Teaser," the "Tom Boxer," and the "Celeste," faster than those of his competitors and manned by abler seamen, Bennett also took advantage of the newly established railroad on Long Island to have his boats bring the dispatches and newspapers from incoming ships to the Long Island terminal of the railroad, from which point they were rushed into New York by locomotive.

The spirit of competition between the newsboats became so heated that all New York joined in the game. Whenever one journal won a notable beat over the others, it became the talk of the town. The victorious paper invariably puffed itself for its feat. One of the many such exploits featured by the *Herald* serves to illustrate the more exciting aspects of journalism in the late eighteen-thirties:

On Friday night last, at 12, Commodore Martin, our high admiral, was quietly asleep on a delicious hard board, in the long cabin or boathouse of Dr. Doane, at the Quarantine Ground, Staten Island. On each side of him were his men, also in the same state of tranquility. At the wharf, under the window, lay our beautiful new boat, called the *Fanny Elssler*—cool and quiet, yet trembling on the top of the moonlit waves like a bird ready to shoot into the eternal blue of the heavens at a moment.

They were waiting for the arrival of the *British Queen,* momentarily expected.

On a sudden, at half past 12, the voice of a big gun was heard booming up the harbor like the voice of distant thunder. The cry was raised outside the log cabin, "The *Queen* is coming," "The *Queen* is coming." Martin—half asleep, half dreaming—was on his feet in an instant; rubbing his eyes and clapping his hat on his head, he looked down the harbor towards the Narrows. A big bright blue light went up to heaven and almost dazzled the brilliant moon. "Rouse, boys, rouse! The *Queen* is coming; there's her blue light."

In another moment, Martin, with his two men, were in the *Fanny Elssler*—sail set, oars splashing, and dashing over the bright wave down to the Narrows. The moonlight was most brilliant, and the shores of Staten and Long Islands were almost as bright as day. As the lovely *Fanny* skimmed like a swan over the silvery wave, another boat, clumsy and heavy, like a tub, came sneaking and swearing after her. It was the news-boat of the Wall Street Press, called the *Dot-and-go-one*.

The beautiful *Fanny* kept her watery way, and in ten minutes' time was, as a certain prince now is, under the lee of the magnificent *British Queen*.

"Steam ship, ahoy!" cried Martin.

"Ay, ay," responded the gallant Captain Roberts.

"The *Fanny Elssler*," roared Martin.

"The what?"

"The *Herald*," responded Martin.

"Oh—stop her," cried Captain Roberts to his engineer. "Throw him a line."

"Martin clinched the line, and in an instant was on the deck of the *Queen*.

"Martin, is that you?" said Captain Roberts. "How in the devil do you always beat?"

"By working harder than my competitors—the way you beat, captain. Where's your private bag?"

"Here are your papers," replied the captain.

"By this time, the news-boat of the Wall Street Press, *Dot-and-go-one*, came alongside, after a great deal of puffing and blowing. In a few minutes the steamer was at the Quarantine Ground. Here she stopped for the physician. Martin, with the private bag for the consignees, jumped aboard the *Fanny Elssler*, and started for the city, *Dot-and-go-one* having started a little ahead; but it was no go. . . .

"Martin jumped ashore, rushed up Broadway, down to 21 Ann Street, and found the lights burning brightly at the *Herald* office. In five minutes all the editors, writers, printers, pressmen, were in motion. The immense daily edition of the *Herald* was about one fourth worked off when the news arrived. The press was stopped—the announcement made: this was the second edition. In two hours it was stopped again, and three columns of news put in and sent by the various mails: this was the third edition. In another two hours six columns were put in: this was the fourth edition—also sent by the mails. By this means we sent the news all over the country—New England, Canada, the South and West, one day in advance of every other paper in New York."

As editors began to understand, and the public to clamor for, spot news, strange ways—including some not altogether honorable— were developed to get important dispatches back to the waiting presses. Once a reporter for Greeley's *Tribune* quietly gathered up the news of an important event, boarded a waiting locomotive, which had been rented by the *Herald,* and ordered the engineer to speed on back to New York, which he did unaware that he was giving Bennett's chief rival the scoop. The *Herald* representative, arriving at the station a minute or two later, did not reach the city till the *Tribune* extra was already on the streets.

To cover important happenings at Albany, editors sometimes quietly installed a battery of compositors on the river boats plying the Hudson, and were thus able to deliver the type already set, to waiting draymen at the pier when the boats docked in New York.

A few years later, in 1846, Webb, Beach, Hale, and Greeley in conjunction with leading editors of several other eastern cities worked out a secret deal whereby they thought they could bring to an end, for all time, Bennett's long-standing boast that he could always beat them in getting the news from Europe.

(Bennett had sent men up to Boston to meet the incoming ships, and rush the news down to New York by train.)

The editors engaged the pilot boat, *William J. Romer,* then believed to be the fastest boat of its kind. At the moment a rupture between the United States and Great Britain appeared imminent over the Oregon Question ("Fifty-four, Forty—or Fight!"), so there was good reason for trying to get news fast. The *Romer* slipped out of port very quietly on February 9, destination unknown. Two days later a short item in the *Boston Transcript* announced: "It is rumored that the Portland folks are going to beat the *New York Herald* in the foreign news by the *Cambria,* now six days out from Liverpool. The *modus operandi* is to have an agent board the steamer off Halifax, cross overland by horses to Annapolis, join the steamer *Kennebec* and run to Portland, and from thence by railroad to Boston. We are inclined to believe this operation will cost more than it will come to."

Meanwhile news of the secret had reached James Gordon Bennett. He had received a letter from a friend in Bangor, Maine, asking, "Are you stocking the road for an express from Halifax?"

Determined to beat his rivals, no matter what the cost, Bennett put a score of his best men to laying the plans for bringing the dispatches from the *Cambria* to the *Herald* in record time. Frederic Hudson, who helped plan the campaign for the *Herald,* told the story in after years:

The expected steamer [Cambria] was commanded by Captain Judkins, a thorough sailor, an energetic navigator, and not partial to what are called "beats." The Cunarders, at that time, ran to Boston only. There was no opposition. Sufficient time was taken to discharge passengers and cargo, and take in coal, at Halifax. They never hurried. Thirty-six hours were occupied in making the run to Boston. The "Holy Alliance," as the *Tribune* and its associates were called, had taken all these facts into their calculations. So, it appears, had the *Herald*.

It became important to notify the agents of the steamer at Halifax of the impending struggle, and inform Captain Judkins, immediately on his arrival, that when he reached Boston he would find that his news had preceded him. Human nature is pretty much the same in England as in the United States. The *Herald,* in this view, published numerous paragraphs on the great race, and sent them to Halifax to be shown to Captain Judkins as soon as the pilot stepped on board the *Cambria*.

"Is an express to beat me to Boston?" asked Captain Judkins. "I'll see about that."

There was never greater activity displayed at Halifax. No Cunarder ever remained so short a time in port; and the *Cambria* made the run to Boston in thirty hours! It was fair to suppose that the "Holy Alliance," entering on such a costly enterprise, would have all its arrangements for speed and success complete from Halifax to New York. It would be unjust to suppose otherwise. Time and space between these two points were therefore to be fully considered by the *Herald*. What did that establishment do under these circumstances? No plans existed east of Boston. The only imperfection in the *Herald* arrangements was in the steamer engaged to connect the Norwich with the Long Island Railroad. She was slow. The only hope of the *Herald* was in making a very quick run from Boston. If it beat, it would be an Austerlitz, a Marengo, and a Jena rolled into one magnificent victory. If defeated, its opponents would call it a Leipsic, if not a Waterloo. If this great overland express was a success, Napoleon Bennett would be sent to Elba. If the *Romer* anticipated the packet-ship, he would go to St. Helena.

Eh Bien! To prevent one and accomplish the other of these contingencies, a fast steamer was necessary to carry the *Herald* messenger across Long Island Sound. There was one steamer, called the *Traveler,* and owned by Commodore Vanderbilt, suitable for this purpose. The *Herald* called on the Commodore, and told the story of the plans of the opposing journalists, and of the importance of the coming news.

"What can I do?" asked the Commodore. "If I can aid you, I will; I like your pluck."

"We want the *Traveler,*" said the *Herald,* "to run across the Sound, land one messenger at Greenport, and then come through the Sound to New York with another messenger."

"Well, well, let me see"; and, turning to a young man, said, "Write out an order for the *Traveler* for Mr. Bennett." Signing the order, the Commodore passed it to the *Herald,* and said, "There's the boat. Keep her till your express arrives. Now go ahead. Good morning."

"One word more, Commodore, will you send one of your smartest captains in her, with orders to keep up the fires and not sleep?"

"Yes; I'll send two."

The *Traveler,* with Captains Scott and Lefevre, was immediately dispatched to Allyn's Point to await the arrival of the news. Mr. Joseph Elliott, of the *Herald,* went in her, prepared to catch Mr. Bigelow in his arms as he jumped from the locomotive to the steamer. The *Boston Transcript* of February 20, 1846, gives the result of this spirited journalistic affair as follows:

"THE EXPRESSES FOR NEW YORK WITH THE CAMBRIA's NEWS

"Mr. L. Bigelow left the Worcester depot on the locomotive Jupiter on Wednesday evening at 11 o'clock; arrived in Worcester in 1 hour and 13 minutes; from thence to Allyn's Point in 2 hours; took the crack steamer *Traveler,* for Greenport, which place was reached in 1 hour and 40 minutes. Here Mr. Bigelow took the locomotive *Jacob Little,* and ran to Brooklyn in 2½ hours, arriving in New York at half past seven o'clock in 8½ hours from Boston. This, we believe, is the quickest time ever made between the two cities, and was run exclusively for Mr. Bennett of the *New York Herald,* beating the *Tribune* combination express 5½ hours. The latter was run via Worcester, Hartford, and New Haven, and arrived at 1 P.M. Thursday."

The scene around the *Herald* office was one of great excitement. The Oregon Question, for a time, was overshadowed by the result of the great race. Mr. Bennett immediately had the news from Europe prepared and thousands of *Extra Heralds* printed; and as the express horse of the "Holy Alliance," covered with perspiration, passed down Nassau Street to the office of the *Journal of Commerce,* the newsboys with the Extras swarmed after him. Among the crowd of spectators in front of the Herald Building was Colonel James Watson Webb, much amused with the scene before him. He had refused to join in the overland express.

David Hale of the *Journal of Commerce* was the first of the publishers of the big Wall Street sheets to realize that in the field of news-gathering, Bennett was practically unbeatable. But, being an eminently practical man, Hale resolved to try out the old adage, "If you can't beat 'em, join 'em." He was the first of the opposition editors to enter the office of the despised *Herald*. He wasted no time in coming directly to the point with Bennett.

"I have called to talk about news with you. Have you any objection?"

"None whatever," replied Bennett. "I am always pleased to talk on that subject."

"We propose to join the *Herald* in getting news," continued Mr. Hale. "Have you any objection to that?"

Bennett agreed to consider the matter. They discussed, at great length, the whole problem of news-gathering. At the close of the Moral War, they did work out a mutually satisfactory arrangement. Soon thereafter these two papers were instrumental in the establishment of the Associated Press.

During 1838-39 two additional means of speeding news-gathering were developed. The first was the establishment of a Pony Express from Washington to New York. The second, and more sensational, was the use of carrier pigeons. In the development of the latter, Bennett co-operated with two brilliant newspapermen, Arunah S. Abell of the *Baltimore Sun,* and D. H. Craig of the *Boston Daily Mail*. The experiment began in Baltimore, where the pigeons were trained for their tasks. The Pigeon Express first operated between Washington and Baltimore. Later, relays of pigeons carried the tiny pellets of news northward to Philadelphia and New York. A bird coop on top of the *Herald* building was the terminal point for the winged messengers, and was maintained as an auxiliary service by the *Herald* many years after the telegraph had been perfected.

Craig, operating from Boston, would travel north to Halifax, first and nearest port of call for all British ships. There he would board the mail steamer with his birds, carefully summarize all important news from the old world as the ship headed south. Hours before the boat docked at Boston, his pigeons had reached home; the type had been set; and presses were rolling off the Extras of the *Boston Daily Mail*. As soon as this press run was completed the title page of the *New York Herald* would be substituted for that of the *Mail,* and another run of extras prepared. These were then forwarded to New York by train or ship.

To thwart Bennett, Craig, and Abell, competing editors even

went so far as to engage sharpshooters to shoot the carrier pigeons. In the intense desire to get news first, editors spent sums unheard of a few years earlier. Bennett, on one occasion, arranged to pay Craig a bonus of five hundred dollars for every hour by which he could beat the other papers with the news.

The long and hazardous voyage across the Atlantic was almost cut in half with the coming of the steamship. In late April, 1828, all New York thrilled to the report that Britain's two new trans-atlantic steamers, the *Sirius* and the *Great Western,* were steaming into the harbor on the same day. Bennett had devoted much space to a discussion of the possibilities of just such an event; and when it did occur, the *Herald* blazoned the news in extras. Like so many other nineteenth-century enthusiasts of scientific progress, Bennett was certain that steamships, railroads, and newspapers were rapidly destroying petty jealousies and national antipathies. In their place, he saw arising a mutual love and respect, growing out of a more accurate knowledge of one another's good qualities, which must of necessity result in "the onward march of mind, genius, enterprise, and energy, towards the perfectibility of men, and the amelioration of our physical, social, moral, and commercial condition."

To the press the coming of the steamship, said Bennett, would reduce the unfair advantages of the larger and wealthier sheets. No longer would there be the need to maintain expensive pilot boats, so that even the smallest newspaper could get its news as soon as the largest.

When the *Sirius* returned to England, one of its passengers was the editor of the *Herald.* Bennett, on a combined pleasure and business trip, returned to the Old World for the first time since he had left it in 1819. The *Herald* was left under the capable management of Frederic Hudson. With typical Scotch foresight, Bennett auctioned off most of his personal belongings before taking the trip, in case any mishap would befall him while he was gone.

Back in England, the *Herald* publisher was received as a man of considerable prominence. He conferred with the editors of leading papers; he spoke with merchants, bankers, engineers, politicians, and the common folk. His curiosity was insatiable. He wanted facts—facts—and still more facts. Into his copious notebooks and in lengthy letters to the *Herald* went a flood of information and impressions. Back home, too, went trunks full of books, documents, government reports, and a mass of other material for future study.

He attended the coronation of Queen Victoria. Then, having devoted a month to England, he went back to the scenes of his boyhood. At Edinburgh he heard again the dialect of the North; he saw the flowers and the trees which he had known as a child; he wandered the narrow crooked streets, trod by his heroes of yesteryear. And for all his shell of hardness, Bennett was as soft and emotional inside as ever. He was still a romantic soul, and, as he confessed in his letters, he was so overcome that he quite forgot about the *Herald,* New York, London, and the great wide world.

From Edinburgh he went, by mail coach, to Aberdeen and then to Keith for a surprise visit to his family. Walking slowly from the village tavern where he had arranged to spend the night, James Gordon Bennett trod the well-known road to his home, chuckling with delight as he recognized long-forgotten fields, hills, houses, and tiny cottages.

His mother, two sisters, and a host of other relatives, goggle-eyed with wonder and admiration, plied their unexpected visitor with a thousand questions. His father and brother were both dead.

Relating to readers of the *Herald* the joy he experienced to be back, if only for a day, with his own kith and kin, he reported how he had said to them:

This narrow, picturesque vale is the scene of my infancy and childhood. Here I first felt the throb of existence. Here is the first school I entered, and there is the water in which I used to lave my young limbs. . . . Beyond these hills, all is a foreign land to my heart and soul. I have only two homes and two places to which my heart is bound; New York and New Mill both fill my bosom—the one the scene of my manhood, the other of my childhood.

How happy I feel to see you again; but I could not live here a month! New York is the center of a great empire . . . the empire of mind, intellect and civilization . . . and there I must live.

The next day, Bennett was on his way to Glasgow; thence to Ireland; and then to France and other parts of the continent.

By mid-October the editor was back at his desk. Not only had he seen much, and talked with many people. He had also engaged six of Europe's ablest newspapermen, functioning respectively from London, Glasgow, Paris, Berlin, Brussels, and Rome, to write exclusively for the *New York Herald*. Thus, once again, Bennett pioneered in still another field of journalism. He was the first editor to arrange for systematic news coverage of Europe through his own foreign correspondents.

That fall and winter he worked out arrangements for special correspondents for the *Herald* from Mexico, the Republic of Texas, and Canada. And a little later the same year—1838—the *Herald* began to pull advance proof sheets of its most important news, and send these, without charge, to the smaller inland papers. This gratuitous service came as a godsend to scores of editors. Not only did they reprint these items, giving credit to the *Herald* (thus spreading its name), but most of them went out of their way to reciprocate, by sending advance news from their own communities to the *Herald*.

These "news-slips" of the *Herald* may well be considered as the immediate forerunner of the Associated Press.

During 1839 the *Herald* started to give full and complete coverage to the annual conventions, gatherings, and synods of all religious groups and denominations. At first there was a hue and cry against this but as the reports were factual, and the names of all participants were mentioned, in less than two years' time, the religious bodies welcomed the men from the *Herald*. In 1840 reporters began to cover the churches of New York, reporting the text of the sermons. Once again, the immediate reaction by the churchmen was one of hostility. "Is there no place," they asked, "sufficiently Holy or Sacred where the men from the *Herald* will not come prying and snooping?" But here, too, the hostility was short-lived, for Bennett had given strict orders that all church services were to be reported, not only with accuracy, but with dignity and decorum. He also insisted that the names of the ministers be given due prominence.

A personal tour through the South was made by Bennett in 1839, the first to be made by any leading New York editor. At Philadelphia he interviewed Nicholas Biddle. At Baltimore he spent a full week; and in Washington he called upon the President, Martin Van Buren:

When my turn came I went up to His Excellency. He held out his hand. It was soft and oily. I took hold of it, gently, by the very hand, too, which has quizzed him most unmercifully during the last four years. . . .

"How do you do, Mr. Bennett?" said Mr. Van Buren, with a half smile.

"Pretty well, I thank you," I responded, with another half smile.

I looked into his face—his eyes wandered over the carpet, probably thinking at that moment of the meeting of Agamemnon and Achilles. I was almost on the verge of bursting into a horse-laugh, at the vagaries of human nature, but being in the presence of the Chief of the Democratic party, I restrained myself.

I sat down on the sofa, crossed my legs, and looked very knowingly into the fine hickory fire blazing on high. . . .

The discussion, said Bennett, was "a little on local politics—a little on land speculation—a little on the weather."

The article concluded: "Ten years ago I knew Mr. Van Buren as a senator, when he had no more idea of being president than I had. What a remarkable illustration of the free institutions of this land! Forty or fifty years ago, Mr. Van Buren was a poor boy in Kinderhook, unnoticed, unknown, unheralded—now he is President of twenty millions of people, and a territory second in size to all Europe."

That summer Bennett made the rounds of the famous watering places, from whence he sent in colorful reports on the doings of Society. One of his contemporaries, describing this new departure on the part of the editor, declared: "Most persons go to Saratoga to waste the best hours of the summer—Mr. Bennett is wiser. He goes there to work. There he sees hundreds of persons and obtains a knowledge of society and themes for public use. He sees Mr. Cunard, who is just announcing his proposed line of British steamers. In his quiet and unobtrusive way the Editor receives the salutations and listens to the conversations of many of the distinguished sojourners at the place. Mr. Van Buren [president] is there. Mr. Clay, General Scott, and many others are there.

"He discovers no papers arrive there on Mondays—so arranges

at once to have the *Herald* reach there on that day, and follows
this up with 14 elaborate letters on Life at the Springs. Everybody
at the Springs will now know there is a New York paper that
fashionable people will be amused by. Always at work, always
finding new ways of building his paper—that is Bennett."

The following winter, just a few weeks before the Moral War
broke out in all its fury, the *Herald* invaded the most exclusive
social event of the season—the Breevort Costume Ball. To the utter
disgust of most of the guests, William Attree, attired in the shining armor of a medieval knight, was there as the *Herald's* representative. Philip Hone expressed the outraged feelings of New
York socialites when he wrote in his diary:

. . . to submit to this kind of surveillance is getting to be intolerable,
and nothing but the force of public opinion will correct the insolence,
which, it is to be feared, will never be applied as long as Mr. Charles A.
Davis and other gentlemen make this Mr. Attree "hail fellow, well met,"
as they did on this occasion. Whether the notice they took of him, and
that which they extend to Bennett when he shows his ugly face in Wall
street, may be considered approbatory of the daily slanders and unblushing impudence of the paper they conduct, or is intended to purchase
their forbearance toward themselves, the effect is equally mischievous.
It affords them countenance and encouragement, and they find that the
more personalities they have in their papers, the more papers they sell.

Thereafter, every important event became the subject of elaborate
spreads by the *Herald*. The splendor of the gowns and costumes,
the elaborateness of the decorations, an estimated value of the jewelry worn, the parade of youth and beauty—all these were reported
in great detail. All those present were listed, except that this was
done by writing merely the first and last letters of each name, separated by asterisks to equal the missing letters. The innovation
was a huge success. On one occasion, to the horror of the blue-
bloods and to the delight of his readers, Bennett devoted four full
pages to a major social event. So great was the reader response to
this new feature, that within a few years every paper had its society
editor.

Bennett's sole criteria for the inclusion of any new feature was
simple: If it is something in which a considerable number of peo-

ple are interested, then it is worth reporting, for those people will want to read about it. Sporting events had their innings next. Up to the mid-forties, they were noticed only by a few small weeklies. The *New York Herald* inaugurated regular sports event reporting and James Gordon Bennett, himself, wrote one of the earliest stories. It appeared in the *Herald* of October 10, 1840:

THE RACES

The October meeting of the New York Jockey Club generally lasts during the first week of this month, but owing to the election, and other exciting matters being on the *tapis,* it was thought desirable by the managers to compress all the races into one day's sport, hoping thereby to attract a large number of sporting men, as well as a considerable portion of the travelling community now in the city. The sun seldom rose brighter than on Tuesday; and, long before 9 o'clock in the morning, lots of smart turn-outs might be seen, with their occupants, on the *qui vive* for the South Ferry. The dennet, the tilbury, the tandem, the britska, and the barouche, for the more exclusive—and the wagon and omnibus for those who preferred a merry party, were all mixed together on board the ferry boats, whilst pedestrians innumerable were wending their way to the Jamaica railroad station, all anxious to be early on the scene of action.

"We arrived at the grand stand about half past ten o'clock, and found Mr. Botts, the secretary of the club, who had made the most admirable disposition for the accommodation of the company. . . .

By this time many of the spectators had got tired of the sport and were on the move for town; but, as the fifth race was expected to be the most interesting, most of the "Club" stayed to witness it, although it was past four o'clock before the horses were saddled. After considerable delay, the following came to the post for a purse of $400. . . .

As the shadows were beginning to lengthen, home was the word, and in a very brief space, the vehicles were in motion, and the thimble riggers and the blacklegs were all scrambling off towards the railroad cars, until two trains were nearly filled. Such a motley crowd never was seen before in one travelling apparatus. Happily, however, they all got safe to the South Ferry, and the whole affair passed off to the great satisfaction of the knowing ones, and without the slightest accident.

Determined to give his readers full and complete reports on the debates in Congress, Bennett went to Washington early in 1841, where he established the first bona fide corps of reporters ever assembled by any outside newspaper. Chief of the *Herald's* Washington news bureau was an able correspondent and a first-class shorthand reporter, Robert Sutton.

Just as Sutton and Bennett completed their plans, the former was told by Senator Samuel Southard, President pro tempore of the Senate, that the *Herald* could not have access to the reporters' desks in the Senate chamber. When asked why this discrimination was being made, Senator Southard referred Sutton to an old Senate rule, which provided that only reporters from papers "printed and published in Washington" were permitted to occupy those seats.

Bennett, who knew the Washington picture as well as anyone, charged that this action was taken at the behest of the Washington newspapers "in order to maintain a monopoly of Washington news, and to rob the public treasury, under the color of public printing. . . ." Henry Clay had stated on the floor of Congress in 1838 that funds to the amount of $420,000 had been paid out to the three Washington dailies, the *Globe,* the *National Intelligencer,* and the *Madisonian.* (It was not until 1873 that the Congressional Record as we know it today, was established.)

Why, asked Bennett, was such a large sum of money being paid out of the public treasury to these papers? To the reply of the politicians who said that it was necessary to remunerate these papers for reporting the debates, Bennett retorted that the remuneration was excessive, and furthermore it was the function of newspapers to report congressional debates without being paid for them. This he now proposed to do, and promised to give a "daily report and circulation of these debates, better and more comprehensive, without asking a cent of the public treasury."

The political bigwigs made a last-ditch fight to keep the exclusive rights on reporting the activities of Congress in the hands of their favorite organs. But Bennett would not yield. He addressed himself to Henry Clay asking for aid in his effort to secure "freedom of the press" for all newspaper correspondents at the nation's capital:

New York, June 5, 1841

Hon. Henry Clay,

Sir: The peculiar circumstances of the case will be my apology for troubling you with the present note.

I have organized, at an expense of nearly two hundred dollars per week, a *corps* of reporters, to give daily reports of the debates in both Houses of Congress. In the House there is no difficulty, but in the Senate there is a rule, I am told, excluding from the reporters' seats all not connected with the Washington press. Now I conceive this exclusion to be hostile to the public interests. I can and will give daily reports of the Senate, without asking any of the printing, or indirect remuneration of that body, but I am met with a rule that certainly is illiberal and injurious both to private enterprise and public advantage.

I address myself to you as one of the most liberal and enlightened members of your body, for the purpose of requesting that a motion may be made for the repeal of the rule in question. No individual in this land will sooner see the propriety and public advantage of such motion than yourself.

> *I am, sir, with great respect,*
>
> JAMES GORDON BENNETT

Clay did intervene—and in the fall of 1841 the obsolete ruling was to all intents and purposes abolished. Sutton and the other *Herald* men took their places in the news gallery. The Washington news monopoly was broken for all time.

For a good many years there had been much speculation by New Yorkers about Bennett's state of single blessedness. Friends asserted that his bachelorhood was due, first, to his early poverty, later to his complete preoccupation with the *Herald*. Enemies whispered that he was "diseased," "impotent," "unnatural," and that no decent, self-respecting woman would have him.

The editor's personal explanation, which, of course, he published in the *Herald,* stated: "There is one drawback, there is one sin, there is one piece of wickedness of which I am guilty, and with which my conscience is weighted down day and night. I am a bachelor. I am unmarried, and what is worse, I am so busy that I have no time to get a wife, though I am passionately fond of female society. For this great sin I have no apology to make. I can only throw myself, heart, soul, feelings, and all, upon the compassion of my enchanting and beautiful female readers. I know well it is my duty to get married and obey the laws of God and nature, but formerly to me the female sex appeared all so beautiful, all so enchanting, all so fascinating that I became bewildered and confused, and now I am so engaged in building up the *Herald* and reforming the age that actually I have scarcely the time to say 'How do ye do.'"

Whatever the reason, the fact remained that Bennett was a bachelor till he was forty years of age. When Cupid did, at long last, aim a shaft at the editor, he scored a bull's eye. It took place at the wedding party of one of his chief assistants, William Attree. The celebration was a gala affair, with writers, actors, singers, joining in the festivities. Among those present was a young lady in her early twenties, Miss Henrietta Agnes Crean. A comparative newcomer to the United States, Miss Crean supported herself by giving piano lessons. Attree's bride was a friend and pupil of the young lady.

That Bennett was smitten with the charms of the music teacher was apparent from the next day's *Herald,* where the Attree wedding party received more than a column of space. Of the many distinguished guests, only one received undue notice—Miss Crean. Said the *Herald:* "The young lady of the distinguished Irish family of Crean (recently arrived from Dublin), afforded a fine specimen of the beauty and talent to be met with among the higher order of her sex in Ireland. She was the *belle* of the evening. She is descended from one of the most ancient families in Ireland—a family that has furnished history with deeds of heroism, long before the subjugation of the bloody Anglo-Normans. Her figure is most magnificent—her head, neck and bust, of the purest classical contour. There was a quiet and finish in her sweet looks, her graceful movements, which we have never seen surpassed in London, Paris or Washington."

Determined to lose no time, Bennett proposed to Attree the very next day that Mrs. Attree and Miss Crean join the two men for a ride into the country. This was done—and thereafter Bennett made rapid progress in his courtship. When and how he found time to press his case, is hard to imagine, for he was busier than ever with the *Herald* for the combined attacks of the other papers against him were just getting under way.

Less than three months after he met Henrietta Crean, on June 1, 1840, and at the moment of the most furious onslaught against himself and his journal, there appeared a feature article on the front page of the *Herald* which read:

To Readers of the Herald

Declaration of Love—Caught at Last—Going to be Married—New Movement in Civilization

I am going to be married in a few days. The weather is so beautiful—times are getting so good—the prospects of political and moral reform so auspicious, that I cannot resist the divine instinct of honest nature any longer—so I am going to be married to one of the most splendid women in intellect, in heart, in soul, in property, in person, in manner, that I have yet seen in the course of my interesting pilgrimage through human life.

. . . I cannot stop in my career, I must fulfill that awful destiny which the Almighty Father has written against my name, in the broad letters of life against the wall of Heaven. I must give the world a pattern of happy wedded life, with all the charities that spring from a nuptial love. In a few days I shall be married according to the holy rites of the most holy Christian church, to one of the most remarkable, accomplished and beautiful young women of the age. She possesses a fortune. I sought and found a fortune—a large fortune. She has no Stonington shares, or Manhattan stock, but in purity and uprightness, she is worth half a million of pure coin. Can any swindling bank show as much? In good sense and elegance another half a million—in soul, mind and beauty, millions on millions, equal to the whole specie of all the rotten banks in the world. Happily, the patronage of the public to the *Herald* is nearly $25,000 per annum, almost equal to the President's salary. But property in the world's goods was never my object. Fame, public good, usefulness in my day and generation—the religious associates of female intelligence—the progress of true industry—these have been my dreams by night and my desires by day.

In the new and holy condition into which I am about to enter, and to enter with the same reverential feelings as I would heaven itself—I anticipate some signal changes in my feelings, in my views, in my purposes, my pursuits. What they may be I know not—time alone can tell. My ardent desire has been through life, to reach the highest order of human excellence by the shortest possible cut. Associated, night and day, in sickness and in health, in war and in peace, with a woman of this highest order of excellence, must produce some serious results in my heart and feelings, and these results the future will develop in due time in the columns of the *Herald*. Meantime, I return my heartfelt thanks to the enthusiastic patronage of the public, both of Europe and of America. The happy estate of wedlock will only increase my desire to be still more useful. God Almighty bless you all.

JAMES GORDON BENNETT

A postscript announced that he had no time to waste upon the editors who attacked him till after the marriage and the honeymoon.

On Saturday afternoon, June 6, James Gordon Bennett and Miss Crean were joined in holy wedlock at St. Peter's Catholic Church.

Thereafter, all through the summer, the *Herald* devoted a great deal of space to the newly married couple, what they did, where they went, and what an amazing effect the marital tie had upon Bennett, and through him, upon the whole field of journalism. "If the *Herald* has already reformed . . . it comes from a fairer, a dearer, a softer, a purer source."

Mountains, hitherto impossible to scale, were readily ascended with a wife at his side, said Bennett.

Describing his wife, he wrote, "[she] composes with the same brilliancy with which she plays." He told *Herald* readers how she patterned a piece of music upon the roaring water of the Niagara. On another occasion, she heard a girl in the street crying "straw-w-w-berries, straw-w-w-berries" with a peculiar combination of notes which caught her fancy. "After breakfast she struck the same notes on the pianoforte, and out of the simple cry of the strawberry girl, she has composed a very amusing and original air."

The newlyweds were harassed, abused, and in general treated with great disrespect both at Saratoga, Niagara, and upon their return to New York—for the Holy Allies had by this time whipped up a public frenzy against Bennett which knew no bounds of decency. Attempts were even made to get the manager of the Astor House to cancel the suite of rooms Bennett had engaged for himself and his wife upon their return to New York in August.

Throughout her first year of married life, gossips spread their whispered tales about Mrs. Bennett. After the birth of her son, James Gordon Bennett, Junior, on May 10, 1841, the chorus of whispers grew louder. Not only was she charged with being extravagant, haughty, a social climber, and the daughter of ne'er-do-wells, but there was buzzed about the word that she had committed

—well—imprudences with other men, which weren't just talked about! Mordecai Noah went as far as he dared in printing these rumors in the *Star*. Beach, of the *Sun,* went one step further and asserted in its columns that Bennett's claim to the paternity of his child, of which he boasted so annoyingly, was subject to some not very unreasonable doubt.

Bennett, furious at the insinuation, sued for libel. Beach, through his lawyer, pleaded guilty, but tried to place the blame upon one of his reporters. The reporter, however, swore that he was given specific instructions by Beach on what to write. The case dragged in the courts for many months. Beach was found guilty and sentenced to pay a fine of $250.

The very mildness of the sentence is indicative of how strong public sentiment still was against Bennett, who charged editorially, "From the facts and affidavits in our possession we can unfold one of the most diabolical conspiracies to destroy and blast by perjury, slander and defamation the reputation and peace of a high-principled, faithful, domestic and affectionate wife and her infant child, merely because the husband of that wife has succeeded in establishing and maintaining against all rivalry, the *Herald* newspaper in New York."

Beach, according to Bennett, was not the originator of the scheme, but was caught merely because he was a low-minded and vulgar person with less cunning than the others. "Private slander, secret espionage, and all sorts of tricks" were used to destroy him, his family peace, and the *Herald,* said the editor. "Spies were deputed to watch my home in Chambers Street, and if a shutter was opened or closed, it was marked and told of as something very mysterious. If I went to Saratoga—to Rockaway—or to any other public place— little knots of the 'salt pork' aristocracy would get together and circulate every species of slander and falsehood against my family."

Bennett gave his readers the whole family background of both himself and his wife. She came of an honorable, respectable, and chivalric Irish stock, he asserted, and did not have to hide her past nor that of her relatives as did some of her persecutors.

There were many who resented the attacks upon Mrs. Bennett and her child, and yet, it was Bennett himself who made both his wife and child public property by constantly writing about them in his paper. A man cannot parade his own wife in his own paper, day after day and week after week, and then complain too loudly if his opponents seize upon the opportunity to do the same. Bennett had done too much name-calling himself to be able to gain much public sympathy.

Mrs. Bennett remained steadfastly by the side of her husband despite the slander. She bore him another son, named Cosmo after her husband's dead brother, but the boy passed away before his sixth birthday. Two daughters were also born into the family; one of them died while an infant; the other, Jeanette, lived to old age.

As soon as young James and Jeanette were old enough to enter school, Mrs. Bennett went abroad, and after 1850, most of her time was spent in France, Switzerland, Italy, England, and Ireland.

Eighteen-forty was the year when all America seemed to be marching in torchlight parades, guzzling hard cider, and singing songs about how "Tippecanoe and Tyler, too" would redeem the country from the extravagances of Van Buren. Although the *Herald* proclaimed itself an "armed neutral" in the conflict and gave equal prominence to doings and sayings of both Whigs and Democrats, it threw its support to General Harrison. Bennett explained his position by saying, "I don't like Harrison—but I like Martin Van Buren even less." Furthermore, he insisted that the defeat of Van Buren's party for at least one presidential term "would produce a salutary effect upon the morals, the ideas, and the temper of the politicians."

The shouting and tumult for William Henry Harrison had no effect whatsoever upon the seasoned political observer. A few weeks before the November elections, Bennett published a long list of the price fluctuations of basic commodities in the United States, from the years 1827 to 1840, to which he appended this pertinent observation: "The present policy of the federal government in financial affairs is more nearly right at this moment than it has been for ten years past, yet the probability remains that General Harrison will be elected, and Mr. Van Buren defeated, because the price of wheat, cotton, and wool has fallen off from the range of former years. Song and hard cider may affect the loafers without wives, and office seekers without breeches—but prices touch the pocket, and the pocket touches a nerve that vibrates to the breast, among all calm thinking, and reflecting men with wives and children."

While the speeches of the leading orators of the day were reported in full, the *Herald* devised a unique plan to cover those of the lesser lights, whom it announced "must be satisfied with miniature portraits and graphic sketches of their performances." The speech of Colonel Hunt of South Carolina, who preceded Daniel Webster at a huge Long Island rally, was presented in this fashion: "Fellow citizens: I trust that in addressing an audience, strangers to me personally—Fellow citizens—a cry of the U. S.—and has—has filled with dangers—Sound democracy.—All our hopes depend—money power—U. S. bank—all—hopes—aristocracy who opposes it. . . ." and so on for two full columns.

In the 1844 elections, the *Herald* again supported the victorious candidate, James K. Polk, although it had declared at the time of his nomination that "a more ridiculous, contemptible and forlorn candidate was never put forth by any party. . . . Mr. Polk is a sort of fourth or rather fortieth rate lawyer and small politician in Tennessee, who by accident was once Speaker of the House. . . . He was rejected even by his own state as Governor—and now he comes forward as candidate of the great democracy. . . . Oh, what a ridiculous finale." The *Herald* added that there could be but one result—the election of Henry Clay, while the Democratic party would be scattered to the four winds of heaven.

Likewise in 1848 the *Herald* climbed aboard the winning bandwagon, by its support of General Zachary Taylor. No sooner were the results known than Bennett hastened to send the President-elect a congratulatory letter, reminding him that they had met back in 1840. "I want nothing, personally, of any administration," wrote the now highly successful and affluent publisher, "but wisdom in its management, and the public good for its leading purpose. As an independent journalist and an early friend of your election, I can offer you a warm support when you are right, with a respectful dissent when I am convinced you may be wrong. . . ."

A bitter political controversy broke out in 1841 between Bennett and Governor Seward of New York. The major issue involved was that of whether state funds should be used to support parochial schools. Bennett was a vigorous opponent of this measure. The heavy Irish Catholic population in New York was urged by its Bishop, John Hughes, to use its power to get the legislature to pass the measure. Immediately the *Herald* turned its guns upon the Bishop. The war between the paper and the Bishop continued almost without interruption for over three years; and the more the Bishop took up the battle for his position, the hotter grew the attacks upon him from Bennett. He was charged with being deficient not only in common sense, but honesty as well. He was told that the methods he used were creating a wave of ill feeling and hatred against all Catholics. He was warned that it was a highly dangerous tactic for him to try to organize his church into a political club.

Bishop Hughes countered by calling Bennett an apostate, and even went so far as to excommunicate him from the Catholic Church. In the spring of 1844, Bishop Hughes issued a public letter to Mayor Harper defending his own position and denouncing that of Bennett. In reporting one of the Bishop's speeches, he said, the *Herald's* account the next morning had it "studded with gems of its own ribaldry; and made some half a column of editorial remarks in that mock gravity of which Bennett is capable. . . .

"Considering his talents, his want of principle, and the power of doing mischief which circumstances have placed within his reach," wrote Hughes, "I regard him as *decidedly* the most *dangerous man,* to the peace and safety of a community, that I have ever known, or ever read of." And he told how he had discovered Bennett "in the sanctuary itself—like a serpent in Paradise—endeavoring to sow discord among my clergy, and to seduce two of them, even by name, into alienation from their duty to God, and towards their Bishop."

But Bennett had the last word—and the cause for which Bishop Hughes fought so hard, failed to materialize. Said the editor, in a final telling blow at the churchman:

The conduct of the Bishop in 1841 gave the Irish a preponderance in 1842, which created in its turn a reaction in the American mind in 1843, resulting in the organization of the Native American party last Spring, and whose operations we have all seen. But all these movements, here as well as in Philadelphia, can be traced with the accuracy of mathematical calculation, back to Bishop Hughes's first entrance into Carroll Hall as a political agitator, and the motives which impelled the Bishop then can be guessed at now with a good deal of certainty. He was the first dignitary of the Catholic Church, in this free and happy land, that ever attempted such a movement, and we trust that he may be the last of the same faith that may ever thus disgrace his holy calling. In all these movements he has most wofully mistaken his duties. He has most wofully mistaken his position in this city, in this country, and in this age. He has forgotten that he is living in a land of freedom and universal toleration, in a republic of intelligent men, and in the nineteenth century.

Coming fresh from the seclusion of his cloister, he imagined when he became a Bishop, that he was living in the fourth or fourteenth century. His policy would, indeed, have been in keeping with the spirit of those dark ages. It is precisely similar to that conduct by which the priesthood destroyed the Roman Empire—decided who should wear the purple, and finally delivered that old heroic nation into the hands of the Northern barbarians. It is precisely similar to that interference of the hierarchy in political affairs which overwhelmed the Italian republics of the Middle Ages with irreparable ruin. It is precisely similar to that conduct which lighted up the fires in Smithfield and the Grass-market. It is precisely similar to that course of policy which whitened the valleys of Piedmont with the bones of thousands slaughtered in civil war. It is precisely similar to that policy which has torn and distracted unhappy Spain. It is, in fact, the same accursed interference of ecclesiastics with the affairs of State, which has, in all ages, brought such disgrace on Christianity, and crushed the liberties of mankind. Need we say that it is utterly at variance with the precepts of Christ and the spirit of his religion? No. We all know that it is in open and blasphemous defiance of the principles of Him who came to proclaim universal peace and good will, as they were developed in his sermons on the mountains of Judea and on the shores of Galilee.

The visit of Charles Dickens to the United States in 1842 was the high point of the year. Never had any literary celebrity received such a reception! The Boz Ball in New York was the most splendid that city had ever devised. Bennett gave it a full eight-page spread. But New York was not alone in its hero-worship of the young Englishman. From New England to the Middle West he was feted, dined, and the focal point of a never-ending adulation.

"I can do nothing that I want to do," wrote Dickens to a friend, "and see nothing that I want to see. If I turn into a street I am followed by a multitude. If I stay at home, the house becomes, with callers, like a fair. . . . I go to a party in the evening, I am so inclosed and hemmed about by people, stand where I will, that I am exhausted for want of air. I dine out, and have to talk about everything, to everybody. I go to church for quiet, and there is a violent rush to the neighborhood of the pew I sit in, and the clergyman preaches *at* me. . . . I can't drink a glass of water, without having a hundred people looking down my throat when I open my mouth to swallow. Conceive what all this is! . . . I have no rest or peace, and am in a perpetual worry."

The early forties were a time of many new religious movements, and to each and all of these the *Herald* gave full coverage. The Millerites, for example, who were sure that the second coming of Christ would take place on April 23, 1843 (later revised to October, 1844) had won a large following all through the East, so Bennett reported faithfully what they said and did.

Then there were the Mormons, or Latter-day Saints. Hated, feared, and misrepresented by most of the press, they found in the *Herald* the one paper which would give a faithful account of their doctrines and doings. For his good work on their behalf, the Mormons not only bestowed upon Bennett an honorary degree from their "university" at Nauvoo, Illinois, but also made him a brigadier general in the Nauvoo Legion. The good news had to be made public, so he penned an article about it.

Rising in the World

We are rising very rapidly in this sinful world. A short time ago, the Corporation of Nauvoo, Illinois, conferred upon us a freedom of the city. How far this freedom extends we know not, but we suppose it embraces a vast number of DELICIOUS PRIVILEGES, *according to the Mormon Creed.* The next step was to raise us to the dignity of LL.D., a regular Doctor of Laws, by the University of Nauvoo, *an honor which we highly price,* and which is as good, and perhaps better, than that conferred on General Jackson by the University of Harvard, or that on his Excellency, Edward Everett, by the University of Cambridge, in England. But this is not all. Yesterday,—blessed be the day!—we received by a special messenger from Illinois, the intelligence that that state had gone entirely for the Mormons and the locofocos, in the elections; and also an enclosure which contained the parchment, *conferring a high military rank upon us,* of which document the following is a true copy—the original being in our salamander safe, with the titles of the *Herald* building. . . .

There's honor—there's distinction—there's salt and greens for a modest, simple, calm, patient, industrious editor. We now take legitimate rank, far above Colonel Webb, Major Noah, Colonel Stone, General George P. Morris, or all the military editors around and about the country. We are inferior in rank—and that but half a step—to good old General Jackson—he being Major-General and LL.D.—we being Brigadier and LL.D. also.

In an hour after the arrival of this precious document, but before I received it, I found myself two inches taller, three inches more in circumference, and so wolfish about the head and shoulders that I could have fought a duel. . . .

The Bennetts visited Europe in 1843. During the course of this visit the editor visited Ireland, and a considerable controversy arose because of his differences with the Irish reformer, Daniel O'Connell—a controversy which was played up both in the London and New York papers.

Shortly before his trip abroad, Bennett announced that he was prepared to sell out the *Herald,* lock, stock, and barrel, for on October 26, 1842, an advertisement in bold-faced type declared:

The intention of the undersigned in retiring from the *Herald* is to proceed to London as soon as practicable, and to establish in that capital a daily and weekly newspaper, for the purpose of defending, explaining, and exhibiting to Europe the institutions, laws, morals, resources, movements and tendencies of the United States, which are now subject—from imperfect knowledge and strong prejudices, to misrepresentation and falsehoods of all kinds and from all quarters. He also intends to establish a branch newspaper in French and English in Paris.

The *Herald* is now completely organized in every point as follows:

Materials for printing, consisting of ten presses, types, news boats, etc., costing $25,000.

Herald Building, having granite columns and brick walls; six stories high, costing $30,000.

Aggregate average circulation of the *Herald,* 30,000.

Aggregate annual cash receipts of the *Herald, New York Lancet,* and other publications as per cash book, $130,000.

Annual profits of the whole establishment, according to industry, genius, and enterprise in its management, $15,000 to $25,000.

Applications for further information are directed to be made to the proprietor.

JAMES GORDON BENNETT

Whether no satisfactory offers were made to him, we do not know. At any rate, the decision to sell was withdrawn a week later.

Horace Greeley, whose *Tribune* had been founded in 1841, soon became one of Bennett's most potent rivals. Greeley, sensing the tide of social and political unrest, made himself and his paper spokesmen for the underprivileged. By so doing he drew down upon himself the wrath of the more conservative organs. At the same time he won, almost at a stroke, a large and enthusiastic band of readers, who supported all causes espoused by the *Tribune*. Albert Brisbane, father of the late Arthur Brisbane, along with a host of other social reformers, was one of the early contributors to the *Tribune*.

With but a few rare exceptions, the two great editors, Bennett and Greeley, were always at odds with one another.

"These new philosophers," wrote Bennett scornfully of Greeley and his associates, "who arrogate to themselves superior intelligence and fuller conceptions of truth, and discover such excessive fretfulness and bad temper, whenever the tendency of their doctrines is pointed out, no doubt mean well. We are willing to admit that they desire to see virtue prevailing and vice driven away abashed from society. They wish well to humanity; but all their absurd theories, all their erroneous reasonings, all their disorganizing schemes, are the result of an entirely mistaken view of human nature and human society.

"They are eternally declaiming about the universal misery and crime which exist on all hands. Everything is wrong in their eyes. Everybody is suffering. The world is in their eyes one vast lazarhouse. Now, all the misery, and suffering, and corruption exist only in their own diseased imagination. They regard everything with a jaundiced eye. Their own feelings are morbid. They are oppressed with a moral nightmare. They can only see the dark side of the picture. Like the owl in the ruined tower, who, drooping his fringed eyelids, hoots at the morning sunshine, they refuse to come out into the open day, and wrapped in darkness, call out when told of the sun in the heavens, where is it?"

More significant to journalism than the railroad, the steamship, or the use of carrier pigeons was a strange electrical device, the telegraph, perfected by a Boston school teacher, Samuel B. Morse. His long struggle to win recognition and some support from Congress culminated at last in the successful sending of a message from Washington to Baltimore on June 3, 1844.

Perhaps the first to grasp its significance to the newsgathering fraternity was James Gordon Bennett. No sooner had he been informed of what Morse had done than he wrote, "The magnetic telegraph at Washington has totally annihilated what there was left of space."

The effect of this new invention, he contended, would be to make of journalism a more potent force than ever before. "The public mind will be stimulated to greater activity by the rapid circulation of news. The swift communication of tidings of great events will awake in the masses of the community still keener interest in public affairs."

As rapidly as telegraph lines were established, the *Herald* made use of them. In 1846 it scooped the whole New York press by printing, in full, the text of Henry Clay's speech at Lexington, Kentucky, on the Mexican War. Expert stenographers took the speech, rushed it by a system of pony express the eighty miles to Cincinnati—the nearest telegraph station—and sent it over the wires to New York. The cost was high, but the scoop was worth it. Later, when Bennett's reporters were on the trail of a big story, they would arrange to keep the telegraph wires open for themselves by filing long passages from the Scriptures till their own stories were complete.

The Bennetts once again left for an extended European tour in June, 1846, and did not return till the following October. In the meantime, the *Herald's* editor, sure that a war with Mexico would break at any moment, had worked out detailed arrangements to cover that conflict. As early as January, 1845, in co-operation with the *New Orleans Crescent City,* he had organized an overland mail express which beat the regular mails by four full days, to the consternation of the Post Office, which sought to impede this by arresting one of the owners of the New Orleans paper. The *Baltimore Sun* and the *Philadelphia Ledger* were made part of the new coalition to cover the conflict with Mexico. And all through that war, these papers were able to report direct news from the warring fronts, from one to five days ahead of any other paper.

It was the *Herald* which made public the Treaty of Peace between Mexico and the United States. This scoop caused the Washington correspondent of the *Herald,* Mr. Nugent, to be held for questioning by the Senate, for the government was not yet ready to release the text of the treaty at the time it was made public.

Among the many special correspondents for the *Herald* in out-of-way places, was Thomas O. Larkin, long the United States Consul at Monterey, when California was still part of Mexico. Larkin stayed on in California after it was annexed to the United States, and from time to time reported to the *Herald* on events in that remote region.

One day there arrived a report from Larkin telling that gold had been found in California, and to prove it he enclosed some flakes of the precious metal. At first Bennett paid no attention to the report, but as additional letters from Larkin arrived telling of the excitement on the American River, Bennett had the samples of metal brought forth. "Let us see," said he, "if this is gold. If it be the pure article, and Mr. Larkin's statements prove correct, we are on the eve of one of the most extraordinary events of the age."

On December 8, 1848, the report from the assayist revealed that the samples were almost pure gold. Bennett at once published the whole report together with Larkin's letter. Soon all New York, then the whole East, then the whole country, was talking about the precious metal. The California Gold Rush was on. And, of course, the *Herald* sent a corps of special reporters to cover this exciting drama of the far west.

From Europe, during 1846 and 1847, both the editor and his wife sent lengthy and interesting letters to the *Herald* on European manners, politics, science, fashions, and the press.

The newspaper press in Paris [reported Bennett in his letter of January 22, 1847] is one of the most remarkable engines in France. In government, religion, morals, modes, philosophy, literature, and commerce, it is more or less a potent element, exercising an influence not only over Paris and France, but over the whole surrounding continent.

There are over fifteen daily newspapers published in Paris, each possessing a distinct character and circulation of its own, but all forming a general similitude in management and design, somewhat different from the Press of London, and more perhaps resembling the journals of New York.

The circulation of all the daily Paris journals is probably over one hundred and fifty thousand sheets per day—that of London about one half that number. Before the July Revolution, Journalism was restricted and expensive, though perhaps equally powerful as a moral and political weapon. . . .

The whole daily newspaper Press of Paris may, however, be divided into three classes—first, those supporting the Orleans dynasty; second, the advocates of the exiled Bourbons; and third, the Republicans. One half, if not two thirds, of the whole circulation belongs to the Orleans dynasty, although the individual journals divide on the ministry. A fourth or more may belong to the legitimatists, or Carlists, and the remainder are the republicans. One of the daily journals adheres to Fourierism, or a sort of social democracy; but it has a limited circulation, and more limited influence.

The most profitable, popular, and widely circulated journals are those which occupy a sort of independent position, and are found generally in opposition to the ministry. The same feature marks the Press in London, and also in New York. This is a curious and remarkable fact in the history of modern Journalism in every free and civilized country. . . .

The manner, or mode by which the Parisian Press is conducted, is very different from that of London, but it has some features in common with that of New York. There are probably over three hundred literary persons of all kinds, and every degree of talent and genius, attached to the Paris Press. They are generally composed of young adventurers from the provinces. Thiers, Guizot, and many other distinguished men, commenced their career on the Press, either as contributors of editorial articles, literary reviews, theatrical notices, or *feuilletons,* as the literary portion of the journal here is called. Each journal of importance has an editor, one or two sub-editors, besides several contributors, reporters, and critics, who furnish the diversified character of the sheet. These literary gentlemen go into the best society here, and I have seen some of them at Guizot's *soirées,* at the Tuileries, and in other high walks of life. In this respect, the estimation put upon literary merit is very different in

Paris to what it is in London. In the latter metropolis, none but the
professions—the army and navy—are considered fit to associate on equal
terms with rank and power. Intellect and genius, if not set off with epau-
lettes or throat-cutting instruments, are consigned to the outer regions
of human society, where no gentlemen are found. . . .

The Paris newspapers will, for months, luxuriate in wordy editorials,
full of theory, fine sentiment, and well put language. They do not deal
so much in practical writing, or diversified articles, as the London or
New York Press does. The Spanish marriages, and the extinction of
Cracow, have occupied the newspapers here nearly four months. These
two topics have been turned and twisted again and again, into every
possible shape—the government journals defending, and the opposition
attacking. The discussion is only just coming to a crisis, either in the
retirement of Guizot, or his retention. English or American readers
would soon get sick, tired, and tormented by the eternal iteration of the
same topic—marriage, marriage, marriage—Cracow, Cracow, Cracow!
The collection of foreign or domestic news—the publication of novel and
extraordinary events, in any department of life, which generally form
the staple of English or American journals, are not cared for here—not
attended to—and little heeded. A new idea on an old subject, no matter
how odd, is more sought after than new and frequent occurrences. . . .

The editors, critics, and reporters of the Paris Press write and prepare their articles with comparative leisure, in their little ornamented
cabinets, and then go to work, varnish their boots, put on their white
gloves, sally out to a restaurant to dinner, and close the evening at the
theatre or the salon. There are few who possess the originating, energetic spirit which you sometimes find in London or New York. In one
respect the Paris Press is peculiar. Its editorial columns, and all that
influence, are regularly sold to the highest bidder, in favor of any kind
of speculation—theatrical, financial, or political. The price of theatrical
notices and similar things is regulated on the same principles, precisely,
which rule the price of beef and mutton. I have some curious facts on
the subject.

J. G. B.

And Bennett's picture of the Europe of 1847 reads like a report
on Europe in 1942:

. . . There is an evident restlessness in the minds of men in this
quarter of the world, which must find a vent somewhere, one of these
days. Vesuvius and Ætna generally give some intimation before an erup-
tion. The old and new dynasties of western and central Europe are
giving way to the spirit of the age, bit by bit. From the frontiers of
Russia to the shores of the Atlantic, these ideas are growing and fer-

menting. It is a singular fact, nevertheless it is true, that in Russia and in the United States alone, are the forms of government and the institutions of society considered permanent, settled, and satisfactory to their respective people. Their calmness or forms of government reign paramount. Yet the one is a pure despotism, and the other a pure democracy. A country with a government and institutions at any point between these two extremes, is in a continual ferment—in a constant state of excitement—in one eternal conflict, that never will end till either one or the other extremes is reached. The time is coming when either Russia must overrun all Europe to the ocean, and create a mighty modern empire on the ancient Roman model, or Europe will become a great family of republics, and overrun Russia, and blot out her present existence. In the meantime, let the people of the United States, till then, get the highest prices for their corn and cotton.

PART IV

SLAVERY, SECESSION, AND WAR JOURNALISM

12. Friend of the South

It was nearly midnight when the scratchy pen ceased its spirited journey back and forth across the sheets of paper, and the silver-gray head, the long hooked nose, and squinting eyes were lifted. The New Year's editorial was finished—an editorial filled with the same high spirits and good cheer for the country as a whole, that Bennett felt flowing through his own spare frame.

He looked pridefully about his office, that small, stuffy, and far from tidy room which was the very heart and brain of the *Herald* whose every impulse and action was his to initiate, to formulate, to modify or destroy.

The first half of the nineteenth century was at an end. The year 1850 was a-borning.

Bennett had good reason to be pleased and to view the future with confidence. He was the most talked about editor, his paper the most influential daily, in the whole United States. He was rich—very rich. He had fought his way to the very top of the heap in the face of tremendous odds. He had few real friends, but a host of fawning admirers and an even larger army of bitter opponents. He knew that each day a host of politicians, reformers, preachers, business men, farmers, and laborers would eagerly scan the columns of the *Herald*. He knew, too, that every rival editor in New York waited expectantly for the earliest edition of the *Herald*, to cull, clip, and crib the many items of news which only the *Herald* had been able to acquire.

The *Herald* had long since emerged from the dark and dingy cellar where it was born. It was now housed in an imposing brick and granite structure at the corner of Nassau and Fulton Streets. In huge letters the name of the paper and its proprietor stretched across the entire front of the building. The basement, which extended far out under the street, was filled with printing presses and folding machines, the very latest and best that money could buy. The street floor was devoted exclusively to the business offices (then called counting rooms) where Mrs. Bennett's brother, Robert Crean, supervised some three score cashiers, bookkeepers, ledger clerks, advertising solicitors, and secretaries. The second floor housed the large and busy editorial staff; the offices of Mr. Hudson, the managing editor; the reference library; and the inner sanctum —Mr. Bennett's private office. Directly above was the *Herald's* job-printing plant, once considered a highly lucrative venture, but which was soon to be discarded to make way for the ever-expanding force of the *Herald* itself. The proofreaders were also quartered on the third floor under the watchful eye of Billings Hayward, whose sole aim in life was to keep misspelled words, improper hyphenations, and broken type from disfiguring the pages of the *Herald*.

The top floor housed the compositors (sometimes a hundred) who translated the scrawls of the reporters and editors into type.

The business office was open only twelve hours each day. The presses thundered through the night and early morning hours. Even the editorial offices, which operated on a twenty-four-hour basis, had their hours of quiet. But not so the top floor. It was a beehive of activity day and night, workday, holiday, and Sabbath, as silent men picked steadily away at the type.

The editor-in-chief, referred to behind his back as the Old Man by his associates and employees, drove himself at the same speed he did his entire organization. Each morning at half-past seven he entered his office to begin his daily adventure (for he scorned to call it work). There were the many personal letters to be attended to first. Then followed reports from his large staff of foreign and native correspondents, each to be checked for its timeliness as news, or for its value as an indicator of social, political, or economic trends. A sheet of paper—with instructions to the appropriate editor, with suggestions for verification or elaboration of specific facts, with notes for use in future editorials, or with questions to be sent to the correspondent—was attached to each report by Bennett.

When the heavy volume of mail had been taken care of, the editor would apply himself to the newspapers. These had already been carefully gone over by his assistants, who marked the items they considered of importance. A mid-morning breakfast of dry toast and tea usually accompanied the perusal of the press. As soon as the necessary notations were made, Bennett summoned one of his many secretaries familiar with shorthand which was then called phonography. An editorial assistant who then worked on the *Herald* has described these dictation sessions:

He speaks with some rapidity, making his points with effect, and sometimes smiling, as he raps one of his dear political friends over the knuckles. Having concluded his article with—"that will do," he gives the head of another article and dictates it in a similar way, and then, perhaps, another, and another, till the reporter sighs at the amount of the work he has before him, and he is told that that will be enough for "today."

The presence of another gentleman is now required. He may not be a phonographer, but one who is able to seize the points of a discourse, and fashion them with some force and elegance of expression, or even to illustrate them. Mr. Bennett invites him to a conversation on a particular topic upon which both have been thinking, and then gives his own view, which he desires to see written out. All the while his assistant editor takes notes, so as not to miss the points or spirit of the desired article, and thus having prepared himself with matter enough to fill two columns, he is permitted to withdraw.

A third gentleman is now called. He is, perhaps, engaged in the news department, or in the money article department, or in reporting for the courts. His opinion is wanted as to whether or not there is any subject connected with his department that requires editorial comment. If so he is told to state the case, and the comments are in due season made in such a way as to have an effect where it is most required.

Noon has now arrived, and visits are received for an hour or so, while the collaborators on the journal are completing their labors, which they finish by two o'clock, so that the manuscripts may be inspected. They are taken to Mr. Bennett's room. He reads them, marks them for their several places in the paper, and sends them to the room of the printer. When they have been put into type they are sent down to the editorial rooms for revision, where they are examined once more, and are then seen by the public. Whether they are beheld the next day, or the day after, will depend upon circumstances.

Each afternoon was devoted to a tour of the establishment, from fourth floor to basement. Editors, reporters, printers, pressmen, copyreaders, and the men in the counting room were queried for suggestions or given advice. The tour invariably ended in the office of Frederic Hudson, where the two friends compared notes and decided on all matters of major policy. These conferences usually ended about six o'clock. Then the publisher hurried home to dinner.

In the evening, between eight and nine o'clock, Bennett returned to his office to check last-minute news, to dictate an article, or to pen an editorial over which he had been pondering during the day. Except when big news stories were about to break, he left his office shortly after ten o'clock. The day's work was done.

The decade opened with a bitter struggle in Congress for the speakership of the House of Representatives. The political forces of the North and the South were almost evenly divided. Howell Cobb of Georgia was finally elected by 102 votes to the 100 cast for Robert C. Winthrop of Massachusetts.

Debate began at once on the Fugitive Slave Law and the Wilmot Proviso. Henry Clay presented his famous Compromise which Congress passed but which left only anger and bitterness in the North as well the South. Daniel Webster, on March 7, argued for Clay's position. In this speech Webster argued that "every foot of soil in the United States and the Territories has a settled character as to freedom or slavery," which the laws of man could not change. The Southern and Middle states rejoiced in Webster's declaration and hailed his speech as the greatest of his career. But in the North and especially in New England, the great Daniel was denounced as a traitor. He was compared to Benedict Arnold and to the Devil himself. They called him "a recreant son of Massachusetts." Whittier mourned him in verse as a lost leader and Sumner declared that Webster, by this speech, had struck a fatal blow at freedom and constitutional rights.

Bennett waxed enthusiastic over Webster's stand. The Compromise of 1850, contended the *Herald,* was a sensible proposal which would appeal to the great mass of citizens who valued the preservation of the Union. It struck a body blow at both the "ultra-Southerners" as well as the "fanatical abolitionists." The passage of the Fugitive Slave Bill was likewise subscribed to by Bennett who demanded that President Fillmore use his office to enforce the act. When leading citizens and officials of Massachusetts, Wisconsin, and other states advocated refusal to heed the new law, the *Herald* read the riot act and called them "incendiaries, rebels, and traitors whose opposition to the law was not freedom but anarchy."

The heightened political tension was temporarily relieved by P. T. Barnum's masterly salesmanship in presenting Jenny Lind, "the Swedish nightingale," to America. Barnum's superb showmanship put Jenny Lind on the front pages of every metropolitan paper, including the *Herald.* Bennett was shrewd enough to understand the publicity tricks being used by Barnum to elicit mass audiences for his latest "find." The editor proceeded to lecture Barnum in his editorial columns against the fantastic publicity he was building up for his prodigy, but most of all, Bennett objected to the fabulously high admission prices which were being asked on opening nights. When admission prices were later reduced to three, four, and five dollars, Bennett proclaimed his victory in the *Herald.* Barnum was in no way averse to the editor's campaign against him, for it gave plenty of free publicity and brought even larger throngs to the concerts of Jenny Lind.

When Jenny Lind completed her successful tour of the United States, the press which had received her so enthusiastically, cast her aside with equally spirited disdain. The *Herald's* review of her tour was most caustic: "She has been principally engaged in singing pieces of operas and catches of all kinds, which were considerably more of the clap-trap style than in accordance with the rigid rules of classical music. When she returns to London and makes her reappearance in opera, she will have to prune away a great deal of her ad libitum redundancies in which she indulged during her career in this land."

In September of 1850, the *Herald* scooped both the British and

American press in its publication of the official British Navy List of the War of 1812, thus revealing for the first time, to the public, the extent of the losses to the British in warships and armed vessels during that conflict. According to the report which had been made by the Admiralty to the House of Lords, nearly a quarter of the entire tonnage of the British Navy had been destroyed or captured by the Americans. The *Herald* quoted Sir Charles Napier as having publicly stated that orders had been given to British officers to stay away from American ships when these were found equal in men and guns to their own. Bennett's anti-British feelings paraded jubilantly across the pages of the *Herald* as he blared the devastating report to the public. The facts, he said, must speak for themselves, and they seriously challenged the boasted power and efficacy of the British Navy.

On the home front, the fighting editor launched a bitter attack upon Tammany Hall's candidate for District Attorney, John Graham. The attacks continued up to the very day of the election and were largely responsible for the defeat of the candidate. A few days after the election, on November 9, as Bennett and his wife were walking down Broadway, the defeated candidate accompanied by his two brothers administered a severe cowhiding to the editor. True to form, Bennett told the story in an editorial the next day: "Yesterday morning about ten o'clock, the ninth inst., I was walking down Broadway with my wife. On reaching the corner of Broadway and White Street I was assaulted by a gang of rowdies and ruffians headed by John Graham, late candidate for District Attorney, and his brother De Witt Graham—an employee in the Custom House under Hugh Maxwell—and also Charles K. Graham, another brother, with a ferocity and violence that seemed to justify the belief that murder or manslaughter had been premeditated by the assailants. Two police officers of the Sixth Ward—whose names I do not know—witnessed the assault but made no effort to preserve the peace of the city from such a gang of ruffians."

Bennett's denunciation of Graham was no greater than his ardent advocacy of the election of Fernando Wood as Mayor. Wood, too, was a Tammany candidate and, like Graham, was defeated in

1850. But unlike Graham who would soon be a forgotten figure, Fernando Wood stood on the threshold of a long and lucrative career as Mayor of New York. Municipal politics at the time were of the worst. The Board of Aldermen was commonly referred to as "The Forty Thieves." It sold ferry leases and street-railway franchises to the highest bidder and authorized claims for tremendous but purely fictitious accounts. William (Boss) Tweed was a member of the Board of Aldermen at this time.

Fernando Wood, a tall, handsome, and well-groomed Philadelphian, had aligned himself with the forces of Tammany as soon as he came to New York, and at the early age of twenty-eight had been elected to Congress.

Bennett's support of Fernando Wood was to continue for many years, but the editor had no illusions, personally, as to the type of character he was supporting. Time after time, the *Herald's* editorials had pointed out the low and sordid levels of municipal politics. "Our city legislators," wrote Bennett, "with but few exceptions, are an unprincipled, illiterate, scheming set of cormorants, foisted upon the community through the machinery of primary elections, bribed election inspectors, ballot-box stuffing and numerous other illegal means. . . . The consequence is that we have a class of municipal legislators forced upon us who have been educated in bar-rooms, brothels, and political societies; and whose only aim in attaining power is to consummate schemes for their own aggrandizement and pecuniary gain."

By 1854, Wood had built up such a powerful machine and was so confident of election as Mayor that when opponents made public some of his shady business transactions of earlier years, Wood declared, "The people will elect me Mayor though I should commit a murder in my family between now and the election." The *Herald* again espoused Fernando Wood enthusiastically and closed its eyes to the mass frauds committed at the polls. Wood was declared elected by 1,456 votes.

Old General Webb, choleric with indignation, penned a scathing editorial in the *Courier and Enquirer* which pretty accurately portrayed the feelings of honest and law-abiding voters:

"With a majority of 17,366 against him," wrote Webb, "Mr.

Wood is Mayor! Supported by none but ignorant foreigners and the most degraded class of Americans, Mr. Wood is Mayor! In spite of the most overwhelming proof that he is a base defrauder, Mr. Wood is Mayor! . . . On New Year's Day he will go to City Hall, and he will go there to give the lie, in the face of every man, woman, and child in this city, to the maxim—That Honesty is the Best Policy. Have things indeed come to this? . . . We cannot believe it."

On the national scene, in 1850, many Southerners were clamoring for further territorial expansion of the United States. This expansionist movement cast a covetous eye upon Cuba and the other isles of the West Indies. Strong financial and military support was given to a General Lopez who, in the spring of 1850, led an invading expedition against the Spanish Government in Cuba. James Gordon Bennett, who was a strong expansionist himself, refused to support the Lopez expedition. He believed that the majority of the people of Cuba were loyal to the Spanish Government. So long as that condition prevailed, he maintained, neither the United States nor its individual citizens should foster revolution in Cuba. And in conformity with his long-established policy of acquiring first-hand information about controversial problems and policies, he and Mrs. Bennett sailed for Havana at the end of November, 1850. The editor and his wife were received in regal style by Havana society and the Spanish Court. No other outstanding American publisher had ever visited the island. The powers-that-be were determined to make the stay of their distinguished visitors as pleasant and profitable as was humanly possible. The *Official Court Journal* of Havana declared with true Latin grace: "We had the pleasure of admiring Mrs. Bennett, of New York— so remarkable for her judgment, and whose manifest talents attracted the greatest interest. She was attired with perfect taste, and her exquisite dress was observed with the deepest attention."

Time was when Bennett had shouted from the housetops of New York that it needed more as well as better newspapers. Horace Greeley's success with the *Tribune* had not been entirely to Bennett's liking. When, in September of 1851, Henry J. Raymond and a group of wealthy men launched still another rival morning paper—the *New York Times*—the editor of the *Herald,* as well as the editor of the *Tribune,* was definitely displeased. They had good reason to be displeased. Raymond was no starry-eyed novice to journalism. Young—he was only thirty-one; able—Webb called him the best writer who had ever worked for him; energetic— he had all the driving force of Bennett, but wrote ever so much faster; and experienced—he had worked ten years on newspapers under Greeley and Webb; Henry J. Raymond was bound to at- tract many readers, not a few of whom would come from the fol- lowing of his competitors.

A staunch Whig, of the moderate school, Raymond had a far more pleasing personality than Greeley and was a much better speaker. Thurlow Weed and Seward saw great promise in the young man. He was more to their liking than the erratic Greeley. Accordingly Raymond was drawn into the inner circle of New York state's controlling politicians. Raymond was elected to the Assembly in 1849. The following year he was its Speaker; and in 1854 he was elected Lieutenant-Governor. Greeley—forever hun- gering for political office—permitted Weed to talk him out of mak- ing a fight for the gubernatorial nomination that year. Later, when Greeley said he would accept the Lieutenant-Governorship, Weed talked him out of that too. When the *Tribune's* editor learned, a few days later, that the position had been given to his rival Henry Raymond, he was sure that Seward and Weed had double-crossed him. Greeley complained bitterly that his political life was at an end; and he wrote a long bitter letter to Senator Seward formally dissolving the partnership between himself, Seward, and Weed. Meanwhile he bided his time, waiting six years for the appropriate moment to deliver a political body blow to his former comrades.

With the active backing of George Jones, an Albany banker who had once served on the business staff of the *Tribune,* and a few more prominent business men, Raymond launched the *New York Times* in September, 1851. The paper was capitalized at $100,000, an unbelievably great sum at the time. The best of printing equip- ment was purchased. Raymond picked his editorial staff carefully from among the working journalists of the city, while Jones, with equal care, organized the business office.

Greeley, fearful of what was to come, had notified all his news-boys that if they attempted to handle the newspaper they would automatically forfeit their rights to distribute the *Tribune*. Greeley lost few carriers—but he did lose three of his best editors, a dozen good printers, as well as the assistant foreman of the composing and press rooms, to Raymond.

The whole of New York was liberally drenched with advance notices of the forthcoming publication. The *Times,* it was announced, at a penny per copy would be "at once the best and the cheapest daily family newspaper in the United States."

Raymond, following in the footsteps of Bennett, stressed the *news value* of his paper, and pledged to make it "as good as the best of those now issued in the City of New York." He promised his prospective readers it would not become the champion of every ism that appeared above the horizon, nor would it brazenly attack or sneer at Morality, Religion, Industry or Education. Its policy would rather be one of seeking "to be CONSERVATIVE, in such a way as shall best promote needful REFORM. It will endeavor to perpetuate the good, and to avoid the evil, which the past has developed. While it will strive to check all rash innovation, and to defeat all schemes for destroying established and beneficent institutions, its best sympathies and co-operation will be given to every just effort to reform society, to infuse higher elements of well-being into our political and social organizations, and to improve the condition and the character of our fellow men. Its main reliance for all improvement, personal, social, and political, will be upon Christianity and Republicanism; it will seek, therefore, at all times, the advancement of the one and the preservation of the other. It will inculcate devotion to the Union and the Constitution, obedience to law, and a jealous love of that personal and civil liberty which constitutions and laws are made to preserve. While it will assert and exercise the right freely to discuss every subject of public interest, it will not countenance any improper interference, on the part of the people of one locality with the institutions, or even the prejudices of any other. It will seek to allay, rather than excite, agitation, —to extend industry, temperance, and virtue,—to encourage and advance education; to promote economy, concord, and justice in every section of our country; to elevate and enlighten public sentiments; and to substitute reason for prejudice, a cool and intelligent judgment for passion, in all public action and in all discussions of public affairs."

The *Times,* from its inception, was a serious competitor to the *Herald* and the *Tribune.* Within a fortnight it boasted a circulation of 10,000. This figure was doubled within the first ninety days —a fact which led its editor to boast that only two other papers in the whole country exceeded it in bona fide circulation. But this amazing growth in circulation was due in large measure to the fact that Raymond did not have to worry about income or expenditures. His backers had plenty of money and were prepared to feed the kitty for a long time before expecting any return. Raymond was content to draw only fifty dollars per week as his salary. Despite these advantages, the amounts on the red side of the ledger mounted steadily for more than a year before the tide began to turn. Not until its fifth year did the *Times* show a goodly profit.

Many years later, at the time of Henry Raymond's death in 1869, Bennett, then in his seventy-fourth year, wrote a lengthy obituary of his younger rival. He freely admitted Raymond's superb journalistic qualities but at the same time felt the need to explain to himself as well as his readers the special circumstances which made the success of the *Times* possible.

At the time of its launching in 1851, rationalized Bennett—

. . . The demand for morning newspapers in the city was greater than the supply. The machinery and facilities of the *Herald* establishment, for instance, were not equal to the morning's demand for the *Herald* at that day. The surplus of readers unsupplied offered a fair margin for a new journal, which it was the good fortune of the *Times* to seize upon, and, in bringing forward this new journal, Mr. Raymond's experience had taught him to abandon the old school of the old stage-coach and sailing-ship epoch of the *Courier and Enquirer,* and to fall in with the new school of the *Herald,* of the new epoch of steamships and railways. The *Times* was established on the *Herald* idea of the latest news, and, as Mr. Raymond comprehended it, upon the *Herald* idea of editorial independence. We had, in fact, opened a new placer,—a regular White Pine silver mine; and numerous diggers undertook to work the vein at various points. Thus the *Times* came into the field, and from the margin suggested to begin with a penny paper, it gradually built up a constituency of its own, and became an established success. But had we possessed in 1851 our lightning presses and stereo-typing facilities of the present day, there would have been no opening for the *Times,* as there is no opening here now for a new morning newspaper, except upon an enormous outlay of capital, with the hazards of heavy losses for a year or two, and then a collapse.

Raymond lost no time in joining the other editors in their de-nunciation of the *Herald's* advertising methods. It was, he charged, "the recognized organ of quack-doctors" and by virtue of its almost complete monopoly of this unsavory business compelled these doc-tors to pay a double price for their advertisements. Greeley went even farther claiming that the major portion of the *Herald's* circu-lation was to be found "in houses of infamy, in gambling hells, and in grog shops and drinking saloons of the lowest character." These, said Greeley, are the only ones interested in the advertising columns of the *Herald*—advertising which "no decent paper pub-lishes."

The occasions when any of the other papers were able to scoop the *Herald* on an important piece of news were few and far be-tween. Raymond had one such scoop to his credit. It occurred late in 1854. The steamer "Arctic," enroute to New York from Liv-erpool, with many important Americans aboard, was long over-due. Not a word had been heard from it for weeks. Anxiety and apprehension for the ship, its passengers and crew mounted with each passing day. Rumors circulated that the "Arctic" had been lost at sea. During the night of October 10, the *Times* city night ed-itor was told that a solitary survivor had reached the city, but since he could get no definite verification of this fact, he prepared a brief statement reporting the rumor. His work ended, he boarded a pass-ing horse-car at three in the morning for his home. Up the street, an excited passenger jumped aboard the rear platform of the street-car. The city editor, half-dozing on his seat, was suddenly stirred into alertness as he caught bits of conversation between the con-ductor and the passenger: "'Arctic'"—"Only man who got in"—"*Herald* office."—The City editor was all ears. Damn it all, the *Herald* would once again carry an exclusive story!

Raymond's friend and biographer, Augustus Maverick, told the story shortly after Raymond's death:

Out of the car dashed the *Times* man; down Broadway he tore; across the Park, and up to the printing-room of the *Times* he rushed. There he found the foreman placidly putting on his coat, in preparation for departure. "Stop the Press!" was the first order uttered. "Why?" inquired the foreman. "Because the *Herald* has got hold of a survivor of the 'Arctic,' and is trying one of its old games; but we'll beat yet!"

A bell tinkled; a message went down the speaking-tube which led from the composing-room to cellar; the great press stopped. A workman in the press-room was called up, and these words passed:

"South, you know the *Herald* office; they've got hold of a story about the 'Arctic,' which belongs to all the Press, and they mean to keep it, and cheat us out of it. I want a copy of it. I want you to get it in any way you can; will you do it?"

"How do you know they've got it?"

The circumstances were recited.

"All right!" said South; "I'll get it, provided you don't ask me any questions."

The promise was given. South departed, to return a few minutes afterwards, with the information that the *Herald* office was all alight (the hour was four o'clock in the morning); that the press-room was fast-locked, and that all the carriers and newsboys had been excluded.

"What shall I do?" asked South.

"Get the first copy of the *Herald* that comes off the press," was the order instantly given. "Buy it, beg it, steal it! anything, so long as you get it; and tomorrow you shall have fifty dollars for your trouble."

"Enough said," observed South.

Twenty minutes later, he appeared in the office of the *Times* (then at the corner of Beekman and Nassau Streets) with a copy of the *Herald,* containing Mr. George H. Burns's narrative of the loss of the "Artic," entire, printed in double-leaded type.

Meanwhile, the whole force of the *Times'* compositors had been routed out of their beds, by messengers sent in urgent haste; each man stood at his "case," "stick" in hand, and when South returned, waving the next morning's *Herald* triumphantly over his head, a mighty "Hurrah!" went up, which might have been heard for several blocks. The *Herald* "copy" was cut up into four-line "takes"; in an hour the whole story was in type; and the people of the *Herald,* blissfully unconscious that a copy of that journal had been adroitly abstracted, withheld all their city circulation until nine A.M., sending off only the mail copies containing the long-expected relation of the dreadful disaster. By eight o'clock in the morning, the *Times* was procurable at all the news-

stands in the city, and its subscribers had received the news an hour
before. Edition after edition of the *Times* was called for; and its Hoe
press ran without intermission from seven o'clock in the morning until
two o'clock in the afternoon, to supply the continual demand.

Several years later, in 1861, Henry Raymond seized upon what
he thought was a most favorable opportunity to attack Bennett
in retaliation for the many barbed shafts which the *Herald's* editor
had aimed at the *Times*.

Readers of the December 11 issue were amazed to find the usually
sedate front page of the *Times* given over largely to two caricature
drawings of Bennett. The first of these pictured him in kilts and
full Scotch regalia busily engaged in blowing up a large bag labeled "the *Herald*." A pair of horns peeped out from either side
of his tam o'shanter. The caption of the cartoon, in heavy type,
declared:

BROTHER BENNETT (PROFANELY STYLED "THE SATANIC") INFLATING HIS
WELL-KNOWN FIRST-CLASS, A NO. 1 WIND-BAG, HERALD.

There followed several quotations from Bennett's paper:

From the Herald, Nov. 2.

Whether the *Tribune* or the *Times* has the larger circulation, we are
unable to decide. According to recent accounts, they both of them distribute somewhere between twenty-five and thirty thousand daily.

Of this we are not certain, but concerning the *Herald*, there can be
no doubt. Its daily sale of papers averages from one hundred and five
thousand to one hundred and thirty-five thousand.

From the Herald, Nov. 3.

It remains doubtful whether the *Times* or *Tribune* will be discovered
to be ahead, but in no case will it appear that both of them together
have one-half as many subscribers as the *Herald*, which sells from one
hundred and five thousand to one hundred and thirty-five thousand of
its daily issue.

From the Herald, Thursday, Nov. 7.

We have attained a daily issue as high as one hundred and thirty-
five thousand. Next to the *Herald* comes the *Tribune* and the *Times*,
but far in the rear, for we presume that neither the *Times* nor the
Tribune can boast of an average beyond twenty-five thousand dailies.

From the Herald, Saturday, Nov. 9.

In regard to our circulation, we did not say that it was one hundred and thirty-five thousand every day; but that it exceeded one hundred thousand every day.

Then in much larger type the *Times* went on to declare:

How the Aforesaid First-Class Wind-Bag Was Punctured by the Following Wagers Offered by the Times.

$2,500 that the *Herald's* daily issue is not...........135,000
2,500 that it is not..............................105,000
2,500 that it is not..............................100,000
2,500 that it is not.............................. 75,000
2,500 that the *Times'* average daily issue is over...... 25,000
2,500 that it is over............................. 30,000
2,500 that it is over............................. 40,000
2,500 that it is over............................. 50,000
2,500 that it is over............................. 75,000

The conditions of the wager were that half the amount be deposited in a bank, and that the whole sum be handed over by the winner to aid destitute families of volunteers in the Federal Army.

The second cartoon on the front page of the *Times* was labeled:

Disastrous Result!

Brother Bennett Resorts to the Consolations of Religion

It showed the wind-bag punctured and collapsed, while Bennett himself, exhausted and dying, lay beside it on the ground.

Below the cartoon were two more quotations from Bennett's journal:

From the Herald, Dec. 5.

Betting, even when fair, is against our religion, and we cannot consent to let him have the information he seeks in that way.

From the Herald, Dec. 7.

Mr. Mephistopheles Greeley and that little villain Raymond are greatly moved upon the subject of the relative circulation of the *Herald* and their own petty papers, and are affected to tears about the matter. We are sorry for them; but their attempts to inveigle us into a silly bet are absolutely in vain. The practice of betting is immoral. We cannot approve of it. It may suit Greeley and Raymond, who have exhibited very little morality in the conduct of their journals, but it will not do for us.

Many a *Times* reader wrote in protesting against such a low and stupid performance on the part of their editor. The attack didn't hurt Bennett or the *Herald*. Certainly it gained no new readers for Raymond's paper. He soon thereafter regretted having indulged in the attack.

Bennett was far from dead; and the influence of the *Herald,* because of its extensive and factual news coverage, spanned the continent. British, French, Italians, and Latin Americans in large measure saw the United States only as reflected in the columns of the *Herald*. It was the only American paper available in every large city throughout the world.

The vitriolic editor was the object of every tongue and every eye, no matter where he went in his adopted land. George Washington Bungay, a well-known free-lance artist and writer during the forties and fifties, told how vast crowds would gather in front of the hotels where Bennett would stop on his frequent trips about the country. "Whether he be more notorious than popular," wrote the cautious Bungay in 1854, "I will not assume the province of determining, but I will hazard the remark that the people of the United States would go farther and give more to see him than they would to see the President or any member of the United States Senate."

The abuse heaped upon Bennett in the North melted away perceptibly below the Mason-Dixon line. To the plantation and slave-owning gentlemen of the South, the editor of the *Herald* was a courageous, intelligent, and noble man. They liked his paper and they liked him, even as they hated and reviled Greeley, Bryant, Raymond, and Webb. One of these Southern gentlemen—from Charleston, South Carolina—published a book in 1852 entitled *Glimpses of New York* wherein, with considerable wit and perspicacity, he analyzed the leading personalities and institutions of the metropolis. His flattering description of Bennett is completely out of tune with the rest of the book, but that fact in itself is a clue to the high esteem Bennett enjoyed in the South.

At the head of the heap stands James Gordon Bennett, and by his side stands that engine of terror to all evil-doers, the *Herald,* and there they are likely to remain as firm as the Rock of Gibraltar. Bennett is undeniably the "Napoleon of the Press." Forrest, in one of his pithy speeches, said "he was the best abused man in the world"; but this remark will apply much more justly to Bennett. Since I have had the opportunity to become acquainted with his private character, I will give you my idea of him as a man—it being utterly unnecessary to speak of him as an editor, for the world knows him in that light. In his habits he is as regular as the sun, or as the clock on Trinity Church; yea, more so, that sometimes varies—he never does! Moral in his conduct as any man you can find in a day's travel, even in this dense population; and I would rely upon his word with as much assurance of its being correct as I would upon John C. Calhoun's. To his family and friends his purse has no bottom, and I believe he has given as much or more to charitable purposes unostentatiously than Jenny Lind. I had as soon go to Bennett, though comparatively a stranger with no claims upon him, for a favor, as to any man I ever met. I do not speak this from the card, but from having heard others speak, who had received his benefaction. In his intercourse and dealings with fellow men, he is particularly correct; he pays his printers, and, in fact, all who are in his employment, not only the best prices for their services, but promptly and without a wry face. It is proverbial with the printers that he who works on the *Herald* is "sure of his pay." I do not eulogize this as a virtue; I only mention it because, from what has been said of Bennett, it is wrongly thought by some that his is tricky, and not disposed to deal squarely with mankind in general.

I would as soon attempt to bribe Bennett to write or publish anything contrary to correct principles, as to induce the President of the United States to commit high treason.

As a politician (we cannot rank him as a statesman exactly), he has as clear perception and foresight as any editor in America. His course for the last half dozen years has been strictly national. The policy adopted by our Government, in many instances, originated with and was advocated by him. His ideas of retrenchment and reform of governmental abuses are lucid and practicable, and must, if our Government exists much longer, be adopted. The manner in which he advocates measures smacks of Salamagundi, ex necessitate rei, having various editors, and not infrequently is Jack-Randolpish! His style is not purely Anglo-Saxon, because he has not time to digest and critically correct his composition. His leaders are never stale or rehashed, and nine hundred and ninety-nine editors out of a thousand in the month's time would become dumbfounded, or be compelled to revamp their leaders. Not so with Bennett. He is always new—ever varied and spicy. Ridicule is one of his great fortes, which is the strongest lever to operate effectually on the minds of men.

At about the same time that *Glimpses of New York* was coming off the presses, someone else, also anonymous, drove up to the main entrance of the *Herald,* just after Mr. Bennett had entered the building. The cab driver called to one of the clerks, and handed him a small cylindrical package addressed to Bennett and marked "Private and With Care." Above the address was written, "Native silver and copper ore from the Cuba Mountains with letter inside the box."

Bennett tore off the outer wrapping which disclosed a small pasteboard box marked, "Specimens and private documents from the interior of Havana for Mr. Bennett (only). Should he be out of town keep for him."

After a few vain attempts to remove the lid, the editor turned the box over to Frederic Hudson, who started cutting off the lid with his pen-knife. A thin trickle of what looked like white sand poured out through the opening. Hudson became suspicious, and threw a small quantity into the fireplace, where it exploded with a loud flash. Detectives were called. The box was soaked in water and then carefully opened. It was an ingeniously constructed infernal machine, filled with enough explosives to have killed anyone close at hand when it was opened.

The would-be assassin was never apprehended, although Bennett later claimed to know his name. The whole episode—unlike the many thrashings which had been inflicted on the editor—was played down and hushed up by the *Herald.* Bennett was quite obviously shaken by his narrow escape, but to his friends and enemies alike he boldly announced, "We will not be deterred from the performance of our duty, were we aware that there was a whole manufactory of torpedoes in full operation for our benefit."

During the year 1850-51, the *Herald* devoted much space and many editorials to advocating enlargement of the Erie and Black River Canals. Its persistent advocacy of these measures, which, it argued, would benefit farmers, laborers, and merchants alike, forced the State Legislature to authorize expenditures for these improvements in the summer of 1851.

To Bennett, too, must go the credit (which many Americans now concede to be a dubious honor) of suggesting that the United States send an expedition to Nippon to explore the possibilities of breaking that island kingdom's century-long isolation from the rest of the world. The articles stirred up a great deal of discussion among exporters, importers, and maritime interests. Soon Washington was buzzing with the novel idea. President Fillmore and his cabinet agreed to it, and soon thereafter Commodore Matthew Calbraith Perry was on his way to the Land of the Rising Sun.

When Louis Kossuth, the celebrated Hungarian patriot, arrived in New York, December 5, 1851, he was greeted with a popular enthusiasm exceeded only by that which had greeted La Fayette in 1825. The warm-hearted and liberty-loving Americans cheerfully subscribed to the bonds Kossuth sold to them. They were eager to help the oppressed Hungarians gain their freedom from the despotic Hapsburgs. Kossuth even spoke to a special meeting of Congress, assembled in his honor. The press of the Republic gave him a tremendous build-up wherever he went. That is, all except the *New York Herald*.

Once again Bennett was roundly denounced by his newspaper rivals. He was called a tory, a reactionary, a tool of monarchy, an unwanted and unwelcome adopted son of the republic, who had never learned the meaning of freedom and brotherhood. But these charges failed to deter him. Bennett, far better than any other editor in the country, knew European politics from first-hand observation as well as close study. He contended that the Hungarian patriot, by a series of foolish acts and speeches, was himself largely responsible for the collapse of the short-lived Hungarian Revolution. He had, said Bennett, not only alienated a large and important segment of the Hungarians themselves, but more than this he had forced the Hapsburgs into a close political alliance with the Russian Czar—all of which spelled defeat for the Hungarians as well as increased oppression and persecution against enlightened Austrians as well. Bennett was particularly opposed to the sale of bonds by Kossuth to Americans—bonds which, he contended, were worthless and could never be redeemed. And when Kossuth, who lost all sense of proportion as to his own importance under the bright glare of publicity, began lecturing Americans on how to run their own country—Bennett became furious. His editorials grew more stinging. His correspondents and reporters played up every false, absurd, or derogatory utterance made by Kossuth. Before a year had passed, many other papers were becoming critical of the Hungarian, too. By the time he left the United States in 1853 the great wave of popularity had completely subsided. In fact, Kossuth left under a cloud of rumors, misapprehension, and ill feeling (largely unjustified) to which James Gordon Bennett and the *Herald* were the most potent contributors.

Meanwhile the political pot was boiling as never before. Except for the Deep South, where voters were few and homogeneous in their economic interests, political confusion was the order of the day, with New York the most confused of all. Whigs and Democrats were still the two major parties—but within each of these there were bitterly contesting factions, slashing and bludgeoning each other with unremitting fury. The very names of the factions —then so all-important—sound meaningless today. There were the Hard Shells and the Soft Shells as well as the Half Shells. There were Wooly Heads and Silver Grays. There were Know-Nothings and Temperance Men. And there were Anti-Renters, City Reformers, United Americans, German-Democrats, and Republicans.

The *Herald* claimed that the Know-Nothings were an offshoot of the Order of United Americans. The latter, by its constitution, forbade its lodges to participate in politics. Its members were able to evade this provision by founding an outside secret organization. They called themselves the Know-Nothings. Their chief aims were, first, direct hostility to all Catholics, and, second, to pledge their support to no man who was not an American of three generations.

Bennett, for all his bias against the Catholics, looked upon the Know-Nothing Movement as utterly at odds with the whole spirit and purpose of the Declaration of Independence and the Constitution of the United States. He assigned reporters to dig up the facts about the secret political society. Not a week passed during the years 1851 to 1854 that the *Herald* failed to blast the Know-Nothings.

As time for the presidential nominations of 1852 rolled around it became apparent that the Democrats were almost evenly divided in their allegiance to James Buchanan, Lewis Cass, and Stephen A. Douglas. Their nominating convention in June was deadlocked, till an appropriate dark horse in the person of Franklin Pierce of New Hampshire was accepted as a suitable compromise candidate. Brave, courtly, engaging; a New Englander, and yet very friendly to the South—such was General Franklin Pierce. Bennett had known Pierce for many years, saw in him a suitable candidate for the presidency, and threw the weight of the *Herald* on the scales for Pierce from the very start of the campaign.

The Whigs, likewise torn with dissension, met in convention a fortnight after the Democrats. To Seward and Weed, those astute political wire-pullers and manipulators from New York State, goes the credit for putting over on the Whigs the candidate who, quite unknowingly, wrecked their party. Their candidate was none other than old "Fuss and Feathers," General Winfield Scott. The hero of the Mexican War accepted, but soon discovered the appalling difference between a military and a political campaign.

Horace Greeley, still a power among northern Whigs, had declared through the columns of the *Tribune* early in 1850 that there could be no compromise on the matter of extending slavery to the territories. No candidate must ever be endorsed who supported such a measure. Better by far, argued Greeley, to see "the Union a thousand times shivered" than assist those who would plant Slavery on Free Soil. Hence, when the Whig convention declared in favor of the very measure which Greeley had so long denounced, and when it selected as its standard bearer the Southerner, General Scott, there were many who expected the *Tribune* to make an open break with the Whigs. Greeley was disappointed and disgusted, but he went along, albeit far from enthusiastically, for the Whig candidate.

No sooner had the news of General Scott's candidacy been announced than the *Herald* launched a full-scale attack against him. It cited the views expressed in a letter written by Scott ten years

earlier. The general had then written that in his opinion all natu-
ralization laws should be repealed and all foreign born should be
forbidden the right to become citizens or to vote. The only exceptions to these rules, Scott wrote, should be for those foreigners who
had served a minimum of two years in the armed forces of the
United States.

The only chance for the Whigs to win the election of 1852 depended upon lining up the heavy foreign-born vote in New York,
Pennsylvania, Ohio, Indiana, and Illinois. Something had to be
done—and quickly—to counteract the action of the *Herald*. Scott's
campaign managers settled upon a line of action never before used.
They decided to send the old general on a barnstorming tour
through the West, to win over the heavy contingent of German and
Irish voters. But, of course, it was at no time to be admitted that
the trip was made for that purpose, so a suitable excuse was found.
The general had been at one time appointed by Congress as one
member of a committee to select a site for a Western Military
Asylum. Here was the excuse, ready-made.

Blue Lick Springs, Kentucky, was one of the spots under consideration for the asylum. The General, with a huge retinue of
advisers, campaign managers, political hangers-on, publicity men,
musicians, and newspapermen, set out for Blue Lick Springs.

Bennett had reporters on hand to cover the more than half a hundred stops made by the train as it zigzagged from town to town.
And at every stop old "Fuss and Feathers" solemnly explained to
the waiting throng that he was not on any campaign tour. The
Herald reporters gleefully announced the speeches were all of a
pattern. General Scott extolled his love of all Americans, but there
were none so fine as the sturdy sons of Europe who had fled
tyranny to enjoy the blessings of a New World, where all persons
were equal. He revelled in the rich brogue of the Irish or the thick
guttural notes of the Germans. He shook hands with them. He
praised their intelligence. He welcomed them as fellow Americans.

It was a wearing journey, a tragi-comedy, and the brave warrior
himself must have marveled at the words and sentiments his lips
uttered. When the journey ended, the *Herald* printed a lengthy
report (which was widely reprinted) under the title:

The Modern Epic

Fifty-Two Speeches of Major General Winfield Scott, Embracing a Narrative of a Trip to the Blue Licks and Back to Washington in Search of a Site for a Military Hospital.

The Illiad of the Nineteenth Century

General Scott's statements, his southern background; and the fact that the Whigs had declared in favor of the 1850 Compromise Act— all these things counted for nothing in the eyes of James Gordon Bennett. To him, the fact that Greeley and other abolitionists gave their support to Scott was proof positive that Scott must be defeated. In fact, since it was the Seward-Weed combination which had nominated Scott, Bennett argued that the General was merely the mouthpiece of those two dangerous abolitionist demagogues. Sewardism was killing the Whigs. But the issue—the real issue of the campaign according to Bennett was one of Sewardism and Disunion versus the Constitution and the Union.

When the votes rolled in, the Whigs and their candidate were completely inundated. Pierce carried every state but Kentucky. Tennessee, Vermont, and Massachusetts. The tragic defeat was augmented by the fact that the two great national leaders of the Whigs, Henry Clay and Daniel Webster, died on the eve of the election which sounded the death knell of their party.

The Democrats were jubilant but none more so than the tall thin man with the squint eyes, who ruled the destiny of the *New York Herald*. To his great army of readers he gave forth the glad tidings. The people—the common people—by their good sense had repudiated those mad and reckless forces of abolitionism, who cared not if they wrecked the Union, so long as they could abolish slavery. Sewardism was defeated. Abolitionism was defeated. Sectionalism was dead. The Compromise of 1850 had been endorsed by the electorate. And the new president, Franklin Pierce, would be the spokesman of a united people!

The new president, shortly after his election, wrote to a friend: "I have not been insensible to the vast influence of the *Herald* throughout the late canvass. Will you assure Mr. B. when you write him that I appreciate both the motive and the ability, and at the same time present to him my sincere acknowledgements."

There were other issues, too, about which the American people argued during these years. Over cracker barrels and cider barrels; atop the rail fence and around the roaring fireplace; at debating and elocution societies; at lyceums; at church socials and at husking bees—young America as well as the older folk talked about such new-fangled things as postage stamps and the Women's Rights Movement. The latter had already given birth to a group of dauntless pioneers: Lucretia Mott, Elizabeth Cady Stanton, Martha Wright, Susan B. Anthony, and Lucy Stone. And there was also Mrs. Amelia Bloomer, who, not content to struggle for mere political equality for her sisters, argued that there was equal need to free their bodies from the shackles of thralldom by adopting a new garb suitable for the new freedom that was soon to be theirs. Serving as her own fashion plate she designed and wore (to the consternation of many and the amusement of some) a costume consisting of a straw hat, a short jacket, a knee-length skirt, gaiters, and loose Turkish trousers. Bloomerism was a much-debated question in the early fifties.

Spiritualism with its raps and taps was founded in 1849 by the Fox sisters. Almost overnight the spirit world was knocking on walls and doors and tables in the dim or darkened rooms of a thousand mediums to the utter amazement of the curious masses, come to behold these strange phenomena. Legislatures debated the merits of a law to suppress impostors.

Another large section of the public was captivated by vegetarianism. Then came Dr. Graham (with a type of flour which bears his name) to teach America not only *how* to eat but *what* to eat. Devotees of hydropathy claimed that water was the only true cleansing and healing fluid. The drugs and medicines of the pharmacopoeia were frauds. Water alone was the cure-all. Alcohol was roundly condemned. The Temperance Movement swept like a prairie fire across the northern states during 1851-1853.

To these many movements, the *Herald* devoted a great deal of attention. It refused to take up the cudgels on behalf of any of them. It reported their growth, their claims and counter-claims, and it told its readers much about the leading personalities in these many crusades. But the *Herald* itself laughed good-naturedly at all of them.

One of the most unique social philosophies of the day was that introduced to the United States by Albert Brisbane, father of Arthur Brisbane. It was known as Fourierism, named after its founder the Frenchman, Charles Fourier. It proposed to solve the social, economic, and political problems of the world by reorganizing society into a series of more or less self-contained communistic communities, known as Phalanxes. Brisbane interested Horace Greeley, Charles A. Dana, Ralph Waldo Emerson, Nathaniel Hawthorne, James Russell Lowell, and many other eminent writers in his pet scheme. A number of Fourierist communities were established during the 1840's. One of the largest and most successful, the North American Phalanx, was in New Jersey.

The *Herald* devoted a great deal of space to what went on at the Phalanxes, in part because it was colorful and unique and, in part, because Greeley espoused Fourierism. On one occasion (August 30, 1852) nearly four full columns were devoted to "A Day at the Phalanx." The *Herald's* correspondent began his story by telling how a member of the Phalanx asked him if he was a *Herald* reporter.

"Do you expect him?" I asked.
"Oh, yes, he will be here. . . ."
"Why do you think he will be here?"
"A reporter has been here every time a lecture was given, and Horace Greeley lectures here tonight. The *Herald* is the only paper that sends a reporter, and its reports have brought us more visitors than we can accommodate."

Shortly thereafter the celebrated editor arrived.

He did not wear the old white coat, but was so dandified that I scarcely knew him. He wore a superfine black dress coat and black pantaloons, with a stylish white vest; he was not only shaved (with a fashionable goatee beneath his chin, whose foxy redness curiously contrasted with his extremely pale face) but he had on a clean shirt and a fashionable brown leghorn hat, with a low crown. In this disguise I would not have recognized him, but for his hobbling gait, his bent figure, and my attention being attracted by the fact of a person in such a dress carrying a bundle under his arm done up in a dirty pocket handkerchief, and a huge pair of filthy boots, which furnished a striking comment upon the other parts of his dress.

The emancipated females, both young and old, all wore bloomers. This was "the first thing that strikes one on entering the precincts of the Phalanx." The reporter tried to be broad-minded, but reluctantly concluded that the Bloomer costume "is not half so becoming to the female figure as the long dress, which was evident from the improvement in appearance of the young ladies when they doffed it at another period of the day, and assumed the more feminine garb. As for the elderly ladies, it makes them look so much worse, that if they 'saw themselves as others see them,' they would never wear it again. It is only tolerable on very young girls, and, even in their case, it might well be dispensed with. . . ."

Even the men were non-conformists. Some wore long beards extending down their breasts. Some wore their hair in ringlets down their backs. Others wore their hair and beards "like Christians." All in all, their variety in dress was as diversified as their variety in ideas.

Among the many discussions going on about the place was one between Professor Conquest Cross of Kentucky, "a southern Whig and slaveholder, and a group of Fourierists. One of the latter threatened the South with Northern arms "if abolition should not be soon carried, and the doctor from Kentucky returned the compliment with a very effective fire. He said he should like to see the Northerns leaving their homes, and coming on a *filibustero* expedition to the South. They would never go back alive."

ABOLITIONIST—But England would help us. She hates slavery.

DR. CROSS—England would help you! No, she would help us.

ABOLITIONIST—But England hates injustice and hates slavery.

DR. CROSS—She loves herself more than she hates either. I want to know what you would do with the slaves if they were set free? We all want to set them free, if it can be done.

ABOLITIONIST—I would do nothing with them; I would leave them to do for themselves.

DR. CROSS—Then you would be more cruel to them than we are who take care of them. The best argument against their emancipation is the condition of your colored population in New York and Massachusetts. They are not practically free. You will not eat, or drink, or associate with them. They are debased thieves and drunkards. This is what your emancipation does for them.

ANOTHER ABOLITIONIST—I would rather have six niggers about me than one Irishman.

MR. BLANCHARD—I don't blame the Southern people for slavery so much as the New York merchants who encourage it. I only blame the Southern people because they prefer English manufactures to those of their own countrymen.

DR. CROSS—We only prefer our own interests, just as you do yours. You have no claim upon us, for you do us all the injury you can. We purchase in the cheapest market and sell in the dearest.

MR. BLANCHARD—But we are all of one country, and we ought to study each other's interests.

DR. CROSS—That is the consolidation doctrine, which I do not hold, though I have been a whig for thirty years. This policy only tends to make the federal government powerful at the expense of the sovereign independent States.

The accommodations, activities, and aspirations of the Fourierists was then presented in a friendly fashion. Greeley's speech, which was reported in full, is unimportant, but the description of the *Tribune* editor as a public speaker is interesting:

Mr. Greeley then rose, and was speechless for a few moments, looking around the audience in a kind of vacant stare. At last he broke silence, in a low, indistinct tone of voice, and with a furious motion of his body, swaying backwards and forwards, as if it were impossible for him to stand perpendicular and erect. There seemed to be a hinge in his middle, and whenever he put his head forward his whole body, down to his waist, went with it; when he drew back his head the same hinge-like motion was visible about his middle, and some of his audiences must have felt alarmed lest he should break in two at that particular point, like a tree cut almost through with the ax. He is not a very effective speaker, being apparently incapable of eloquence, either in manner or matter. He has a good deal of stammering and hesitation, and his voice is so weak that he cannot be heard at any distance. There is an affectation of simplicity of language and style, but it so borders on the colloquial or mere commonplace conversation, that it does not tell on the audience, especially if it be an educated and enlightened one.

To the rapidly growing metropolis, the transportation problem and the crime problem were becoming increasingly important in the early fifties. Transit companies lashed at each other and openly bribed and threatened to win the right of operating their horse-cars on the main streets. The franchise for Broadway was looked upon as the most lucrative. One company offered to pay the city one hundred thousand dollars per year for ten years for that franchise. William Tweed and his fellow members on the Board of Aldermen quite openly sold these valuable public rights to the highest bidder. As the year 1852 drew to a close, the *Herald* reported with a note of dismay that the grand total of six hundred and fifty omnibuses were rattling through the streets of New York. It demanded more horse-cars. Soon thereafter a new line was installed extending from City Hall as far north as 23rd Street.

On November 11, 1853, the *Herald* announced that after that date, all of the city's police were to wear uniforms. The uniform selected consisted of a blue coat with brass buttons, gray trousers, and a blue cap. The cap was to carry the number of the officer as well as the word "police" in large letters. This action by the Board of Police Commissioners was truly revolutionary. So revolutionary, in fact, that almost the whole police force revolted against it. They held meetings, they signed petitions, they wrote letters to the press declaring that no respectable American would wear livery and that the action by their superiors was a violation of their rights as free men. The controversy continued for several weeks. The Board was adamant. Many police resigned their jobs. The others reluctantly yielded to the innovation.

The verdict of the voters in the 1852 election was accepted with little grumbling on the part of the losers. The bitterness and turbulence died down. To the outward eye, Bennett's analysis was fundamentally correct: sectional warfare had given way to national unity. Not since 1830 had the ever-present issue of slavery been so completely relegated to the background as a major problem. Even President Fillmore, in his last message to Congress in December, 1852, passed it by without mention.

The dead calm was short-lived, broken on the one hand by the hotheads from the South who were determined to press home their victory; on the other, by the astute undercover moves of Seward to bring about action in Congress which would arouse the country.

And, last of all, by President Pierce's open support to the pro-slavery forces.

As so often in the past, the controversial issue came to the foreground in the discussion as to the organization of new states. Senator Stephen A. Douglas, on January 4, 1854, presented a bill on the question of the organization of the Nebraska Territory. The report, while claiming to function within the Compromise Act of 1850, was in actuality so drawn that it could easily be interpreted otherwise. During the debate, Senator Dixon of Kentucky proposed an amendment which would repeal the Act of 1850 in so far as it prohibited slavery in any of the territories of the United States. Douglas incorporated Dixon's proposal in a new bill which opened up a whole new section of western lands to slavery. It was Seward who had suggested the amendment to Dixon knowing well that this proposal would plunge the country once again into the "irrepressible conflict."

Political organizations were again riddled by the slavery issue. The *New York Evening Post* and many other northern Democratic papers broke with their party. The despised Abolitionists overnight won many new recruits, augmenting their ranks not only from the vast masses of the foreign born, laboring and agricultural groups, but also from merchants, bankers, and professional men. The stage was set for the rise of a new party. Its program was already drafted in an editorial published in the *National Era* which denounced the Douglas Bill as a gross violation of a sacred pledge and a criminal betrayal of precious rights. It was, wrote the fiery Abolitionist journal, "part and parcel of an atrocious plot to exclude from a vast unoccupied region immigrants from the Old World and free laborers from our own States, and convert it into a dreary region of despotism inhabited by masters and slaves."

When in March, the Kansas-Nebraska Bill (for such it was called) was passed by the Senate amid the boom of cannon fired by Southern enthusiasts, Senator Chase of Ohio remarked to the senior senator from New York, "They celebrate a present victory, but the echoes they await shall never rest until slavery itself shall die."

Even the *Herald* doubted the wisdom of the action by Congress

and of President Pierce in supporting it. Bennett had no sympathy
for the abolitionists, to be sure, but he was equally firm, at least for
the moment, in wanting to see no further extension of slavery. The
situation brought about a short-lived peace between Greeley and
Bennett. Both rallied behind the standard of the Republican Party
which entered the campaign of 1856. Greeley was enthusiastic about
the Party and its standard-bearer, General John C. Fremont. The
editor of the *Herald* went along reluctantly. He accepted the Republicans as the lesser evil.

Bennett, while shifting his political alliance, did not for a moment give up blasting against the abolitionists. At the very time
when that movement was gaining momentum almost everywhere,
the *Herald's* editor felt sure it was falling apart. Early in 1855 he
wrote a lengthy article to prove his point. As evidence he cited
recent curtailments affecting the abolitionist newspapers in New
York City:

> Abolitionism in the North is in a state of decay—rapid decay. The
> present hard times have put it to the test, and it is sinking under the
> pressure. This fact has been strikingly illustrated within the last few
> months, in the curtailment of the daily anti-slavery journals of this city.
> The last and most striking example among them being the cutting down
> of the *Journal of Commerce,* to the extent of about one-third from its
> late ambitious but ruinous dimensions.
>
> In the matter of curtailment the *Tribune* led the way, in a marked
> reduction of its size, and in the substitution of a cheap and inferior
> quality of paper in place of a comparatively expensive article. Next, our
> junior Seward organ,—the *Times,* adopted the same expedient of "mak-
> ing both ends meet." Next the *Sun* in the reduction of its sheet, at a
> single blow diminished its annual bill for white paper to the extent of
> ten or twelve thousand dollars. Lastly, the *Journal of Commerce,* the
> founder of the whole school of our modern anti-slavery journals, has
> from the same cause been driven to the same extremity. It opens the
> New Year very considerably shorn of its fair proportions. Another such
> downward step, including its limited and rather private circulation, will
> bring it fairly within reach of that "Robert Macaire" of Wall Street, the
> *New York Express.*

The year Bennett reached his sixtieth birthday (1855), there was
founded London's first successful penny paper, the *Daily Telegraph.*

Its founder, J. M. Levy, boasted of the fact that his new journal was an imitation of the highly successful *New York Herald*.

The greatest failure of the year fell to P. T. Barnum who went bankrupt to the tune of more than half a million dollars. The editor of the *Herald* took advantage of the misfortune to write a moralistic editorial on

THE FALL OF BARNUM

The author of that book glorifying himself as a millionaire from the arts and appliances of obtaining money under false pretenses, is, according to his own statements in court, completely crushed out. All the profits of all his Fejee Mermaids, all his wooly horses, Greenland whales, Joyce Heaths, Negroes turning white, Tom Thumbs, and monsters and impostures of all kinds, including the reported $70,000 received by the copyright of that book, are all swept away, Hindoo palace, elephants, and all, by the late invincible showman's remorseless assignees. It is a case eminently adapted to "point a moral or adorn a tale."

It was in 1855 that an anonymous gift of a ten-piece silver service set valued at more than $1,500 was given to Bennett. Each piece bore an engraved sentiment, highly flattering to the editor. He was called "the advocate of right and justice," "the truthful exponent of American interests," "the most abused editor in America" and "an example to the rising generation." All in all, it was a grand tribute, though skeptics maintained the old man had sent it to himself.

Less pleasant were the many libel suits brought against the *Herald* and its publisher. One of these, brought in 1853, won $10,000 for the plaintiff but was later reduced, by court order, to $6,000. The case, which attracted nation-wide attention, also brought back into the public eye the long-forgotten but notorious Ellen Jewett case.

The libel case itself opened as sensationally as any drama. It began, not in court, but in a lengthy communication, published in Greeley's *Tribune* on the morning of February 23, 1855, under the title of: A CARD FROM MR. FRY. Addressing himself "To the Public," Mr. Fry wasted no words in opening up his attack:

When James Gordon Bennett of the *New York Herald*, whose course as editor drove one weak-minded man to commit suicide, and caused nine other able-bodied ones to horsewhip him through the streets of

New York—when this man, some 6 years ago, discovered in me the first operatic or theatrical manager who dared to refuse him black-mail, and one who had ignored the very existence of his polluted journal, by withholding from it advertising and denying to any of its editorial or reporting crew the privilege of the free-list—when this Ishmaelite of the Press perceived his black-mail occupation in danger, he formed the deliberate plan to attack me through the columns he controlled. With diabolic malignity he sought to ruin my business, and blast my character, lest other managers might follow my example, and withdraw from his job-office the theatrical printing, the black-mail profits upon which—or profits over and above what any printer should charge—to the extent of $12,000. to $20,000. a year, have built up and sustained, and are still a chief support of his paper. . . .

Bennett, according to Fry, had repeatedly charged in the *Herald* that the Astor-place Opera House, which Fry managed, was the common resort of prostitutes and gamblers. Nor was that all, for he had also written that when Fry appeared before the audience to address them, it was "in his favorite character—of an ape"; that Fry himself was "a half-starved musical adventurer, who could not pay his landlady his board bill."

Fry unfolded before the readers of the *Tribune* a long and sordid tale of vicious libels committed against him by the publisher of the *Herald*. By virtue of these many attacks made against him, Fry claimed losses to himself in excess of $25,000. His patience exhausted, his reputation damaged, and his bank account nearly depleted, Fry determined to take legal action against his tormentor.

I therefore selected about a dozen out of the hundreds of libels he had published against me, and commenced a civil suit for damages. He at once perceived that his case was desperate, and that his only hope was to stave off a trial. He engaged 7 lawyers . . . from the most distinguished members of the profession down to the Tombs pettifogger who had run the risk of being domiciled at Sing Sing on a charge of perjury. With the aid of this legal army he managed to have the trial put off, upon one pretext or another, for *five* long years—the judges never seeming to think that justice, to be justice, should be speedy as well as certain.

When the trial came on, *four* important witnesses of mine were dead, and among them Judge Noah, who had told me he was ready to come on the stand at any moment and give evidence that within his personal knowledge Bennett had at various times, under threat of publication in the *Herald* of the name of an unfortunate man who happened to be in the house of Rosina Townsend on the night Ellen Jewett was murdered, extorted from him sums in all amounting to $13,000 and that, not content even with this large amount of blackmail, which laid the foundations of his fortune, he continued to demand more, and finally drove the poor man to commit suicide.

Fry maintained that notwithstanding his loss of important witnesses—some from death, others from "fear of attacks by the *Herald*," the jury, in December, 1853, awarded him $10,000 in damages against Bennett. Six of the jurymen, he claimed, had at first wanted to set the amount at $20,000.

Following this decision, Bennett's battery of attorneys began action to set aside or, at any rate, delay payment for as long a time as possible. The lawyers had filed a total of fifty exceptions to the decision—and at long last were granted a new trial on *one* point, and only one.

In the meantime, Bennett cried loudly in his editorials against this attempt to muzzle him. He charged that the very freedom of the press was at stake. In an editorial of Sunday, February 18, 1855, he wrote, "We are violating no rule when we say that it was notorious that the plaintiff in that case [Fry vs. Bennett] was sustained by a large clique of wealthy men, comprising what are vulgarly known as the 'cod-fish aristocracy,' who lavished influence, money, and intrigue in order to crush a journal which has been hostile to them as a class, and unfriendly to their schemes. . . ."

Fry concluded his open letter with the statement that he was for a first and last time to make his position clear to the public:

Let me assure James Gordon Bennett that, poor as I am, and rich as he is, I have still the means and determination to continue the suit till he shall be suitably punished. Politicians, proverbially base and timeserving, may quail before him; craven managers of theaters may still pusillanimously pay him vast sums of black-mail in overcharges on their printing bills; lawyers may fear him; and some witnesses, like vile cowards, may not dare to give the testimony that would effectually blast him,—but I still have full faith that another intelligent jury, composed, like the first, of New York mechanics . . . will award a verdict as formidable as the old one.

Mr. Bennett will have to learn that there is at least one man who does not fear him, and that man is
EDWARD P. FRY

Still another libel case which attracted widespread attention was that of Daniel E. Sickles (later a Civil War hero) versus James Gordon Bennett. This trial took place in 1857. Bennett's attorneys had done their best to postpone the case. The District Attorney opposed further delay, arguing that three complaints for libel were ready to be made against Bennett as soon as this one was disposed of. "I am prepared to show," said the District Attorney, "that this defendant has been twice convicted in this Court of libel, and received its clemency in the shape of a pecuniary fine; and that he has been, also, convicted in the Court of Oyer and Terminer, for an infamous publication concerning one of the judges of this court. And in that Court, also, he was leniently dealt with. I can, also, if it be deemed necessary, produce judgement records from the civil courts to prove that he is an incorrigible libeler."

In his closing address to the Court, District Attorney Graham declared:

Who is James Gordon Bennett? No prosecution you can institute against him involves the liberty of the press. The press disowns him as a member. No press will defend the licentiousness of his journal. Do we not all know, as a matter of fact, that when the press of our city gave to the great champion of European liberty [Kossuth] a testimonial in the shape of a public dinner, there was no seat at that table for the editor of the *Herald,* or any person connected with his infamous establishment. No ticket for that dinner was sent or sold to him; and if I am not mistaken, none were allowed to be sold to the persons connected with his nefarious establishment.

Graham then summed up the long and scurrilous record of the *Herald* and concluded with a final castigation of its editor:

My client is determined to give the author of this libel an opportunity to confront—I was going to say, his peers—but where the peers of this man Bennett would come from, I know not. That twelve such men live at this time upon the face of the earth, or that twelve such men have, at any one period of existence of our globe, disgraced it by their existence, is a fact which to the credit of the human species, I distinctly deny. If you were to congregate and concatenate all the monsters that have ever disgraced the human form, I doubt whether you would be able to find among them twelve bad enough to make the peers of this infamous wretch.

In the spring of 1855 New York booksellers prominently displayed *The Life of Horace Greeley*. Its author was a brilliant young Englishman, James Parton, who declared in his preface to the biography that "Horace Greeley is wholly innocent of this book. . . . I undertook the task simply and solely because I like the man, because I gloried in his career, because I thought the story of his life ought to be told."

The biography was an altogether too flattering portrait of the editor to be accurate. But the book was well received, gave new fame to the man it described, and established Parton as an up-and-coming author.

At the close of 1855 the booksellers announced another biography *Memoirs of James Gordon Bennett and His Times*. The author's name did not appear upon the book, but in its place were the words: "By a journalist."

This biography was as uncritical of its subject as was Parton's. The book did not have the success of its rival. People said quite openly that Bennett had hired someone to write this flattering biography out of envy of the book on Greeley. Such was not the case.

The author of the *Memoirs of James Gordon Bennett and His Times* was a brilliant man by the name of Isaac C. Pray. Pray had been a highly successful actor, playwright, musical and drama critic, as well as editor of the *New York Journal of Commerce* and the *Ladies' Companion*. Pray had known Bennett for many years, and for two years—1850 and 1851—had been the music and drama critic for the *Herald*. He resigned the position to take over the managership of the National Theatre, one of the largest in New York City.

A few years ago, in 1932, there was published a book entitled *An American Procession* by William A. Croffut, which throws some light on the writing of the biography of Bennett by Isaac C. Pray.

Croffut, who was born in 1835, came to New York as a boy to learn shorthand. When Croffut had mastered the art of stenography, his teacher sent him to a potential employer. This happened to be Isaac C. Pray, who lived in a luxurious home at 23 Irving Place. Mr. Pray hired the young man to act as secretary and general messenger for which he received eight dollars per week. The very first task Croffut was given to perform was that of delivering a sealed package to James Gordon Bennett. It was a thrilling first assignment:

In a few minutes I found my way to the den where the elder Bennett forged his thunderbolts. It was at the top of a building adjoining the American Museum at the junction of Broadway and Park Row, and Underhill had pointed it out to me as a fearsome cavern where ambitious reporters were tortured. I trembled as I handed the great man the parcel.

The Scotch editor who terrorized New York at that time was, as I recall him, rough-hewn and bony, six feet high, with a harsh and strident voice, a crescent of white whiskers under his chin, and so terribly cross-eyed that when he looked at me with one eye, he looked out at the city hall with the other.

"Who from?" he bluntly asked, without taking the document.

"Mr. Isaac C. Pray," I answered.

"Nothing to do with Mr. Isaac C. Pray! Nothing to do with Mr. Isaac C. Pray!" he exclaimed angrily. But he took the parcel and tore off the envelope, disclosing a quantity of printed matter. With a savage gesture he flung it out the door into the hall, fixed me with one good eye, and shouted, "I don't want it! I won't have it! Carry it back and tell him to keep his stuff!" And he turned his back on me. . . .

I was reassured by my reception at Irving Place, where the author pleasantly accepted the package, merely exclaiming, "Yet that fool once got his living as a proofreader!"

Pray then explained to Croffut: "I have undertaken to write a life of Mr. Bennett, rather against his protest. He doesn't like the idea wholly and gets angry about it. He is odd, but will come around all right. These are some of the early proof sheets and I wanted to give him a chance to revise them and correct any errors. Bennett does not want his life written at all, and declares he will not contribute a word."

A few days later the young messenger was again sent to deliver a batch of proofs to Mr. Bennett at the *Herald* office, and again the old gentleman refused to take the copy and ordered Croffut out of the building.

"It was obvious," wrote Croffut, "that Mr. Pray had imposed upon himself a terribly difficult task; to write a friendly biography of an unfriendly man without the active assistance or even the tacit sympathy and acquiescence of the subject of it, and even under his prohibition."

Bennett was called a public scold, a virago, a vixen, and a Xanthippe, by his competitors, one of whom prepared a ducking stunt for him at the Battery while another actually erected a gallows on which to hang him.

13. Prelude to War

Aʟʟ ᴛʜʀᴏᴜɢʜ the night the milling crowds surged about the newspaper offices, shouting, booing, cheering, whistling, as the reports of the election were announced. The staff at the *Herald* worked like madmen, from printer's devil to publisher. They were determined to keep their reputation of always being "first with the news."

Not till three o'clock in the morning, when it was evident that Buchanan had been elected to the presidency, did James Gordon Bennett don his hat, coat, and muffler and call it a day. For the first time in his long career, Bennett realized that the candidate he supported had been defeated. He paused on the stairway, returned to his office, called in one of the reporters, dictated a congratulatory message to the new president-elect, then hurried home.

The 1856 election had been a three-cornered affair. James Buchanan of Pennsylvania, Democratic nominee, polled 1,838,169 votes. John C. Fremont, candidate of the newly organized Republican Party, garnered 1,341,264 votes. Millard Fillmore, the last Whig president, carried what remained of his once powerful party (under the name of National-American Party) to its final electoral contest. He received 874,534 votes. How purely sectional the new Republican Party was is shown by the total vote it received in the slave states—1,194.

Whereas Bennett beat a hasty retreat to the triumphant party of Buchanan, believing that the defeat of the Republicans would ruin their chances of a comeback, shrewd observers thought otherwise. The *Springfield Republican* editorialized while the results of the election were still unknown: "Of the two contestants, the Republicans can alone afford to be beaten. With the Democracy, defeat is destruction. The party is only held together by its alliance with the national treasury and the slaveholder. Separated from one, it becomes useless to the other, and its power is gone. But a reverse cannot break the Republican column. . . . Whether it enters upon the affirmative exercise of its mission now, or four years hence, is to all seeming the only question of today. . . . It can afford to wait, if the country and the world can afford to have it."

On the wide prairies of Nebraska and Kansas the issue was no longer debated with words or settled with ballots. Strong and reckless men from the Deep South and the North were pouring into the region, ready to win their point with lash and pistol, with faggot and breech-loading rifle. The *Tribune,* the *Times,* and the *Post* joined in the campaign to send militant free-soil advocates to the disputed territory. Reverend Henry Ward Beecher told a gathering of churchmen that his church would pay for half the guns required for the free-soil immigrants, adding that a Sharpe's rifle was a greater moral agency than the Bible in the impending conflict. Greeley raised thousands of dollars for the same purpose, as he pounded hard on the theme that "the duty of the people of the Free States is to send more true men, more Sharpe's rifles, and more howitzers to Kansas."

Violence was not confined to Kansas. Broken heads and bruised bodies became almost commonplace in the larger cities. Even the halls of Congress had their taste of blood when Senator Preston Brooks of South Carolina beat his colleague, Charles Sumner of Massachusetts, into insensibility in his Senate seat. To the fine old scholar and poet, William Cullen Bryant, the North must rise in its wrath to end such barbarism. "Violence," he wrote in the *New York Post,* "reigns in the streets of Washington. . . . Violence overhangs the frontiers. . . . In short, violence is the order of the day; the North is to be pushed to the wall by it, and this plot will succeed if the people of the free States are as apathetic as the slaveholders are insolent."

Bennett, too, viewed the rising tide of passion with alarm and apprehension. But he placed the blame upon the rabid abolitionists. He wrote scathing editorials against Beecher and other clergymen, for their "slanderous political sermons." Every public figure who supported the Republicans was lampooned and lambasted. Greeley, Bryant, Raymond, Webb, Dana, and every other editor was flayed and lashed in the *Herald's* editorials. They were called traitors to the Union. The defeat of Fremont was placed at their doorstep, a defeat which, said Bennett, "has caused another furious flare-up over the niggers."

Name-calling on all sides descended to a new low. Greeley called Bennett and the *Herald* "nigger drivers," to which Bennett retorted by calling Greeley a "nigger-worshipper," and "Massa Greeley."

Bennett leaped to the defense of the Kansas-Nebraska Act, adding belligerently that his was "about the only Northern newspaper that had the moral courage to come out boldly in its support." He let the world know that for two score years "through good and evil report, the *New York Herald* has been the only Northern journal that has unfailingly vindicated the constitutional rights of the South."

The anathema heaped upon the editor in the North was canceled out by the way he was lauded in the South. His was the only New York paper with a growing subscription list in Dixie. The *Herald* was the champion of the southern cause, and because of this its news and views were gravely and unquestioningly accepted among planters, bankers, and business men from Richmond to New Orleans. A correspondent for the *Springfield Republican* told its readers how amusing it was "to see the greed with which the *Herald* is snatched up and devoured on its earliest arrival here in the evening; and what is worse, to see the simplicity of these Southern fellows who seem to pin their whole faith in it."

When Chief Justice Taney announced the famous Dred Scott Decision in 1857, the *Herald,* though ready to back up that decision to the limit, nevertheless feared its effects upon the country,—"a bombshell, which will at once reopen the slavery agitation in all its length and breadth."

Shaken off, his late political associates were henceforth to be referred to in the *Herald* as "Black Republicans." These were the men who "want to plunge us into a fearful conflict between the nigger-worshippers and the nigger drivers, North and South." On rare occasions he would also fire a round at the fire-eaters of the

South. They too, he said, were jointly responsible with the Black Republicans for the plight of the country. Between them they "were doing their best to destroy this fair political fabric, raised by the wisdom and cemented by the blood of our forefathers."

Bennett's mood alternated between one of deep despair for the safety of the Union and one of high optimism. He grabbed at every straw in the wind to fortify this more sanguine outlook, as, for example, the fact that the *Tribune's* associate editors, George Ripley and Charles A. Dana, augmented their income by writing articles for *Appleton's Encyclopaedia,* or Greeley's anti-slavery lecture tours. Facts such as these, announced Bennett triumphantly, "show that nigger worship is nearly at its close; that anti-slavery agitation is going down, and that whenever it becomes defunct, the *Tribune's* nigger circulation will collapse."

The *Herald* never would admit that the *Tribune* could be considered seriously as a *news* purveyor. And as for the much-touted *Weekly Tribune* (which, in truth, had a much greater national influence than that of the *Herald* or any other paper), it was dismissed by Bennett as representing neither a business want, nor the spokesman for any great interest, social, religious, or political. "People can breakfast, dine and sup with the most perfect equanimity without having perused the *Weekly Tribune,* though whether they can sleep without its aid is not quite so certain."

President James Buchanan and the *Tribune's* editor had become acquainted back in the middle Forties, when Buchanan was Secretary of State in the cabinet of President James K. Polk. When Bennett and his wife made their lengthy tour of Europe in 1846-47, they had carried with them a number of letters of introduction to important personages abroad, written by Buchanan. The two men maintained contact with each other for several years, but a difference of opinion led to misunderstanding followed by a complete rupture of relations.

Buchanan knew full well the value of having Bennett on his side; so when the editor indicated his eagerness to go along with the new chief executive, Buchanan lost no time in accepting him back as a friend. "I rejoice that our former friendly relations are to be restored. I can assure you I am truly sorry they were ever interrupted; and this not only for my own sake, but that of the country. The *New York Herald,"* he added, "exercising the influence which signal ability and past triumphs always commands, can contribute much to frustrate the sectional party which now so seriously endangers the Union, and to restore the ancient friendly relations between the North and the South."

Replying to a letter of congratulations from Mrs. Bennett, the President, on April 14, 1857, told her of his delight in knowing that Bennett had promised his wife that he would stick by Buchanan's administration through thick and thin. "Thus far," continued the President, "he has given it a powerful support with occasional aberrations, for which I am always prepared and do not complain. He is an independent man and will do just what he pleases—though I know there is an undercurrent of good will towards me in his nature and he is disposed to treat me fairly. . . ."

Bennett did, indeed, stick by the Buchanan administration through thick and thin. Its policy of drift and open appeasement to the pro-slavery forces was upheld by the *Herald* as sound and sensible statesmanship. When it was denounced in the House of Representatives as "the most profligate and corrupt Administration ever known to this government since its organization," the *Herald* pooh-poohed the charges as the mad ravings of abolitionist agitators and quoted with approval a letter from the President to Bennett in which he protested against such unkind charges, adding, "In performing my duties I have endeavored to be not only pure but unsuspected."

Buchanan, happy at the thought of such a staunch champion, gave the *Herald* access to reports well in advance of other papers. He let its Washington correspondents get advance tips on changes in policy or personnel, and on at least one occasion, the President himself sent to Bennett an advance copy of his proposed message to Congress.

Harper's Weekly of July 10, 1858, devoted its lead article to the colorful career of James Gordon Bennett. It was the first ever to appear in any major American periodical about Bennett which made a serious attempt to evaluate his place and that of the *Herald* in the annals of journalism, and told how the *Herald,* in the twenty-three years since its founding, had fought its way to the head of newspaper literature in the United States.

No American journal at the present time can compare with it in the point of circulation, advertising or influence. Its most bitter assailants concede to it unrivaled sagacity and enterprise in the collection of news. Its friends regard it as a universal guide. It has, naturally, been much abused. Abuse is the necessary price of success in any business; and it must be admitted that Mr. Bennett has not given himself much pains to conciliate his rivals. His plan has ever been rather to court than to avoid controversy; his lance is always in rest; and his powder invariably dry. But whatever rival journals may have said in their wrath, no one can seriously deny the merit of the *Herald* without impugning the judgement or the morals of the community which for twenty years has given it a generous and undivided support.

Harper's was likewise the first to credit Bennett with two major reforms in the business of journalism.

He was the first newspaper proprietor in the United States who had the courage to refuse to advertise or supply his paper on credit. No one who is unacquainted with the business can realize the mischief which the credit system did to the press of olden time. Newspapers were uniformly crippled by the dishonesty of their patrons. No man thought it wrong to cheat a newspaper. . . . Mr. Bennett broke up this ruinous system; he refused to sell papers or to take advertising save for cash; and all his competitors hastened to follow the example he had had the boldness to set.

In the second place, he set the example of a newspaper independent of politicians. . . . At the time the *Herald* was started, the support of some influential politician was considered essential to the success of a newspaper. It was deemed preposterous for a journal to hope to thrive without at least a Governor, a Senator, or a handful of Congressmen to endorse it. Mr. Bennett disabused the public mind on this head. He had learned that political patronage, like protective duties, is really more injurious than beneficial to the paper patronized; and he had sickened of the base selfishness which prompted ambitious men in every sphere of life to seek to use the press, and to turn around afterward and repudiate the obligation. Mr. Bennett was the first editor who taught the press of the country the duty of self-dependence; who set the fashion of looking to the public alone for patronage, and of treating all individuals, whether great financiers or social leaders, as subordinates and not masters. For this great reform he deserves to be remembered as long as the United States can boast of an independent press.

Looking back across the years, we ask ourselves how could James Gordon Bennett have been so consistently wrong in his evaluation of the trend of public sentiment on the burning issues of the day? His usual perspicacity was completely missing. He was, we suspect, so blinded by his own position on these issues that he refused to see the trend of the times. That Bennett was not the only editor to suffer from this fault demands no extensive research. On the eve of July 4, 1859, he wrote an editorial reeking with complacency and congratulations to the Republic for its good health: "While three of the European powers are absolutely at war, and all the others trembling upon the brink of the abyss into which France, Austria and Italy have been plunged . . . we stand at peace with all men, respected at home and abroad, and without a standing army to eat out the life-blood of the people. . . . We stand without embarrassing or perplexing questions of any sort, and that the bond between the States is, notwithstanding all the groans of the croakers and the howls of fanatics, stronger today than it was fifty years ago."

A fortnight later, complacency was forgotten as the *Herald* launched into an extensive exposé of the pernicious slave trade, whose very hub and source, it claimed, lay not in the South but in New York, Boston, Portland, Bristol, New Bedford, and other New England ports. Look close, shouted the *Herald,* and you'll find that many a staunch contributor to the abolition movement makes his money out of hauling slaves. The odor of sanctity and the odor of fat profits from this inhuman business are strangely intermingled. Bennett's reporters had been told to "get the facts," and get the facts they did. They told their readers just where the slave-traders were built and outfitted, by whom they were owned, and the profits of the business. An article of August 15, 1859, summarized the situation in these words:

"It is estimated that the slave fleet which leaves New York, Boston, and other eastern seaports in a single year numbers some 40 vessels of different sizes, varying from 100 to 400 tons, and capable of carrying from 300 to 600 slaves each. Every vessel is manned by crews of from 15 to 25 men, including captain and officers, making a total for the whole fleet of about a thousand men. The whole of the capital invested does not probably exceed $4,000,000 upon which, as we have shown, a profit of $11,000,000 is realized."

On the same day, the editor-in-chief presented his version of what these unsavory facts really meant. Appropriately, he captioned his editorial:

The Black Republicans and Their African Slave Trade Schemes

While Thurlow Weed was performing his last great feat on the anti-slavery tight-rope, the people were amused with the Kansas humbug. Henry W. Beecher clanked his chains in the tabernacle; Professor Silliman sent Sharpe's rifles to Kansas, and three thousand clergymen, with their black coats and white chokers, went through a staid and solemn minuet of the Roger de Coverley style, to the tune of "Shriek for Freedom." The Black Republicans, under the advice of their great rope-walker, have taken care to provide an abundance of music for the coming political festival, and the African drum will be beaten with tremendous energy. The Black Republican organs will pipe to the same tune, and have already begun. They know more about the slave trade that is being carried on in the States than anybody else, and continually give us the fullest particulars. They have every facility for doing so; for the traders being fitted out by themselves, they of course know all about the matter.

We are glad to see that they have combined their slave trade scheme so well. It includes great profits, no personal risk, and an abundance of political capital for the Black Republican Party.

The long-dreaded storm came at last. It came at a time and a place and under circumstances as fantastic as those in a mystery thriller. No other newspaper in the whole country gave such complete coverage as did the *Herald* to the strange events and personalities emerging out of the attack on Harpers Ferry by John Brown and his followers in the fall of 1859.

Readers of the *Herald* on the morning of October 19 were almost shocked out of their wits at the sensational headlines on the front page of the paper, and the story which followed:

FEARFUL AND EXCITING INTELLIGENCE.

NEGRO INSURRECTION AT HARPERS FERRY.

EXTENSIVE NEGRO CONSPIRACY IN VIRGINIA AND MARYLAND.

SEIZURE OF THE UNITED STATES ARSENAL BY THE INSURRECTIONISTS.

ARMS TAKEN AND SENT INTO THE INTERIOR.

THE BRIDGE FORTIFIED AND DEFENDED BY CANNON.

TRAINS FIRED INTO AND STOPPED—SEVERAL PERSONS KILLED— TELEGRAPH WIRES CUT—CONTRIBUTIONS LEVIED ON THE CITIZENS.

TROOPS DESPATCHED AGAINST THE INSURGENTS FROM WASHINGTON AND BALTIMORE,
&c.,   &c.,   &c.,

SPECIAL DESPATCHES TO THE HERALD

Washington, Oct. 17, 1859

A telegraph despatch has just been received by the Secretary of War from Mr. Garrett, President of the Baltimore and Ohio Railroad, stating that a serious affair has occurred at Harpers Ferry, where the United States Armory and the bridge are in possession of a large band of armed men, said to be abolitionists, but thought to be Armory men. The guns from the Armory have been taken for offensive use, and the leaders notified our men that no trains shall pass the Armory and Bridge. Our officers were fired upon, and a laborer nearly killed. The wires being cut, we got our advices from the next station. He asks the Secretary of War to get the government to allow the military of Washington and Baltimore to go on in the three o'clock train this afternoon, and render them such assistance as may be necessary. The Cabinet are now in session upon the matter.

The government immediately ordered that a company of marines from Washington barracks should leave this afternoon, under the command of Colonel Harris, for Harpers Ferry, and if necessary any further assistance that may be required.

Colonel Robert Lee, of the army, will command the United States forces. He leaves in the afternoon train with a company of marines, and will be joined on the Ohio Railroad by a company of volunteers from Maryland. Troops have been ordered from Old Point.

Washington, Oct. 17, 1859

A passenger who has just arrived here, who left Harpers Ferry this morning, having been detained there for upwards of five hours, corroborates the statements received today by the Secretary of War.

This gentleman, who is an intelligent man, states that a Negro insurrection of a formidable character, headed by white men, is in active operation. They are fully armed with muskets and other arms, which they had seized at the Armory. They had, when the train left, taken all of the white citizens, so my informant says, and held them as prisoners. They number one hundred and fifty, and recruits were coming in constantly from the surrounding country.

My informant says that they told him that they would have, by one o'clock today, over seven hundred Negroes and white men. The object of this movement was to obtain their freedom.

They had cut off all the avenues of communication with the town, and refused to let any leave the place. They allowed the train that my informant was in to pass, after a detention of five hours, giving the conductor only five minutes to decide; if not, they would seize them and lock them up in the Armory. He says they barely escaped with their lives.

The Secretary of War received some time since an anonymous letter, stating that a foray would be made by Negroes headed by white men, upon Harpers Ferry, Wheeling, and other points in Virginia, about the middle of October. At the time he thought nothing of it, and gave it no attention whatever; but it looks from this movement as though they have been organizing for some time, and intended to carry it out.

The moment the first telegraphic dispatch reached the *Herald* office, things began to happen. Both Bennett and Hudson knew that here was a mighty big story. Instructions were immediately wired their reporters in Washington, Baltimore, and Richmond. Others were routed out of their beds in New York and sent forth to get the whole story, accurately and in detail, as well as the story behind the story. Some were put on the trail of abolitionist leaders to get their reactions to the events at Harpers Ferry. Still others were sent to speak with public officials, with military men, with scholars, with the man on the street, with leaders of the heavy foreign contingent in New York, and even with free Negroes living in the North.

While the presses were being held back to await last-minute dispatches that hectic night, Bennett dictated his first of a great many editorials on the Harpers Ferry Insurrection:

A most strange and almost incredible piece of information comes to us by telegraph from Baltimore. It represents that a mob of Negro insurrectionists, numbering several hundred and led on by white men, had seized on Sunday night upon the United States Arsenal at Harpers Ferry, possessed themselves of the arms of the government there deposited, sent wagon loads of rifles into the interior, stopped and fired into passing trains, planted cannon upon the bridge over the Potomac, cut the telegraph wires, seized and kept in custody the peaceable and orderly citizens of the place, levied contributions upon the hotels and provision stores, shot several persons, and otherwise committed dreadful havoc and onslaughts, against the peace and sovereignty of the people of the United States.

Our Baltimore despatches leave us altogether at sea in regard to the origin and cause of the outbreak, but our special despatch from Washington gives more particulars. From this, we learn that the Secretary of War has been officially informed of the dangerous extent of the movement. It appears to be a regular Negro conspiracy or insurrection, planned and organized for some time past and led on and directed by white men. The Secretary had information months since of the existence of such a conspiracy, and of the intention of the Negro plotters to seize upon the Arsenal at Harpers Ferry, possess themselves of arms wherewith to arm the slaves of Virginia and the neighboring States, establish themselves at Wheeling and other points, and regain their freedom. He seems to have given no credence to the story when he first heard it, but it now becomes fearfully verified.

It is difficult to understand how such a movement could have had any success, particularly in a section of the country where the slaves are but few in number, and we are especially at a loss to conceive how they could have gained possession of the Arsenal against the officers and workmen of the government. But it seems too true that the blacks have actually gained the upper hand at Harpers Ferry. At all events, troops have been sent against them from Washington and Baltimore, and to-morrow will probably bring us news of a terrible conflict, in which the Negroes and their white abettors will be made to pay dearly for their temerity.

Apropos of this exciting news, we recollect a very significant passage in one of Gerrit Smith's letters, published a month or two ago, in which he speaks of the folly of attempting to strike the shackles of the slaves by the force of moral suasion or legal agitation, and predicts that the next movement made in the direction of Negro emancipation would be an insurrection in the South. Is this the first act in that programme? —and are those white abolitionists spoken of in our despatches emissaries of the peaceful Gerrit? If not, is the insurrection part of that "irrepressible conflict" which is so dear to the heart of William H. Seward?—and is it intended to affect the next Presidential contest? Time will show; but one thing appears certain—that the outbreak has assumed startling proportions, and may prove the first act of a terrible drama.

The fortnight following John Brown's raid at Harpers Ferry brought to a white heat the passions of North and South alike. Abolitionists had found their martyr, the slaveholders their devil, in the old gentleman who lay wounded at Harpers Ferry.

Newspaper editors and reporters found themselves lashed by the same emotional storms which swept over the public. Hence, instead of giving their readers a factual account of what had taken place, they consciously or otherwise slanted almost every news dispatch to agree with their own outlook on the whole slavery issue. Bennett, for all his rabid hatred of John Brown and his fellow abolitionists (to which he gave full vent in his editorial columns), nevertheless maintained his stature as the ace news man of the day. He insisted that every available fact on the case be printed. He told his editors that Brown and his fellow conspirators were to be permitted to state their position fully and freely in the columns of the *Herald*. These instructions were adhered to without deviation. No other paper gave such a complete picture of the whole episode.

Bennett, for all his insistence upon factual reporting, was not above using tricks of journalism to sway his readers. For example, the *Herald* of October 19, along with its lengthy report of the successful repression of the revolt, carried on the same page Senator Seward's stirring speech at Rochester in which he had announced the "irrepressible conflict" between the slave and free states. To the average reader, it would appear that John Brown's raid at Harpers Ferry was the direct result of Seward's speech. That, of course, was what Bennett wanted to convey. As a matter of fact, Seward's speech had been made a considerable time before the insurrection.

In an editorial introduction to Seward's speech, Bennett wrote:

"The first overt act in the great drama of national disruption which has just been plotted by that demagogue, William H. Seward, has just been closed at Harpers Ferry. It opened in treason, robbery and murder, and has appropriately closed in the blood of the misguided fanatics who lent themselves to the doctrine of the 'irrepressible conflict.' No reasoning mind can fail to trace cause and effect between the bloody and brutal manifesto of William H. Seward on the banks of the Genesee, and the terrible scenes of violence, rapine and death, that have been enacted at the confluence of the Potomac and the Shenandoah. . . ."

The very extensive report on what had taken place at Harpers Ferry called forth even more extensive headlines than had appeared on the previous day. In fact, multiple headlines for newspapers were born at this time. Bennett set the pace; others followed in his footsteps. The headlines of that day (October 19) summarized the report:

THE ABOLITION OUTBREAK IN VIRGINIA.

THE NEGRO INSURRECTION AT HARPERS FERRY.

SEIZURE OF THE ARMORY.

ARRIVAL OF TROOPS FROM VIRGINIA, MARYLAND AND WASHINGTON.

FIGHTING IN THE STREETS.

BATTLE AT THE BRIDGE.

NINE CITIZENS AND FIFTEEN INSURRECTIONISTS KILLED AND WOUNDED.

THE INSURRECTIONISTS TAKEN IN AN ENGINE HOUSE.

ATTACK OF THE TROOPS ON THE BUILDING.

ONE MARINE MORTALLY AND ONE SLIGHTLY WOUNDED.

TWO INSURRECTIONISTS KILLED AND ONE SERIOUSLY WOUNDED.

CAPTAIN JOHN BROWN, THE LEADER, REPORTED MORTALLY
WOUNDED.

SKETCH OF HIS CAREER.

GOV. WISE ACTIVELY ENGAGED IN SUPPRESSING THE REVOLT.

BETWEEN THIRTY AND FORTY, IN ALL, KILLED AND WOUNDED.

STAMPEDE OF TWO OR THREE HUNDRED SLAVES.

END OF THE OUTBREAK.

VIEWS AND OPINIONS OF THE BLACK REPUBLICAN ORGANS.

THE VIRGINIA INSURRECTION OF 1831 AND THE TENNESSEE
OUTBREAK OF 1856.

THE VERY LATEST,
&c.,   &c.,   &c.,

Two days later, on the 21st, the *Herald* reported the verbatim discussion between John Brown and the members of Congress who
interviewed him on the 19th. No other reporter had as yet been in
to talk to Brown. The *Herald's* report of that historic interview
was the only one made by any newspaper in the country. It is docu-
mentary evidence of great historical value on one of the most vital
episodes in American history. It is presented here with one slight
editing to eliminate repetitious questions and answers:

THE HARPERS FERRY OUTBREAK

VERBATIM REPORT OF THE QUESTIONING OF OLD BROWN BY
SENATOR MASON, CONGRESSMAN VALLANDIGHAM, AND OTHERS.

HE REFUSES TO DISCLOSE THE NAMES OF HIS ABETTORS, BUT
CONFESSES TO INTERVIEWS WITH JOSHUA R. GIDDINGS,
AND ENDORSES GERRIT SMITH'S LETTER.

HE DECLARES THAT HE RECEIVED HIS WOUNDS AFTER
SURRENDERING.

HIS STATEMENT TO THE HERALD REPORTER

&c.   &c.   &c.

FROM OUR SPECIAL REPORTER

Harpers Ferry, Oct. 19, 1859

"Old Brown," or "Ossawattomie Brown," as he is often called, the hero of a dozen fights or so with the "border ruffians" of Missouri, in the days of "bleeding Kansas," is the head and front of this offending—the commander of the abolition filibuster army. His wounds, which at first were supposed to be mortal, turn out to be mere flesh wounds and scratches, not at all dangerous in their character. He has been removed, together with Stephens, the other wounded prisoner, from the engine room to the office of the armory, and they now lie on the floor, upon miserable shake-downs, covered with some old bedding.

Brown is fifty-five years of age, rather small sized, with keen and restless grey eyes, and a grizzly hair and beard. He is a wiry, active man, and should the slightest chance for an escape be afforded, there is no doubt that he will yet give his captors much trouble. His hair is matted and tangled, and his face, hands and clothes all smouched and smeared with blood. Colonel Lee stated that he would exclude all visitors from the room if the wounded men were annoyed or pained by them, but Brown said he was by no means annoyed; on the contrary he was glad to be able to make himself and his motives clearly understood. He converses freely, fluently and cheerfully, without the slightest manifestation of fear or uneasiness, evidently weighing well his words, and possessing a good command of language. His manner is courteous and affable, and he appears to make a favorable impression upon his auditory, which, during most of the day yesterday, averaged about ten or a dozen men.

When I arrived in the armory, shortly after two o'clock in the afternoon, Brown was answering questions put to him by Senator Mason, who had just arrived from his residence at Winchester, thirty miles distant. Col. Faulkner, member of Congress, who lives but a few miles off, Mr. Vallandigham, member of Congress of Ohio, and several other distinguished gentlemen. The following is a *verbatim* report of the conversation:—

MR. MASON—Can you tell us, at least, who furnished money for your expedition?

MR. BROWN—I furnished most of it myself. I cannot implicate others. It is by my own folly that I have been taken. I could easily have saved myself from it had I exercised my own better judgment, rather than yielded to my feelings.

Mr. Mason—You mean if you had escaped immediately?

Mr. Brown—No; I had the means to make myself secure without any escape, but I allowed myself to be surrounded by a force by being too tardy.

Mr. Mason—Tardy in getting away?

Mr. Brown—I should have gone away, but I had thirty odd prisoners, whose wives and daughters were in tears for their safety, and I felt for them. Besides, I wanted to allay the fears of those who believe we came here to burn and kill. For this reason I allowed the train to cross the bridge, and gave them full liberty to pass on. . . .

Mr. Mason—But you killed some people passing along the streets quietly.

Mr. Brown—Well, sir, if there was anything of that kind done, it was without my knowledge. Your own citizens, who were my prisoners, will tell you that every possible means were taken to prevent it. I did not allow my men to fire, nor even to return a fire, when there was danger of killing those we regarded as innocent persons, if I could help it. They will tell you that we allowed ourselves to be fired at repeatedly and did not return it.

Mr. Mason—If you would tell us who sent you here—who provided the means—that would be information of some value.

Mr. Brown—I will answer freely and faithfully about what concerns myself—I will answer anything I can with honor, but not about others.

Mr. Vallandigham—(member of Congress from Ohio, who had just entered)—Mr. Brown, who sent you here?

Mr. Brown—No man sent me here; it was my own prompting and that of my Maker, or that of the Devil, whichever you please to ascribe it to. I acknowledge no man in human form.

Mr. Vallandigham—Did you get up the expedition yourself?

Mr. Brown—I did.

Mr. Vallandigham—Did you get up this document that is called the constitution?

Mr. Brown—I did. They are a constitution and ordinances of my own contriving and getting up.

Mr. Vallandigham—How long have you been engaged in this business?

Mr. Brown—From the breaking out of the difficulties in Kansas. Four of my sons had gone there to settle, and they induced me to go. I did not go there to settle but because of the difficulties.

Mr. Mason—How many are engaged with you in this movement? I ask those questions for your own safety.

MR. BROWN—Any questions that I can honorably answer I will, not otherwise. So far as I am myself concerned I have told everything truthfully. I value my word, sir.

MR. MASON—What was your object in coming?

MR. BROWN—We came to free the slaves, and only that.

A YOUNG MAN—(in the uniform of a volunteer company) How many men in all had you?

MR. BROWN—I came to Virginia with eighteen men only, besides myself.

VOLUNTEER—What in the world did you suppose you could do here in Virginia with that amount of men?

MR. BROWN—Young man, I don't wish to discuss that question here.

VOLUNTEER—You could not do anything.

MR. BROWN—Well, perhaps your ideas and mine on military subjects would differ materially.

MR. MASON—How do you justify your acts?

MR. BROWN—I think, my friend, you are guilty of a great wrong against God and humanity—I say it without wishing to be offensive—and it would be perfectly right for anyone to interfere with you so far as to free those you willfully and wickedly hold in bondage. I do not say this insultingly.

MR. MASON—I understand that.

MR. BROWN—I think I did right, and that others will do right who interfere with you at any time and all times. I hold that the golden rule, "Do unto others as you would that others should do unto you," applies to all who would help others to gain their liberty.

LIEUT. STEWARD—But you don't believe in the Bible.

MR. BROWN—Certainly I do.

MR. MASON—You considered yourself the Commander-in-Chief of these "provisional" military forces.

MR. BROWN—I was chosen agreeably to the ordinance of a certain document, commander-in-chief of that force.

MR. MASON—What wages did you offer?

MR. BROWN—None.

LIEUT. STEWARD—"The wages of sin is death."

MR. BROWN—I would not have made such a remark to you, if you had been a prisoner and wounded in my hands.

MR. VALLANDIGHAM—Have you lived long in Ohio?

MR. BROWN—I went there in 1850; I lived in Summit county, which was then Trumbull county; my native place is in York State; my father lived there till his death, in 1805.

MR. VALLANDIGHAM—When in Cleveland did you attend the Fugitive Slave Law Convention there?

Mr. Brown—No. I was there about the time of the sitting of the court to try the Oberlin rescuers. I spoke there publicly on that subject. I spoke on the Fugitive Slave Law and my own rescue. Of course, so far as I had any influence at all, I was disposed to justify the Oberlin people for rescuing the slave, because I have myself forcibly taken slaves from bondage. I was concerned in taking eleven slaves from Missouri to Canada last winter. I think I spoke in Cleveland before the Convention. I do not know that I had any conversation with any of the Oberlin rescuers. I was sick part of the time I was in Ohio with the ague. I was part of the time in Ashtabula county.

Mr. Vallandigham—Did you see anything of Joshua R. Giddings there?

Mr. Brown—I did meet him.

Mr. Vallandigham—Did you converse with him?

Mr. Brown—I did. I would not tell you, of course, anything that would implicate Mr. Giddings; but I certainly met with him and had conversations with him.

Mr. Vallandigham—About that rescue case?

Mr. Brown—Yes, I did; I heard him express his opinions upon it very freely and frankly.

Mr. Vallandigham—Justifying it?

Mr. Brown—Yes, sir; I do not compromise him certainly in saying that.

A Bystander—Did you go out to Kansas under the auspices of the Emigrant Aid Society?

Mr. Brown—No, sir; I went out under the auspices of John Brown and nobody else.

Mr. Vallandigham—Will you answer this: Did you talk with Giddings about your expedition here?

Mr. Brown—No, I won't answer that, because a denial of it I would not make, and to make any affirmation of it I should be a great dunce.

Mr. Vallandigham—Have you had any correspondence with parties in the North on the subject of this movement?

Mr. Brown—I have had correspondence.

A Bystander—Do you consider this a religious movement?

Mr. Brown—It is, in my opinion, the greatest service a man can render to God.

A Bystander—Do you consider yourself an instrument in the hands of Providence?

Mr. Brown—I do.

A Bystander—Upon what principle do you justify your acts?

Mr. Brown—Upon the golden rule. I pity the poor in bondage that have none to help them; that is why I am here; not to gratify any personal animosity, revenge or vindictive spirit. It is my sympathy with the oppressed and the wronged, that are as good as you and as precious in the sight of God.

A BYSTANDER—Certainly. But why take the slaves against their will?

MR. BROWN—I never did.

BYSTANDER—You did in one instance, at least.

STEPHENS—(the other wounded prisoner here said, in a firm clear voice)—You are right. In one case I know the Negro wanted to go back.

BYSTANDER—Did you ever live in Washington city?

MR. BROWN—I did not. I want you to understand, gentlemen—(and to the reporter of the *Herald*) you may report that—I want you to understand that I respect the rights of the poorest and weakest of colored people, oppressed by the slave system, just as much as I do those of the most wealthy and powerful. That is the idea that has moved me, and that alone. We expected no reward except the satisfaction of endeavoring to do for those in distress and greatly oppressed as we would be done by. The cry of distress of the oppressed was my reason, and the only thing that prompted me to come here.

A BYSTANDER—Why did you do it secretly?

MR. BROWN—Because I thought that necessary to success; no other reason.

BYSTANDER—And you think that honorable? Have you read Gerrit Smith's last letter?

MR. BROWN—What letter do you mean?

BYSTANDER—The *New York Herald* of yesterday in speaking of this affair mentions a letter in this way:—"Apropos of this exciting news we recollect a very significant passage in one of Gerrit Smith's letters, published a month or two ago, in which he speaks of the folly of attempting to strike the shackles off the slaves by the force of moral suasion or legal agitation, and predicts that the next movement made in the direction of Negro emancipation would be an Insurrection in the South."

MR. BROWN—I have not seen the *New York Herald* for some days past; but I presume, from your remark about the gist of the letter, that I should concur with it. I agree with Mr. Smith that moral suasion is hopeless. I don't think the people of the slave states will ever consider the subject of slavery in its true light till some other argument is resorted to than moral suasion.

MR. VALLANDIGHAM—Did you expect a general rising of the slaves in case of your success?

MR. BROWN—No, sir; nor did I wish it; I expected to gather them up from time to time and set them free.

MR. VALLANDIGHAM—Did you expect to hold possession here till then?

Mr. Brown—Well, probably I had quite a different idea. I do not know that I ought to reveal my plans. I am here a prisoner and wounded, because I foolishly allowed myself to be so. You overrate your strength in supposing I could have been taken if I had not allowed it. I was too tardy after commencing the open attack—in delaying my movements through Monday night, and up to the time I was attacked by the government troops. It was all occasioned by my desire to spare the feelings of my prisoners and their families and the community at large. I had no knowledge of the shooting of the Negro [Heywood].

Mr. Vallandigham—What time did you commence your organization in Canada?

Mr. Brown—That occurred about two years ago, if I remember right. It was, I think, in 1858.

Mr. Vallandigham—Who was the Secretary?

Mr. Brown—That I would not tell if I recollected, but I do not recollect. I think the officers were elected in May, 1858. I may answer incorrectly, but not intentionally. My head is a little confused by wounds, and my memory obscure on dates.

Dr. Biggs—Were you in the party at Dr. Kennedy's house?

Mr. Brown—I was the head of that party. I occupied the house to mature my plans. I have not been in Baltimore to purchase cats.

Dr. Biggs—What was the number of men at Kennedy's?

Mr. Brown—I decline to answer that.

Dr. Biggs—Who lanced that woman's neck on the hill?

Mr. Brown—I did. I have sometimes practiced in surgery when I thought it a matter of humanity and necessity, and there was no one else to do it, but have not studied surgery.

Dr. Biggs—It was done very well and scientifically. They have been very clever to the neighbors, I have been told, and we have no reason to suspect them except that we could not understand their movements. They were represented as eight or nine persons; on Friday there were thirteen.

Mr. Brown—There were more than that.

Q.—Where did you get arms to obtain possession of the armory?

A.—I bought them.

Q.—In what state?

A.—That I would not state.

Q.—How many guns?

A.—Two hundred Sharp's rifles and two hundred revolvers—what is called the Massachusetts Arms Company's revolvers, a little under the navy size.

Q.—Why did you not take that swivel you left in the house?

A.—I had no occasion for it. It was given to me a year or two ago.

Q.—In Kansas?

A.—No, I had nothing given me in Kansas.

Q.—By whom; and in what state?

A.—I decline to answer. It is not properly a swivel; it is a very large rifle with a pivot. The ball is larger than a musket ball; it is intended for a slug.

REPORTER OF THE HERALD—I do not wish to annoy you; but if you have anything further you would like to say I will report it.

MR. BROWN—I have nothing to say, only that I claim to be here in carrying out a measure I believe perfectly justifiable, and not to act the part of an incendiary or ruffian, but to aid those suffering great wrongs. *I wish to say, furthermore, that you had better—all you people at the South—prepare yourselves for a settlement of that question that must come up for settlement sooner than you are prepared for it.* The sooner you are prepared the better. You may dispose of me very easily. I am nearly disposed of now; but this question is still to be settled—this Negro question I mean; the end of that is not yet. *These wounds were inflicted upon me—both sabre cuts on my head and bayonet stabs in different parts of my body— some minutes after I had ceased fighting and had consented to a surrender,* for the benefit of others, not for my own. (This statement was vehemently denied by all around.) I believe the Major (meaning Lieut. J. B. Stuart, of the United States Cavalry) would not have been alive; I could have killed him just as easily as a mosquito when he came in, but I supposed he came in only to receive our surrender. There had been loud and long calls of "Surrender" from us—as loud as men could yell—but in the confusion and excitement I suppose we were not heard. I do not think the Major, or anyone, meant to butcher us after we had surrendered.

An Officer here stated that the orders to the Marines were not to shoot anybody; but when they were fired upon by Brown's men and one of them killed, they were obliged to return the compliment. Mr. Brown insisted that the marines fired first.

AN OFFICER—Why did not you surrender before the attack?

MR. BROWN—I did not think it was my duty or interest to do so. We assured the prisoners that we did not wish to harm them, and they should be set at liberty. I exercised my best judgment, not believing the people would wantonly sacrifice their own fellow citizens, when we offered to let them go on condition of being allowed to change our position about a quarter of a mile. The prisoners agreed by vote among themselves to pass across the bridge with us. We wanted them only as a sort of guarantee of our own safety; that we should not be fired into. We took them in the first place as hostages and to keep them from doing any harm. We did kill some men in defending ourselves, but I saw no one fire except directly in self defense. Our orders were strict not to harm any one not in arms against us.

Q.—Brown, suppose you had every nigger in the United States, what would you do with them?

A.—Set them free.

Q.—Your intention was to carry them off and free them?

A.—Not at all.

A BYSTANDER—To set them free would sacrifice the life of every man in this community.

MR. BROWN—I do not think so.

A BYSTANDER—I know it. I think you are fanatical.

MR. BROWN—And I think you are fanatical. "Whom the Gods would destroy they first make mad." And you are mad.

Q.—Was it your only object to free the Negroes?

A.—Absolutely our only object.

Q.—But you demanded and took Col. Washington's silver and watch?

A.—Yes; *we intended freely to appropriate the property of slave holders to carry out our object.* It was for that, and only that, and with no design to enrich ourselves with any plunder whatever.

Q.—Did you know Sherrod in Kansas? I understand you killed him.

A.—I killed no man except in fair fight; I fought at Blackjack Point and Ossawattomie, and if I killed anybody it was at one of these places.

Another significant document—often referred to but rarely quoted —was the interview by a *Herald* reporter with Gerrit Smith on October 31. This was considered by some historians of journalism as the first official interview to be published in a daily paper. Others claimed that credit for Horace Greeley, who had interviewed Brigham Young in August, 1859. The actual facts are, as we have shown in an earlier chapter, that it was James Gordon Bennett himself who undertook and published the first interview—that with Rosina Townsend, keeper of the house of ill fame where Ellen Jewett was murdered, in 1836.

The interview with Gerrit Smith and his neighbors by the *Herald* was high-grade journalism. It, too, gave to its readers a totally different impression of the make-up of the leading abolitionists from that which its editor held. The impression of Gerrit Smith revealed in the interview stood in sharp contrast to Bennett's vitriolic outbursts against the man. There were many people who gleefully pointed to the obvious contradiction between the news and the editorial pages of the *Herald*. Bennett cheerfully admitted the fact. He enjoyed nothing better than to have some powerful politician or wealthy merchant call his attention to this apparent inconsistency, so rarely found in the other papers. The old man would listen seriously, then burst into a chuckle. "My good man," he would retort, "of course there are contradictions between my news and my editorial pages on many occasions. And why not? Editorials represent opinion, attitude, point of view. News, if it be news at all, must be a straightforward and impartial recording of what is said, or done, or contemplated. The editor whose views are always in accord with what appears in his news columns is either a dolt, a weathervane, or what is more likely, he sees to it that his news columns are doctored to fit his opinions. My paper is first of all a *news* paper, not a journal of opinion. That is why the *Herald* is the most widely read paper in the world. People in all walks of life, many, perhaps most of whom care naught for my personal views, buy the *Herald* and read it eagerly, because they know it will give them the news, full, complete, and without bias."

Such was the consistent journalistic philosophy which made it possible for Bennett to urge his men to get and print reports on matters which ran completely counter to his own opinions. Such was the philosophy which made possible the visit by a *Herald* reporter to the home of Gerrit Smith, as reported in the *Herald* on November 2, 1859:

Eleven miles from the Oneida depot, on the Central Railroad, perched well up on the hills of Madison County, is the quiet little village, or settlement of Peterboro. The last census shows it to have been at that time a collection of three hundred and forty-seven souls; and as it is by no means a progressive locality, and as the natural increase by birth and decrease by death about keep each other balanced, it is reasonable to conclude that the number of its inhabitants is about the same now. It is a pretty village, the houses and stores being clustered mainly on the north and south sides of a long green, surrounded with trees. At the east end of this green—it would be dignified with the name of park in a city—is the once popular Peterboro Academy, now dilapidated in exterior and degenerated internally; and at the west end is the Fay

House, the sole hotel or tavern of which the settlement can boast. The street at the west end stretches a little to the south, beyond the green, and contains a few straggling residences and the village church. On the south side of the green are some fifteen private dwellings and that important institution, the Post Office. On the north side we find six or eight dwellings, two drug stores, a tailor's shop, two groceries, one country drygoods store, a corner building, of a glaring yellow color, bearing the sign of the Peterboro Hotel, but with its doors and windows all closed, and the residents of the Hon. Gerrit Smith, ex-member of Congress, abolitionist, and supposed accomplice of the Harpers Ferry insurrectionists.

Though to outward appearance everything is dull, no little excitement exists in the village, and indeed in most parts of the country, on the subject of the Harpers Ferry affair. In all circles that event and the rumored connection of Gerrit Smith with the insurrectionists form the staple of conversation. The wildest rumors are of course afloat, and conjectures that speak but illy for the intelligence or common sense of the community are freely bandied about.

The first person with whom I had any conversation on the subject was Mr. P. Farrell, a strong Republican, landlord of the hotel at the Oneida Railroad depot; and as I found his sentiments very generally re-echoed during my progress through the county, it may be of some interest to report exactly what was said.

"Is there much excitement about here in regard to the Harpers Ferry affair?" I asked.

"Yes, sir," emphatically replied Mr. Farrell. "I guess Gerrit Smith is considerably excited about that matter. He is telegraphing from here all the while. His nigger was over here day before yesterday quite late, with dispatches. The telegraph office was closed, and he had to remain until morning. The old gentleman, evidently, is a good deal uneasy."

QUESTION.—What is he uneasy about? Does he fear an arrest?

MR. F.—Well, I don't know that he fears anything where his principles are involved; but then he is agitated and uneasy about it, and I suppose he is very much cut up about Old Brown.

Q.—Suppose a warrant should come here for his arrest on a requisition from the Governor of Virginia, do you think he would go?

MR. F.—Well, so far as he is concerned himself, if let alone he probably would not resist it.

Q.—Would anybody else resist?

MR. F.—I guess it would be tough work to attempt to get him out of Madison County.

Q—Why? Would the people offer any violent opposition to an officer?

MR. F.—An officer! Why it would take a regiment of soldiers to get him away. Yes, sir, the people would resist. They'll never let Gerrit Smith go to Virginia; that you may bet on.

Q.—Do they so generally sympathize with his abolition sentiment, then, in this county?

Mr. F.—No, they do not. But then there's scarcely a man in the county who has not at some time or other asked a favor of Gerrit Smith, and no one ever came away unsatisfied. Aside from politics, he's every man's friend. And when that's so, it is difficult to make people consent to let such a man be arrested and taken off to another State.

Q.—Then the people hereabouts are fond of Mr. Smith?

Mr. F.—Fond of him? I guess they are. No one can help it, for he's a noble old fellow.

Q.—You say he's sorry for Ossawatomie Brown, as they call him? Do you suppose he was personally well acquainted with him?

Mr. F.—Oh, yes. Brown was here constantly some years ago. He bought cattle to take to Ohio. His two sons were here with him, and he had a big law suit growing out of a wool contract, in which Timothy Jenkins was his lawyer. He was a fine, honest-appearing fellow, and was generally liked.

This was the substance of the conversation; but when I left Oneida for Peterboro on the following [Sunday] morning, the landlord remarked as I stepped into the buggy—"Tell Gerrit that if those Harpers Ferry fellows take him, it must not be from here. We'll make the old house a fort first!"

I drove from Oneida, eleven miles up hill to Peterboro, on a Sunday morning, over an indifferent road. Once during the ride I drew up at a little roadside tavern for the customary refreshments—water for the horse and whiskey for the driver. The occupants of the barroom were three men well advanced in years—the landlord and two of his neighbors—one lame, the other partially blind, and the third very deaf. The cheerful log fire was tempting; and so, throwing off my shawl and pulling off my gloves, I took a seat on the wooden bench in front of the grate. Now, thought I to myself, here I am in search of information—feeling the public pulse, as it were, and ascertaining what the popular sentiment is in respect to this dangerous affair in Virginia, and its probable consequences. Here is an opportunity to learn the opinions of three honest, disinterested men of the rural districts, and a little investment, accompanied by a proper degree of caution, may accomplish my object. Acting upon the mental suggestion, I invited my three elderly friends to the bar, and as rye whiskey was the only beverage to be procured, we "took the drinks round," I, of course, very lightly, and the invited guests rather more solidly. After beating about the bush for some time warily, so as not to startle the bird, I approached the subject upon which I most desired information. "Anything new from Harpers Ferry?" I inquired. Two of my friends gazed at me with astonished looks, and the partially blind man, even, seemed to stare inquiringly. The landlord was the first to speak.

"Whose Harper, and whar's his ferry?" he asked. "I don't know nothing about him."

I was nonplussed. "Why, you've heard of the outbreak in Virginia, and Gerrit Smith's supposed complicity with the plot for a Negro insurrection?" I inquired.

"No, I haven't," was the reply. "Have you, Jake?"

"Well, strikes me I did hear su'thin about it," replied another of the rural districters; "but I should think Gerrit Smith would be tired of niggers; 'taint six months since a nigger raped a little white girl, five years old, here in Clocksville, while her father lay dying in bed, and she has been near dead ever since. It's all along of these darned abolitionists that such things happen. I'll say it, if I am a Republican."

It was not many minutes before I left this tavern, where the occupants knew nothing about Mr. Harper or his ferry, and where I had made so poor an investment. (Memo—the whiskey only cost three cents a glass.)

I reached Peterboro during church time on Sunday, and found in the hotel the usual number of idlers generally gathered about a country tavern. As I stepped out of the buggy and entered the hotel, inquisitive glances were bent upon me; but taking them only for the customary curiosity of a country settlement, I soon sought my room and a conversation with Mr. Fay, the landlord.

"Did the Harpers Ferry affair create much excitement in this place?" was my inquiry.

"Yes, a great deal," was the landlord's reply.

Q.—How does your townsman, Gerrit Smith, feel about it?

L.—Well, he's quite excited and uneasy. He seems to feel bad.

Q.—Do you suppose if a warrant should come along for his arrest he would be taken away without difficulty?

L.—No, sir. He would not be taken away at all, unless those arresting him had more guns than we can muster in town.

Q.—Have you reason to suppose he would himself resist arrest?

L.—He would if his friends wished that he should.

Q.—Would they counsel resistance by force?

L.—I think they would now, because of the declaration of Governor Wise, that he wished a mob would take Gerrit Smith to Virginia, and his threat against him if he caught him there. Otherwise I think much would have depended on the manner of the arrest.

Q.—That is, I suppose, if Governor Morgan should decide to yield him up on a requisition from Virginia, and the authority of the officer was undisputed, there would be no resistance?

L.—Well, if a single officer came here with a warrant from Governor Morgan, and Mr. Smith desired to go quietly, the people might consent to have him taken. But even then I think there would be difficulty, for he has friends here and all over the county who are opposed to his going any way.

Q.—Political friends, do you mean?

L.—Oh, no. There are many of his best friends who would never support him politically; but almost all the people like him. He does a vast deal of good here, and so plain and so simple in his way of living for a man of his means. He employs a large number of people, too, about his premises, independent of his large charities.

Q.—Talking about his charities, I suppose he is preyed upon a good deal by the designing?

L.—Yes, a great deal, by people from all parts, who come here and pretend to sympathize with his political views. They are constantly bleeding him, and he is always moved by a tale of distress, so that others, too, have a chance of making money out of him out of all sorts of charitable pretenses.

.   .   .   .

It would probably astonish some of our ultra Southern brethren to see the residence of Gerrit Smith. It is just as unlike a conspirator's castle, or an insurrectionist's fort, or a Negro stealer's depot, as can well be imagined. No black muzzled muskets—no bristling bayonets or bowie knives—no revolvers—not even one of Old Brown's pikes, can be seen anywhere about the premises. There are two or three colored servants at work on the premises, but they look as little as possible like savage runaway slaves, ready to burn and ravish and murder. I looked over towards the house, and saw a fine little boy, about eight or ten years of age, romping on the stoop with two dogs. Even the animals failed to suggest anything of an incendiary, desperate character to my mind. They were handsome, useful watch dogs, gentle as lambs with their youthful playmate, and just such as a well-to-do farmer might love to possess. And here let me say that Mr. Smith cultivates some forty acres of ground adjoining his residence for his own family use.

A very little inquiry amongst such citizens as I chanced to meet convinced me that the excitement here has been intense, and the interest deep-seated, in all that relates to the Harpers Ferry affair. Where ever I asked the question I found but one answer—*The men of Peterboro would never consent that Gerrit Smith should be taken to Virginia. They would resist the officers of the law, first, to the extent of their power*. But the most absurd ideas prevail. By some I was assured that Gerrit Smith's house was watched by volunteers every night, in the fear that a Southern mob might carry him off in the night, after the fashion of Kansas border ruffianism in the days of old Ossawatomie Brown. By others I was seriously informed that the apprehension was not so much that Gerrit might be arrested, as that he might be shot—assassinated by some emissary of Governor Wise. Mr. Smith's neighbors evidently believed that the Southerners regard him as a terrible and powerful enemy, and have no idea that he is only looked upon by every sensible man as a crazy but honest abolition fanatic.

I soon discovered that poor Mr. Smith is about as excited and mistaken as his friends. Indeed, I am quite convinced that the agitation consequent upon the Virginia outbreak has not only impaired his health, but is likely to seriously affect his excitable and illy-balanced mind. *He is a very different man today from what he was twelve months since.* His calm, dignified, impressive bearing has given place to a hasty, nervous agitation, as though some great fear was constantly before his imagination. His eye is bloodshot and restless as that of a startled horse. He has lost flesh, and his face looks as red and as rough as though he had just returned from one of Old Brown's Kansas raids. It may be that he chafes and frets at the silence and inactivity imposed upon him by his friends, rather than dreads any responsibility for the past; but, however this may be, he appears an altered man, and his true friends must deeply regret an affair that can so agitate and so distress him.

Mr. Smith's views as to the Sabbath are as peculiar as are his political sentiments. He follows rather the Jewish doctrine, and makes Saturday his day of rest. He is, therefore, always visible and ready for business on the Sabbath. Having been apprised of this fact, I sought an interview with him on Sunday, armed with a letter from a near relative. I found this unnecessary, however, as Mr. Smith at once recognized our former slight personal acquaintance.

A few words sufficed to convince me that any attempt to obtain from Mr. Smith any information as to the actors in the Virginia invasion, or his connection therewith, was useless. I frankly avowed a desire to hear his sentiments upon that subject. "Sir," said Mr. Smith, starting like a frightened deer, "I can't speak a word with you on that matter. I can't say a word—not a syllable, even to my most intimate friends." "But," I argued, "I do not, of course, desire any disclosures or any word from you that could implicate or injure anyone."

"I can't speak about it at all," replied Mr. S., "I am going to be indicted. If any man in the Union is taken, it will be me. It would not be proper to say a word about it. I ought not to say one word. I am advised not to approach the subject at all. *I am going to be indicted, sir, indicted! You must not talk to me about it."*

I subsequently conferred with a near relative and close adviser of Mr. Smith, and expressed to him a desire to obtain some statement that, while doing injury to none, might, on the other hand, remove erroneous impressions and lay facts before the public.

"Sir," he said, "Mr. Smith does desire to make such a statement himself, and can scarcely be restrained from doing so. But if he should, he would do it in his own manner, and strike the thing square in the face, let who might be injured. He is, however, strongly advised not to do so in the present condition of affairs, and has agreed to abide by the judgment of his counsel. *When he does tell his story, it will be found that many now only partially suspected are more implicated than he himself is. But at present he will say no word to any person.*"

I made some inquiries about Captain Brown, and found that he was here last spring for several weeks, a guest at Gerrit Smith's house, and that while here *a number of the most prominent leading Republicans visited him, and were for days in consultation with him.*

As I viewed Gerrit Smith, the man of sturdy frame and large heart, I could not resist drawing a contrast in my own mind, between him, with his earnest, disinterested, but misdirected philanthropy, and his wily, calculating, selfish co-laborer, William H. Seward; the one an honest abolitionist—the other a political anti-slavery man. How wide the distinction between the generous although almost criminal acts of the one, and the cool, well-weighed, carefully prepared professions of the other. Truly, there is as much difference between the manly heart and the politician's gizzard, as physically between the massive form of the Abolitionist and the insignificant figure of the agitator. I could not help thinking that Southern men, who have seen them both, must have much more respect for the sturdy champion of the Negro than for the cunning demagogue who rides the black hobby only so far as it is safe and useful. The former has before now refused to shake the hand that would fasten a fetter on a human being. The latter, with Spaniel-like amiability, has tendered the grasp of friendship to a Southern opponent who has insulted him only to find it haughtily rejected. Yet, would not a Southern gentleman respect the former far more than the latter?

A comical instance of Gerrit Smith's connection with the Negro is related by his neighbors. Some years ago an eccentric Southern gentleman died, leaving forty Negroes their freedom, "providing Mr. Smith would transfer them to New York State and provide for them." This Mr. S. of course consented to do, for he declares he cannot use his money more satisfactorily than in procuring freedom for the slave. But when the time came for the exodus of the darkies, they were informed that Gerrit was a cannibal, and only wanted to get them to New York to cook and eat them. The poor Negroes were so scared that many refused to leave their State and chose to remain in servitude, and others ran away as soon as they could get a chance, leaving only seven out of the forty to reach Peterboro.

I believe that Brown's visit to his [Smith's] house last spring was intimately connected with the insurrection, and that it is the knowledge that at any moment, either by the discovery of papers or the confession of accomplices, his connection with the affair may become exposed, that keeps Mr. Smith in constant excitement and fear. . . .

When the jury brought in its verdict against John Brown, finding him guilty of murder; of treason against the Commonwealth of Virginia, and of inciting the slaves to insurrection, Bennett hailed the verdict as eminently just. However, he contended there was more to be done. The federal government was urged to bring to trial all accessories of Brown, including, by all means, Seward.

"It will never do for the administration to permit itself to be held responsible for charging W. H. Seward with the high crime of treason, without proceeding against him as a traitor. . . . Let the Government act."

But the government of the otherwise so pliable President James Buchanan failed to act.

The political implications of what had taken place were soon to be translated into votes by the people of the State of New York. Such Black Republican organs as the *Tribune,* the *Times,* the *Evening Post,* and the *Courier and Enquirer,* wrote Bennett, "look at the dangerous results of Seward's doctrines each from a different standpoint, but all treat it with the same imbecile palliation and unmanly sycophony. The fanatical philosophers of the *Tribune* hate the man, but love the traitor-ultraism of Seward, and sing covert elegies about the epitaph of old Brown. The wishy-washy *Times* palliates the doctrine while pretending to deplore its results. The hoary-of-service (Webb) at the *Courier and Enquirer* looks upon Seward as his deity upon earth, and strives to defend him from the results of his own troublesome doctrines. And the poet of the *Evening Post* endeavors to joke over the bloody scenes of Harpers Ferry."

Seward's political future hung in the balance. Bennett worked like mad to whip up the voters against him and his Republican machine. But the voters refused to look upon Seward as a traitor.

They saw in him their hero—the champion of the common people—
and the next president of the United States. When the votes had
been tallied, Seward and his party were swept into office. Bennett
became disconsolate and heartsick. Seward, he told his readers, was
the "Arch-Beelzebub of American politics." The others, Sumner,
Chase, Wilson, Giddings, Gerrit Smith, and Hale, were but satel-
lites "revolving round the greater abolitionist sun, and vainly attempting to fly from the centripetal force that controls them." According to Bennett, William H. Seward was the most unscrupulous
adept in pecuniary and political profligacy that the country had ever
produced.

Attempting to discover how it was possible for a man with the
record of Seward to win the state elections, Bennett decided that it
was due to the general political demoralization of a substantial section of the voters, who refused to vote. Hence the best-organized
machine could carry the day. These voters (more than 200,000 in
New York State) had been "palsied into supineness and inactivity,
preferring rather to do nothing, than to co-operate with iniquity of
any kind." As a consequence, there had taken place the loss "by
default, of an important election, and a victory in behalf of the
most atrocious disunion dogmas that ever have been sprung upon
the public."

Looking over the election returns from a number of other states
—Michigan, Illinois, Massachusetts, Wisconsin, and Ohio—which
had taken place in November, 1859, the editor of the *Herald* refused
to admit that public opinion was rapidly crystallizing around the
very men whom he denounced as traitors. His only explanation was
the same as that given for the New York elections. The good, the
honest electorate stayed away from the polls. Yet in their hands
rested the future of the Republic. Should they continue their boycott of the polls, then one could easily foresee the dreary prospects
for the country's advance. It would mean that William H. Seward
would most likely be the next president of the United States!

Bennett proceeded to picture what would happen with Seward
in the White House. Outbreaks such as the one at Harpers Ferry
would not be suppressed, but would be condoned and even encour-
ged, contributing to them such indirect aid as the federal admin-

istration could afford. "Missouri would be invaded by abolitionists from Kansas and Illinois; Kentucky and Tennessee would be attacked from Ohio; the plan of Brown to take possession of Maryland and Virginia would be attempted from Pennsylvania and New York, and 'the day of calamity' would come which Gerrit Smith foretold, when 'fire, rape and slaughter' shall fill up the measure of affliction. Where then would be the civilization, progress, happiness and onward advancement of the United States? Abolitionism, aided by President Seward, its high priest and apostle, would be rampant in its aggressive measures."

Such was the fearful prospect. Never had the aging editor felt so hopeless and helpless. Yet give up the fight he refused to do. Instead, he called upon the confused and non-voting citizens to rise in their might as voters of a great and good republic to smite and destroy the organs of Black Republicanism while there was still time.

14. *"Let the South Secede!"*

Out of the turbulent political arena there arose, in the late summer and early fall of 1858, a new and hitherto unknown figure. If he appeared to be important, it was only because the derision and contempt heaped upon him by editors and political wire-pullers was so widespread. But within a year, these same elements were forced to acknowledge that the object of their venom had become a major presidential threat.

The *Herald* took notice of Abe Lincoln only after it discovered that agents of Senator Stephen Douglas had appealed to Tammany for a fund of $50,000 to be used in the Illinois senatorial campaign. Douglas had been considered good presidential timber as early as 1856. He was a powerful speaker, an able debater, and a shrewd political manipulator. His hold on northern democrats was very strong. That he, with his national prestige and great abilities, should appeal to Tammany for financial aid, caused the *Herald's* editor to ponder what type of man the new contender from Illinois might be.

Bennett had on many occasions issued orders that the names of certain persons were not to appear in the columns of the *Herald*. It seems likely that he may have issued an order of this kind respecting Abraham Lincoln, for the *Herald* departed from its usual policy of complete news coverage of political campaigns by ignoring the man from Illinois who had challenged the seat of Senator Douglas. Bennett viewed Lincoln as just another abolitionist.

Other New York papers, such as the *Times, Tribune* and *Evening Post*, gave full coverage to the celebrated Lincoln-Douglas debates. The *Post* even went so far as to send a special correspondent to cover them. Not so the *Herald*. It ignored or played down Abe Lincoln till he made his trip East to speak at the Cooper Union

Institute in February, 1860, under the auspices of the Young Men's Central Republican Union. Only once, prior to this time, had Bennett devoted an editorial to Lincoln, the occasion being a discussion of the Lincoln-Douglas debate in Chicago.

The *Herald,* on the morning of February 28, gave its readers the full text of Lincoln's New York speech, including parenthetical notations of the laughter or applause which punctuated the address.

"ANOTHER REPUBLICAN ORATOR ON THE STUMP," was the caption of the article. It reported that an unusually large number of ladies were present. Another fact, unique in political campaigns, according to the *Herald,* was the admission charge of twenty-five cents. But the entrance fee proved no deterrent to the audience, which continued "to pour in in considerable numbers till the large hall was about three-quarters full."

The Club which payed Lincoln his fee of $200 and all other bills, was left with a net profit of just $17. Total income had been $367, and a great many free tickets had been given away to swell the crowd.

William Cullen Bryant, editor of the *Evening Post,* introduced Mr. Lincoln to his first New York audience.

The man from the West was described by the *Herald* as a tall, thin, and dark-complexioned, apparently quick in his perceptions. "He is rather unsteady in his gait, and there is an involuntary comical awkwardness which marks his movements while speaking. His voice, though sharp and powerful, at times, has a frequent tendency to dwindle into a shrill and unpleasant sound. His enunciation is slow and emphatic." A peculiar characteristic of his delivery, we are told, was the remarkable mobility of his features, "the frequent contortions of which excited the merriment which his words alone could not well have produced."

The article and the speech were framed in other strange bits of news: "A Mother Destroys the Body of Her Illegitimate Child by Burning It in a Furnace"; the report on the use of a new street-sweeping machine, which had swept Broadway from Fourteenth Street to the Battery; a publicity plug for Barnum's Museum, announcing a new and strange creature, "supposed to belong to the ourang-outang species, but having all the appearances of a human

being"; the report of a fire in Canal Street; of a law lecture by
Judge Clerke; of a tribute to the late Daniel Fanshaw by the New
York Typographical Society; of missionaries sailing for China; and
of a little girl who was caught stealing letters from a postbox. There
was also information that widowed Mrs. Blount, the daughter of
the man who wrote *The Star-Spangled Banner,* "would give some
reading at the Hope Chapel to raise funds for the support of her
children."

Following the Harpers Ferry raid, political lines grew more
taut than ever before. Into the rapidly swelling ranks of the Republican party poured radical Democrats, disgusted Whigs, rampant
free-soilers, and abolitionists. Into it also poured the foreign-born,
conscious of their strength and dignity as "citizens" rather than
"subjects." Politicians, big and little, smelling victory in 1860 with
all that it would mean in jobs and contracts, hopped aboard the
Republican bandwagon. Nor were the financiers and industrialists
far behind. All in all, it was as strange and varied in its multiple
make-up and philosophy as was possible.

The Democrats, meanwhile, were breaking at the Mason-Dixon
line. In the North, Douglas was trying to reconcile the Dred Scott
Decision with the rights of popular sovereignty. But Jeff Davis,
speaking before the state convention in Mississippi, put the issue in
bold, blunt terms: "Our countrymen have two courses before them.
One leads by tortuous construction through civil strife to the destruction of the best hopes of republican government. The other,
through peace and prosperity, mounts to an eminence which looks
down on a continent of equal, sovereign, confederate States. We are
now near the point at which a selection is to be made. For myself,
I say, if a President be elected on the platform of Mr. Seward's
Rochester speech, let the Union be dissolved. The success of such a
candidate would indeed produce an irrepressible conflict. I love and
venerate the Union of these States; but I love liberty and Mississippi
more."

The hosts of the Republican Party assembled in Chicago in mid-
May, 1860. There were a number of candidates—but none had the
backing or the national spotlight accorded Seward. The practical
politicians were determined to allow nothing to go into the party

platform that smacked of abolitionism. When Josiah R. Giddings
of Ohio proposed the inclusion of that section of the Declaration
of Independence which declares all men to be created free and
equal, the convention voted it down.

Seward had many powerful enemies at the convention. Most
potent of all, was a moon-faced, apple-cheeked, white-haired individual of middle age bearing a credential from far-off Oregon. In
his heavy boots, broad-brimmed hat, and crumpled suit, he looked
every inch a farmer. This was Horace Greeley, editor of the *New
York Tribune,* the man who had sworn years earlier to have his
revenge on Seward. Greeley, whose influence was very great among
the humbler midwestern delegates, worked like a beaver to line up
enough votes to stave off the nomination of Seward. When the convention opened on the sixteenth, the Seward forces gained the upper
hand, and, flushed with victory, pressed for an immediate selection
of the presidential candidate. Greeley, at the close of the second
day, wired his paper that Seward was in the saddle and would be
nominated. That night, the anti-Seward forces caucused late, and
when they adjourned, had agreed to unite their forces behind Abraham Lincoln of Illinois. When the ballots were counted on the
morning of the eighteenth, Seward was defeated. Greeley had done
his work well.

The nomination of Lincoln came as a bombshell to the nation.
Almost alone, among the New York press, in expressing its grati-
fication and pleasure at the choice, was the *Evening Post.*

The surprise and chagrin of Republican organs was as nothing
when compared to the blasts of invective poured out by the pro-
Democratic journals. The *Buffalo Daily Courier* claimed Lincoln
had never held public office of any credit; that he was known only
as a slang-whanging stump speaker of a class with which every
party abounds and of which every party is ashamed. He represented neither principle nor program—only bitter hatred against
Seward. The *Binghamton Democrat* remarked wryly that the people were now expected to accept a slang nickname (Old Uncle Abe)
in lieu of fitness. Bennett wrote that the Republicans had passed
over such able, though misguided men as Seward, Chase, and

Banks, to take on a fourth-class lecturer who couldn't even speak good grammar.

From the South the language was much stronger. Typical was the comment of the *Charleston Mercury:* "A horrid-looking creature he is, sooty and scoundrelly in aspect, a cross between a nutmeg dealer, the horse-swapper, and the night man. . . . He is a lanksided Yankee of the uncomeliest visage and the dirtiest complexion. Faugh! After him, what decent white man would be President?"

A young and ardent German-American Republican, who had known Lincoln in Springfield as a lawyer, who had covered his debates with Douglas for the *Cincinnati Commercial,* and who was soon to join the staff of the *Herald,* wrote in his autobiography many years later: "It seemed to me incomprehensible and outrageous that the uncouth, common, Illinois politician . . . should carry the day over the eminent and tried statesman [Seward]."

The year of Abraham Lincoln's nomination and election to the presidency of the United States was, in one sense, the high point in influence of the *New York Herald*. Its circulation (77,000 daily and 82,000 Sunday) was, without a doubt, the largest of any other newspaper in the world. It exceeded that of the "Old Thunderer," the *London Times,* by fully 25,000 and that of its leading daily competitors in New York, the *Sun,* the *Tribune,* the *Times,* and the *Evening Post,* by 17,000, 22,000, 42,000, and 57,000, respectively.

The story of the hectic days between May and November, 1860, is the story of the most bitter presidential campaign in United States history. Every issue of the *Herald* carried at least one report of physical encounters between the rapid partisans of Lincoln, Douglas, and Breckenridge. While Bennett penned editorials filled with malice and hostility toward the candidate, he also published lengthy news items which were frequently favorable to Lincoln. Carl Sandburg records one such instance in his biography of Lincoln:

There came to Springfield a correspondent for the *New York Herald*, a scribbler whose name was never signed to his articles. And while his newspaper was hurling shrapnel, javelins, and poison at Lincoln, editorially, he was sending columns of reportorial fact and impression of just the opposite character. His policy as a writer and his personal feelings about Lincoln were as different from the editorial page of the *New York Herald* as day is from night.

He likes Lincoln's looks, face, ways, and wrote: "Mr. Lincoln's face is a study—especially when lighted up. I have never seen a picture of him that does anything like justice to the original. He is a much better-looking man than any of the pictures represent. I do not understand why people call him Old Abe. He displays no appearance of age except deeply indented wrinkles on his brow, and the furrow plowed down his bony cheeks. You hardly detect the presence of frost in his black glossy hair."

Then the correspondent did a bold deed. He compared Lincoln's looks to those of two respectable Easterners, and gave Lincoln the best of it. "I do not understand why Mr. Lincoln is represented as being so prodigiously ugly. Put him alongside Mr. Charles O'Connor and Mr. James W. Gerard—both of which eminent gentlemen have ridiculed so much his supposed ugliness—and if he would not appear 'as Adonis to a satyr,' he would at all events be set down as the finest-looking man of the trio. He affects not the elegancies of refined socity, does not care to imitate New York aldermen in the matter of yellow kids, but is altogether a plain, blunt, unostentatious man. . . . In all of the photographs, his face wears a stony, rigid, corpselike expression, as if they were taken from a piece of sculpture, whereas in conversation he has great mobility and play of features. When he is thus animated, you fail to perceive anything ugly or grotesque about him."

That "scribbler" of the *Herald* was the young German-American referred to earlier in this chapter. Born Ferdinand Heinrich Gustav Hillgard, he had migrated to the United States in 1853, a young man of eighteen years. Soon thereafter he changed his name to Henry Villard. He studied law for a time in Springfield, Illinois, but soon shifted his activities to the field of journalism, writing first for German language papers and later for the American press. By 1860, Villard was well established in his field. Immediately following the nomination of Lincoln at Chicago, the young newspaper man went to New York. There he renewed his acquaintance with Frederic Hudson, the *Herald's* dynamic managing editor. Hudson was impressed by the intelligence, resourcefulness, and writing ability of Villard; and when he learned that the young man was personally acquainted with Lincoln, he proposed that Villard return to Springfield, to report on Lincoln for the *Herald*.

Thus it was that the reports from the *Herald's* special correspondent at Springfield were both factual and friendly, while its editorials were biased and denunciatory. Villard remained on to cover Lincoln's activities till the President-elect left for Washington. He was the only member of the working press who accompanied the new chief magistrate on that train from Springfield, Illinois, to Cincinnati, Ohio, by personal invitation of Lincoln.

Through Villard's foresight Lincoln's farewell address to his friends at Springfield was saved from oblivion. No shorthand reporter was on hand at the railway station. That speech—which had been made extemporaneously—Villard asked Lincoln to write out in full immediately after the train got under way. This Lincoln did.

In detailed and matter-of-fact fashion, the *Herald* of November 8, 1860, informed its readers that the Republican candidate had carried fifteen states (Connecticut, Illinois, Indiana, Iowa, Maine, Massachusetts, Michigan, Minnesota, New Hampshire, New York, Ohio, Pennsylvania, Rhode Island, Vermont, Wisconsin), which gave him an electoral vote of 169, as against 66 for Breckenridge, 49 for Bell, and 20 for Douglas. (The *Herald* conceded California, Georgia and Louisiana to Breckenridge and Oregon to Douglas.) Lincoln had won New York State but had lost the city, where his opponents had garnered 62,657 votes to his 33,069. In spite of the victory by the Republicans, Congress would still be safely Democratic, said the *Herald,* with a majority of eight in the Senate and twenty in the House.

Of all the dark days in the nation's history, none were blacker than those between the election of Lincoln and his inauguration as President.

Secession and dismemberment of the United States was no longer an idle threat. South Carolina took the lead almost as soon as Lincoln's election was assured, to be followed in quick succession by six of her sister states. James Buchanan sat quietly in the White House doing nothing to stop the disintegration. Fire-eating Southerners became ever more outspoken. Northern industrialists and merchants, fearful of the loss of lucrative southern markets, beat a hasty retreat from the position they had taken only a few weeks earlier. They were prepared to make almost any kind of a compromise to appease the South. Once again the abolitionists were blamed for the sad state of the nation, and in many northern cities their leaders were beaten, tarred, and feathered or prevented from speaking.

The President-elect refused to make a declaration as to his policy. Hotheads demanded that he follow the lead of old Andy Jackson who thirty years earlier promised to march federal troops into the seceding states and hang every secessionist leader to the nearest tree or lamp post. Others proposed a compromise deal be worked out with the South to save the Union; while yet another group favored letting the Southern states go their own way in peace.

Bennett demanded forthwith that Lincoln make public the policy he intended to pursue. This policy, he argued, must of necessity be one of conciliation. But when no word came from the new chief executive, Bennett angrily referred to him as the man who had once split rails and was now splitting the Union. The *Herald* editor announced that if the Southern states broke away from the Union they were merely following a pattern and procedure that had been used by the founding fathers against British tyranny. This pattern they had handed down to later generations as a legitimate instrument for the expression of public opinion.

The sentiments which Bennett voiced were repeated, with minor variations, by such other influential New York dailies as the *Journal of Commerce,* the *Express,* the *Day Book,* the *Daily News,* and two foreign-language dailies, the *Courrier des Etats Unis* and the *Staats-Zeitung.*

Bryant of the *Evening Post* took a firm stand against secession. Peaceful secession he called an absurdity which no government could tolerate, for such a policy could mean only one thing: undermining its own credit, its own ability to function, and the faith of its citizens in its future. "If a state secedes it is in rebellion, and the seceders are traitors."

Raymond of the *Times* took an equally strong position, and the *World* followed suit.

But the most widely read of all Republican journals, Horace Greeley's *Tribune,* took a vacillating position, which left its wide army of loyal readers thoroughly befuddled, and thus helped to bring further confusion into the already muddy stream of public opinion.

On November 9, Horace Greeley was very sure that a state has no right to remain in the Union and defy the laws; but to withdraw "was quite another matter." He admitted Bennett's contention that the right of secession, though revolutionary, nevertheless did exist. A few days later Greeley asserted that the Union should be preserved only so long as it was "beneficial and satisfactory to all parties concerned." To detain forcibly those who wished to leave, he contended, was fatal to the Union. All through November, December, and well into January, the *Tribune* took a position which differed little if any from that of its bitter enemy, the *Herald*.

If the Southerners in their great majority no longer wish to be a part of our United States, then let them go in peace. Such was the position of Greeley. Much as he would hate to see the loss of so much as a single star from the federal flag, he would far rather suffer that loss than to employ military force to keep the people of the South in the Union. As late as January 14, 1861, he sounded the same note: "If the people of the Slave States, or of the Cotton States alone, really wish to get out of the Union, I am in favor of letting them go as soon as that result can be peacefully and constitutionally attained." All he asked in return was that they make their decision, without intimidation, by a fair and impartial balloting on the question at issue. "I want no States kept in the Union by coercion; but I insist that none be coerced out of it."

Greeley, and for that matter many other Northerners, believed that if the South were magnanimously permitted to secede in peace, it would soon realize the folly of its ways and return, chastened, to the Union. This policy, which Greeley termed one of "masterly inactivity," would, he was certain, bring the great majority of the Southerners back to their senses and cause them to disown their rabble-rousing fire-eaters. Greeley took this position as late as March, 1861, arguing that if Lincoln's administration followed this tactic the Union would be saved in short order, and leaders of the secession movement would soon "dangle at every cross-road in the South" at the hands of their own aroused neighbors.

Appeasement was in the air everywhere in the North. To the people south of the Mason-Dixon line, the peaceful inclinations of the North merely strengthened their determination to push forward with the rupture. In January of 1861 there was put forward in all seriousness by a great number of Northern Republicans and Democrats, the Crittenden Compromise which proposed making the Missouri line of 36' 30", a new and permanent line across the country to separate Slave and Free territory. The *Times,* the *Evening Post,* the *World,* and even the *Tribune* opposed this scheme, but the *Herald* gave it full support; and when William B. Astor brought a petition in its favor to the *Herald* office, it acquired 140 signatures within a few hours.

Suddenly Greeley completely reversed his position. Screaming editorials appeared in the *Tribune* with headings that cried: "No Compromise!", "No Concession to Traitors!", "The Constitution As It Is!" Then a few days later, the editor of the *Tribune* modified the new stand: Let the Federal Government buy up and free all the slaves in Delaware, Maryland, Missouri, Texas, Arkansas, and Louisiana! The cost was estimated at about $100,000,000 and the whole job could be completed in fifteen years.

The *World* had its pet solution; so did the *Express,* the *Sun,* and the *Journal of Commerce.*

But of all the proposals, none was more fantastic than that of James Gordon Bennett. He had, of course, favored the Crittenden Compromise and he had asked Lincoln to repudiate the Republican platform. But shortly after New Year's Day, 1861, he suggested that the Southern states convene their own constitutional convention, adopt such amendments to the Constitution of the United States as they deemed necessary, and then submit these amendments to the Northern states for their adoption. In this fashion, Bennett was certain, the Union could be preserved, that is, all except New England. But New England, contended the editor, was such a well of provincial meanness, self-conceit, bigotry, universal fault-finding, and hypercritical opposition to anything and everything, that its loss would be a blessing to the rest of the country.

Sounding this theme again the next day, January 5, he asserted that of the nation's five million voters, "it is within bounds to say that four million three hundred thousand are conservative in sentiment and prepared to concede to the South their reasonable demands." These voters, he was sure, would not pause "in choosing between the happiness and prosperity which will flash upon the country out of concord, and the misery which perseverance in the chaotic byways of Abolition would produce." Therefore, once the South had formulated its amendments to the Constitution, "let mass meetings everywhere call upon our Northern State Legislatures to summon together constituent State conventions." Uniting the common people under the cry of "The Union must and shall be preserved," Bennett was certain that such a movement would sweep the country, and might even "produce its rebound in the frozen consciences of Massachusetts and Vermont." But should the New Englanders reject the plan, they might well be compelled to form their own rigid abolitionist republic, with Greeley, Garrison, or Wendell Phillips as president—or perhaps annex themselves to Canada.

The *Herald,* always sensitive to economic disturbances, had reported in mid-December that the Northern states had suffered a loss of four hundred seventy-eight million dollars since the election of Lincoln. Mayor Fernando Wood, whose political supporters included most of the opposition to the Republicans, used the political turmoil to further his own ambitions. At a tumultuous mass meeting on December 15, his followers adopted a resolution which declared that they believed their southern brethren were engaged in "the holy cause of American liberty." To them, the meeting extended its heartfelt sympathy.

On January 8, Mayor Wood went even further. This time he sent a message to the City Council suggesting that New York secede from the United States and establish itself as a free and independent city-state. "Why may not New York," suggested the Mayor to his Council, "disrupt the bands which bind her to a venal and corrupt master—to a people and a party that have plundered revenues, attempted to ruin her commerce, taken away the power of self-government, and destroyed the Confederacy of which she was the proud Empire City? Amid the gloom which the present and prospective condition of things must cast over the country, New York, as a *Free City,* may shed the only light and hope for a future reconstruction of our once blessed Confederacy."

However, when once the War Between the States got under way, public opinion united behind the federal government. Fernando Wood realized then that the sentiments he had uttered a few weeks earlier would list him as a traitor, so he did a quick about-face and became a most vociferous patriot.

The strain of those fateful months told upon everyone, but upon the President-elect they must have been truly terrific. Villard, in one of his letters to the *Herald,* mentioned that Lincoln had lost forty pounds from his spare frame in the course of less than a year. And he told how pale and careworn Lincoln looked, overwhelmed as he was, not only with the responsibility of the ship of state, but with a crew part mutinous, part indifferent to its fate or their own. In addition, the President was immersed in a sea of groveling tidewaiters, fawners, sycophants, and parasites, greedy for office. "His ears and eyes must learn to be closed at certain times. His lips must be trained to less ready response. If not, the crowd of cormorants and place-hunters will unbalance and overwhelm him," concluded Villard.

In the meantime, the *Herald* came forth with a new idea. North America, it proclaimed, was too large for any *one* government, "but establish two and they will in good time cover the continent." The alluring concept of imperialist expansion drew a number of Bennett editorials. In one of these he pictured the two great republics (United States and Confederate States) as friendly allies. The former would annex Canada, while the latter would take under its banner Mexico, Cuba, and all other lands and islands of the Caribbean. Continuing his pipe dream of conquest, Bennett predicted that "Northern troops may yet have to repel invaders of the possessions of slave-holders in Mexico, and Venezuela, and our fleet will joyfully aid in dispersing new Spanish armadas on the coast of Cuba." Nor was this all. In turn, he foresaw how the legions from Louisiana, Alabama, and South Carolina would aid their Northern cousins on the banks of the St. Lawrence or under the very walls of Quebec!

Shifting suddenly from his dreams of conquest, Bennett let loose another novel idea upon his readers. Forgetting for a moment all the horrible names he had heaped upon the President-elect, he now turned to him with a suggestion which if followed, would not only avert the impending ruin of the country but invest Lincoln's name "with an immortality far more enduring than would attach to it by his elevation to the presidency." The scheme, in brief, was that Abraham Lincoln, instead of going to Washington to be inaugurated President of the United States, step out of the national picture and go home to Springfield. This time Bennett was certain he had a surefire idea, and lectured Lincoln on it. Why, if he would only withdraw at this time, and surrender his claims to some man acceptable to both sections of the country, it would "render him the peer of Washington in patriotism." But should Lincoln fail to heed these words of wisdom, should he persist "in his present position in the teeth of results as his election must produce, he will totter into a dishonoured grave, driven there perhaps by the hands of an assassin, leaving behind him a memory more execrable than that of Arnold—more despised than that of the traitor Cataline!"

Meanwhile the presidential train, on its roundabout journey from Springfield to Washington, carried the untried leader of a divided country toward its destination. Henry Villard's respect and admiration for Lincoln grew with each succeeding day. To the *Herald* he reported his impressions of finding the President a man of immense power, force of character, and natural talent. But more than that he found him to be "so sincere, so conscientious, so earnest, so simple-hearted, that one cannot help liking him," for he possessed all the homespun common sense with which his friends accredited him.

The official policy of the *Herald* was one of forever finding fault with and belittling Lincoln. His speech at Columbus was called one of "foolish consolations," and the *Herald* bluntly advised him that if he could do no better, "let him say nothing." When he passed through Buffalo the President was pictured as a man whose face and forehead were furrowed by a thousand wrinkles; his hair was unkempt, his clothing badly arranged, and altogether he looked more like some newly arrived foreign immigrant than the first man of the land.

As the train neared New York, where the Republicans had planned an impressive and elaborate welcome, the sardonic Bennett in a lead editorial asked his readers: "What will Mr. Lincoln do when he arrives? What will he say to the citizens of this great metropolis? Will he kiss our girls, and give a twirl to the whiskers he has begun to cultivate? Will he tell our merchants, groaning under the pressure of the greatest political convulsion ever experienced in America, that 'nobody is hurt' or that 'marching troops into South Carolina' and bombarding its fortresses is 'no invasion'?"

When Lincoln did arrive, the crowd which greeted him was sadly lacking in spontaneous enthusiasm, all of which pleased the *Herald* no end.

Due to the threats made upon Lincoln's life, his entry into Washington was made in secrecy—a fact which Bennett made much of for several days.

Henry Villard, whose reports on Lincoln were so completely at variance with those of his editor, decided to function exclusively from the nation's capitol. The *Herald,* which had first call of his services, paid him twenty-five dollars per week; the *Cincinnati Commercial* and the *Chicago Tribune,* each fifteen. His was, in fact, the earliest of all the syndicated news services which emanated from Washington. "Bennett and Frederic Hudson of the *Herald,*" wrote Villard in his autobiography, "offered to engage me as a telegraphic correspondent, and, as they conceded my condition that I should be free to speak through the *Herald* as a sympathizer with the Republican party, I came to an understanding with them. My enterprise was to be a sort of supplement to the Associated Press, whose then Washington correspondent was very inefficient, but was kept in his place on account of his long services."

Washington in those days preceding Lincoln's inauguration was altogether different from what it was during the long years of war that followed. Its regular population of 60,000 was already swelled by 10,000 visitors, office seekers, politicians, businessmen, speculators, staunch Union men, and equally staunch Confederates. Except for the few large public buildings, Washington was still nothing but an overgrown village. The streets, with few exceptions, were unpaved; the stores small; the homes mostly low wooden or brick structures. Neither street-cars nor omnibuses plied the streets. Restaurants were few in number and none too good, but there was an ample supply of bars and taverns. Altogether, Washington had the easy-going and indolent character of the South, rather than that of the hustling, bustling North.

At last came the day of the Inauguration. The whole country was tense with excitement, wondering what would be the policy of the first Republican president. At its conclusion, everyone breathed easier. The *Times* and the *World* praised it as a statesmanlike job. The *Evening Post* considered it simple in style, concise and pithy in manner, generous and conciliatory in tone, and convincing in argument. The *Tribune* commented that while it showed Lincoln meant to act cautiously and provoke no unnecessary hostility, there could be no question that he intended to be equally firm in seeing to it that the laws of the land were obeyed and executed. The speech proved, wrote Greeley, that the United States still lives "with a Man at the head of it."

The *Daily News,* on the other hand, warned its readers to beware the honeyed phrases of the President. The other Democratic organs were equally skeptical. But it remained for James Gordon Bennett to take the lead in denunciation and ridicule of Lincoln's inaugural speech:

It would have been almost as instructive if President Lincoln had contented himself with telling his audience yesterday a funny story and let them go. His inaugural is but a paraphrase of the vague generalities contained in his pilgrimage speeches, and shows clearly either that he has not made up his mind respecting his future course, or else that he desires, for the present, to keep his intentions to himself.

The stupendous questions of the last month have been whether the incoming Administration would adopt a coercive or a conciliatory policy towards the Southern States; whether it would propose satisfactory amendments to the Constitution, convening an extra session of Congress for the purpose of considering them; and whether, with the spirit of the statesmen who laid the cornerstone of the institutions of the republic, it would rise to the dignity of the occasion, and meet as was fitting the terrible crisis through which the country is passing.

The inaugural gives no satisfaction on any of these points. Parts of it contradict those that precede them, and where the adoption of any course is hinted at, a studious disavowal of its being a recommendation is appended. Not a small portion of the columns of our paper, in which the document is amplified, look as though they were thrown in as a mere make-weight. A resolve to procrastinate, before committing himself, is apparent throughout. Indeed, Mr. Lincoln closes by saying that "there is no object in being in a hurry," and that "nothing valuable can be lost by taking time." Filled with careless *bonhommie* as this first proclamation to the country of the new President is, it will give but small contentment to those who believe that not only its prosperity, but its very existence, is at stake. . . .

In a word, the inaugural is not a crude performance—it abounds in traits of craft and cunning. It bears marks of indecision, and yet of strong coercive proclivities, with serious doubts whether the government will be able to gratify them. It is so clearly intended to admit of a double, or even of any possible interpretation, that many will content themselves with waiting for the progress of events, in the meanwhile seeking in it for no meaning at all. It is neither candid nor statesmanlike; nor does it possess any essential of dignity or patriotism. It would have caused a Washington to mourn and would have inspired Jefferson, Madison, or Jackson with contempt. With regard to the ultimate projects of Mr. Lincoln, the public is no wiser than before. It is sincerely to be trusted that he is yet ignorant of them himself.

Seward the astute politician was a key figure in the new Cabinet. Aware at last of the dizzying speed with which the country was rushing toward civil strife, he did an about-face from his former position, and brought all his weight to bear upon the President to move for quick and appropriate compromises with the seceding South. With this change in policy, Seward, in the eyes of Bennett, underwent a remarkable metamorphosis. He was no longer the arch-betrayer of the Union, but rather one who "if he perseveres in the course which he has beyond peradventure determined on, will make for himself the highest name in the history of statesmen, patriots, and benefactors of the Republic." Sure that Seward would bend the administration to his will, Bennett gleefully referred to the platform, adopted less than ten months earlier by the Republican Party at Chicago as "the fossil of a bygone time."

Lincoln refused to follow Seward's suggestion. Days passed with
no word from the White House as to major policy—and meanwhile the rolling tide of secession mounted ever higher, spreading
northward till the nation's capital itself became an island, cut off
from the loyal states.

Bennett fumed at Abe Lincoln's procrastination. Not a day went
by that the editor did not refer to the administration as cowardly,
mean, or vicious, and to the President himself as "the incompetent,
ignorant, and desperate 'Honest Abe.'"

Except for the *Evening Post,* even the administration organs
turned from support to criticism. "Wanted—A Policy" wrote Raymond in the *Times,* as he tried to prod the President. He charged
that the administration "exhibited a blindness and a stolidity without parallel in the history of intelligent statesmanship," and Lincoln was accused of having spent time and strength in feeding rapacious politicians "which should have been spent in saving the
Union."

Horace Greeley demanded that the President "Come to the
Point!" By this time he did not seem to care what kind of a program Lincoln would propose. "If the Union is to be maintained at
all hazards, let the word be passed along the line. . . . If the secession of the Gulf States—and of any more that choose to follow—
is to be regarded as a fixed fact, let that be proclaimed. . . ."

Drift and demoralization; disintegration and decay—that seemed
to be the logical outcome of the election of Lincoln. A sense of
futility and a sense of desperation, twin brothers of the chaos,
gripped the nation.

Bennett, as the spokesman for a powerful but unorganized group
of Northern interests, finally decided that name-calling was not
enough. Action was needed—but not the kind of action demanded
by Raymond or Greeley. Bennett suggested something far more
drastic:

It is becoming too evident that, so far as a vicious, imbecile, demoralized Administration possesses power, the hideous horrors of civil war
are about to be forced upon the country. The deliberations of Mr. Lincoln and his advisers have been shrouded in mystery; but the very con-
cealment they have affected has betrayed their iniquitous purposes.

Amid the contradictory reports that have lately prevailed, unmistakable facts have compelled a tardy and reluctant acquiescence in the conviction that aggressive measures are contemplated against the seceding States, and that hostile demonstrations, upon an extensive scale, have for many weeks formed part of the design of the government. Ominous and painful uncertainty has, at length, given place to the fearful prospect of an internecine strife between the North and the South, which is inevitable unless the troops that are being sent southward, more patriotic than their leaders, shall emulate the example of French soldiers when ordered to fire upon the people, and refuse to imbrue their hands in the blood of their fellow-citizens. . . .

"Irrepressible conflict" has thus succeeded in developing the outlines of a fearful shadow over the land; but it is to be hoped that the very armies which are soon to be brought face to face will shrink from permitting it to acquire a bloody substance. Far better that the Union should be dismembered forever than that fraternal hands should be turned against one another, to disfigure the land by slaughter and carnage.

The masses of the population reprobate the blood-thirsty imbecility of the Washington government. They are forewarned, by the gigantic footsteps with which anarchy has been progressing, that a military despotism is imminent, which may reduce the country to the lowest place in the scale of nations. In the annals of history there would be found no parallel of a people, from such a height of prosperity as the United States have attained, so recklessly plunging its future destiny into an abyss of ruin, if the present mismanagement of affairs is allowed to continue.

The popular sentiment is everywhere peaceful, and the time cannot be distant when the shameful manner in which Mr. Lincoln and his Cabinet are sacrificing the welfare of the land, and betraying its most sacred interests, will call forth an outbreak of indignation before which even Republican fanaticism and intolerance will tremble.

On the next day, April 10, Bennett proposed vigilante action to depose the Administration. "Our only hope now," he wrote, "against a civil war of an indefinite duration seems to lie in the over-throw of the demoralizing, disorganizing and destructive [Republican] sectional party, of which 'Honest Abe Lincoln' is the pliable instrument."

15. *"The Union Must Be Saved!"*

T HE LAST blow has been given to the fabric of freedom, raised at such cost by the Fathers of the Republic," declared the *Herald* on April 12, in an editorial entitled "The War Has Begun."

On the same page, prominently displayed, was a cut of the new Confederate flag.

The presses roared day and night pouring forth new editions of the *Herald* to feed the news-hungry crowds. Each day a new record was established, until an all-time high of 135,000 copies was reached on the fifteenth of April, 1861.

The attack on Fort Sumter by the Confederates galvanized the people into action. For the first time, they felt that war was upon them. Reveling in their new-found unity and fired with a desire to fight all traitors, angry crowds surged about homes and offices and business establishments of the most outspoken "friends of the South."

On the night of April 14, a hostile mob surged about the *Herald* building and there was loose and angry talk about demolishing the plant. The excitement outside was as nothing compared with that within the *Herald* building. Printers, reporters, clerks, and proofreaders barricaded doors and windows. The crowd on the streets hurled threats and imprecations at the paper and its editor. Finally, according to Horace Greeley, they demanded that Bennett himself appear before them, and they demanded as well that the Stars and Stripes be unfurled over the building.

The *Herald* later denied the charges made by the *Tribune,* calling them "false, mean, and malicious." It declared, "In regard to the display of the American flag, no one has asked us to do so. It was unnecessary to take that trouble. The glorious flag of the Union is our flag, and long may it wave."

The *Tribune* countered by repeating its charge once more, adding that it was unfortunate for the *Herald* that it did not even possess an American flag but had to send out for one at the last moment. There were undoubtedly, continued the *Tribune,* enough Secession flags on hand at the *Herald.*

Bennett had, in the meantime, done a right-about face in policy and displayed not one but a score of American flags. The *Herald* claimed that the crowds milling about its offices on the night of the fourteenth were merely excited patriots, anxious to read the latest bulletins or buy the latest papers.

Actually, the mob had come determined to do damage. There was no flag available, so a *Herald* office boy hurried out through a rear entrance, reached a Broadway bunting store, and returned with a banner in the nick of time. The flag was duly displayed, and Bennett, standing so close to it he was all but wrapped in its folds, bowed profusely to the mob.

Fearful of any future mob action, and determined never to be caught unprepared again, the elder Bennett purchased a small arsenal of rifles and ammunition, which were stored behind special panels in the offices of the *Herald.* The guns were kept in perfect working order for a great many years as a grim reminder of the hectic night of April 14, 1861.

On the very next day, the day that President Lincoln issued his call for 75,000 volunteers, the *Herald* announced that the time for peace meetings was ended. It pledged its support, and that of all Northern Democrats, to a successful prosecution of the war against the unscrupulous fire-eaters. War had come from the South, said the *Herald,* and the South must be vanquished. The Union must be preserved, no matter what the cost. Then, speaking for the business interests of New York, the *Herald* went on to say that these interests demanded the war be of *short* duration. "Business men can stand a temporary reverse. They can easily make arrangements for six months or a year. But they cannot endure a long, uncertain, and tedious contest."

On the sixteenth, Bennett wired his special correspondent in

Washington to return at once to New York for instructions. Villard left by the night train wondering all the while what his new instructions were to be.

On reaching the *Herald* office [wrote Villard in describing the event], I found an invitation to accompany him [Bennett] in the afternoon to his residence at Washington Heights and to spend the night there. As was my host's regular custom, we drove from the office up Broadway and Fifth Avenue and through Central Park to the Heights. I had seen Bennett only twice before, and then but for a few minutes each time, and the opportunity to learn more of this notorious character was therefore not unwelcome to me. I must say that his shameful record as a journalist, and particularly the sneaking sympathy of his paper for the Rebellion, and its vile abuse of the Republicans for their anti-slavery sentiments, made me share the general prejudice against him to such an extent that I had been thinking for some time of severing my connection with the *Herald,* although the agreement had been strictly kept. With his fine tall and slender figure, large intellectual head covered with an abundance of light curly hair, and strong regular features, his exterior would have been impressive but for his strabismus, which gave him a sinister, forbidding look. Intercourse with him, indeed, quickly revealed his hard, cold, utterly selfish nature and incapacity to appreciate high and noble aims.

His residence was a good-sized farm house in parklike grounds, with no great pretensions either outwardly or inwardly. On the drive and during the dinner, at which his one son—a fine-looking, intelligent youth of twenty—was the only other person present, he did nothing but ask questions bearing upon the characteristics and doings of President Lincoln and the circumstances of my acquaintance with him. After dinner he disclosed his true purpose in sending for me. First, he wanted me to carry a message from him to Mr. Lincoln that the *Herald* would hereafter be unconditionally for the radical suppression of the Rebellion by force of arms, and in the shortest possible time, and would advocate and support any "war measures" by the Government and Congress. I was, of course, very glad to hear this, and promised to repeat these assurances by word of mouth to the President. The truth was that the *Herald* was obliged to make this complete change in its attitude, there having been ominous signs for some days in New York of danger of mob violence to the paper. Secondly, he wanted me to offer to Secretary Chase his son's famous sailing yacht, the "Rebecca," as a gift to the Government for the revenue service, and to secure in consideration thereof for its owner the appointment of lieutenant in the same service. The last wish I thought rather amusing, but I agreed to lay it before Secretary Chase, to whom I had ready access as the representative of the

Cincinnati Commercial, his strongest supporter in Ohio. My host retired early, and was ready before me in the morning for the down drive, on which I accompanied him again. Mr. Hudson—the managing editor, a fine-looking man, and one of the most courteous and obliging I ever met, with extraordinary qualifications for newspaper management— told me in the course of the day that Mr. Bennett was very much pleased with me and had increased my weekly allowance to thirty-five dollars.

Villard found the return trip to Washington far more exciting than the one already completed. Trains were not running beyond Baltimore. Troops were on the march. Forces of the militant Confederacy seemed to be everywhere. It was only with the greatest of difficulty that Villard managed to rent a horse, upon which he made the trip into the Nation's capital. In the space of less than four days, the city had undergone a startling transformation. The halls, lobby, and sitting rooms at the Willard were almost empty. The clerk at the desk informed Villard, "We are going to shut up this hotel tomorrow, and this meal will be the last you can be served here." The young reporter could scarcely believe his ears or his eyes. The thousand guests at the Willard had dwindled overnight to less than twenty. Stores and private homes were locked up and deserted. The streets were empty. Only the roads leading out of the city were crowded—crowded with panic-stricken men and women and children—fleeing North and West and East to avoid being trapped by the Confederates. All railroad, mail, and even telegraphic services between Washington and the North had been abruptly broken off. The executive heads of the government of the United States were as completely isolated from their people as though they had been suddenly moved to an island in mid-ocean.

"From what I saw myself and learned from others," wrote Villard, "I was oppressed by the thought that the Government was in a most perilous plight, that this must be known to the rebel authorities through the many willing and eager informants who left Washington daily for the South, and that, with the audacity they had so far shown, they would without fail take advantage of this, their great opportunity, and gain possession of the capital by a *coup de main.* The circumstances were so favorable to an attempt of this kind that I felt sure it would be made, and was prepared to hear at any moment of the appearance of a rebel force in the streets. I did not understand then, nor could I ever understand, why the rebel hands were not stretched out to seize so easy a prey—a seizure that might have resulted in the immediate triumph of the insurrection."

It went without saying that President Lincoln was highly gratified with the news brought to him by his friend Villard as to the position Bennett would take, for Lincoln knew full well the strength and power of the *Herald,* both at home and abroad. Its power for good could be as great as its power for mischief. Not wishing to trust himself merely to the word of one of Bennett's employees, the President soon thereafter raised the question of Bennett and the *Herald* at one of his cabinet meetings. They agreed, for all their hatred of the old man and his scurrilous paper, that a direct and earnest appeal for administration support must be made to Bennett. Among those proposed for this rather delicate task was Thurlow Weed. Seward remarked sarcastically that no better man than Weed could be chosen to insure the complete failure of the mission, for Seward knew that next to himself there was perhaps no person in the whole country more repugnant to Bennett than Thurlow Weed. These two men had been bitter enemies for nearly thirty years; and though both of them had lived for long periods at the Astor House, neither would condescend to speak to the other. Lincoln declared that Weed was the man whom he believed best fitted to speak to Bennett, and Weed, after much hesitation, agreed to do his best.

Upon my arrival in New York [wrote Weed in his autobiography], I called upon my friend Richard Schell, between whom and Mr. Bennett I knew that intimate relations existed. Mr. Schell readily undertook to arrange an interview, and in a couple of hours afterward called at the Astor House with a message from Mr. Bennett inviting me to dinner that afternoon. In stepping out of the cars at the Washington Heights Station I met Mr. Bennett, who had gone out in the same train. After a cordial greeting we were driven in his carriage to his mansion on the Heights. We then walked for half an hour about the grounds, when a servant came and announced dinner. The dinner was a quiet one, during which, until the fruit was served, we held general conversation. I then frankly informed him of the object of my visit, closing with the remark that Mr. Lincoln deemed it more important to secure the *Herald's* support than to obtain a victory in the field. Mr. Bennett replied that the abolitionists, aided by Whig members of Congress, had provoked a war, of the danger of which he had been warning the country for years, and that now, when they were reaping what they had sown, they had no right to call upon him to help them out of a difficulty that they had deliberately brought upon themselves. I listened without interruption for ten minutes to a bitter denunciation of Greeley, Garrison, Seward, Sumner, Giddings, Phillips, and myself, as having, by irritating and exasperating the South, brought the war upon the country. I then, in reply, without denying or attempting to explain any of his positions, stated the whole question from our standpoint. I informed him of facts and circumstances within my knowledge, showing conclusively the deliberate design of severing the Union to prevent California from coming into it as a free State. I gave him the then unknown particulars of an interview of Messrs. Toombs, Stephens, and Clingman, members of Congress from Georgia and North Carolina, with General Taylor. The object of that interview was to induce General Taylor, a Southern man and slave-holder, to veto the bill permitting California to enter the Union as a free State. It was a stormy interview, with threats of disunion on one hand and of hanging on the other. The facts were communicated to Senator Hamlin of Maine, and myself, within ten minutes after the interview closed. Jefferson Davis, General Taylor's son-in-law, though not present was, as General Taylor believed, the master spirit in the movement. General Taylor's death and the compromise measures under the auspices of his successor, Mr. Fillmore, bridged over rebellion for the time being. I then called Mr. Bennett's attention to the condition of things in 1860, when the results of the census disclosed the fact of an unmistakable numerical and political ascendency of freedom over slavery. This ascendency crushed the Southern hope of extending slavery into free territory, that having been the object of the repeal of the Missouri compromise and the only national issue then pending. I then reverted to the Democratic National Convention of 1860, startling Mr. Bennett with the assumption that that convention was deliberately demoralized by its leaders for the purpose of throwing the government into our hands, and thus furnishing the pretext desired for secession. I claimed that the harmonious nomination of an available candidate would have insured the success of the Democratic ticket, but that the convention was broken up by leading Southern men, into whose hands General Butler and Caleb Cushing played. Two Democratic candidates for president were placed in the field, with the knowledge and for the purpose of giving the election to Mr. Lincoln, and then, before a word was spoken or an act performed by the incoming administration, a predetermined course of secession and rebellion was entered upon.

No one knew better than Mr. Bennett the truth, the force, and the effect of the facts I presented, but his mind had been so absorbed in his idea of the pernicious character of abolition that he had entirely lost sight of the real causes of the rebellion. He reflected a few minutes, and then changed the conversation to an incident which occurred in Dublin in 1843, at an O'Connell meeting which both of us attended, though at that time not on speaking terms. In parting Mr. Bennett cordially invited me to visit him at his office or house as often as I found it convenient. Nothing was then said in regard to the future course of the *Herald,* but that journal came promptly to the support of the government, and remained earnest and outspoken against the rebellion.

It was charged that Mr. Bennett's changed course was occasioned by the mob which surrounded his office, and it was also charged that the *Herald* had been bought up by the administration. Both of these accusations were utterly unfounded. Up to the time of my interview with Mr. Bennett, several weeks after the threatened violence, there was no change in the course of the *Herald,* nor was one word spoken, suggested, or intimated in our conversation conveying the idea of personal interest or advancement. My appeal was made to Mr. Bennett's judgment, and to his sense of duty as an influential journalist to the government and Union. That appeal, direct and simple, was successful. The President and Secretary of State, when informed of the result of my mission, were much relieved and gratified. Mr. Lincoln frequently expressed to me his desire in some way to acknowledge his sense of obligation to Mr. Bennett, and some two years afterward, when the French mission was open, the President authorized Mr. Wakeman, the surveyor of the port, to offer it to Mr. Bennett, which, however, he declined. Our personal and social relations being thus reestablished, they continued throughout his life.

The nature of the support which James Gordon Bennett gave to the Lincoln administration during the ensuing years of war and politics was anything but consistent. True, he never became a defeatist as did so many of his rival editors when they saw the fortunes of war running heavily against the Union. But beyond that the support he gave to the Administration was slight indeed. In the meantime, his feud with Horace Greeley, William Seward, and the abolitionists lost none of its fire or venom. And though he let fly a continuous barrage of editorial shafts at the hotheaded Secessionists, he also quoted with approval, on more than one occasion, the words of Jefferson Davis, Alexander Stephens, General Robert E. Lee, and other responsible heads of the Confederacy.

Bennett was nearly sixty-six years of age when the War Between the States began. (He always called it "The American War" in the columns of the *Herald*.) His paper, for all its editorial unpopularity, was without a peer as a news-gathering and news-purveying agency. It covered the field with greater thoroughness, accuracy, and speed than any of its rivals. This the public knew, and that was why they bought the *Herald*.

Any great crisis invariably brings with it an increased demand for news, rumors, gossip, and reports on the personalities and issues involved. Wars are the most potent crises; and of wars, none creates the tensions and anxieties of a civil war. This Bennett knew well. Consequently, long before the opening of hostilities between the North and the South, the staff of the *Herald* had been called in for frequent consultations with Bennett and Hudson to prepare for the conflict that was sure to come. The editorial staff was enlarged and revamped. Some of the men were assigned to the study of European military tactics and history; others to acquaint themselves with the campaigns of Washington, Jackson, Scott, and the lesser generals in the nation's wars. Files and government records were searched for data on military equipment and ordnance; on locations of forts, railroads, highways, bays, and rivers; on population, agriculture, manufacturing, and other resources of every State and Territory. Artists and typographers were put to work drawing maps, pictures of troops and leading personalities. The editor-in-chief re-read the campaigns of Napoleon and Wellington, of Frederick the Great and Marlborough, of Caesar and Hannibal. The numerous special correspondents throughout the country (and especially those in the South) were ordered to send in detailed reports on changes in public opinion; on changes in the cost of living, and the flow of goods, traffic, and personnel by railroad, steamer, canal boat, or omnibus.

The *Herald,* by virtue of its long and consistent advocacy of the rights of the South, had a thousand sources of information upon which to draw for information in that part of the country, compared to a handful for the other large New York dailies. These contacts were maintained, and often augmented, by the *Herald* during the long years of conflict. True, many Northerners, including some high government and military officials, were very suspicious of the *Herald* all through the war—and some of the reports published by Bennett as well as many of his scathing editorials gave not a little justification to their fears.

On the other hand, no other paper was ever able to equal the full and complete war coverage of the *Herald*. Its correspondents were with every army; they covered every major and most of the minor engagements, both on land and at sea. And the trained staff of experts in the home office were able to supplement the reports from the fronts with detailed information of every kind, thus giving a full picture to their hundreds of thousands of readers. Government officials, from President Lincoln and the cabinet members down, read the *Herald*. So, too, did military officials, speculators, army contractors, and the editors of every important rival paper. The home folks in a thousand towns and villages scanned its pages for reports on what their boys were doing. And out in the army camps—even up to the lines of battle themselves—went the news vendors, their mule-driven wagons loaded with the latest issues of the *New York Herald*.

There were *Herald* correspondents in Florida, Texas, Arkansas, Alabama, and North Carolina; others functioned regularly from Washington, New Orleans, Wilmington, Cincinnati, St. Louis, and Chicago. Some were at Fort Monroe and Harpers Ferry. William Young and F. G. Chapman sent in splendid reports from the Army of the Potomac. D. P. Coningham reported the operations of the Army under General Meade, and he marched with General Sherman to the sea. E. D. Westfall covered the battles of Chattanooga and Lookout Mountain. Oblivious to hardship and danger in their determination to get the news were William H. Stiner, J. A. Brady, G. W. Clark, D. B. Randolph Kein, Edwin F. De Nyse, Oscar G. Sawyer, and General F. F. Millen. Among the best of these was Charles Henry Farrell who reported the battle at Antietam, Grant's siege of Vicksburg—and, as a final job, the surrender of General Robert E. Lee at Appomattox Court House.

And there were ace war correspondents like Villard and Osbon, of whom more later.

The *Herald* had the first complete coverage on Bull Run, on Shiloh, and Yorktown. "The *Herald* is constantly ahead. We are obliged to copy from it," wrote Greeley's chief war editor. With almost unceasing regularity, it was Bennett's paper which "got there fustest with the mostest." Gettysburg, Pea Ridge, Corinth, Stone River, and Mine Run, Vicksburg, New Orleans, and Mobile Bay, not to mention the battles in Missouri—all these were given to the public, first and in greatest detail by the *New York Herald*.

Money was no object; expense meant nothing—all that counted was to get the news—and get it *first*. He once refused to pay the cost of a horse, killed in battle, because his correspondent was a day later than the *World's* man in reporting the fight. "A horse which couldn't beat the *World* isn't worth paying for," remarked the old man, sarcastically. But to men who showed ability, speed, verve, and imagination, Bennett was ever ready to pay more than they asked for. To one of these, who sent in a bill for one dollar for a short telegraphic dispatch, Bennett paid twenty-five dollars instead. Time after time he would order his business office to pay correspondents double or triple the established rate if the story was a good one. He knew, too, that his men, knowing that a bonus was sure to be had for a job well done, would strain every nerve and muscle to achieve the impossible in accuracy, color, and speed.

Bennett gloried in the fact that his paper outdistanced all others. "We have beaten them regularly in Southern news" was no idle boast on his part. It was an undeniable, unpalatable fact which every other editor knew to be true.

With war a hard fact, not a mere probability, the New York press forgot its talk about concessions, appeasement, and unpreparedness of the North for any conflict. Not only did it clamor for war—but it wanted the whole thing over and done with before summer was ended. Yesterday's fears gave way to a boastful overconfidence. The *Times* argued that only a few months would be required to starve out the South. The *Evening Post* predicted in mid-June that the cause of the Confederacy was already doomed, and that Jeff Davis meant to make a last desperate stand at Manassas. The *Tribune*—whose pacifist editor had opposed the use of force—now went all out in its cry for blood and victory.

Lincoln found the new Greeley policy as unwelcome as the old, for the President was bending every effort to hold the vacillating border states within the Union as the first trial of arms between the North and South began. Greeley, on the other hand, now demanded the immediate occupation of every border state which had not made an immediate response to Lincoln's call to arms. The people of Virginia, Tennessee, and Kentucky were traitors, one and all, shouted the ex-pacifist. Governor Hicks of Maryland was labeled a "snivelling, whiffling traitor," and the "worn-out race of emasculated First-Families" of Virginia and Maryland were told to bow before the onward march of the sturdier stock of the Yankee pioneers.

The news value of the *Tribune* during the spring and early summer of 1861 was very slight. Its whole tone and tenor were hysterical. It shrieked, it threatened, it scolded, and it denounced. Its columns were filled with rumors and counter-rumors; and with advice, mostly useless, to the government, to merchants, the public, to labor, and the farmers. It bragged and it boasted. It sniveled and sneered. It demanded action!—Action!—ACTION! And, as Benjamin Butler and others close to the Washington scene later confessed—this demand for action by the Federal forces as expressed by the *Tribune* in its new slogan "ON TO RICHMOND," exerted great pressure on the Administration, paving the way for the disaster at Bull Run.

When the stunning news of the Bull Run defeat became public knowledge, Greeley, strangely oblivious to his own part in the misfortune, launched into a most bitter attack upon Lincoln's administration for its blundering stupidity. What apology, what excuse, asked Greeley, has the government to offer to its humiliated and astounded citizens for such unpardonable action? A new set of generals and a new set of advisers for the President—this, charged the *Tribune,* is imperative at once.

The *Herald,* for all its political zigzags, took a far more realistic position of what had to be done after that first great disaster. First reports received pointed to a possible victory for the Union forces—and the *Herald,* on July 22, carried the headlines: "BRILLIANT UNION

VICTORY." The following day, its readers learned that what had happened was: "DESPERATE CONFLICT AND REPULSE OF UNION TROOPS BY AN OVERWHELMING FORCE." But even so, the *Herald* failed to print the whole sorry story of the debacle, as sent to it by Henry Villard. The correspondent had told all in his lengthy report—but Bennett was fearful of publishing it without careful pruning. However, since he was now fully cognizant of the body-blow which the North had received, Bennett refused to become panicky. Instead, with clear head and calm hand, he wrote out his analysis of the situation. He told his readers to forget their dreams of easy victory. The war would be hard and long. People must work and fight. Every minute was precious. The Union must be saved. "The war," he concluded, "now ceases to be an uninterrupted onward march of our forces southward. The government in a single day and at the Capitol of the Nation, is thrown upon the defensive, and under circumstances demanding the most prompt and generous efforts to strengthen our forces at that point. Every other question, all other issues, and all other business, among all parties and all classes of our loyal people, should now be made subordinate to the paramount office of securing Washington. The loyal states within three days may dispatch twenty thousand men to that point; and if we succeed in holding the Capitol for twenty days we may have by that time two hundred thousand men intrenched around it. Action, Action, Action! Let our Governor, and state and city authorities, and the state and city authorities of every loyal state come at once to the rescue and move forward their reinforcements without waiting for instructions from Washington."

Villard's experiences in reporting that first test of arms between North and South was as exciting as any by war correspondents of later years. News of the impending battle jammed the roads with thousands of excited men, women, and children out to see the fun. Ladies in all their finery, and gentlemen in top hats and swallowtail coats, poured southward from Washington in buggies, carts, and omnibuses. They brought along huge picnic baskets, stuffed with food and drink. Altogether, it was to be a gala occasion as "Johnnie Reb" got his much-deserved trouncing.

The Union soldiers, ill trained and ill led, took their first baptism of fire very well. The Confederates made several withdrawals all of which brought overconfidence to both officers and men of the Federal forces, and it was upon the news of this first phase of the battle that Bennett and other publishers spread the word of Union victory.

It was late afternoon when the Rebels took the offensive. They struck at the flank and rear of the Federal forces with great force and suddenness. Villard, from a vantage point close by, saw what happened. Surprised, confused, and alarmed the Union forces cracked. The panic spread like a prairie fire through the ranks, creating utter confusion along the whole front. "Now came the disastrous, disgraceful end," wrote the conscientious and heart-broken reporter:

Without any formal orders to retreat, what was left of the several organizations yielded to a general impulse to abandon the field. Officers and men became controlled by the one thought of getting as far as possible from the enemy. Three-fourths were quickly reduced to the condition of a motley, panic-stricken mob. Not that resolute efforts were not made by the General-in-chief and some of the commanders under him to insure an orderly retreat. They were all in vain. The morale of the army was entirely gone, and the instinct of self-preservation alone animated the flying mass.

When I rode away from Keyes's brigade towards the stone bridge, this rearward movement had not yet reached its full dimensions, but the Warrenton turn-pike was already swarming with fugitives from the battle-field, going towards Centreville. I made inquiries at the bridge from every passing officer as to the whereabouts of General McDowell's headquarters, but no one could direct me to them. I concluded to wait at the bridge for developments. I had not watched the tide of runaways for more than twenty minutes when one of Hunter's staff officers came dashing down the pike on horseback. I stopped him to repeat my question about McDowell, when he exclaimed excitedly, "You won't find him. All is chaos in front. The battle is lost. Our troops are all giving way and falling back without orders. Get back to Centreville," and galloped on. I waited a while longer till other officers and the increasing flow of retreating soldiery confirmed the news of the general retreat, and then resumed my ride.

A quarter of a mile to the east of the bridge, I found the turn-pike blocked by a double line of army wagons, ambulances, and other vehicles, that extended as far as I could see and made further progress on the pike impossible. Fortunately, the persons in charge had already opened a way through the adjacent fields by pulling down the fences. But it occurred to me at once to what further disaster to the Union army this choking up of their main line of retreat might lead. I took it upon myself to call the attention of a passing officer of the quarter-master's department to this danger, and he at once proceeded to try his best to remove the tangle. Time and again, owing to such obstacles, I had to leave the turnpike and proceed through the fields, even having to open a way myself by pulling down fences. I was lucky enough to find no obstruction on the small suspension-bridge over Cob Run. A short distance beyond this I came upon another blockade, in which were involved a number of hackney carriages with members of Congress, some of them known to me, who had driven out from Washington that day and were trying to get to the front to witness the great victory which the favorable course of the action up to the afternoon had led them to expect. They had heard nothing of the defeat, and would not believe me when I told them the bad news.

I passed on, and had not left them more than five minutes when I was startled by the sound of artillery in close proximity behind me. A rebel cavalry detachment with a battery section, sent to cut off our retreat, had suddenly emerged from the woods to the south of the turn-pike, and commenced shelling it. A shell exploded over and on the roadway, and some of the rebel cavalry dashed up, yelling with all their might. The turnpike and the adjacent fields became instantly the scene of a wild panic. The teamsters jumped off their wagons and ran away as fast as they could. Even ambulances with wounded were deserted. The retreating soldiers all the way from the stone bridge were seized with fright, and started on a full run through the fields in swarms of hundreds and thousands, throwing away their arms and accoutrements, knapsacks, haversacks, and blankets. Within a few minutes after the first rebel gun had been fired, a wild, senseless rabble came rushing by me on foot, horseback, and muleback. A good many soldiers detached animals from wagons and galloped off on them. The members of Congress and other civilians also abandoned their private vehicles, and joined afoot in the race for safety. Among the fugitives there was a well-known newspaper correspondent, who had caught and mounted bareback a badly bleeding artillery horse, and was urging him to extreme speed by merciless cudgelling. The terrified crowds presented a pitiful and humiliating sight. Starting again, filled with greater fear than before for the fate of the army, I rode all the way amid runaways, soldiers and officers of all ranks—I noticed among them fellows with the straps of majors and lieutenant-colonels—and a mixture of civilians, to Centreville, where I arrived shortly before six o'clock, travel-stained,

dust-covered, and about as tired, hungry, thirsty, and disgusted with all
the world as a human being could well be.

For all his weariness and disgust, Villard was first and foremost a newspaperman. He knew that he had a great, if dismal,
story to tell. He knew he had a good chance to reach Washington,
eighteen miles distant, ahead of his rivals and score a master scoop
for the *Herald*. He saddled his horse and set out in the gathering
twilight toward the capital. The roads were choked with immense
trains of army wagons, as well as by camps of soldiers and teamsters on either side, which compelled Villard to dismount and
cautiously pick his way for hours through the tangled mass of
men, mules, and supplies. He told of passing innumerable groups of
runaway soldiers, some of whom "being hidden from view by the
darkness, amused themselves by sending forth rebel yells so as to
frighten the passers-by into the belief that they had fallen upon a
rebel ambuscade."

About daybreak the weary reporter passed the camp of a regiment of "ninety day volunteers from Pennsylvania. Their term of
service had expired the day before the bloody conflict began, so,
with the very sound of battle in their ears, they had insisted upon
marching back to their homes." Such was the martial spirit of
many of the troops at the time, sadly remarked Villard.

Washington lay silent and deserted in the early morning sunlight
as the *Herald's* correspondent, hungry and haggard after more
than eighteen hours of great fatigue and excitement, made his way
to his rooms.

"I had no right to rest," observed Villard, "before I had done
my duty to the *Herald*. During the night ride I had thought out
what seemed to be the best course in reporting the battle. My
knowledge of the details of the fighting was very limited, but I
had picked up enough information for an intelligible and nearly
correct summary of what had occurred. I determined, therefore, to
prepare first a succinct report of say six hundred words for transmission by wire when the telegraph-office opened at seven A.M.
. . . Next I would allow myself six or seven hours' sleep, and in
the afternoon endeavor to collect further material for a fuller ac-

count by the last evening mail. It took me only half an hour to write out my despatch, so that before leaving it at the main telegraph-office I had time for an early breakfast at Willard's Hotel. The despatch reached its destination before eight, and was printed at once as an extra. It was the first revelation to the New York public of the extent of the national disaster, and as such created a great sensation but was not immediately credited."

After a few hours' rest, Villard set out to gather more detailed information from men at the War Department, but they, alas, knew less of details than he did. Villard returned to Arlington, where McDowell's headquarters had been re-established. From Captain Fry and other responsible officials, who dictated for him their impressions and recollections of the battle, the young reporter obtained the first comprehensive picture of what had taken place as well as the reasons for the disaster. Chief among these reasons were "the incapacity of commanding officers, the lack of courage and discipline among the troops, and above all, the nonfulfillment of General Scott's promise [Winfield Scott was still commander-in-chief of the U. S. Army] that 'if [General] Johnston joined Beauregard, he should have [General] Patterson on his heels.' "

It was six o'clock that evening before Villard returned to the capital, loaded with facts and observations. There was not enough time left to write out the lengthy report and send it north on the mail train, so he wired Bennett for permission to telegraph the whole story. Permission.was granted.

"I commenced work at half-past six," Villard later wrote, "and was through at half-past ten. Two office-boys kept running to the main telegraph-office with the successively finished sheets of the manuscript, so that, within a few minutes after my work was done, the last installment was being flashed to New York. I felt well satisfied with what I had written and confident that it would prove quite a hit for me. Alas! when it reached me in print, I discovered, to my great disgust, that so much of it had been stricken out or altered that I could no longer feel any pride in the mutilated remnant as my own production."

In the person of B. S. Osbon, the *Herald* had another ace war correspondent. He had been hired by Frederic Hudson many years before the war to cover the ships and docks of the New York water-front. Osbon was more than just a good newspaperman; he was also a good seaman and an able signal officer. He was a reserve petty officer in the navy as well.

When in early April, 1861, Lincoln ordered an attempt made to relieve the Union troops at Fort Sumter, Osbon went along with the expedition on the revenue cutter, "Harriet Lane," the only newspaperman in the fleet. Osbon heard the first shots fired from the batteries in Charleston which set into motion the Civil War. He was an eye witness of the bombardment of Sumter, as well as of the surrender of it to the Confederates by Major Anderson. And from that gallant officer he obtained a first-hand report of what had transpired. Osbon hastened back to New York as fast as he could to tell the whole thrilling tale to the readers of the *Herald*.

By virtue of his own abilities, supplemented by some appropriate wire-pulling by Hudson and Bennett with the administration, Osbon was given a special commission by the Secretary of the Navy which permitted him "to accompany naval expeditions in any staff capacity to which the commanders might appoint him, provided these did not interfere with the regulations of the Navy."

Well written, dramatic, and factual, the articles which Osbon sent in to the *Herald* (and to *Harper's Weekly*) during the long years of the conflict were eagerly read and as eagerly quoted and re-printed by other papers. But the high point of his career as war correspondent came in the spring of 1862, when he served as signal officer under Admiral Farragut, who was then engaged in break-ing the Confederate stranglehold on the mouth of the Mississippi. Osbon's report on the battle for New Orleans and the forts along the river covered three whole pages in the *Herald*. It was the long-est, yet most dramatic, piece of reporting that had come from the front line.

By virtue of his position as signal officer, Osbon occupied a most vital post in the naval operations. At the same time, this position, from the point of view of a reporter, was second only to that of standing at the side of the Admiral himself, for it was Osbon who gave the signals to the other members of Farragut's fleet, as these orders were issued by the Admiral. He knew the exact position of every ship, and what they were supposed to do, even before they did it. In turn, reports from the other vessels to Farragut passed through Osbon's hands before they reached the Admiral himself.

During the midnight hours of a cloudy night the ships moved silently into their allocated positions. "It was a solemn time," wrote the naval correspondent. "On the stroke of two, with my own hands I hoisted to the mizzen peak a pair of red lanterns, which was the signal to get under way."

High in the mizzen-rigging, above the smoke of battle, from where he gave his orders, was the commander, Admiral Farragut. "With his feet on the rat-lines and his back against the shrouds, he stood there as cool and undisturbed as if leaning against a mantel in his own home."

With notebook in hand, and with a watch lashed to his sleeve, Osbon did double duty, jotting down the orders from the flag officer as well as his own notes on the battle for the *Herald*.

About four in the morning, with the battle at its height, the Admiral's ship ran aground on a sandbar. A Confederate ram, perceiving the plight of the ship, shoved a fire-raft up under the port quarter. At the same moment a large shell from nearby Fort St. Phillip exploded squarely on the main deck. The grounded ship was soon ablaze in both places. The situation was desperate. Osbon threw a heavy overcoat over his head, rolled several heavy shells across the burning deck, uncapped them, and threw them overboard onto the fire-raft which exploded and sank. The flames on deck and along the sides were soon extinguished, the ship got off the sand-bar, and the Admiral led his victorious squadron past the forts. The blockade had been broken. New Orleans would soon be in Federal hands.

Amid the cheers of the men and officers for his bravery, Osbon left for Washington on Farragut's dispatch boat. At Fort Monroe he told the story of Admiral Farragut's exploit to President Lincoln and Secretary of War Stanton before going to report to the *Herald* for his next assignment.

Following the debacle at Bull Run, the administration issued a call for an additional 300,000 men to serve in its armed forces. A new general was placed in charge of the army. Search and seizure of people suspected of being spies or helping the Confederacy mounted rapidly. Washington became an armed camp, in preparation for anticipated attacks by the rebels. In the North and West, business boomed as never before; prices rocketed; and soon a new song was on the lips of the legions of men and boys as they swung along the highways leading to the fields of battle. They sang words of determination:

We are coming, Father Abraham, three hundred thousand more,
From Mississippi's winding stream, and from New England's shore;
We leave our ploughs and workshops, our wives and children dear,
With hearts too full for utterance, but with a silent tear
We dare not look behind us, but steadfastly before:
We are coming, Father Abraham, three hundred thousand more.

Upon the head of Horace Greeley poured the unleashed abuse of every irate and disappointed editor, politician, and civilian. He became the convenient scapegoat at whose door was laid the primary responsibility for the defeat at Bull Run, by his insistent cry of "On to Richmond."

Poor Greeley broke under the strain. He developed brain fever and then, to cap the climax, wrote a pathetic private letter to Lincoln asking: "Can the rebels be beaten after all that has occurred, and in view of the actual state of feeling caused by our late awful disaster? If they can—and it is your business to ascertain and decide—write me that such is your judgement, so that I may know and do my duty. . . . If the Union is irrevocably gone, an armistice for thirty, sixty, ninety, one hundred twenty days—better still for a year—ought at once be proposed. . . . Send me word what to do. I will live till I can hear it, at all events."

As in every other war, so too in the War Between the States, many innocent people were jailed or mistreated. The *Herald* (whose editor many patriots would gladly have seen behind the bars) reported regularly on the latest notables to be detained in prison or fort or concentration camp. Particular attention was given to Fort Lafayette, in New York Harbor. On one occasion, Bennett suggested it would fascinate future historians to delve into its record of Civil War inmates, including as it did not only Baltimore police-men and maritime adventurers, rebel financiers and diplomats, but also the Honorable Pierce Butler (husband of Fanny Kemble, the famous actress) as well as "the handsome, amiable, but misguided secessionist Mayor Berret of Washington, D. C." On one occasion it commented, "Three more candidates for the hospitalities of the Hotel de La Fayette passed through the city yesterday afternoon, enroute to their winter quarters."

The nation's capital, long notorious for its strong contingent of leading citizens outspoken in their support of the South, lost many with the outbreak of hostilities. But there were also many who re-mained—those whom Bennett labeled "rebels in crinoline." During the Buchanan administration, said Bennett, "these fascinating fe-male secessionists held the government and the destinies of the country in their delicate little hands." Even the French Revolution, he contended, had failed to produce "a circle of feminine politicians more accomplished, more sagacious and industrious."

These witty and charming rebels had only contempt for the new administration. They intrigued as never before, and kept a steady flow of vital information moving southward to their friends and relatives in the Confederacy. The Government, with great reluc-tance, decided that they were a danger to the country, and ordered their ring leaders arrested or placed under strict observation till the end of the war.

The new star on the military horizon was General George B. McClellan, an ambitious and dashing figure, who made bold prom-ises to wipe out the Confederates as soon as he had reorganized the shattered and demoralized Federals. Out in the West meanwhile, another general, the man who had been the first standard-bearer for the Republican party, issued a proclamation, which for a time threatened to disrupt the Administration.

General John C. Fremont was commander of the Union forces west of the Mississippi River. On September 1, 1861, he announced that henceforth the State of Missouri was under martial law. Per-sons found with arms in their possession were to be court-martialed, and if found guilty were to be shot. Furthermore, "the property, real and personal, of all persons in the State of Missouri who shall take up arms against the United States, or who shall be directly proven to have taken an active part with their enemies in the field, is declared to be confiscated to the public use, and their slaves, if any they have, are hereby declared freemen."

Fremont's action was hailed by the anti-slavery press as a measure of greatest significance. Lincoln, on the other hand, when he learned of the proclamation, lost no time in countermanding the order. He wrote Fremont that "the Confederates would very certainly shoot the very best Northerners in their hands, in retaliation. Furthermore, to liberate the slaves and confiscate the property of traitors to the Union would alarm many southern Union friends and turn them into enemies, as well as ruin our rather fair prospect for Kentucky." Shortly thereafter Fremont was relieved of his command.

Greeley, Bryant, Raymond, and a host of lesser editors immediately turned their guns upon the President. But James Gordon Bennett came to his support declaring that "of late months [Lincoln] has justly earned the reputation of a wise and energetic statesman." The President had not only the task of "contending in battle array with the insane faction of nigger-drivers at the South, and putting down with a strong hand their murderous and suicidal treason," but likewise he must be forever mindful "that the original cause of the evil began with the machinations of fanatical nigger-worshippers at the North, and that to them are mainly owing our present troubles."

"The moderate and effective rebuke contained in his letter to Major-General Fremont," continued Bennett, "is eminently worthy of admiration, both for the dignified and courteous language in which it is couched, and the death-blow it strikes at all attempts of badly advised local commanders to overstep the legitimate sphere of their military duties."

It was just at this time that the Polish patriot, Count Gurowsky, then visiting in Washington, confided to his diary, "Mr. Lincoln has already the fumes of greatness, and looks down on the press, reads no paper—that dirty traitor, the *New York Herald,* excepted. So, at least, it is generally stated."

Sandburg and other historians question the accuracy of the Count's statement. Certain it is that the *Herald* was read by Mrs. Lincoln as well as by most members of Lincoln's official family. The canny editor never overlooked any bets as to possible sources of information at the capital. Staff members in Washington were instructed to establish themselves on terms of friendship and intimacy with all heads of departments and their chief subordinates. Cabinet members were carefully scrutinized to determine by what policy the *Herald* would be most effective in getting them to unburden themselves to its reporters. Some were bulldozed by thunderous editorials; on others the flattering word was used. Villard admitted that with respect to Seward, "the *Herald* made a regular practice of bestowing upon him extravagant eulogies, bordering on ridiculous exaggeration, in order to smooth the way to his confidence for its correspondents."

To the fury of its rivals, and often to the consternation of the administration, the *Herald* was forever printing bits of news and gossip well in advance of all others. There were many in Washington who sought in vain to plug the leaks, or who became unduly reticent on future policy for fear the information would somehow find its way to Bennett's reporters. General McClellan, for example, in the early summer of 1862, refused to take anyone into his confidence as to when and how he planned to make his big move against the Confederates. When asked to tell his plans to the President, McClellan declined, and is said to have replied that if he did so, they would appear in the *New York Herald* on the following day, for in his opinion Lincoln could not keep a secret.

Perhaps the most effective of Bennett's many undercover men in Washington during the early portion of the Lincoln administration was a suave and elegant man-about-town and adventurer whom the editor had met back in 1838, and who, since that date, had been on the *Herald's* confidential payroll on many occasions. That little time had been lost by this middle-aged glamour boy to do his master's bidding is evident from a letter, marked "Private and Confidential" which President Lincoln wrote to Bennett on September 22, 1861:

My dear Sir:

Last evening Mr. Wikoff solicited me for a pass, or permission to a gentleman whose name I forget, to accompany one of our vessels down the Potomac today, as a reporter of the *Herald,* saying the Sec. of the Navy had refused, while he had given the privilege to reporters of other papers. It was too late at night for me to see the Secretary, and I had to decline giving the permission, because he, the Sec., might have a sufficient reason, unknown to me. I write this to assure you that the Administration will not discriminate against the *Herald,* especially while it sustains us so generously, and the cause of the country as ably as it has been doing.

Your Obt Servant,

Abraham Lincoln.

Henry Wikoff, labeled "the Chevalier" by Bennett, had moved in both French and English court circles for many years, and was the welcome guest of New York's upper crust. Hence, he had no difficulty in making himself an intimate of the first lady of the land. Mrs. Lincoln possessed none of that uncanny ability of her husband to weigh and measure the personalities about her. Wikoff soon discovered she was proud, vain, and eager for flattery. He lost no time in securing her confidence and good will by fulsome praise for all she did, or said, or wore. Villard, who was a forthright person, disliked the blandishments of Bennett's White House confidant. He remarked in his memoirs that on many occasions he had heard Wikoff compliment Mrs. Lincoln "upon her looks and dress in so fulsome a way that she ought to have blushed, and banished the impertinent fellow from her presence." Instead, "she accepted Wikoff as a majordomo in general and in special, as guide in matters of social etiquette, domestic arrangements and personal requirements, including her toilette, and as always welcome company for visitors in her salon and on her drives."

Cynical old Bennett instructed his staff to play up Mrs. Lincoln to the limit. This they did—and with a vengeance. She was pictured as taking the lead of Washington society "with as easy grace as if she had been born to the station." In her purchases at the fashionable stores she displayed such exquisite taste "that all the fashionable ladies of New York were astir with wonder and surprise." Her state dinner to Prince Napoleon was "a model of completeness, taste and geniality." Every glittering phrase, every cloying adjective, every approving metaphor was used to magnify the charms and virtues of Mrs. Lincoln, till they became buffoonery to all but the first lady herself and her fawning friends.

"Good old Bennett," people would say with a knowing wink— "Good old Bennett has not overstated the case one iota when he says of Mrs. Lincoln that 'this Kentucky girl, this Western matron, this republican queen, puts to blush, and entirely eclipses the first ladies of Europe—the excellent Victoria, the pensive Eugenia, and the brilliant Isabella.'"

Month after month the comedy of adoration continued in the columns of the *Herald*. When Mrs. Lincoln left Washington for a summer vacation on Long Island, Bennett's reporters reported each trivial incident at great length. And when other papers spoke out against her many extravagances at a time when all true citizens were expected to make sacrifices, the *Herald*, with tongue in cheek, went to her defense. This so pleased Mrs. Lincoln that she wrote Bennett a warm letter of thanks for defending her against the unkind comments of the other papers; and she invited the publisher and his wife to visit the Lincolns at the White House.

Wikoff's usefulness to Bennett at the capital came to an end during the winter of 1861-62. Shortly before Christmas the *Herald* had published what it claimed to be lengthy extracts from President Lincoln's forthcoming message to Congress. Administration leaders and rival editors were outraged and demanded a congressional investigation into the matter. The Judiciary Committee, to whom the investigation was assigned, lost no time in summoning Wikoff to testify. The Chevalier admitted that he was the person who had telegraphed the excerpts to the *Herald*, but he bluntly refused to reveal his source of information. He was ordered arrested and thrown into jail on a contempt charge, but still refused to speak, beyond admitting to the Speaker of the House that he had been sworn to strict secrecy by the person from whom he had obtained the information.

General Sickles, who had sued Bennett for libel in 1857, was retained as counsel for the Chevalier. The case dragged on and on. At last, upon advice of counsel, Wikoff made a startling confession.

His informant, he announced, was John Watt, head gardener for the White House. Watt was called, and corroborated the statement. The gardener confessed to having seen the President's message lying on the library table in the White House. He had scanned through it hurriedly, but such was his amazingly retentive memory (so he said) that on the following day he had been able to quote whole sections correctly to Wikoff.

Meanwhile there was no secret as to Wikoff's close friendship with Mrs. Lincoln. Therefore, when the Judiciary Committee after closed hearings voted to absolve Wikoff and to accept Watt's tale as true, rumors spread that pressure from "on top" had been applied to bring in that verdict. Years later, the long-time Washington correspondent for the *Boston Journal*, Benjamin Perley Poore, wrote about the case: "Mr. Lincoln had visited the Capitol, and urged Republicans on the committee to spare him disgrace, so Watt's improbable story was received, and Wikoff was liberated."

During the conduct of the case, the *Herald* denied any tie-up whatsoever with Wikoff. It heaped ridicule upon him instead. Its publication of the extracts from Lincoln's message to Congress it now declared to have been nothing more than a "shrewd surmise." Bennett suddenly became concerned with stopping "the nigger-lovers" and all others opposed to Lincoln from their "infamous attempt to break up the domestic relations of the President, and sow misery in his family."

It was at the time of the Wikoff scandal that Lincoln made Edwin M. Stanton his Secretary of War. The hard-headed Ohioan threw himself into his task with fervor. One of his first acts was to take into his hands the complete control of all telegraph lines and to centralize the problems of censorship which up to then had been both slipshod and overlapping. Newspapers had printed as news the wildest rumors, which the government was forever belatedly denying or attempting to trace to their source. Correspondents at the front had been forced to depend upon such deals as they could work out with the commanding officers. If these generals liked the men or their papers, or were anxious to get favorable newspaper attention, they permitted the correspondents a great deal of leeway. If they were men with a natural distrust of the newspapermen, they did not. General William T. Sherman, for example, who was a very outspoken man among his friends as to how the war was conducted, had made some very unorthodox remarks, which were overheard by a newspaperman, who sent them in to his paper. The next day, headlines told a startled public: "GEN. WILLIAM T. SHERMAN INSANE!" This took place December 11, 1861. Sherman almost lost his command, and the United States, one of its finest generals as a result of that headline. Under the circumstances, one can appreciate Sherman's bitter hatred of all war correspondents thereafter. He is known to have remarked, when informed that three reporters had been killed in action, "That's good! We'll have dispatches now from Hell before breakfast."

Villard observed that there was too great an eagerness on the part of volunteer officers (so many of whom were aspiring politicians at home) to get themselves favorably noticed by the press "even at the cost of indiscretions." On the other hand, he admitted that the members of the press, so eager to get news at all costs, were too often indifferent to the military interests involved. In his opinion, "the harm done by war correspondents far outweighs any good they can possibly do. If I were a commanding general I would not tolerate any of the tribe within my army lines."

Secretary of War Stanton thought he could correct most of the evils by a rigid censorship. At first he announced that "All newspapers publishing military news, *however obtained,* not authorized by official authority, will be excluded thereafter from receiving information by telegraph and from transmitting their publications by railroad."

No sooner had his decision been made public than the newspapers, with a unanimity never before known to journalism, roared their disapproval. Cabinet members, department heads, members of the House and Senate, and Lincoln himself—all were deluged by a flood of protests. Bennett, Greeley, Raymond, and Bryant joined in a journalistic united front to force suspension or modification of Stanton's order.

Opposition was, in part, successful. The very next day Stanton amended his ruling to permit the publication of "past facts, leaving out details of military forces, and all statements from which the number, position and strength of the military forces of the United States can be inferred."

16. War Journalism

Stanton's rules on censorship, even though slightly modified, placed heavy obstacles in the path of every newspaper. Many editors reluctantly accepted the decision, notified their readers that they must be prepared to receive less up-to-the-minute news, and let it go at that. Others, bitterly resentful at Stanton's action, unloosed their heaviest editorial guns against the administration. How, they asked, could a free people be expected to give their very lives to defend a Union whose government took away from them the rights of a free press?

Of the handful of editors who lost no time in trying to find new sources of information to keep their readers' attention, none was more resourceful than James Gordon Bennett. Just as, on the eve of the conflict, he had organized his staff to funnel every available bit of information into the offices of the *Herald,* so now, with the heavy hand of Stanton and his censors clamping down on the day-to-day news of the armed forces, Bennett planned to unearth other, but equally interesting, intelligence, with which to bypass the blue pencil and shears of the War Department.

One of these, he had already discovered—the casualty lists. Families and friends of the men in the armed forces of the Union grew tense and taut at the news of each new battle, fearful of the fate of their beloved ones in the army. The long period of waiting and uncertainty was distinctly bad for civilian morale, although that much-used term had not yet entered into the vocabulary of the nation.

When, prior to the new censorship, the *Herald* had listed the names, addresses, and regiments of men killed in action there had been an immediate rise in circulation, as well as a demand for copies of the *Herald* from all of the towns and cities where the families of the deceased resided.

More than half a million men were already enrolled in the Federal forces at the beginning of 1862. As many more were likely to be called up before the end of the conflict. Meantime, battles and skirmishes were taking place almost continuously along a zigzag front from the Atlantic Ocean to west of the Mississippi River.

"Get the names of the dead men on every battle field as soon as you can," ordered the publisher. "But that alone is not enough. Get the names of the wounded. Find out their condition, and if possible, ask them if they have any message they wish relayed to their relatives. Get the facts, and get them quickly."

The already large staff of *Herald* men at the front was augmented by many new men, whose sole job it was to get the names of those killed, wounded, or missing after each engagement. The men from the *Herald* were soon busy checking up in every field hospital, and at every hastily prepared burial field. They checked with regimental officers and company commanders as to the correct spelling and the right address of each man lost or wounded. More than that, it was not long before the *Herald's* reporters were out on the battlefields taking notes, succoring the wounded, and getting their precious lists of names while the fighting still raged about them. Needless to say, the daily lists of killed, wounded, and missing as published in the *Herald* swelled circulation by the thousands. Within short order, the army itself was checking those lists against its own more belated reports. A special staff of letter-writers in the *Herald's* office forwarded the messages and mementoes to the folks back home. Into its offices, in return, came letters of thanks for the good work done by the *Herald*. There came, too, hundreds of letters requesting the assistance of the paper in locating sons, sweethearts, and husbands.

What Bennett had started, other papers copied—but none were prepared to spend the large sums that he did on getting the news.

Bennett had likewise informed his reporters that if any of them were taken prisoner, their families would be taken care of; supplies of essential food and clothing would be forwarded to the prisoners as soon as the *Herald* knew their whereabouts; and every effort would be made to secure their release as quickly as possible.

Secure in the knowledge that both themselves and their families would be taken care of, the *Herald's* reporters took risks unparalleled by those of other papers. Many were captured and imprisoned. But this did not stop them. They bribed guards to smuggle news of their whereabouts to the *Herald*. They wrote intimate eye-witness accounts of life in prison camps or behind the enemy lines, which released or exchanged prisoners carried with them, tucked away in their tobacco pouches, sewed between the lining of their jacket or trousers, or hidden in the heels of their heavy shoes. One such prisoner of war, immediately upon his release from Libby Prison, hastened to New York, made his way to the office of the *Herald*, tore off one of the big brass military buttons from his coat, and handed it to one of the editors. "There," he said, "you will find a letter in that." The button was hollow. In it, on tissue paper, was a letter describing affairs in the enemy capital, Richmond. The letter, when published, took up almost a full column in the *Herald*.

Frederic Hudson, the managing editor, years later told how instructions were issued to every *Herald* correspondent to obtain rebel newspapers. "Neither trouble nor expense were to be spared in their acquisition. Contrabands and deserters, abandoned camps and villages, were searched for them."

From these papers, the Southern Bureau in the *Herald* compiled lists of the military forces of the Confederate Army. From time to time, in incomplete form, these would then be published in the *Herald* to the amazement of the War Department and the consternation of the enemy.

On one occasion, June, 1862, Bennett decided to "shoot the works." The whole roster of the Confederate Army was published. New York and Washington were agog at the revelations. In Richmond it caused a crisis in the War Department, where several clerks were placed under arrest, charged with having furnished the information.

Hudson, in his *History of American Journalism,* relates an incident which took place the very evening of the day the *Herald* had published the Confederate roster. A *Herald* staff writer, boarding

the Fourth Avenue horse-car after his day's work, chanced to meet
a fellow journalist, George N. Snow, then employed by the *Tribune.*

"If anything were wanting to show the intimacy between the
rebels in Richmond and the office of the *Herald* in New York,"
remarked Snow, "the list of the rebel army, as published this morning, is that thing."

"What do you mean?" asked the *Herald* attaché.

"What do I mean? That roster of the rebel army could only have
been obtained from the rebel war office. That is quite enough I
should think," replied Snow, with a touch of professional jealousy.

"Why, Snow, you don't mean to say that the *Herald* obtained
that list direct from the War Department in Richmond? That information was wholly made up from advertisements and local news
paragraphs of the Southern newspapers which were run through
the lines."

"Nonsense," said Snow. "Don't you suppose that the *Tribune* and
the *Times* could have done the same thing?"

But neither Greeley nor Raymond ever thought of gathering
information in that manner. Greeley, bitter as ever at his long-time
rival, demanded editorially in the *Tribune* a day or two later that
Bennett "Let us know from what source, and through what chan-
nels, the *Herald* has twice procured for publication the alleged
muster-rolls of the rebel armies. Let us see by what means the
Herald has been repeatedly supplied with rebel newspapers."

Again, again, and yet again, the *Herald* found ways of getting
the information which the public demanded. To be sure, it did
have its conflicts with Stanton, who at least on one occasion threw
into jail one of its correspondents, a Dr. Ives, under suspicion of
being a spy. On the other hand, Bennett made it a point to pass on
to Stanton many bits of advance information regarding the enemy.
To Bennett, this was bread cast upon the waters in full expectation
of a multiplied return. The editor had not erred in his calculations.
Stanton was hard-boiled and realistic. He both hated and despised
the owner of the *Herald,* but knew that he stood to lose more than
he would gain by failing to reciprocate for the information passed
on to him by Bennett. Most of his dealings with the publisher took

place through intermediaries, but on at least one occasion, May 2, 1862, the Secretary of War wrote a personal letter to James Gordon Bennett:

DEAR SIR:—I take the liberty to inclose to you some observations respecting the present state of things as they appear to me. The great question involved in the rebellion has always seemed to me in a great measure a commercial question, and the history of the Federal Union shows that the commercial interest was one of the strongest inducements to the formation of the government. We have experienced the misfortune of the dissolution of the Union in our Commercial interests most sensibly (using that word in its most general sense), and have proved the wisdom of the framers of the Constitution by our loss in the destruction of their work—a wise and liberal system of domestic and foreign commerce. To the re-establishment of commercial relations I look, under Providence, for the restoration of the government, and that work, I regard, in a great measure, accomplished by the open ing of the ports occupied by our forces. Of course, I consider the destruction of the enemy at Yorktown and Corinth as necessary conditions.

Holding these views, I think the public mind should be directed to this state of the question, and therefore venture to submit it to you.

Yours truly,
EDWIN. M. STANTON.

Of the many men who knew Bennett well, few could exceed James Parton, the biographer of Horace Greeley, in their detestation and loathing of the cynical editor. "It would be incorrect to call him a liar," wrote Parton in his critical study of Bennett in 1870, "because he is wanting in that sense of truth by violating which a man makes himself a liar." Nor, added Parton, could he be called a traitor, "for his heart knows no country; nor an infidel, for all the serious and high concerns of man are to him a jest." Citing verse and chapter from the life and deeds of Bennett to prove his points, Parton concluded: "That region of the mind where conviction, the sense of truth and honor, public spirit and patriotism have their sphere, is in this man a mere vacancy."

Yet, in the face of this merciless castigation, Parton, himself a first-class journalist, waxed almost lyrical in his descriptions of Bennett's enterprise and ingenuity in conducting the *Herald* during the Civil War. Never for an instant, Parton averred, did Bennett relax his endeavors to obtain the earliest and fullest intelligence from the seat of war, and never did any journal *in any country* maintain so great an expenditure for news. Every man in the field representing the *Herald,* wrote Parton, was more than authorized, "he was encouraged and commanded, to incur any expense whatever might be necessary either in getting or forwarding intelligence."

"There were no rigid or grudging scrutiny of reporters' drafts; no minute and insulting inquiries respecting the last moments of a horse ridden to death in service; no grumbling about the precise terms of a steamboat charter, or a special locomotive. A reporter returning from the army laden with information, procured at lavish expense, was received in the office like a conqueror coming home from a victorious campaign; and he went forth again full of courage and zeal, knowing well that every man employed on the *Herald* was advancing himself when he served the paper well. "One great secret of success the proprietor of the *Herald* knows better than most;—he knows how to get out of those who serve him all there is in them; he knows how to reward good services; he knows a man's value to him. There is no newspaper office in the world where real journalistic efficiency is more certain to meet prompt recognition and just reward than in this."

These were the reasons the *Herald* maintained its leadership for so long as the most widely read and quoted newspaper in the world. Bennett, on more than one occasion, admitted that if he were editing the *Herald* for his own personal reading, its contents would be very different from what they were in his attempt to give the public what it wanted.

All through the war the *Herald* continued to appear as a triple-sheet (twelve-page) paper, 22 inches by 32 inches in size. The paper was of good quality; the type was neat; the layout attractive; and the printing clean and clear. The price was raised from two cents to three cents per copy in December, 1862; and again in August, 1864, the price was jumped still another cent to meet increasing costs of labor and raw materials.

At the war's close, Frederic Hudson computed the total costs of war journalism alone for the *Herald* as amounting to $525,000—a sum unequaled by any other paper up to that time, and exceeded in only a few cases during World War I.

Several of the most outspoken pro-slavery papers in New York were either suppressed or forbidden the use of the mails. Of these the *Journal of Commerce,* the *Brooklyn Eagle,* the *Day Book,* and the *Daily News* were the most important. The powerful German *Staats-Zeitung* and the French *Courrier des Etats Unis* were under government surveillance; the *World* and the *Express* managed to continue through the war, though both of them were leaders of what Bennett called the "copperhead press." Bad as he considered them, he thought them no worse than the "niggerhead press," represented by the *Times,* the *Tribune,* and the *Evening Post.* These three, on the other hand, classified the *Herald* as being not only in the camp of the enemy but as being the most dangerous of all.

The *Evening Post,* which had followed a policy of consistent support of the Lincoln administration, claimed that the Democratic press consistently magnified all rebel successes and minimized all Federal victories, abused the President and his Cabinet, calumniated the able and energetic generals such as Grant and Sherman, but held up the worthless and incompetent military leaders as "master generals of the age."

Bennett, in reply, suggested that the *Post* first learn to distinguish between fact and fancy before it lectured the opposition press; and he urged Bryant to return to his poetry, a subject with which he was more adept than journalism or military tactics.

With greater vehemence, Bennett lunged at the *World.* This journal, said Bennett, "came into existence by robbing the government, and became notorious by its managers palming off on the soldiers straw hats and linen pantaloons—all boys' sizes at that—for regular army uniforms." Now, in the summer of 1862, it was zealously "at work" endeavoring to destroy confidence in the financial system of the government, and thus indirectly assist the treasonable designs of Jeff. Davis and Company.

Fortunately for the people, argued Bennett, no one ever looks at the *World* "except the secession sympathizers in our midst," and besides, "its financial ideas, like the straw hats and linen pantaloons, are all 'boys' sizes.' "

But the real fury of the aging editor was as usual reserved for Horace Greeley. In an editorial of August 12, 1862, entitled "Sedition and Disunion at the North—Wendell Phillips and Horace Greeley," Bennett demanded prompt action by the Federal government to stop these "disunion orators and the organs of treason and sedition" in the north from giving aid and comfort to the enemy.

Citing a speech by Phillips wherein that orator called upon his abolitionist followers to pray God to humble the nation, put despair into the hearts of the Cabinet, and send Lincoln fleeing on horseback from the capital, to return "on the arms of a million adult Negroes," Bennett asked, "What is this but treason?"

"According to Wendell Phillips, Mr. Lincoln and his Cabinet are wholesale robbers and murderers of the blackest dye, and his generals are as bad, and they ought to be overthrown by revolution— by 'systematic, matured, intelligent interference by the mass of the people.' "

The *Herald* then quoted from recent editorials by Greeley to prove him of the same stripe. "The object of these attacks," wrote Bennett, "is evidently to bring the army and the government into public contempt, and to prevent enlistments, because the President will not issue an emancipation proclamation. . . . Last fall Greeley contended that the South, upon the principles of the Declaration of Independence, had a right to secede; and he published a song against the Union flag in which he called upon the people to pull it down 'as a rag' and a 'flaunting lie.' He is now laboring day and night in the same direction. How long will the people have to complain that only the radical disunionists are exempt from the operation of the orders of the government, and that abolitionists and niggers may say and do what they please with impunity?"

The *Herald* was conspicuously silent about its own political past. Greeley, meanwhile, was to be taken to the public whipping post as often as opportunity availed. In December, he was again the subject of a lengthy editorial, "Greeley as a Political Cheat and a Hypocrite."

Greeley, at this time, was involved in a battle with his old associate Thurlow Weed and with A. Oakey Hall, District Attorney for New York City. Gloating at the troubles of his rival, Bennett called him a wretched old criminal, "who attacks jobbery in his paper and practices it in person, and who eats no meat at dinner, but sups his full of bloody horrors whenever he can inveigle our troops into a rebel trap." He also assured his readers that they were in for a choice performance: "Stripping the lion's skin off of the ass is nothing compared to the cruel operation which Messrs. Weed and Hall are now performing." These two knew their opponent well. "Thurlow Weed took Greeley when the rascal had not two pair of breeches to his legs, and gave him a clean shirt, a good dinner, and a new pair of boots," while Oakey Hall was at one time Greeley's counsel when the editor needed to cover up some nefarious transactions over which we kindly throw the veil of generalities."

Gleefully, the *Herald* quoted at length the accusations made by Thurlow Weed and Oakey Hall against Horace Greeley. Weed, himself an old hand at political chicanery, charged that "the *Tribune* has been represented in the lobby at Albany for many years by an assistant editor, who is a brother-in-law of Mr. Greeley, and who is understood to have a finger in all the pies baked in the Albany lobby. One or more assistant editors are understood to be equally diligent and successful in gun contracts and other jobs in Washington, while half a dozen other assistant editors of the *Tribune* rejoice in foreign appointments."

New York's District Attorney, Oakey Hall, fortified Weed's attack by admitting that "having been during several years counsel for various persons desiring to advance or oppose legislative or contract interests, I found in every matter the direct influence of Mr. Greeley."

Every juicy bit of testimony was used by Bennett to castigate poor Greeley, who, said Bennett, had "descended from stage to stage of vice and degradation." Gift enterprises and lotteries, he added, "are as familiar to Greeley as the nose on his face." But his chosen element is the corruption of lobbying, "and he wallows in it like a pig in the mire."

In part at least, Bennett's attacks upon Greeley were due to the fact that Greeley represented a rising tide of public opinion in the North which demanded the liberation of the slaves. Hundreds of

thousands of persons who were prepared to make any needed concessions to prevent war from breaking out at the time Lincoln took
office, and who up to the time of the Bull Run disaster were prepared to mete out rough treatment to Northern abolitionists in their
ranks, were by the middle of 1862 saying that sooner or later chattel
slavery would have to be abolished.

On August 20, 1862, Greeley wrote one of his most powerful editorials, "The Prayer of the Twenty Millions." It was addressed to
Lincoln and it told him that "a great portion of those who tri-
umphed in your election, and all who desire the unqualified suppression of the Rebellion now desolating our country, are sorely disappointed and deeply pained by the policy you seem to be pursuing
with regard to the slaves of the Rebels. . . ." Greeley demanded an
end to the timid, pussyfooting policy of the administration on the
slave question. His editorial was immediately reprinted and spread
broadcast over the country in hundreds of thousands of copies. As
such it gave added impetus to the demand for action by the Administration.

A few days later, President Lincoln made a formal reply to
Greeley's open letter.

Executive Mansion, Washington
August 22, 1862

HON. HORACE GREELEY:

DEAR SIR: I have just read yours of the 19th, addressed to myself
through the N. Y. Tribune. If there be in it any statements or assump-
tions of fact which I may know to be erroneous, I do not now and here
controvert them. If there be in it any inferences which I may believe
to be falsely drawn, I do not now and here argue against them. If
there be perceptible in it an impatient and dictatorial tone, I waive it
in deference to an old friend, whose heart I have always supposed to
be right.

As to the policy I "seem to be pursuing," as you say, I have not
meant to leave anyone in doubt.

I would save the Union. I would save it the shortest way under the
Constitution. The sooner the National authority can be restored, the
nearer the Union will be "the Union as it was." If there be those who
would not save the Union unless they could at the same time *save* slavery, I do not agree with them. If there be those who would not save
the Union unless they could at the same time *destroy* slavery, I do not
agree with them. My paramount object in this struggle *is* to save the

Union, and is *not* either to save or to destroy slavery. If I could save the Union without freeing *any* slave, I would do it; and if I could save the Union by freeing *all* the slaves, I would do it; and if I could do it by freeing some and leaving others alone, I would also do that. What I do about slavery and the colored race, I do because I believe it helps to save this Union; and what I forbear, I forbear because I do *not* believe it would help to save the Union. I shall do *less* whenever I believe what I am doing hurts the cause, and I shall do *more* whenever I shall believe doing more will help the cause. I shall try to correct errors when shown to be errors; and I shall adopt new views so fast as they shall appear to be true views. I have here stated my purpose according to my view of *official* duty, and I intend no modification of my oft-expressed *personal* wish that all men, everywhere, could be free.

Yours,

A. LINCOLN.

As a matter of fact, the President had drafted and read to his Cabinet his proposed Emancipation Proclamation on July 22, but at Seward's suggestion it was laid aside for the time being. All Lincoln wanted was an appropriate Union victory as a peg upon which to hang his proclamation. That victory came in late September, with the Battle of Antietam. The next day Lincoln announced that he was giving the seceded states one hundred days—till January 1, 1863—in which to return to the Union. Rebel states which failed to lay down their guns by that time were given notice that their slaves would thereafter be considered as free men.

The radical wing of the Republican Party was jubilant, and rallied to the support of Lincoln as never before. "It puts us right before Europe," exulted the *Evening Post*. "It brings back our traditions; it animates our soldiers with the same spirit which led our forefathers to victory under Washington; they are fighting today, as the Revolutionary patriots fought, in the interests of the human race. . . ."

Most jubilant of all was Greeley who wrote that the end of the rebellion was at hand. The Emancipation Proclamation likewise meant the beginning of a new life for the nation. And the *Tribune* concluded: "GOD BLESS ABRAHAM LINCOLN!"

James Gordon Bennett, on the other hand, was greatly disappointed to find Lincoln yielding to the radicals. He took solace from the fact that the President had supposedly informed an Illinois dele-gation that there was no way of enforcing the Emancipation Proc-lamation, so perhaps it was a mere sop thrown to the abolitionists to stop their attacks upon the administration. A few days later, he wrote that if put into effect it would ruin the free white labor of the North and West by bringing into the labor market hordes of cheap and docile ex-slaves. Still later, and still smarting from what he believed to be a most grievous concession to the abolitionists, Bennett wrote, "While the Proclamation leaves slavery untouched where his decree can be enforced, he emancipates slaves where his decree cannot be enforced. Friends of human rights will be at a loss to understand this discrimination. As a war measure it is un-necessary, unwise, ill-timed, impracticable, outside the Constitution and full of mischief."

Lincoln had requested that the liberated slaves "abstain from all violence unless necessary in self defense." To the *Herald* such a request carried with it the hint to do otherwise. Its editor reminded his readers of the Irish student who witnessed from his room in Old Trinity, a proctor being ducked in the college tank, and there-upon called out, "Boys, don't nail his ear to the pump!" "Of the same solemn character is the injunction of Mr. Lincoln to the Negro in his Proclamation," wrote Bennett.

The *Herald's* somewhat turbulent honeymoon with President Lincoln was at an end. It spoke out more frequently against him. It attacked his Cabinet. It cried for the reinstatement of General McClellan as Commander-in-Chief of the armed forces of the Union. "As a friend of President Lincoln," wrote Bennett, January 16, 1863, "we must tell him seriously and earnestly that the country has had enough of the military plans and combinations of Mr. Sec-retary Stanton and General Halleck. They have been tried in the balance and found wanting in every essential for military success. . . . But how are their places to be filled? We can tell the President how. Put Gen. McClellan at the head of the War Office, and abolish the office of General-in-Chief, and McClellan will do the work which Stanton and Halleck combined will never accomplish. . . . We have had enough of them. They have brought our cause and our hopes to the verge of ruin. The crisis demands their removal,

and the country will rejoice again with McClellan's appointment
to supersede them both. He is our man in the hour of danger. . . ."

Lincoln did not heed the warning nor follow the advice. He was,
thought Bennett, too much the politician, skilled at riding two
horses at one time, letting now the radical, now the conservative,
get a "leetle ahead."

The year 1863 marked the turning point in the War Between the
States. It was the year when the Draft Act came into being—the
first of its kind in the United States. It was the year when Congress authorized the President to suspend the writ of *habeas corpus*
in cases where persons were suspected of disloyalty to the United
States. It was the year when Lee invaded Pennsylvania and lost the
three-day battle at Gettysburg. It was the year when Vicksburg
yielded to the hammering blows of General Grant. It was the year
when Federal forces gained control of the mighty Mississippi and
cut off Louisiana and Texas from the rest of the Confederacy. It
was the year of the Draft Riots in New York. And it was a year
of political turbulence, when the fate of Lincoln's administration
hung in balance. It was the year when General Sherman, on his
march through Georgia, ordered the arrest and court-martial of the
New York Herald correspondent, Thomas W. Knox, for sending
in reports to his paper for publication without first submitting them
to the general. Knox luckily got away by merely being ordered to
stay outside the army lines. But to General Sherman, this incident
was the last straw of unfortunate experiences with newspapermen.
"I will never again command an army in America," wrote the
irate general to his wife, "if we must carry along paid spies. . . ."

To lighten the reading matter during this awful period of blood-
letting, the *Herald* used to go out of its way to report incidents and
anecdotes about the President and his Cabinet. In one of these,
which concerned Lincoln's aching feet and burning bunions to
which a young Jewish chiropodist was giving relief, it reported:

Dr. Zacharie trimmed the feet of President Lincoln and all his Cabinet. He is a wit, gourmet and eccentric, with a splendid Roman nose,
fashionable whiskers and an eloquent tongue, a dazzling diamond
breast-pin, great skill in his profession and an ingratiating address. . . .
Dr. Zacharie has made his debut on the national stage to cut the Pres-

idential corns. When Dr. Zacharie called at the White House, Secretary Stanton mistook him for some visionary Greeley or Jewett, refused to listen to him. But Zacharie passed on into the President's private reception room and as soon as Mr. Lincoln saw him he held out his foot and complained of corns.

On another occasion, the newspaper suggested that the President and his wife visit New York for some much-needed relaxation, especially to enjoy the music of the new opera season, just beginning:

How grateful will be the change between Washington and New York! It will be a translation and transformation as by the magic lamp of Aladdin. From the hospitals of sick and wounded soldiers, camps of contrabands, corrals of army horses and hordes of hungry politicians, to the shops of Broadway, the concerts of the Park and fascinations of Opera! We expect a series of victories over the rebels in the meantime so that our great father, or great grandfather as some of the Indians call him, may pack up and pack off from Washington for a few days with a light heart and an easy conscience. We want President Lincoln as well as Mrs. Lincoln to come during this May campaign of Maretzek. We want the President to compare for himself the strategy of Maretzek with the strategy of the War Office; the harmony of the Italians with the discords of the politicians; the music of Mazzoleni with the jargon of the Cabinet; the delicious strains of Guerrabella with the tedious orders of General Halleck.

New York's Tammany machine, with its tremendous contingent of foreign-born (mostly Irish) voters, continued to be hostile to the Lincoln administration throughout the war. When the first drawing of the draft numbers began in July, that resentment and hostility were fanned into a flame of opposition which brought on a minor Civil War within the city itself.

The Draft Riots began on the morning of July 13 at the headquarters on the corner of 46th Street and Sixth Avenue. They continued for four days. One of the city's main armories was captured. Negroes were clubbed to death. The homes, stores, and other business establishments of well-known abolitionists were wrecked, looted, or burned. The local police force was overcome. Both Governor Seymour and Mayor Opdyke, known for their opposition to the Federal administration, were slow to move in quelling the mobs which surged through the city's streets, shouting, looting, and killing.

Both the *Herald* and the *World* at first looked somewhat sympathetically upon the rioters, referring to them as "the people" or "the laboring men of the city"—but within a day both papers changed their position and joined the rest of the press in demanding the sternest of measures to suppress the mob.

On the night of the thirteenth, a vast mob gathered to march on and destroy the *Tribune* and hang its editor. Chanting, "We'll hang old Greeley to a sour apple tree, And send him straight to Hell," the mob poured down upon Printing House Square. The police guarding the *Tribune* were overwhelmed; fires were started in half a dozen spots in the building; desks, tables, type forms, and printing presses were smashed; Greeley and his assistants escaped in the nick of time. The editor was chased into a Park Row restaurant, where he hid under a table.

After four frightful days, the riots were brought to a close. The city was a shambles. More than a hundred buildings had been burned; several times that many had been damaged or looted. More than two thousand persons had been killed and over eight thousand wounded; which meant a casualty loss on a par with that suffered by the Union forces at Bull Run. From the rioters the police and soldiers captured over eleven thousand firearms as well as great masses of clubs, daggers, swords, and other instruments of destruction.

According to Herbert Asbury, who devoted several chapters of his book, *The Gangs of New York,* to the Draft Riots, military and police authorities were constantly being hampered by Democratic members of the State Legislature and the city's Board of Aldermen who seized the opportunity to embarrass Lincoln and his administration:

These worthy statesmen frequently appeared at Police Headquarters, and at a time when houses were being looted and burned and Negroes tortured and hanged, when business was at a standstill and the streets were filled with surging mobs, demanded that the police and soldiers be withdrawn from their districts, complaining that they were murdering the people. A Democratic Police Magistrate held a special session of his court, brought forward a test case, and solemnly pronounced the draft law to be unconstitutional, and urged the people to resist its enforcement. Most of the prisoners taken by the police during the last two days of the rioting, and during the search for stolen goods, were immediately freed through political influence, and were never brought to trial. Many of the gang leaders of the Five Points, the water front and other criminal infested areas were caught leading their thugs on looting expeditions, when politicians rushed to their aid and saved them from punishment. When the rioting had ceased only twenty men, out of the thousands who had formed the mobs, were in jail. Of these nineteen were tried and convicted, and were sentenced to an average of five years each in prison.

Whereas all the other papers devoted their front pages to the riots, not so the *Herald*. War news and world news came first, so far as Bennett was concerned. The reports on the riots raging all about the *Herald* building were placed on the inside editorial page. More than that these reports were both brief and disconnected, whereas every other paper gave detailed descriptions of the whole sordid affair. In view of Bennett's long career as the ace newsgatherer, one can only conclude that for personal or political reasons he gave orders to his staff to play down the riots.

A fortnight later, however, on August 3, Bennett devoted a lengthy editorial to "Poor Greeley and the Recent Riots." Bennett accused the Radical Republicans of trying to make political capital out of the riots. But alas, "Poor Greeley" had again "failed as dismally in his pet enterprise of strengthening his party by the riots, as in his gold pen, strawberry plant and other lottery schemes for increasing the circulation of the *Tribune*."

One can almost see the gleam in the squint eyes, and the broad grin on the thin lips, as Bennett flayed and heaped ridicule upon his editorial opponent. Not only did Greeley fail to make political capital out of the riots, but

. . . the *Tribune* philosopher has not even acquired a reputation for ordinary bravery by his participation in the late exciting scenes. In vain he now talks of concealed riflemen and hand grenades and cannon, and threatens what he would have done if the rioters had only attacked his office again. This playing Bombastes Furioso after the fighting is over excites more ridicule than admiration. It reminds us of rare Jack Falstaff, who took to his heels at Gadshill and counterfeited death at

Shrewsbury, but was always ready to brag tremendously when his foes were dead or put to flight. Kindly disposed as we are towards poor Greeley, we feel bound to say that his doughty deeds and heroic exploits will never furnish themes for the poet or historian, or subjects for the sculptor and the painter. On the first day of the riots he took refuge in a restaurant, and Dame Rumor reports that he there concealed himself in a refrigerator. If this be true, it is a singular instance of the power of fear; for poor Greeley is so rigid a vegetarian that no one would have thought him capable of getting into a meatbox, even to save his life. When the riot had somewhat subsided, and poor Greeley deemed it prudent to emerge from his hiding place, he proceeded to disguise himself by pulling his trowsers out of his boots, washing his face and hands, and adjusting his white hat jauntily on one side of his head. These slight alterations in his personal appearance disguised him so effectually that his best friends did not know him, and it was with some difficulty that the persons who came to take him away in a carriage could be induced to believe that the comparatively respectable looking individual before them was really Horace Greeley. It was only when he produced a leading editorial, hastily written upon the back of a greasy bill of fare, that his friends admitted his identity and consented to convey him to Jersey City for safety.

Bennett was getting his revenge for Greeley's rejoicing at the mobbing of the *Herald* in April, 1861.

No sooner had the riots become a thing of the past when a bitter state political campaign was launched in New York. Bennett had intimated that it would be advisable to postpone elections till after the war was over, but this idea was so thoroughly denounced by all that he said no more about it. And for once the *Herald* refused to take any side in the gubernatorial campaign. On election day, November 2, the paper summed up its views of the campaign in an editorial as follows:

A Good Riddance

The labors of the battalion of political orators who for several weeks have been stumping the state close today. By 12 o'clock tonight the dismal platitudes of Governor Seymour, the profane comicalities of Governor Yates, the vindictive copperheadism of Booby Brooks, the tedious twaddle of Chevalier Forney, and all the electioneering clap-trap, rant and cant of the whole tribe of these political spouters on both sides will come to an end, and the people of the State will have a season of rest. Let the people rejoice!

All through the spring and summer the *Herald* had taken a highly critical position toward Lincoln. But late in October, when Lincoln was faced with another grave crisis in his Cabinet, Bennett, once again, became more friendly. Good-naturedly, he wrote, "Ordinarily Honest Old Abe does not display much energy and spirit. So long as he is left in peace to read Artemus Ward's book and crack his own little jokes, he is happy." And then, expressing renewed confidence in Lincoln's ability to handle the emergency, he added: "Old Abe is ready to meet it. We should not be at all surprised to learn that at this moment Lincoln had a masked battery ready to open up on Chase and blow him to atoms whenever he is ready." The President's more recent acts and statements, in the opinion of the *Herald,* suggested that Lincoln was taking a more constructive and conservative point of view, to the perplexity of the abolition radicals. The *Herald* praised him for standing firm against these radicals by letting them know that he, and not they, was responsible for the acts of his administration.

"The day is approaching," concluded the publisher, "when the President will be required to make known his policy in regard to the restoration of the rebellious States to the Union. Senator Sumner would reduce them to the condition of Territories, or so much wild land, without local institutions or boundaries of any kind, and from this wild land he would carve out new States and new institutions for them, based upon the eternal expulsion of African Slaves. But Mr. Secretary Chase and the bulk of the radical faction do not care to go quite so far. . . . President Lincoln has broken ground for the next Presidency, and has broadly intimated that his platform will be that of the conservatives; that his policy will be the restoration of the seceded States as soon as any or all of them may choose to return, and with their local institutions, including Slavery, just as the war may practically have left them."

As the showdown between Lincoln and the leading members of his Cabinet appeared imminent, Bennett determined once again to throw his paper into the fray. Each day he launched his attacks against the radicals. From the copious files and confidential reports of the *Herald* his writers fashioned devastating articles crammed with instances of stupidity, mismanagement, inefficiency, and corruption on the part of the radicals and their underlings. The "political" generals were held up to scorn and ridicule—men who wasted the nation's blood and wealth to win laurels for themselves. On the other hand, there was presented the record of the "constructive and conservative" leaders, both civil and military. And these, if the *Herald* was to be believed, were as uniformly good as the others were bad. Lincoln was urged to "look at the record" and then take his stand. "Don't let the Abolitionists bully you any longer, Mr. President."

"These radicals," warned the editor, "care nothing for the Union." They despised and spat upon it while it was intact. They rejoiced when it was broken by the secession of South Carolina, and both Mephistopheles Phillips and Robespierre Greeley urged the other Southern states to secede also. They never supported the war for the Union until they conceived the idea of converting the war into an abolition crusade. The vilest copperhead has no such damnable record. For the President to yield to these men is as great a folly as to enter an insane asylum and submit to the whims and caprices of madmen, monomaniacs, and lunatics:

Of all the issues raised by this war there is none so plain as that in regard to slavery. Undoubtedly the war has killed slavery. It would have killed it if no emancipation proclamation had ever been issued. . . .

President Lincoln has his duty before him, and should do it. That duty is to save the Union, no matter whether slavery be saved or lost. If he is an anti-slavery man he may be happy in the conviction that slavery cannot possibly be saved. We have gone too far for that. If the seceded States came back tomorrow they could not preserve slavery for more than a few years, and that in a galvanized rather than a living form. But, as President of the United States, Mr. Lincoln has nothing to do with this. To use plain words, it is none of his business what becomes of slavery. He is bound to restore the Union and to administer its government justly. Any man who would sacrifice the Union to destroy slavery is as deadly and as dangerous a traitor as the meanest Copperhead who would sacrifice the Union to preserve slavery. The masses of the Northern people are neither pro-slavery nor anti-slavery traitors. They are true Union men, and they want their President to be like them.

Meanwhile, on the basis of the many bits of information which the *Herald* was able to gather on conditions in the Confederate states, it became convinced that a breakdown was near at hand. In early November there came into the possession of the *Herald* a confidential letter, written on April 25, 1863, by L. B. Northrup, Commissary General of Confederate States to the Hon. James A. Seddon, Confederate Secretary of War. Northrup described the many serious agricultural shortages faced by the South. Worst of all was the fact that despite the many urgent pleas by both the government and the army, there had been no extra plantings on needed food crops by the farmers. "It is obvious that something must be done immediately or both the people and the army must starve next winter."

Bennett knew as well as any general that an army travels on its stomach. Northrup's letter merely confirmed the editor's many predictions that the exhausted economy of the South was bound to bring about its defeat, no matter how brilliant its generals or how brave and gallant its soldiers.

Discussing "The Bread Question in the South," Bennett cited some of the tell-tale evidence of its importance for a Union victory. "The rebellion," he wrote, "is already beginning to feel the pangs of a famine, and the winter has not yet set in. How is the poor barefooted rebel soldier's family to live through it when his month's pay in rebel scrip will only buy them two or three pounds of bacon, a few pounds of flour, or a peck or two of corn meal? . . . These facts we have recited, at all events, are sufficient to show the exhausted condition of the rebellion, and that, if within the ensuing six months of consumption without production, the rebellious States are not subdued the country will need nothing further to prove the incompetency and imbecility of President Lincoln's Administration."

When Lincoln and members of his entourage, in mid-November, journeyed to attend the elaborate consecration at what the *Herald* called "Our National Necropolis," the hostile press called it a political stunt. If the President wants to build his fences for re-election, argued some of these, at least he should have the decency not to use the ceremonies at Gettysburg for such a purpose.

The little village was jam-packed with visitors, curiosity seekers,

politicians, soldiers, newspapermen, and folk from the neighborhood on the night before the ceremonies got under way. The *Herald*
was well represented and in its issue of November 20 carried a
detailed account of all that took place. There was a carefully written
article describing the battle which had been fought at Gettysburg,
and its significance to the nation. Another reported the progress of
the presidential party from Washington to Gettysburg with lengthy
descriptions of all leading personalities. Still another told what Gettysburg looked like on the eve of the huge gathering. The Fifth
New York Artillery band serenaded Lincoln at the house where he
was resting. A large crowd gathered outside, calling for the President to come out and make a speech. At last the tall stooped figure
appeared.

"I appear before you, fellow citizens, merely to thank you for this
compliment. The inference is a very fair one that you would hear
me for a little while at least were I to commence to make a speech.
I do not appear before you for the purpose of doing so, and for
several substantial reasons. The most substantial of these is that I
have no speech to make. (Laughter.) In my position it is somewhat
important that I should not say any foolish things."

A Voice: "If you can help it."

Mr. Lincoln: "It very often happens that the only way to help
it is to say nothing at all. (Laughter.) Believing that is my present
condition tonight, I must beg you to excuse me from addressing
you further."

This was Lincoln's *first* Gettysburg address. It was carried only
in the columns of the *Herald*.

In the report on the great day itself, Edward Everett's oration was
printed in full. The procession to the battlefield and the elaborate
program were given complete coverage. At the very end came
these three items, with no description at all: "Music; Dedicatory
Remarks by the President of the United States; Dirge and Bene-
diction."

Lincoln's address was printed in six-point type on an inside page.
There was no build-up for it; no description of how the President
looked, how he spoke, or how the audience reacted to it.

The *Herald* devoted several lengthy editorials during the next few days to the consecration ceremonies at Gettysburg. Edward Everett's speech was highly praised and assured a place among the great orations of history. Lincoln's five-minute talk was evidently considered too commonplace to deserve comment.

Most of the other papers followed Bennett's example and ignored the remarks of President Lincoln. A few, and very few indeed, joined the *Providence Journal* in saying, "We know not where to look for a more admirable speech than the brief one which the President made at the close of Mr. Everett's oration." But many more followed the lead of the *Patriot and Union* of Harrisburg: "We pass over the silly remarks of the President. For the credit of the nation we are willing that the veil of oblivion shall be dropped over them and that they shall no more be repeated or thought of."

If the *Herald* overlooked the Gettysburg Address, it made up for it by inventing speeches for him. On November 21, in a discussion on Lincoln as the American Aesop it reported on a supposed speech that the President had made to members of his Cabinet and some of the foreign diplomatic corps.

"In my position," began the imaginary speech of Lincoln, "it is not wise to talk foolishly and I would therefore not talk at all. . . . As for the 'war for succession,' about which the *Herald* and Mr. Phillips appear crazy, I will say some few words. Men oftenest betray and defeat themselves by overanxiety to secure their object just as the widow Zollicoffer's Negro did down in Bourbon County when he had been eating her cranberry jam. (Laughter.) The widow, while making her jam, was called away to a neighbor who was about to increase the population. 'Sam, you rascal, you will be eating my jam while I am away.' Sam protested he would die first but the whites of his eyes rolled and hung towards the bubbling crimson. 'See here, Sam,' said the widow, taking up a piece of chalk. 'I'll chalk your lips and then I'll know if you have eaten any when I come back.' So saying she passed her forefinger heavily over the thick lips of her darkey, *holding the chalk in the palm of her hand and not letting it touch him.* Well, when she came back, Sam's lips were chalked a quarter of an inch thick and she needed no further evidence against him.

"Now it is much the same about the Presidency. (Loud laughter.)

A good friend of mine declared he would not take it at any price, but his lips were heavily chalked when he came back from Ohio. (Great merriment, with Mr. Chase joining in heartily.) So were General Fremont's out in Missouri when he issued his 'emancipation order.' And General Butler's were not only chalked but had the jam on and had it thick. Senator Seward once chalked very badly but gave it up as of no use when he quarreled with the machine proprietor of his own State. (Loud laughter.) Mingled jam and chalk might be seen on the lips of General Banks; while the same compound formed quite a paste around the office through which his good friend Governor Seymour supplied the wants of nature. (Roars of laughter.) I have never seen any chalk on the lips of Secretary Stanton nor General Halleck but with these exceptions there was scarcely a man connected with the army who did not chalk his lips. (Continued mirth, the foreign diplomatic corps joining in heartily.)"

"The President," continued the *Herald's* report, "who had been sitting curled up in an arm chair with his legs loosely crossed one over the other, now began to rise, slowly untwisting the kinks of his back and towering up like one of the genii released from a jar or jug in which he had been bottled up for centuries under the seal of Solomon. 'Aisy!' exclaimed Mr. Luke Clark with unaffected dismay. 'It's dashing your brains out against the ceiling you'll be or tangling your shoulders in the top notches of the chandelier.' At length Mr. Lincoln reached his full height and said that he did not quite catch the drift. Still later the President was saying to Miles O'Reilly, the poet, 'Tell us if you can, what the people say of us, what they say of Chase, of Seward. You needn't be afraid, Miles, we are not of a thin-skinned family and we know before asking that you have an awkward knack of telling the truth. . . .

"As to his being a candidate for reelection, it reminded him of what old Jesse Dubois said to the preacher at Springfield when he asked from the State House for a lecture on the subject: The Second Coming of Our Saviour. 'If our Saviour,' retorted old Jesse, 'had ever come to Springfield and was lucky enough to get away with his life, he would be too smart to come again.' This is very much my case about succession. . . . As I see you are all buttoning up to

go away, I will not detain you, more especially as Louis Burgdorf
has been making secret signs to me for the last half hour that Mrs.
Lincoln and the child will have cold turkey for their Thanksgiving
dinner if I don't cross over the other side of the building shortly."

War or no war, the year 1864 meant that the voters of the United
States would go to the polls to choose a new administration, or vote
to retain the old one.

Northern Democrats seemed pretty well convinced that their
standard-bearer should be the dashing and politically ambitious
General McClellan. The *Herald* had long praised McClellan as a
splendid military commander. It had intimated, on more than one
occasion, that he was worthy of consideration as presidential timber.
But McClellan had not been able to hold the military spotlight in
1863 as he did the year previous. He was being overshadowed by
a short, stocky, grim-faced, bearded man from down-state Illinois
by the name of Grant. The westerner, in his crumpled uniform,
and with the stump of a cigar jutting out from his mouth, cut no
dashing figure like McClellan. He made no speeches. He wrote no
lengthy letters. He possessed neither eye nor sex appeal. But he won
victories. He was like a bull dog in his tenacity. Grant was rising
fast in the estimation of the country.

Bennett decided to whoop it up for Grant as a presidential candidate. The reporters were ordered to give him the appropriate
build-up. Soon every page of the *Herald* carried some news about
Grant. And the editorial page began to speak of him as "The People's Candidate." Other papers took up the cry, and many disappointed Republicans saw a possibility of riding into power behind
the hard-hitting general. Grant himself, busy with a first-class war
on his hands, was probably unaware of this build-up until it had
gained considerable momentum. The pro-Lincoln organs, meanwhile, decided to blast Bennett for his audacity. Most outspoken was
the *Chicago Tribune,* which was as determined to keep Grant out
of the claws of Bennett as it was to keep Lincoln in the White
House for another term.

"We claim the right to tell this organ of the Five points and the
Thugs of New York," thundered the *Chicago Tribune,* "that it
must keep its copperhead slime off our Illinois General. He has no

attribute, thought, or sympathy in harmony with *Satanic* [nickname for the *New York Herald*]. General Grant is an old neighbor and friend of President Lincoln. The latter has stood by him with the strength of iron from the first. . . . In return General Grant has been true as steel to his friend and Commander-in-Chief. For the *New York Herald* to bring out General Grant is a gross libel on him and an insult to his friends. Unless it keeps its unclean and treacherous hands off of him, it may expect to get 'tomahawked.' " The *Herald* "cannot be allowed to paw and slobber over our Illinois General, and if it has any regard for its 'throat' or its 'fifth rib,' it will take warning and govern itself accordingly."

Back came the *Herald* with the charge that the *Chicago Tribune* was "the sewer into which goes everything too dirty for its New York namesake to print." The *Chicago Tribune* could only reply, "The people want Old Abe to stay where he is until he has finished *his* big job . . . and General Grant to stay where he is until he has finished *his* big job. . . . Let our Western General alone."

The tone of the *Herald* grew steadily more critical of Lincoln, and as steadily more laudatory of Grant. On January 21, 1864, Bennett published a lengthy editorial entitled "PRESIDENT LINCOLN AS COMMANDER-IN-CHIEF—HIS MILITARY INCAPACITY."

No longer was there the bantering about "Old Abe" and his story-telling. This time came a head-on attack. The loss of life, the blundering, the mass of defeats and retreats—all these were placed squarely in the lap of the President. "The official reports of General McClellan and of General Halleck, with the accompanying military views and instructions of President Lincoln," wrote Bennett, "remove all doubts as to the individual really responsible for these aforesaid magnificent military promises and deplorable military failures."

"We say to President Lincoln, the Commander-in-Chief of the Army and the Navy, as the prophet Nathan said to King David, *'Thou art the man.'* "

In clear cold words and phrases, the old editor reviewed the long lists of blunders committed and opportunities missed:

What a budget of blunders is here! Of overwhelming armies wasted in the foolish system of small detachments here and there, each under an independent commander, operating around a great circle against the combined forces of the enemy in the centre. What a deplorable want of military capacity at Washington is here exhibited in golden opportunities disregarded, in battles lost by blundering strategy, in great victories thrown away by hap-hazard changes of military plans and army leaders. The responsibility lies with President Lincoln for all these misfortunes and failures, from the first Bull Run down to the escape of the rebel army across the Potomac. Without education or practical service as a soldier, his experience with the Army of the Potomac has proved that he is equally deficient in the natural qualities of mind essential to the successful military leader.

No braver army ever took the field than our heroic and self-sacrificing Army of the Potomac; yet how different the net results of its arduous and bloody campaigns, under the management of President Lincoln, compared with the results of Grant's campaign in the West. The Army of the Potomac stands today only some forty miles beyond Bull Run, while General Grant has overrun and reconquered an empire. We contend that the man who has subjugated the rebellion in the West is the man to finish it in the East; that General Grant, in a word, is the man to take the place of President Lincoln in view of the speedy and complete extinguishment of the rebellion, and in view of the foreign complications which may follow, calling for a capable military leader at the head of the government when the rebellious States shall have been reduced to submission and peace. General Grant is the man to reestablish the Union in its territorial integrity, and the man to settle our outstanding balances against the Western Powers of Europe. President Lincoln has failed as a military leader, and General Grant is the man to take his place.

The attacks continued day after day. And when Henry Ward Beecher wrote in the *Independent* that the President seemed to be a man "without any sense of the value of time," Bennett seized upon this to claim that even the small amount of intellect with which he was credited by Beecher "is gradually failing under the President's anxiety for re-nomination."

In the meantime, Lincoln's friends had obtained a statement from Grant that he had neither the time nor the inclination to run for President. But within the Cabinet itself almost every man was secretly or openly building his own political machine to win for himself the nomination against Lincoln at the forthcoming Republican Convention.

Those loyal to Lincoln worked like Trojans to secure the support needed for his renomination. In this, the power of James Gordon Bennett was by no means overlooked. His biting pen was doing as much damage as the blundering of the generals. In February, he wrote, "As a joker, Mr. Lincoln is unique. With the caustic wit of Diogenes he combines the best qualities of all the other celebrated jokers of the world. He is more poetical than Horace, more spicy than Juvenal, more anecdotal than Aesop, more juicy than Boccaccio, more mellow than rollicking Rabelais, and more often quoted than the veteran Joe Miller."

On the Democratic side the *Herald* continued to pump for McClellan with redoubled energy as it saw that its boom for Grant had collapsed on the Republican side. Then, in order to throw confusion and consternation into the Republican ranks, it declared that Lincoln would, of course, get his party's nomination again, for he had in his hands the reins and machinery of the party. "He will enter the canvass," continued the *Herald,* "as the embodiment of all the blunders, follies, and corruptions of his administration," and he would carry with him such an unholy band as William Seward, Horace Greeley, General Fremont, and Wendell Phillips. "With this precious freight the great jester will push into the political current as proudly as when in earlier days he strode an Ohio flatboat freighted with his Lares and Penates and a bountiful supply of hog and hominy."

Name-calling and political intrigues were temporarily relegated to second place as the nation awaited word of the Battles of the Wilderness, where the armies of Grant and Lee were locked in mortal combat.

Grant had been placed in command of the armed forces of the Union in March, 1864. The *Herald,* a year later, told the following interesting anecdote about Grant and Stanton:

When General Grant was about to leave Washington to enter upon that sublime campaign which began with the battle of the Wilderness and ended with the downfall of the rebellion, he called upon Secretary Stanton to say good-bye. The Secretary was anxiously awaiting him. During the two and a half years that President Lincoln and Secretary Stanton had managed the Eastern army, it was the first point in their plans to keep Washington heavily garrisoned with troops. Large bodies of men were stationed in the fortifications around the city, and other large bodies were kept within supporting distance. Now that Grant had come into power, Stanton wanted to see that the defence of Washington was not overlooked. Accordingly, after a few preliminaries, the Secretary remarked:

"Well, General, I suppose you have left us enough men to strongly garrison the forts?"

"No," said Grant, coolly, "I can't do that."

"Why not?" cried Stanton, jumping nervously about. "Why not? Why not?"

"Because I have already sent the men to the front," replied Grant, calmly.

"That won't do," cried Stanton, more nervous than before. "It's contrary to my plans. I can't allow it. I'll order the men back."

"I shall need the men there," answered Grant, "and you can't order them back."

"Why not?" inquired Stanton again. "Why not? Why not?"

"I believe that I rank the Secretary," was the quiet reply.

"Very well," said Stanton, a little warmly, "we'll see the President about that. I'll have to take you to the President."

"That's right," politely observed Grant; "the President ranks us both."

Arrived at the White House, the General and the Secretary asked to see the President upon important business, and in a few moments the good-natured face of Mr. Lincoln appeared.

"Well, gentlemen," said the President with a genial smile, "what do you want with me?"

"General," said Stanton stiffly, "state your case."

"I have no case to state," replied General Grant. "I'm satisfied as it is"; thus outflanking the Secretary, and displaying the same strategy in diplomacy as in war.

"Well, well," said the President, laughing, "state your case, Mr. Secretary."

Secretary Stanton obeyed; General Grant said nothing; the President listened very attentively. When Stanton had concluded, the President crossed his legs, rested his elbow on his knee, twinkled his eyes quaintly and said:

"Now, Secretary, you know we have been trying to manage this army for two years and a half, and you know we haven't done much with it. We sent over the mountains and brought Mister Grant—as Mrs. Grant calls him—to manage it for us, and now I guess we had better let Mister Grant have his own way."

The radical wing of the Republicans and smaller unaffiliated groups called a convention in Cleveland at the end of May, 1864, and nominated Fremont as their presidential candidate. Meetings in

Baltimore on June 17, the regular Republican machine renominated Lincoln without any serious opposition. At the end of August the Democrats nominated McClellan. Shortly thereafter, Fremont withdrew from the race and his group threw their support to Lincoln.

During the summer of 1864, Horace Greeley again became the *Herald's* target. The *Tribune's* editor had allowed himself to be made an intermediary for two Confederate "ambassadors" who were in Canada waiting to work out a negotiated peace. The scheme died quickly, and this time not only Bennett, but Raymond, Bryant, and a host of other good Republicans joined in denouncing Greeley for his stupidity and gullibility.

Earlier that summer, a bogus proclamation in which President Lincoln called for the enlistment of 400,000 additional men and set aside a day of fasting and prayer—was sent out to all the newspapers by an erratic journalist. The proclamation had been cooked up in conjunction with some shady stock speculators who hoped to reap a fortune out of the fluctuations which such a proclamation would have on the stock market. To the credit of the press, only two New York papers—the *World* and the *Journal of Commerce* —published the report. Lincoln immediately denounced the statement as a forgery. Federal authorities suspended publication of both papers for several days, and the guilty perpetrator was sent to Fort LaFayette, where he spent fourteen weeks as a prisoner.

As the summer wore on, the *Herald* grew more venomous in its attacks upon Lincoln, charging him with the mass murder of Union troops in order to win political supporters. Lincoln's campaign managers knew that the election was sure to be close, and some means had to be found, if possible, to win over Bennett, or at least to silence his attacks.

One of the political emissaries sent to sound out Bennett reported that the editor asked, "Will I be a welcome visitor at the White House if I support Mr. Lincoln?" Senator Harlan, according to John Hay, considered the influence of the *Herald* on the soldier vote to be so potent that it would not be too big a price to offer Bennett a major foreign mission (ambassadorship) if he would throw his support to Lincoln.

William Herndon, Lincoln's old law clerk and partner, and his first biographer, claimed that a close friend of Bennett came to Washington to report that "if Lincoln would invite Bennett to come over and chat with him, his paper would be all right. Mr. Bennett wanted nothing; he simply wanted to be noticed. Lincoln in talking about it said, 'I understand it; Bennett has made a great deal of money, some say not very properly, now he wants me to make him respectable. I have never invited Mr. Bryant or Mr. Greeley here; I shall not, therefore, especially invite Mr. Bennett.' All Lincoln would say was, that he was receiving everybody, and he should receive Mr. Bennett if he came."

Lincoln evidently hesitated long before making any commitment on the question of offering a foreign mission to Bennett— but as election day drew close to hand, he made the verbal commitment.

One of Bennett's close associates, W. O. Bartlett, who had been doing confidential jobs for the publisher, wrote to Bennett on November 4:

MY DEAR SIR: I am from Washington, fresh from the bosom of Father Abraham. I had a full conversation with him, alone, on Tuesday evening, at the White House, in regard to yourself, among other subjects.

I said to him: "There are but few days now before the election. If Mr. Bennett is not *certainly* to have the offer of the French Mission, I want to know it *now*. It is important to me."

We discussed the course which the *Herald* had pursued, at length, and I will tell you, verbally, at your convenience, what he said; but he concluded with the remark that in regard to the understanding between him and me, about Mr. Bennett, he had been a "shut pan, to everybody"; and that he *expected to do that thing* (appoint you to France) *as much as he expected to live.* He repeated: *"I expect to do it as certainly as I do to be reelected myself."*

I wanted to see you; but I am obliged to do some work in Pennsylvania, about the election, and cannot till my return.

Truly yours,
W. O. BARTLETT.

Bennett did the appropriate last-minute shift in favor of Lincoln. The President kept his word, and a fortnight before his second inauguration sent the following message to the publisher of the *Herald:*

DEAR SIR: I propose, at some convenient and not distant day, to nom-
inate you to the United States Senate as Minister to France.

Your obedient servant,

A. LINCOLN.

This message was, however, kept strictly confidential. Lincoln
did not even notify the members of his Cabinet of the appointment he was considering, although when the rumor did get around,
it was quite generally denied or laughed off as preposterous.

Bennett himself never uttered a word about it publicly to the
day of his death, but his long-time friend and managing editor,
Frederic Hudson, asserted that though Lincoln "unreservedly offered this great prize—the French Mission—to Mr. Bennett . . . it
was respectfully and positively declined. In his letter to the President the editor said his editorial mission was high enough and
honorable enough for him; that he could do more good in the
Herald than in France, and did not want the office."

This is, in all likelihood, the truth, and fits in well with the
whole character of the man. What could be more gratifying to
one in his position than to force the President of the United States
to offer him the most distinguished foreign post that was to be
had, and then to be able to turn it down? Besides, Bennett was
nearly seventy years of age. He wanted no more travel. He felt
he could not leave his one great love—the *New York Herald*.

Once again the President was in the good graces of the *Herald*.
His second inaugural speech was received with approval. Shortly
thereafter, when Lincoln was at the front visiting troops, the *Herald* waxed almost lyrical in its commendation: "Taught by experience, Old Abe now takes the field again, succeeds in extinguishing
Davis and is in at the death of the rebellion. His bulletins from
City Point are so readable that we may offer him a situation on
the *Herald,* after his present term expires, as a war correspondent
in the grand struggle with Europe which is to follow the close of
our civil contest. Should he accept he can have one hundred dollars
a week, his rations and a fresh horse every six months."

Nor was this enough. With his second term as President hardly
begun, the *Herald* proposed him for a third term: "He has so far
eclipsed all other politicians by his movements on both flanks and

in front and rear that we should not wonder if he took the starch
out of them all for the succession in 1868. Who can tell what will
happen?"

Grant, too, came in for his share of glory. When some of the
more radical Republican journals objected to the lenient terms
given by Grant to Lee at Appomattox, Bennett came stoutly to his
defense: "We apprehend no danger from a pardon to the Confederate leaders, political or military. They have played their game of
rule or ruin and have lost it. Refuse them the honors of martyrdom.
They may be left to the judgment of the people they have so cruelly
and selfishly betrayed. With the violent death they have brought
upon their institution of slavery, the cause, the argument and the
party of a Southern Confederacy cease to exist. If four years of this
terrible war have done the work of a century of peace, we must
advance a century now that the work is done."

And an editorial, which appeared on April 15, but evidently
written just before Lincoln's assassination, refused to support those
who clamored for the head of Jeff Davis. "Let him die like Benedict Arnold, in foreign lands, or go, like Judas, and hang himself."

Then came the stunning news of the assassination. "The President is murdered." This, wrote Bennett, is the awful piece of news
which has paralyzed everyone. But the fatal blow, from whence
did it come?

And to this question the editor made his reply: "It is as clear as
day that the real origin of this dreadful act is to be found in the
fiendish and malignant spirit developed and fostered by the rebel
press, North and South."

Forgetful of his own recent bitter attacks on Lincoln, James
Gordon Bennett pondered long and carefully over the strange
career of this man over whom a whole nation now wept in a sorrow
both deep and genuine. Yes, he had been a story-teller, and a pro-
crastinator; he had been a politician, in both the worst and best
sense of that much-abused word. He was a strange and baffling
character, for though he appeared simple enough at first glance,
the more one gazed at him, the harder he became to understand.
In fact, a new kind of historian would be needed "to comprehend
the genius of a character so externally uncouth, so pathetically sim-

ple, so unfathomably penetrating, so irresolute and yet so irresistible, so bizarre, grotesque, droll, wise, and perfectly beneficent as the great original thinker and statesman for whose death the whole land, even in the midst of victories unparalleled, is today draped in mourning."

There might be many among the vanquished, continued Bennett, who rejoiced at the death of the man who led the forces which had beaten them. But such persons, he averred, would soon learn that in Lincoln "the Southern people have lost their best friend, and the rebel leaders one of their wisest and bitterest enemies."

Old Bennett had seen much in his seventy years of life, and he had studied much too. The Old World and the New—he knew them better than most men; and he knew their leaders in art and science, in war and statesmanship. He thought about them now, as he slowly penned the words in which he sought to tell his hundreds of thousands of readers just what kind of a man their late President had been.

Lincoln was something new, something different—the end product of a new dynasty of nation-rulers, yet "as indigenous to our soil as the cranberry crop, and as American in his fibre as the granite foundations of the Appalachian range." He was "the triumph of the democratic principle over the aristocratic." He was the embodiment of a republic, born in the sweat and blood of free men, which free men would ever strive to keep free.

PART V
CLOSING YEARS

17. Mr. Bennett Leaves His Mark

THE BULLET of Wilkes Booth, in taking the life of President Lincoln, gave to the nation, in his place, a stubborn, headstrong, loyal Tennessean, who had been picked as Lincoln's running mate in 1864 with an eye to garnering a doubtful state. Overnight, Andrew Johnson was jerked from semi-obscurity into the white hot light of national interest and attention.

The new President announced that he intended to follow Lincoln's policies regarding reconstruction and rehabilitation of the late confederate states. To this, James Gordon Bennett reacted hopefully: "He begins well."

The *New York Herald* did not fall into line with the forces in Congress, in state legislatures, and in the national press which cried out vindictively for harsh penalties against the vanquished foe. Bennett believed that after four years of war, it would be a hollow victory indeed if the nation were permitted to remain two hostile camps.

The radical Republican forces, led by Congressman Thaddeus Stevens of Pennsylvania, lost no time in attacking both the new President and the policies of his predecessor, which he tried vainly to follow. The *Herald* took up the cudgels on behalf of Johnson, and for several months flayed the radicals for their vengeful spirit, narrow-mindedness, and stupidity.

President Johnson needed every bit of support he could muster, and gladly accepted Bennett's assistance and advice. Before he had been in office six months, President Johnson addressed a confidential letter to Bennett expressing his desire "to confer with you freely and fully" upon the problems of foreign policy. But domestic problems loomed larger, and he was thankful to Bennett for "the able and disinterested manner in which you have defended the policy of the Administration since its accession to power." And, added the President, "it is the more highly appreciated because it has not been solicited."

Although the *Herald,* a year later, found itself parting company with Johnson, it refused to support the move for his impeachment by Congress in 1868 and openly rejoiced when that move failed.

Not far from the *Herald* building—itself the object of national attention because of its owner and his newspaper—was another much larger building which was daily visited by both New Yorkers and out-of-towners. It was the mecca of the curiosity seeker, the super-showplace of the nation. It was Phineas T. Barnum's American Museum at the corner of Ann Street and Broadway.

On July 13, 1865, a spectacular fire not only wiped out Barnum's Museum, but eighteen other buildings as well; and for a time threatened the *Herald* and other large publishing establishments. The *Herald,* in telling the story of the giant conflagration, added many humorous touches to the scenes. It stressed the unusual, the ironical, and the unique: the figure of Jeff Davis had lost its head, and boa constrictors were on the loose in New York City.

Barnum took his loss philosophically and the very next day, with his usual optimism, announced to the world that he would build another and even greater museum to house curiosities and monstrosities such as the eye of man had never before gazed upon. Of course, all this would take money—of which Barnum had little. But the showman was relying on his wits and they had not failed him before. This time, he planned to secure the necessary funds by consummating an audacious real-estate deal in which his long-time foe, James Gordon Bennett, would be left holding the bag.

The publisher had wanted a choice bit of property on Broadway for a long time, but there had been nothing available either in size or location which pleased him. Barnum's corner was perfect. Although not very large (56 by 100 feet) it was ideal, so Bennett suggested a deal to Barnum while the ashes of the American Museum were still hot. The showman did not own the land, but he had a lease on it which did not expire for eleven years. With restrained glee, Barnum immediately arranged to have an exaggerated appraisal made on his leasehold. Barnum's real-estate associate obliged him with an appraisal of $275,000. Armed with this statement, Barnum went to the publisher, informed him of the facts, and then, to clinch the deal, told the canny Scot that to such an old friend as Bennett he was willing to sell his leasehold for the trifling sum of $200,000.

For once, Bennett's eagerness to get possession of what he wanted was too great. Instead of making a careful survey of the property's value, he immediately bought the land from the owners for half a million dollars, and paid to Barnum $200,000 for the lease, thus distinguishing his new holding by making it the highest-priced piece of land in the world.

The publisher had already signed a bond agreeing to pay $248,000 in cash to the owner, Henry W. Sargent (the balance to be held as a mortgage), and had given Barnum a check for $200,000 when he realized how thoroughly he had been taken in by the showman. Bennett was mortified at what had happened and tried to back out of the deal. His attorney called Barnum to his office to cancel the sale.

"Mr. Barnum," said the lawyer, "I have sent for you to say that Mr. Bennett has concluded not to purchase the museum lots, and therefore you had better take back the lease, and return the $200,000 paid for it."

"Are you in earnest?" Barnum asked.

"Certainly, quite so," said the lawyer.

"Really," smiled Barnum, "I am sorry I can't accommodate Mr. Bennett; I have not got the little sum about me; in fact, I have spent the money."

"It will be better for you to take back the lease," observed the lawyer gravely.

"Nonsense," answered Barnum. "I shall do nothing of the sort, I don't make child's bargains. The lease was cheap enough, but I have other business to attend to, and shall have nothing to do with it."

But the matter did not end there. Bennett retaliated by refusing to print Barnum's advertisements in the *Herald*. Barnum at once organized an effective protest. He persuaded all of the members of the Theatrical Managers Association to cancel their advertisements in the *Herald* until Barnum's were reinstated. When the publisher was presented with an ultimatum by the theatrical managers, he told them, "I will not publish Barnum's advertisement: I do business as I please, and in my own way."

The Association thereupon placed a boycott on the *Herald* and withdrew all advertising as well as the lucrative job printing from Bennett's establishment. This represented a loss in revenue of from $75,000 to $100,000, but the obstinate Scot refused to give in. The war between the theaters and the publisher lasted two years. During that time, the *Herald* denounced and ridiculed every concert or play given in any Association theater. The Association, in turn, retaliated by stating in all their advertisements in other papers, "This establishment does not advertise in the *New York Herald*."

Since there was no way to get out from under the white elephant he had purchased, Bennett determined to erect upon the property the finest and most modern newspaper building in the world. For months he busied himself with architects and builders. In the fall of 1865, construction of the *Herald's* new home was begun.

Not until early 1868 was the new edifice completed—an imposing structure with gleaming white marble fronts facing Broadway, Vesey, and Ann Streets. The Broadway entrance of huge black walnut doors was flanked by six heavy Corinthian columns, richly ornamented. The main floor itself had neither lock nor key—symbolic of the fact that there was life and activity at the *Herald* both day and night throughout the year.

Shortly before James Gordon Bennett turned over the active management of the *Herald* to his twenty-five-year-old son, James Gordon Bennett, Jr., there appeared, and was widely republished, the following anonymous poem about the old gentleman:

> *Should History condescend to pen it,*
> *What would its verdict be on Bennett?*
> *'Twould say, if truth were in its page,*
> *He was the scandal of his age;*
> *A coward, liar, pimp and sneak;*
> *A heartless robber of the weak;*

In vice to profit by;—a ferret;
  Extorter of black-mail from merit;
With face like Pan's—if Pan had squinted—
  And heart more foul than face ere hinted.

The wretch, when young and in his prime,
  Was cudgelled many a hundred time—
Knew the full weight of boot or baton,
  Was kicked, cow-hided, whipped and spat-on;
On seat of honor and in face
  Felt all conceivable disgrace;
And when he'd suffered punishment
  Printed the tale incontinent,
Without self-reverent omissions,
  In 2nd, 3rd, and 4th editions,
And signed it with his hateful name
  To make a profit of his shame.

But now, when o'er his dastard head
  Full seventy years their snows have shed,
He's safe from lash, and cane, and stick,
  From spittle, tweak of nose, and kick.
His age preserves him from our blows,
  And we despise him as he goes;
Content, if younger men shall learn
  From his example not to earn
Dishonest wealth in filthy places,
  And think it salvoes all disgraces.
This, should it condescend to pen it,—
  Might History say of Gordon Bennett.

From 1860 on, *Vanity Fair* and other magazines had made Bennett the subject matter of more cartoons (all derogatory) than anyone else in the whole country with the exceptions of Lincoln and Greeley. But, despite this, he was no longer the social pariah he had been a quarter of a century earlier. Both he and his paper had become nationally recognized institutions, the one inseparable from the other. He, who had begun his career as publisher of the

Herald, one man in a cellar fighting against the world, was now a multi-millionaire, with a yearly income of more than three hundred thousand dollars. Besides the costly *Herald* building, he owned many other choice business properties as well as a town house at 425 Fifth Avenue and a magnificent country estate on Washington Heights (181st and Broadway).

James Gordon Bennett had for many years been consulted by presidents and cabinet members, by governors, senators, mayors, and a host of lesser public officials. Foreign dignitaries always made it a point to call on him, for the *Herald* was the only well-known American newspaper in Europe and South America. Churchmen of every creed reluctantly admitted that their sermons and services were given the most complete and unbiased reports in the columns of the *Herald*. Hard-headed business men declared that no other newspaper equaled the *Herald* in the drawing power of its advertisements. Artists, musicians, singers, and authors (especially those who had yet to scale the ladder of public acclaim) swore that no other paper was so generous in its support. And rival editors had long since learned that almost every new device or procedure in journalism had its origin at the *Herald*.

Neither Bennett nor his wife ever made any attempt to break into Manhattan's upper crust. He was both too busy and too independent to bother. His wife, resentful of the harsh and bitter words said about her husband, her family, and herself during the early years of her marriage, spent most of her time in Europe. Thus it happened, that James Gordon Bennett, for all his notoriety, was a mysterious and unknown figure to all but a handful of New Yorkers. And except in the vicinity of his own home or the *Herald* building, he attracted no more attention than any other old gentleman going about his business. For that matter, the pressure of work at the *Herald* had become so great after 1860, that the publisher spent almost all his waking hours there. Even the concert hall and the theater, his favorite sources of relaxation and entertainment, saw him rarely, if at all, after the Civil War broke out. His whole life, his alter ego, was the *New York Herald*.

To most people old age comes as a gradual process. To James Gordon Bennett it came overnight. He had been so preoccupied with his work for so long a period that he failed to realize the cumulative drag of the years till some months after Lincoln's assassination. Then, as the country settled down to the problems of reconstruction, Bennett became aware of a thousand aches and pains, of stiffened joints and creaking legs, of sagging muscles and a great weariness that refused to go away. James Gordon Bennett was an old man, with the proverbial three score and ten years tucked behind him. He must step down from the driver's seat.

Neither Bennett, his son, nor his close friend and co-worker, Frederic Hudson, ever reported what took place when the skipper turned over the ship to his twenty-five-year-old son, but it must have been a dramatic scene for them all. The man who had fought his way to the top of American journalism was turning over his beloved creation to another man. To be sure, that man was his son —but he was untried.

Young Bennett had been reared in the lap of luxury. He was spoiled, self-centered, and high-spirited. His education had been largely acquired abroad, under private tutors. He was tall, like his father; handsome, like his mother; and seemed destined to become notorious only as a sportsman and play-boy.

Hudson and old Bennett must have talked about the youngster hundreds of times, planning how they could get him to feel the same glow of pride and satisfaction in the *Herald* which they possessed. Every opportunity was given to young Bennett to familiarize himself with the techniques and the personnel of the *Herald*. He was given an office and placed on the payroll while still in his teens, but he cared little for the opportunity, and would be absent for weeks on end from the establishment. Not till the close of the Civil War was it possible for his father to get him to make regular appearances at his office; and then these would be of short duration.

Faced with such a situation, one can easily understand the heartaches of both Hudson and Bennett in coming to the decision to turn over control of the *Herald* to the younger man. It was a gamble—a gamble with the most precious thing in the world to James Gordon Bennett. But he had to take that chance. Shortly after New Year's Day, 1866, he called his son into his office and gave him a document which declared that he, James Gordon Bennett, Jr., was now the editor-in-chief of the *New York Herald.* The father and Hudson formally retired from the staff, and for better or for worse gave command to the young man.

The gamble was a fortunate one. The young man, backed by a large and able staff, unlimited funds, the international reputation of the *Herald,* and continued advice from his father, took up his new career with many advantages. Once the main responsibility was his, the younger Bennett settled down to his job with enthusiasm. He, too, had a nose for news, and within a few years made the *Herald* as famous for the manner in which he created exclusive news as his father made it famous as the first and foremost newsgatherer of its day.

Young Bennett took hold of the interview and built it up to amazing proportions, forcing every other newspaper to follow suit. Like his father, he knew that people were interested in knowing what persons in the public eye had to say. He assigned the best reporters on the *Herald's* staff to get the opinions of leading politicians, army officers, scientists, explorers, and other celebrities. This action brought not only good will from those interviewed, but also a great many new readers as well. In fact, the venture proved so successful that within a few years feature writers of the *New York Herald* were crossing the seven seas in search of the great and notorious men of all continents and nations from whom they hoped to get interviews. Every week the pages of the *Herald* carried one or more of these exclusive features. Bismarck, the Iron Chancellor; Napoleon the Third; the Emperor of Brazil; the Prime Minister of Egypt; the Premier of Italy; the Catholic Cardinal Bishop of London; and a host of others gave their interviews to the special correspondents of the *Herald.*

Most spectacular of these men who roamed the wide spaces of the earth for the *Herald,* undoubtedly, was Henry Stanley who had made a bit of a reputation for himself as a free-lance reporter covering the government's campaigns against the Sioux and Cheyenne Indians in 1866-67. Returning to New York at the close of those campaigns, Stanley tried to interest the *Tribune* in giving him an assignment to cover the forthcoming British military expedition against King Theodore of Abyssinia. The *Tribune* was not interested and was equally sure American readers neither knew of nor cared about what might take place in such a distant land.

Perhaps Mr. Bennett of the *Herald* would be interested, thought Stanley. He made his way to the *Herald,* and sent in his card, asking if he could see the editor. Almost immediately he found himself in the presence of a tall, fierce-eyed, imperious-looking young man who said, "Oh, you are the correspondent who has been following Hancock and Sherman lately. Well, I must say your letters and telegrams have kept us very well informed. I wish I could offer you something permanent, for we want active men like you."

Delighted with such a favorable reception, Stanley told young Bennett of his plans. When the editor asked what his terms would be, Stanley replied he was willing to accept either a moderate salary or be paid by the article, adding, "Of course, if you pay me by the letter, I should reserve the liberty to write occasional letters to other papers."

Bennett at once assured him that it was the policy of the *Herald* not to share news in that way, but that it was also the policy of the *Herald* to pay well for "exclusive intelligence." Then, without further discussion, he asked Stanley if he would be willing to carry out his proposed trip on a trial basis.

"Pay your own expenses to Abyssinia," said the editor, "and if your letters are up to the standard, and your intelligence is early and exclusive, you shall be well paid by the letter, or at the rate by which we engage our European specials, and you will be placed on the permanent list."

"Very well, Sir. I am at your service, any way you like."

"When do you intend to start?"

"On the twenty-second, by the steamer 'Hecla.'"

"That is the day after tomorrow. Well, consider it arranged. Just wait a moment while I write to our agent in London."

For nearly two years, Stanley, the roving reporter, sent back his fascinating stories to the *Herald* from Abyssinia, the Near East, the Balkans, and Spain. Then, on October 16, 1869, came a terse wire from his employer: "Come to Paris on important business. J. G. BENNETT."

Stanley caught the very next train from Madrid. The following night he arrived in Paris. He went straight to the Grand Hotel, where the publisher was staying. He went upstairs and knocked at the door of Bennett's suite. In his autobiography, Stanley recorded the conversation which followed:

"Come in," I heard a voice say.

Entering, I found Mr. Bennett in bed.

"Who are you?" he asked.

"My name is Stanley," I answered.

"Ah, yes; sit down. I have important business on hand for you."

After throwing over him his robe-de-chambre, Mr. Bennett asked me, "Where do you think Livingstone is?"

"I really do not know, sir."

"Do you think he is alive?"

"He may be, and he may not be!" I answered.

"Well, I think he is alive, and that he can be found, and I am going to send you to find him."

"What!" said I. "Do you really think I can find Dr. Livingstone? Do you mean me to go to Central Africa?"

"Yes; I mean that you shall go and find him wherever you may hear that he is, and to get what news you can of him, and perhaps"—delivering himself thoughtfully and deliberately—"the old man may be in want: take enough with you to help him should he require it. Of course you will act according to your own plans, and do what you think best —BUT FIND LIVINGSTONE!"

Said I, wondering at the cool order of sending one to Central Africa to search for a man whom I, in common with almost all other men, believed to be dead, "Have you considered seriously the great expense you are likely to incur on account of this little journey?"

"What will it cost?" he asked abruptly.

"Burton and Speke's journey to Central Africa cost between £3,000 and £5,000, and I fear it cannot be done under £2,500."

"Well, I will tell you what you will do. Draw a thousand pounds now, and when you have gone through that, draw another thousand, and when that is spent, draw another thousand, and when you have finished that, draw another thousand, and so on; but FIND LIVINGSTONE."

Stanley did what he was ordered to do. He found Livingstone— and the sensational tale of that discovery, which placed both Stanley and young Bennett among the immortals of journalism, was published in the *Herald* shortly before the death of the elder Bennett.

The young publisher, not content with one paper, launched another, the *Evening Telegram,* in July, 1867; and a few years later, the *Paris Herald.* He developed, or brought over from other papers, the ablest writers and cartoonists to be found. Mark Twain joined the staff in January, 1868, and remained a regular contributor to the columns of the *Herald* until his death. Walt Whitman was on the payroll. So also were such ace reporters as James Creelman, Charles Nordhoff, Januarius A. MacGahan, and a host of others.

The old man found it impossible to break off his work at the *Herald,* so all through 1866, 1867, and most of 1868, he kept up his trips to the *Herald* office. Try as he would, he could not refrain from giving advice and instructions to the men, or dictating articles and editorials. But little by little his visits to the office became shorter in time, and spaced at greater intervals.

Within three years, he had cut down his activity to the extent that he seldom appeared more than twice a week, and then for no more than half a day. But to make up for this curtailed contact with the newspaper, he arranged to have a private telegraph wire installed between the *Herald* and his Fort Washington estate (and later the Fifth Avenue house) so he could keep his finger on the pulse of the paper at all times.

Summaries of every major news development, domestic as well as foreign, were flashed to his home as quickly as they were received at the *Herald.* He, in turn, would dictate instructions, queries, or suggested editorials and feature stories to be flashed back to the editorial staff. Young Bennett, who was a bachelor, lived with his father, so the two were able to consult at will upon problems and policies demanding immediate attention.

In the late summer of 1868, James Gordon Bennett took his final editorial fling at his long-time foe, Horace Greeley. It was occasioned by a withering blast at the Democratic press of New York by the *Tribune.* A great new party organ, the *Democrat,* was about to be launched. Greeley stated he had anticipated such a move for a long time, since "it was impossible for a great party, a party of lusty, zealous and bold men, to forever follow the uncertain leadership of the *Herald,* or to find comfort in the endless columns of twaddle . . . in the *New York World."*

With the fire of battle once more in his squinting eyes, old Bennett took Greeley to task. "He is the man who has driven the common sense, the respectable, controlling conservatism of the country into an attitude of hostility to the Republican Party. He is the source in his party of all its extreme tendencies—all those desperate efforts to remodel the nation in accordance with extravagant and misty theory—those ridiculous vagaries of a dreaming enthusiast, who fancies he is a politician and a statesman."

Greeley was blamed for "all the nigger legislation" of recent date, even as earlier he had brought about the defeat of General Scott in 1852 by his "extravagant agitation . . . his fury, his venomous invectives, and in intellectual antics."

A few days later, Bennett suggested that the Republican Party could solve many of its internal difficulties if it were to send Greeley as Minister to China.

One of the elder Bennett's last editorials, which showed that the fighting spirit of the man and the cutting irony of his pen had not been dimmed by old age, was published on June 2, 1871. Two days previous there had occurred the most spectacular event in New York's social season—the marriage of Boss Tweed's daughter, Mary, to a young man from New Orleans.

The Boss, then at the height of his power, staged a celebration of such splendor and magnitude that the vocabularies of the *Herald's* reporters were taxed to describe it. The bride's trousseau eclipsed, at least in cost, anything ever before seen in America. Delmonico and his staff devoted two whole days to the preparation of the dinner. The music was by the largest and most expensive orchestra obtainable. The gifts to the bridal couple were lavish and ranged from a set of silver pickle forks to a piece of jewelry "with diamonds as large as filberts." These represented a total cash outlay of nearly three-quarters of a million dollars—the gifts of city officials, contractors, speculators, and grafters who had plundered New York's taxpayers out of millions of dollars under the regime of Boss Tweed.

"Seven hundred thousand dollars!" exclaimed Bennett in his

editorial. "What a testimony of the loyalty, the royalty, and the abounding East Indian resources of Tammany Hall! Was there any Democracy to compare with 'thy Democracy' in glory, power, and equal rights under the sun? Never! And it is just the beginning of the good time coming. Don't talk of Jeff Davis and his absurd Democracy; don't mention the Democracy of the Paris Commune, as representing true Democratic principles; but come to the fountain-head of Democracy, the old Wigwam, and you will get it there—if you get within the lucky circle of the 'magic' Ring. There you get into a Democratic placer which gives you, without labor of digging, but with some deep diving, the pearls of Ceylon, the silver of Mexico, the gold of California, and the diamonds of Golconda, South America and Alaska. And they say that, by the 'rule of three,' it all comes out of the Tax Levy, and from the abounding blessings of municipal sovereignty and a municipal and munificent emperor, who needs only a crown of brilliants and a throne of ivory surmounted by a golden peacock as large as life, with an outspread tail blazing all over with diamonds, to rise to the Oriental Splendor of the Great Mogul."

Two distinguished journalists—both on the staff of the *Tribune*—who had come to know Bennett well during his last years, have left us their impressions of him. Junius Henri Browne, in his sketches of *The Great Metropolis,* published in 1869, said of the old journalist: "Privately, Bennett is a very honest and strictly moral man. He owes no one, and so far as I can learn, never did owe a dollar; paying his debts having always been with him the first of obligations. He was never other than industrious and abstemious, and is said to be very charitable without the least ostentation. Ever since his marriage . . . he has been a pattern of domesticity. . . . He is, and always has been, the opposite of gregarious. He never went into society, and the sole instance I can remember of his presence at any festival or public occasion, was at the Sir Morton Peto dinner at Delmonico's in the Autumn of 1865. Then he seemed quite lost and ill at ease. He did not appear to know anyone, nor anyone to know him."

According to Browne, James Gordon Bennett "rises at five; never calls on anybody, but receives courteously and hospitably all who visit him."

Browne also mentioned the fact that the old man still kept close contact with the paper which now bore his son's name on the editorial masthead. "Whenever any event of consequence occurs," wrote Browne, "his opinion is obtained in regard to its treatment for the next day's paper, the name of the required writer being frequently given by him. All the City and leading country dailies are taken to his house every morning. He reads them; marks the articles which strike his attention; makes suggestions as to the editorials; sees proofs often; in fact, supervises the *Herald* very much as he used to when he wrote on the head of a barrel in the Ann Street cellar."

John Russell Young, who distinguished himself not only as a journalist, but as Minister to China as well as Librarian of the Library of Congress, recalls in his *Men and Memories* that his earliest impression of Bennett had been that of a vast sinister shape, which, like some genie from an *Arabian Nights'* tale, had come to overspread and darken the heavens. Then one bleak, cold snowy night, during the winter of 1864-5, a friend drove him out to the Bennett estate at Fort Washington.

"If my imagination had gone into darkened fancies over the ideal Bennett, the man as I saw him drove them away," wrote Young. "Hair white and clustering, a smooth face soon to have the comfort of a beard, prominent aquiline nose, a long, narrow head with abundant development in perceptive faculties, a keen boring eye which threw arrowy glances, bantering rather than hearty laughter, a firm masterful jaw, talk in a broad Scottish accent, which he seemed to nurse with a relish. His speech had the piquant, saucy colloquialisms which stamped his individuality on the *Herald*. His manner stately, courteous, that of a strenuous gentleman of unique intelligence giving opinions as though they were aphorisms, like one accustomed to his own way. Whatever he may have seemed in the columns of his journal, the man as he welcomed us was wreathed in courtesy and good will."

The young writer was thereafter to become well acquainted with the elder Bennett, and visited him at regular intervals till within a month of his death. John Russell Young claimed the old man's sense of humor was intensely keen, but tended to run into mockery "until it seemed almost as though it were the spirit of Voltaire breathing through him."

"His mind teemed with ideas, which streamed into his talk—saucy phrases, invectives, nick-names, keen bits of narrative surcharged with cynical pessimism, which remained, one might fancy, as a legacy of early days of disappointment and trial. For this man had fought the world—had fought it down! The world would not come to his need, and now he reigned apart, looking down upon it with scorn."

During the summer of 1871 Bennett's health began to fail. He gave up his rare trips to the city; he let others take over the labors which had been his for so many, many years. Rising as early as ever, he would wander slowly through his rose gardens, his grape arbor, his fragrant shrubs, his gnarled trees, majestic in their age and sweep. He would drink in the sweet morning breeze from off the Hudson, and perhaps dream of the boy who had played so hard in far-off Banffshire at the dawn of the nineteenth century. For the first time in his long and busy life there was time to dream. No longer need he worry about meeting deadlines with the latest news. No longer need he care what was being said or done by the *Times,* the *Tribune,* the *World,* or the *Sun.* No longer need his active brain keep planning new and better ways of getting news or making news; of planning editorials to shock the public, terrify the politicians, and bedevil his newspaper rivals. Now he could dream.

In slippered feet and dressing gown, he puttered about his garden, chatted to his collection of birds (each of whom bore the name of some politician, preacher, or newspaperman), dozed in the warm summer sun, or sat back in his easychair to dip at will in the books, old and new, stacked high all about him. Time—that most precious of all ingredients, especially to a newspaperman—no longer mattered to the veteran journalist.

Day-dreaming under the roses and ivy, Old Bennett must have been amazed at times to realize how far both he, journalism, and his adopted country had traveled in the half century since he stepped ashore at Boston. Then the republic was young—so young in fact that he had talked with many of the veterans of the Revolution, and many of the founding fathers had still been alive. Then, the nation's western boundary lay somewhere west of the Mississippi River, but most of this territory had been a vast unexplored wilderness. Then, Texas and California, Florida and Oregon, were but geographical names of foreign regions, unknown to all but a handful of Americans.

Then, the husky young republic was proudly announcing its population as nine and one half million persons; now it could boast nearly forty millions. Then, there were but thirteen cities with a population in excess of 8,000 inhabitants; now there were two hundred and twenty-six. Then, industry and manufacturing were in their swaddling clothes, factories were few in number and small in size; now, there were over two million wage earners, working in thousands of establishments, and the value of their yearly output amounted to nearly three and one half billion dollars.

Then, roads were poor, travel slow and every means of communication both cumbersome and sluggish; now the country was covered with a network of railroads. The Union Pacific had spanned the continent in 1869; there were steamships on lakes and rivers and oceans; there were telegraph lines from Canada to Mexico; and there was a transatlantic cable tying the Old World with the New.

Then, the newspapers had been small, poorly printed, highly opinionated, and of dubious news value; now they were large and well printed, and up-to-the-minute with their news, thanks to the telegraph, stereotyping, rotary presses, and a score of other mechanical inventions.

Then, Congress was passing its first great compromise on the slavery issue; now a great civil war and a constitutional amendment had settled that question for all time.

Upon these and a thousand other changes in the whole social and political fabric of the nation to which he gave allegiance, old Bennett must have mused again and again as the sun of his life dipped toward the horizon. And he must have chuckled to himself at his own journalistic escapades, at his naïveté, his audacity, and his tremendous self-assurance in the face of almost insuperable odds.

There was no other man in the whole country who had drawn unto himself the wrath of the clergy, as had James Gordon Bennett. And well might they denounce him, for he smote them hard and often, calling them fools and bigots and the vehicles of superstition. Yet he had always contributed to every denomination which asked for help; and he had carried their sermons to much wider audiences than they themselves could have reached. And when the Reverend Henry A. Brann began his efforts to erect a Catholic church in the Fort Washington area, James Gordon Bennett not only gave him the ground for the church, but a check for $5,000 as well.

The winter of 1871-72 was very hard on Bennett, but with the coming of spring he talked cheerfully about making the trip to Europe with his wife and children—a trip he had originally planned to make in 1871. During the winter, Bennett had been moved back to his palatial Fifth Avenue residence, where three eminent physicians and a host of servants stood in constant attendance. His family had been abroad all winter. They returned early in the spring, only to leave again for France at the beginning of May. Bennett was not well enough to accompany them, but promised to come a few weeks later.

His condition grew worse instead of better. He was no longer able to leave his room. Pondering over his long life, he decided that his time was almost over. To be sure, he was not afraid of death, but he didn't want to die. At last, on May 21, he summoned Archbishop McCloskey, to whom he made his final confession, and from whom he received the last sacrament. He had returned to the church of his fathers.

On the 25th, Bennett suffered a stroke, which left the lower portion of his body paralyzed. His mind was as clear as ever, and he conversed at length with his few close friends whom he had called in to stay with him. Frederic Hudson, who had rushed down from his farm in Massachusetts to be with his friend, reported that Bennett "was fully aware of his approaching end and spoke to his friends with philosophical resignation."

As twilight gathered over the city on June 1, 1872, James Gordon Bennett died in his sleep, surrounded by doctors, nurses, servants, lawyers, and friends—but without a single member of his family present. Only his son returned to New York to attend the funeral.

James Gordon Bennett had made his last bit of news. The announcement of his death was headline copy in the press of the world. And now that he had passed away, his rivals praised him at length, finding virtues which even he would have questioned. The *Herald,* itself, printed no lengthy obituary of its founder but, instead, reprinted, without comment, those of the other leading dailies.

The *Times* was most noncommittal of all, merely calling Bennett a "successful journalist and man of business." Manton Marble of the *World* credited Bennett with being the greatest of all journalists, since it was "the chief function of modern journalism" to supply the public with important news quickly and accurately. Dana of the *Sun* praised Bennett for having emancipated the press of the nation from "sects, parties, cliques, and what is called society."

But it was from his old foe, Horace Greeley, that he received the best tribute and the fairest evaluation. It was an editorial which Bennett would' have relished, for it made no attempt to gloss over his weaknesses.

"It was as a collector of news," wrote Greeley (who within six months was to follow the editor of the *Herald* to the grave) "that Bennett shone conspicuously. Editorially he was cynical, inconsistent, reckless, and easily influenced by others' opinions, and by his own prejudices. But he had an unerring judgment of the pecuniary value of news. He knew how to pick out of the events of the day the subject which engrossed the interest of the greatest number of people, and to give them about that subject all they could read. The quality might be bad, and generally was; but it suited the multitude, and the quantity at any rate was abundant. He had a method of impressing the importance of news upon others in his employ, which inspired many who served him to energetic action, some of them in a remarkable degree, but he inculcated no principle of correctness. The fact is, he was utterly indifferent to the correctness of details or conclusions, provided the principal event of the narrative or argument of the editorial was made clear and published ahead of all competitors. He never tolerated defeat. . . .

"He developed the capacities of journalism in a most wonderful manner, but he did it by degrading its character. He made the newspaper powerful, but he made it odious. Those who recognize this, whether claiming it as his admirers or admitting it contemptuously, know that his personal characteristics had everything to do with forming his paper. He alone made it; it was personal journalism in all senses of the word. He associated with himself a few remarkable men, but they were remarkable as much in consequence of his training as from a natural aptitude for the profession. . . . His hard early career, by embittering his nature, isolated him from friends, unfitted him for friendly relations with any one, for he suspected everybody. His conduct of *The Herald* in its early existence isolated him from society, and all his subsequent great wealth brought no oblivion for what were called his misdeeds. *The Herald,* without acquiring any principle, acquired some decency as it grew great, and the discredit which once attached to any man seen reading it gradually passed away; but it is rather a remarkable fact that Mr. Bennett personally never was forgiven for the scandals of his early career."

At the funeral, every important newspaper editor in New York acted as pallbearer. Services were held at the home instead of at St. Patrick's Cathedral, and the interment took place at the non-sectarian Greenwood Cemetery in Brooklyn.

While still a young man fighting his way up in the world, Bennett had declared, "Praise or dispraise, abuse or condemnation are equally thrown away upon me." Having once set his sights, neither hell nor high water were going to stop him, for he was of that tough and sinewy breed called Scotch. And while he was still fighting his way out of the cellar of Ann Street with his little paper, he wrote the epitaph which might well be his:

"I want to leave behind me no castles, no granite hotels, no monuments of marble, no statues of bronze, no pyramids of brick. Simply

a name—the name of JAMES GORDON BENNETT, as one of the benefactors of the human race, will satisfy my desire and every hope."

"My ambition," he added, "is to make the newspaper Press the
great organ and pivot of government, society, commerce, finance,
religion, and all human civilization."

The power of the Press, as we know it today, is in large measure
the product of his genius.

James Gordon Bennett left his mark.

APPENDIX

APPENDIX

Scotland in the Napoleonic Era

For all its outward placidity, the Scotland into which young Bennett was born in 1795, and from which he departed for America in 1819, was in the vortex of not one, but three waves of revolution—each overlapping the other. First came the agricultural revolution, then the industrial, and last the political.

Out of this multiple dislocation came wealth and power to a few, disaster to many, confusion and a clutching at any vehicle of faith, thought, or action by the great majority. Out of it also came leaders in scientific agriculture, in industrial enterprise, in economics, ethics, and politics. Out of it, too, came the pioneers of land reform, great historians, great poets and novelists, and great critics.

Sir Walter Scott, who lived through this triple attack and whose keen eye and ear took note of these events, wrote in his epilogue to *Waverley* that no other nation in Europe had within the short space of half a century undergone such a drastic transformation as Scotland. The innovation began in 1746 when the English at Culloden disastrously defeated the Scotch who had rallied to the banner of Bonnie Prince Charlie, last of the Stuarts. The victorious British were determined to stamp out, once and for all, the spawning ground of future revolts and insurrections. The Highland chiefs who had rallied to the Stuart banner were hunted down and killed. The whole clan system was broken up; the century-old land tenure system of the clans was wiped out. Their military mode of life was destroyed. People were prohibited from wearing, or even owning, the tartans and the kilts. The British took away from the Highlander his flint-lock gun, his claymore, and his dirk—thus completely disarming him. Worst of all, by taking away his kilts, they took away his pride, for as the fighting men of the glens so often sadly remarked, "A warrior could not battle in trousers."

The destruction of the patriarchal power of the Highland chiefs was followed in quick succession by the abolition of the heritable jurisdictions of the Lowland nobility and barons. These factors, according to Scott, plus the rapid influx of wealth and the extension of commerce, "have since united to render the present people of Scotland a class of beings as different from their grandfathers as the existing English are from those of Queen Elizabeth's time."

Thus the transition which in England took centuries was telescoped into a few hectic decades for the Scotch.

To even the well-educated Londoner at the close of the eighteenth century, Scotland was a more remote, less-understood land than is China to the average American schoolboy of today. The extent of public travel between London and Edinburgh, in those days, can best be gauged by the fact that in 1750 and for many years thereafter there was only one weekly stagecoach between the two capitals. The trip itself took five long days. Not until 1789 was a weekly "fly" coach service begun between Edinburgh and Aberdeen. That trip took three days and the price was two guineas.

The rough terrain, the limited population, and the poverty of the people meant that roads and highways were few in number and always in bad condition. In fact, the agricultural carts of the peasantry had no wheels till after 1770. Almost all overland traffic was carried on beasts of burden along narrow trails. Except for the nobility and the merchants, the mass of the people were as blissfully ignorant of their native land as were the foreigners. They lived and worked and died without ever having gone, even on their most extended journeys, beyond the horizon that daily met the eye.

At that time, said one historian, "It would have been regarded as incongruous to put on the stage or in satire a Scotsman without meanness or pawkiness, or to mention Scotland without allusion to its filth and its poverty." Colonel Fullerton, who visited the country in 1750, testified to the fact that even the farmhouses "were hovels, moated with clay, having an open hearth or fire-place in the middle, and with a dunghill at the door."

Even Edinburgh—social, intellectual and political mecca of Scotland—carried an unsavory odor about it, due in large measure to the general habit of pouring out upon the streets the accumulated filth of the day. Each night, between the hours of ten and midnight, the householder or a servant would open a window to pour the slops out upon the street. It was expected that the person at the window would shout in French, *"Gardez l'eau,"* to warn pedestrians below, who, in turn, were expected to arrest the discharge by exclaiming in the vernacular, "Haud yere haund!" Despite these signals, not a night passed but many a man or maiden was soused by these polluted waters. There are some who claim that the fashion of a man taking the outer side of the walk in escorting a lady, originated in Edinburgh at this time. There was less danger of an overhead drenching to the person hugging the wall.

Edinburgh's obnoxious window nuisance continued till late in the century.

Out of the poverty and the isolation grew superstition and a dread of the new, the unusual, and the untried. It took fifty years to convince the Scotch peasantry that potatoes were good food. When the farmers tried introducing the potato as a commercial crop after 1750 they were met with the sullen refusal of the peasantry to have anything to do with the tuber. So, too, with the turnip, which was introduced to the country in 1740. Cotters were firm in their belief that hairs which appeared in the butter they churned should under no circumstances be removed for fear that, if this were done, the cow which had given the milk would cease to thrive. Young folk would rub shoulders with the bride at a wedding so as to obtain "matrimonial infection."

The introduction of tea drinking to the populace was also a slow and arduous process. A resolution, passed in 1744, is typical of the attitude then prevalent.

"We, being all farmers by profession, think it needless to restrain ourselves formally from indulging in that foreign and consumptive luxury called tea; for when we consider the *slender constitutions* of many of higher rank, amongst whom it is used, we conclude that it would be but an improper diet to qualify us for the more *robust* and *manly* parts of our business; and therefore we shall only give our testimony against it, and leave the enjoyment of it altogether to those who can afford to be *weak, indolent,* and *useless."*

There was much truth to the charge that the Scotland of this period was too poor to give adequate employment or recompense to its talented sons. Under the circumstances, it is quite understandable that the ambitious and energetic made their way to England, France, or North America. London society chortled over the jibe that when a Scotsman left his native soil he never cared to return to it, that though he might *die* for his country, he would not *live in it.* James Watt, the Scotch engineer, whose steam engine set into motion the industrial revolution, had been forced to go to England to make a living. Scotland lost its great architects: James Gibb, Robert Mylne, and the brothers Adam, for the same reason. Its artists, Ramsay, Aikman, and Strange, sought their patrons and public in England. Its institutions of higher learning lost many outstanding professors who were driven to other occupations in order to increase their earning power. David Hume, who was Scotland's greatest philosopher, left his professor's chair to become governor to an imbecile peer. Colin Maclaurin, the brilliant mathematician, became a traveling tutor at several times the fifty pounds per year allowed him by the university. Even Adam Smith, whose *Wealth of Nations* became the Bible of classical political economy, gave up his chair at Glasgow to serve as traveling companion to a youthful duke.

The thick-skinned Boswell seems never to have felt the cruel jibes and jeers of Johnson and his circle about Scotland and its inhabitants. But most of his countrymen winced under the sneers, and were thoroughly embittered by the spleen of these "facetious barbarians" as David Hume called them. "In patriotic efforts to magnify their own qualities," wrote a Scotch historian nearly a century later, "they preposterously over-rated everything and everybody Scottish, till the unread and unreadable *Epigoniad* of Wilkie—that lout of a genius—was declared by Hume and many compatriots worthy of a place beside *Paradise Lost;* and Home's *Douglas* was proclaimed as fine a play as *Macbeth*—which its author thoroughly believed."

The agricultural revolution in its effects upon Scotland was neither so beneficial, as claimed by its proponents, nor so disastrous as charged by the land-reformers. Certain it is that the population, which had inched slowly forward through the centuries, to reach a total of 1,265,380 in 1755, mounted to 1,608,420 in 1801, and then leaped forward within the next twenty years to 2,091,521. Adam Smith, on the other hand, contended, "It is not uncommon in the Highlands of Scotland for a mother who has borne twenty children not to have two alive. . . . Every species of animals naturally multiplies in proportion to the means of subsistence, and no species can ever multiply beyond it. But in civilized society it is only among the inferior ranks of people that the scantiness of human subsistence can set limits to the further multiplication of the human species; and it can do so in no other way than by destroying a great part of the children which their marriages produce."

The introduction of rye grass and clover seed, plus turnips, potatoes, and many fruits and vegetables previously unknown to the Scotch, coupled with the invention of the swing plow (1763), the use of fertilizers, and improved breeds of cattle and sheep—all these added enormously to the national income, and widened the scanty base of foods upon which the common people had been forced to live for untold generations. But one must also bear in mind the confusion arising among the simple villagers and clansmen as their traditional regulations and hoary, tangled customs were swept away like cobwebs. The "commons" were swept away from under the eyes of the bewildered Gaels as the sweep of "enclosure" took its steady toll. This new device took away from the tenant and cotter his age-old right to common fields for pasturage, to the forest and the marshland where he might gather nuts and wild berries, gather wood, or dig peat for much-needed fuel. The process of "enclosure" proceeded very slowly until 1760, but gathered momentum and spread like wild fire during the next half century.

The highland clan chieftains, after their defeat in 1745 by the British, did not give up their time-honored trade as robbers, but merely changed its form. On their own authority they transferred their nominal rights over the property of the clan into a right of private property, and turned ruthlessly upon their own less fortunate kith and kin. George Ensor, an early student of population, declared, "The Scotch grandees dispossess families as they would grub up coppice-wood, and they treated villages and their people as Indians harassed with wild beasts do, in their vengeance, a jungle with tigers. . . . Man is bartered for a fleece or a carcass of mutton."

It was in 1767 that large-scale sheep raising was introduced to Scotland. The large, landed proprietors saw in this a new method of quick, sure, and easy profits. Whole sections of the country were depopulated to make way for the gentle four-footed animals. Most notorious of all these cases—which led at last, in 1792, to a blind and spontaneous uprising on the part of these dispossessed—was the action of the Duchess of Sutherland. Determined to turn her vast properties into a sheep-walk, she had the 15,000 inhabitants on her property hunted down and rooted out, using British soldiers to enforce the evictions, and, when necessary, she burned the huts over the heads of the inhabitants. In this way, the noble Duchess appropriated 794,000 acres of land, which from time immemorial had belonged to the clan. To the expropriated, who numbered about 3,000 families, she assigned 6,000 acres of waste land along the seashore—at a rent of two shillings sixpence per acre. There the remnants of her clan eked out a precarious existence, living, as a contemporary described them, "half on land and half on water and withal only half on both," while 131,000 sheep nibbled their way across the broad lands where the evicted had formerly dwelt.

The Industrial Revolution, which was given its greatest single impetus in 1774 when Watt's steam engine was put to practical use, made Britain the workshop of the world. Steam-power meant coal, and the coal fields lay in the North of England and extended up into Scotland. Then came the power-loom, the spinning jenny, and a host of other basic inventions. Home industry gave way to the shop and factory just as the village gave way to the city, and the proud artisan was largely replaced by the propertyless wage-earner. Side by side appeared great wealth and even greater poverty.

Glasgow, and the whole Clyde River area, mushroomed in a few short years to the leadership of industrial and commercial Scotland. The black smoke of sooty factory chimneys and the dull red glare of blast furnaces and iron works dotted the Scottish landscape. Into the maw of these dark and throbbing industrial plants poured a never-ending mass of raw material and a never-ending mass of raw humanity, both to be fashioned to the order of the day. The dispossesed Highlander and the impoverished Lowlander, who had fought each other for countless generations, rubbed elbows, swapped tales, and gave jointly of their sweat, blood, and tears to the industrial machine and its masters.

The complexity of the domestic social scene was in itself a problem to tax the best minds of the United Kingdom. But there were then, as there are now, many prophets of doom and disaster, and an all too generous sprinkling of those who wanted to hold on to the past, while reaping the advantages of the present. To use a good old western phrase, England had not one, but two bears by the tail, which were rushing her pell-mell into unknown and unchartered waters. New social and economic classes were in the making; the whole face of the nation was undergoing a thorough overhauling; economic crises, arising out of the rapid dislocation, displacement, and depreciation of labor by machinery popped up in the midst of a trade boom the like of which had never before been known. There was need for a far-seeing statesmanship, based upon a careful analysis of the causes and effects of the agricultural and industrial revolutions.

An era of social, economic, and political reform arose despite the Old Tories, George the Third, and his court clique—an era that was closely tied up with the revolt of the American colonies and their establishment of a free and independent republic. This development gained even more momentum during the early days of the French Revolution. Fox, then one of the political leaders of the British, shouted gleefully as he learned of the fall of the Bastille in Paris, "How much is this the greatest event that ever happened in the world, and how much the best!" Pitt, the Prime Minister, though lacking the exuberance of his colleague, wished the New France well, and hoped for much good to arise from its actions. Meanwhile, he had been busily employed trying to put through Parliament various measures of parliamentary reform, wiping out the "rotten borough" system, destroying the most glaring abuses within Parliament itself and setting the finances of the country in order.

But, as the French Revolution moved forward into high gear,

with the guillotine and the terror in the driver's seat, more and more influential Britons turned from endorsement and applause to condemnation and fear. Their spokesman turned out to be, strangely enough, one of the most brilliant and progressive figures who had graced the floors of Parliament, Edmund Burke. The great social upheaval across the channel was not to his liking. "Whenever a separation is made between liberty and justice, neither is safe," he wrote a few weeks after the fall of the Bastille. Later, when Pitt was still assuring his countrymen of a glorious future for the new French Constitution, Burke cried out in alarm, "The French have shown themselves the ablest architects of ruin who have hitherto existed in the world. In a short space of time they have pulled to the ground their army, their navy, their commerce, their arts, and their manufactures."

Day in, day out, Burke argued the menace of the French Revolution. He forgot the rotten core of the overthrown monarchy; he forgot the misery which had begotten the Revolution; he failed to see a single redeeming feature in the whole affair. Instead, he charged the French with having become the arch foes of religion, justice, and civilization whose success would threaten every other nation with destruction. He called for a holy crusade to wipe out and destroy the whole leadership of the French Republic; and when his fellow Englishmen refused to head his call, he cried bitterly, "The age of chivalry is gone; that of sophisters, economists, and calculators has succeeded, and the glory of Europe is extinguished forever."

But Burke was not to stand alone for long. His speeches, and above all, his *Reflections on the Revolution in France,* published in 1790, gave to British merchants, manufacturers, and landlords the arguments they needed to turn against France, as well as to subdue critics and agitators on the home front who wanted a British counterpart of the French Revolution.

Burke, in his *Reflections,* argued his case well. Social systems and constitutions, he maintained, could not be blue-printed in advance by theorists, nor suddenly called into being by the popular vote of an assembly. They were, instead, an organic growth, no more to be suddenly jammed down the throat of a nation than could the whole past be construed as a stupendous error or imposture to be wiped off the national slate at one fell swoop. Social systems, contended Burke, are organisms of long, slow historic growth, containing within themselves living, dead, and dying matter. That which is live and vital must be preserved and extended; that which is dead or dying, lopped off.

What was taking place in Scotland during all this time?

The first faint evidences of any political awakening in Scotland appeared in 1779 and 1780, when the repeated failure of British troops to quell the rebellious colonies across the Atlantic began to produce what a contemporary Scotch writer, Dr. Somerville, called "a great change in the sentiments of the nation at large," with so much time and attention being given to what was happening overseas that it became "a principal object of conversation in every company, and often excited angry debates which impaired the pleasures of social life, and weakened the confidence of friendship."

But Dr. Somerville, if other chroniclers of the period are to be believed, exaggerated the situation, or judged it by what was happening in his own immediate vicinity. To the mass of the population the long-drawn-out war evoked neither strong approbation nor disapproval, for the simple reason that they were not informed as to what was taking place. Newspapers were few in number, high in price, and were not edited for or meant to be read by the common folk. That highly important factor which we call public opinion was largely non-existent at that time, or at best it concerned itself with what less than one-half of one per cent of the Scotch people thought about social and political problems. How true this statement is can be attested to by the fact that as late as 1788 there were only 2,662 persons allowed to vote in the whole of Scotland. More than three decades passed before that narrow base was slightly broadened.

An acute observer, Mrs. Hamilton, summed up the situation in her native land in 1782: "The people here are not such great politicians as in Ireland. There, politics engross the greatest part of discourse in every county; and man, woman, and child enter as zealously into every debate as if they had been perfectly acquainted with all the hidden springs of government. The people here pretend to no such knowledge, but whatever changes happen, either in ministry or constitution, they seem to adopt the maxim of Mr. Pope, that 'whatever is, is right!'"

Nonetheless there was a slow but steady seepage of political ideas from across the seas as well as from London. At a Glasgow political discussion on support of the Crown in 1784, the *Caledonian Mercury* noted with alarm that "hissing" was heard for the first time at a public gathering in that city. At this time, too, voices were being raised for much-needed burgh and county reforms. Even this effort, small and weak though it be, was applauded as indicating that "the spirit of liberty had taken a northern turn."

The county franchise was based on feudal tenure dating back to 1427. Of the many abuses which crept into the law, the most flagrant was the creation of "Parchment Barons" who as such were given the right to vote. These were friends, lawyers, or vassals retained by the peers and wealthy landholders to give them additional votes. When these fictitious voters were taken into account, the sum total of bona fide voters numbered about one person per thousand of population. Of 2,665 voters in 1790, nearly half, or 1,318, were fictitious.

The men who led the campaign for abating this evil were merchants, manufacturers, professional people, and the Scotch intelligentsia. They read the works of Locke and Hume and Adam Smith; of Benjamin Franklin; of Voltaire, Montesquieu, and the French Encyclopaedists; and they read Tom Paine. Many admitted that "that spirit of civil liberty which had arisen in America was now animating Scotland." But to their opponents, these were wild-eyed reformers only echoing "the ravings of political insanity imported from the republicans of the south."

From Glasgow and Edinburgh the movement spread slowly northward to Stirling, Nairn, Perth, Inverness, Dundee, and Aberdeen. In the latter city, John Ewen and Professor William Ogilvie wrote articles and pamphlets on the burning issues of the day.

Prime Minister Pitt, who at that time was instituting many reforms, introduced a Bill in Parliament in 1785 to widen the basis of representation in England. The preamble to the draft indicated the reform should also be extended to include Edinburgh and Glasgow. Pitt, however, was too far ahead of his followers so they voted him down. Not until the end of the Napoleonic era were such reforms to be written into the law of the land.

The political boss of Scotland during all these years was Henry Dundas. Shrewd enough to turn each ministerial crisis to his advantage, a forceful speaker, a clever organizer and political wire-puller, Dundas soon was able to deliver with unfailing regularity thirty-nine out of the forty-five votes of the Scottish members of Parliament. Like Poo-bah in the Mikado he held a multitude of offices: Lord Advocate, Keeper of the Scottish Signat, Treasurer of the Navy, Home Secretary, Secretary for War, and President of the Board of Control for India. Dundas was willing, at times, to vote for reform measures, providing they didn't loosen his control over Scotland. But, in his own private domain, he was ruthless in the measures he used to quell the slightest sign of revolt against his powers.

Suddenly from across the Channel came strange, startling, and disturbing news.

"That a nation whose characteristic for several centuries has been unconditional submission to slavery should have on a sudden, in the twinkling of an eye, been animated by the boldest spirit of liberty and patriotism, is an event to be contemplated with wonder," editorialized the *Edinburgh Evening Courant* on July 25, 1789. And every other paper and politician echoed its words. Men everywhere sought for news on this amazing French development. Scottish newspapers and magazines were few in number, but every issue was avidly read for accounts of the French Revolution. English papers were imported in great quantities; and the leading clubs and coffee rooms were crowded with anxious readers of the London papers as well as the Gazettes from Ireland, Holland, and France.

The Whigs hailed the achievement. The Reform Burgesses at Aberdeen were among the first to toast the Estates General for its action. Others followed throughout 1789 and 1790. The Address of the Whig Club at Dundee is typical of the period:

The triumph of liberty and reason over despotism, ignorance and superstition is an interesting event to the most distant spectators. But the regeneration of your kingdom is rendered doubly interesting to us inhabitants of Great Britain, for the example of your former abusive government proved in the last century extremely prejudicial to ours. It excited in our princes and their ministers an inordinated desire for power which was often hurtful and sometimes fatal to themselves, but always injurious to the state.

Accept, Sirs, our sincere congratulations on the recovery of your ancient and free constitution and our warmest wishes that liberty may be permanently established in France. We observe for the honour of the age and nation that your renovation has been effected without a civil war, and that neither the superfluous domains of the Prince nor the possessions of the Church have been divided among rapacious subjects but converted to the use of the State to which they belong. That some disturbances and even acts of violence should have attended this great Revolution is in no way surprising: that these have not been more numerous is the wonder of every politician. Our hopes are that your example will be universally followed, and that the flame you have kindled will consume the remains of despotism and bigotry in Europe. . . .

The message proceeded to declare that France and Britain should now be able to work in close co-operation "in promoting the peace and prosperity of the two kingdoms, and in diffusing those blessings through the whole extent of the globe."

Note the self-assurance of these Whigs in their belief that Britain (and especially Scotland) have had the blessings of liberty since the year 1688, as the address concluded: "Our climate is cold and our country mountainous. Yet since public liberty has been restored to us by the Revolution, our cities become daily more populated, our inhabitants more industrious, our mountains less barren, and our whole country more healthy and happy. Our Sovereign, the guardian of our constitution and the father of his people, is almost an object of our adoration, and our nobility and clergy form useful and illustrious members of a state where all are subject to laws."

Burke's *Reflections* certainly had a sobering effect on many early enthusiasts for the French Revolution. But in short order his arguments were replied to by that prince of pamphleteers, Thomas Paine. The first part of Paine's *Rights of Man* appeared in February, 1791, to be followed by the second part a year later.

By what right, asked Paine, does Mr. Burke make this unprovoked attack upon the people of France and their National Assembly, when they have not troubled to interfere with the affairs of England?

Paine accused Burke of having poured forth "in copious fury . . . everything which rancour, prejudice, ignorance or knowledge could suggest." Then, point by point, Paine built his argumentative structure in support of the French Revolution and its Declaration of the Rights of Man. Beyond this he indicated the many real grievances that the British people were still suffering under, and with telling effect suggested the way out of the difficulty by quoting La Fayette's phrase, "For a Nation to be free, it is sufficient that she wills it."

As Scotch interest in things political grew, bitter religious controversies were replaced by discussions of secular matters. Farmers, tradesmen, and even some of the mill-hands began to read newspapers. The *Rights of Man* articulated the grievances of the common people and stirred them to action. Riots occurred in Birmingham in 1791 and were followed a year later by similar action at Aberdeen, Perth, and Edinburgh. The contagion, which Burke had warned about, had crossed the Channel, causing alarm even to Mr. Pitt.

The era of reform was ended.

Once the government had turned its back on the reformers and Francophiles it moved swiftly along the road to repeal many hitherto existing liberties. A proclamation against seditious writings was issued in May, 1792—aimed primarily at Paine's troublemaking pamphlet. But such action led, at least momentarily, to increased popularity. "I know," wrote the editor of a Scotch magazine, "that in a small town in the north of Scotland before the proclamation, there was just *one* copy of Paine's pamphlet; and the bookseller of the place declared three weeks ago that he had since then sold seven hundred and fifty copies of it. And a bookseller in Edinburgh told me that he had before the proclamation a good many copies of it that lay so long on his hand that he would gladly have sold them all at two shillings a copy. He has since then sold the whole of these and many more at three shillings and six pence each."

Dundas was burned in effigy in a score of northern Scotch towns and villages. Toll bars were torn down. Soldiers and guards were stoned. Windows in the Lord Provost's mansion were smashed. There were tumult and rioting from May till late summer; and only the quick use of troops rushed in from England brought the disturbances temporarily under control.

Societies of Friends of the People sprang up everywhere. Slogans heretofore unheard of began to resound through the streets and in the market places. Members of the lower classes, "and even boys," reported the Sheriff of Edinburgh, were heard shouting, "liberty, equality, and no king!" Bells were rung by the mobs surging through the streets, and soon every town and hamlet reported that "Liberty Trees" were being planted by the unruly inhabitants, to be stubbornly defended against attempts by police or "gentlemen" to tear them down. Some of these trees were lit up with lanterns and candles and decorated with apples and other fruit; others bore huge scrolls reading "Liberty, Equality and no Sinecures." Sailors in the port towns of Leith and Aberdeen went on strike, or un-rigged the vessels so they could not sail.

"To all lovers of order," says Henry W. Meikle in his excellent study of the period, "the lower classes in Scotland seemed to be rushing headlong down that path of innovation which in France had led to revolution and finally to the massacres of September. It was in vain, therefore, that the Friends of the People strove to dis-tinguish themselves from those wilder spirits who inevitably accom-pany all popular movements. . . . It was at their meetings that 'those with nothing at stake' had picked up their loose notions of equality and liberty, for among the lowest classes it was commonly understood that these involved an equal distribution of property and exemption from all taxation. . . . The Government, by its re-sistance to all reform, was now reaping the fruit of such a policy. . . ."

In February, 1793, the French government declared war against Great Britain. Two months earlier its Convention had decreed that France would offer the aid of her soldiers to all nations who would strive for freedom; and its President had declared, "All Govern-ments are our enemies; all peoples are our allies."

Meanwhile Scotch enthusiasts and French spies were reporting that Scotland was the Achilles heel of Britain. "The English people," reported one of these agents to the French Convention just before war was declared, "like all conquerors, have long oppressed Scotland and Ireland; but it should be noted that these two nations, always restive, and secretly in revolt against the injustice of the dominating race, have acquired at different epochs concessions which have engendered the hope of ultimately regaining their entire independence." He closed his report on this hopeful note: "Nowhere is more joy caused by your victories than in Scotland."

Still another, Citoyen Pétry, was certain that "if Ministerial influence has reduced to silence nearly all the societies for the rights of the people, the members of which they were composed are still alive. The slightest thing will awaken them from the state of lethargy they appear to be in."

Like other nations in more recent times, the French had completely misjudged the spirit and temper of both the English and the Scotch. For the preceding two years in both these countries an ardent war party had been gathering strength. Pitt, with all his adroitness and eloquence, could not stem it. When, at last, the war began, frenzy and alarm swept over the nation. The partisans of Reform and Republicanism became outcasts. All who spoke with calm or moderation about France became forthwith the target of abuse or suspicion.

Tom Paine was convicted of seditious writing. Fox's motion for the removal of certain disabilities for the Dissenters was defeated; and a bill for the abolition of the chattel slave trade was pigeonholed and forgotten. A motion for parliamentary reform was defeated 294 to 105; but the Alien Act, providing for the supervision and (if necessary) removal of aliens from the United Kingdom was passed by an overwhelming majority. The Traitorous Correspondence Act was also quickly enacted. And in 1794 the Habeas Corpus Act was suspended. Green in his *History of the English People,* tells of the results which followed: "Prosecution after prosecution was directed against the Press; the sermons of some dissenting ministers were indicted as seditious; and the conventions of sympathizers with France were roughly broken up. The worst excesses of the panic were witnessed in Scotland, where young Whigs, whose only offence was an advocacy of Parliamentary reform, were sentenced to transportation, and where a brutal judge openly expressed his regret that the practice of torture in seditious cases should have fallen into disuse."

Scotland did indeed feel the full fury of the attack. Snoopers and informers infested every gathering place. Organized bands of rowdies searched out and terrorized the reformers. Troops were everywhere. Judges meted out severe sentences, often upon the slightest evidence. And the clergy, which had been temporarily in eclipse, redeemed itself in the eyes of the ruling class by a continual barrage of sermons based on texts such as: "Fear God and honour the King," "My son, meddle not with those that are given to change," "Who is like unto thee, O people, saved by the Lord?"

Most important of all the trials was that of Thomas Muir who was charged with (1) exciting disaffection by seditious speeches, (2) circulating Paine's *Rights of Man* and other seditious works, and (3) of reading and defending the Address of the United Irishmen in the first General Convention of the Friends of the People.

With a packed jury and a war-mad and hysterical nation behind him, Dundas had no difficulty in convicting this trouble-maker. Muir, himself, in a long address to the jury pleaded guilty to one offense only—and that was not stated in the indictment—the advocacy of parliamentary reform.

But Lord Justice Braxfield in charging the jury made this out to be a crime, too, leaving them to judge "whether it was perfectly innocent or not for Mr. Muir, at such a time, to go among ignorant country people, and among the lower classes of the people, making them leave off their work, and inducing them to believe that a reform was absolutely necessary to preserve their safety and their liberty, which, had it not been for him, they would never have suspected to have been in danger."

Braxfield went on to sum up the position of the ruling class: "A government in every country should be just like a corporation; and, in this country, it is made up of the landed interest, which alone has a right to be represented. As for the rabble, who have nothing but personal property, what hold has the nation on them? What security for the payment of their taxes? They may pack up all their property on their backs, and leave the country in the twinkling of an eye. But landed property cannot be removed."

For his crime Thomas Muir was sentenced to transportation to Botany Bay, Australia, for fourteen years. A month later, another reformer drew a seven-year sentence to the same hell-hole.

Prices were rising, food became scarce, factories multiplied, the war went on, and the reformers, soured in their attempts for social betterment, kept their mouths shut, or functioned in small groups, keeping alive the principles of Liberty, Equality, and Fraternity till a happier and more auspicious time would come.

The war with France which lasted for twenty-one years, broken only by two short periods of peace, ended with the Battle of Waterloo.

The condition of the British army when it entered the war in 1793 was highly reminiscent of what took place in the fall of 1939. Twenty thousand British and ten thousand Hanoverian troops were sent to reinforce the Allies in the Low Countries under the leadership of the Duke of York, who was described at the time as "a royal prince, whose stupidity as a man is only equalled by his ignorance as a general." Lord Grenville declared, "We have no General, but some old woman in a red riband."

The troops themselves were bad for, since the close of the American war, the army had sunk into a wretched condition. "Lax in its discipline, entirely without system, and very weak in numbers. . . . There was no uniformity of drill or movement, professional pride was rare, professional knowledge still more so."

The soldiers were either too young or too old—and though they fought bravely, they were unable to withstand the savage energy of the French. Within less than a year, the whole British force had been chased out of Holland. The French forces seemed unbeatable and rolled steadily on from victory to victory over their neighbors. The generalship of the French army was superb, its morale high, and the whole nation was imbued with the feeling that it was spreading the doctrines of the French Revolution to the far corners of Europe.

Even after Napoleon had proclaimed himself First Consul as well as Emperor, he fortified the French morale with a vision of the rottenness and decay in the enemy governments and the contrasting virility of the new social order set into motion by the French Revolution.

With all of Europe rapidly giving way before the seemingly all-powerful French, the British fought on although they too continued to suffer defeat after defeat. Their first significant victory on land was won March 21, 1801, at Alexandria, Egypt, under Sir Ralph Abercrombie, Britain's best professional soldier. From the point of view of numbers involved—a mere twelve thousand on each side— the engagement was insignificant. From the point of view of moral effect, the results were tremendous, for they proved to the world that there were still troops in Europe which could beat the French in a fair and open fight.

The cost of the war to Britain was enormous. Not only was it necessary to build up gigantic armies and navies, Britain had to become, as well, the paymaster and the arsenal for the numerous allied armies in the field during the long years of war. The public debt mounted to what seemed astronomical figures, in a few short years. New and hitherto undreamt-of methods of taxation had to be devised. In 1797, the monetary crisis became so great that the government authorized the Bank of England to suspend all cash payments. The following year, 1798, the government placed an income tax of ten per cent on all incomes over two hundred pounds.

Out of the long war also came numerous changes in manners and morals. The upper-class Briton, forced to abstain from foreign travel during the war years, frequented the newly established seaside resorts and indulged in sea bathing. There was a shortage of food and the scarcity of flour led to dietary changes for both rich and poor. "The rich were recommended to make no soups or gravies, to take only the prime cut, and leave the others that the poor might buy them. The poor were taught to make soup and rice pudding." Thus was given the first big impetus to the use of rice among the British people.

The high price and limited supply of flour also brought about a complete change in the personal appearance of both sexes. Men ceased to wear powdered wigs and women no longer wore powdered "heads." Although in pre-war Britain only the lower classes allowed their natural hair to be seen, "patriotism" and the high price of flour soon extended this practice to the upper classes.

Knee breeches, for so many generations the very height of fashion, crept downward to become pantaloons which were buttoned or tied below the knee. Shortly after the outbreak of the war, they had lengthened to the ankle, and within a few short years, the full-length trouser had become the correct fashion for all gentlemen. The shoe buckle, too, went out of style, to the dismay of the Birmingham buckle workers. It was replaced by what was sometimes scornfully called "the unmanly shoestring." Swords were no longer worn in Parliament, and soon ceased to be worn at social gatherings except by military officers. Before the war had ended, the plebeian umbrella came into its own. Shirt ruffles and hose for men were discarded, and the well-known three-cornered hat was replaced at the turn of the century by the one generally designated as the sugar loaf.

Morals, too, tightened up during the war. Promenades and masquerades which had once been so fashionable among the wealthy were frowned upon. Operas were dispensed with as unnecessary, costly foreign importations. General sentiment against gambling spread, and the newly inaugurated Sunday School movement established a firm foothold.

Scottish society aped British society with the result that the changes in manners and morals of the British spread northward, usually from three to five years after taking hold in London.

But, particularly in Scotland, perhaps the most significant transformation wrought during the war, was cultural. There was a rapid growth of journals and periodicals. In 1782, there existed in all of Scotland only eight small newspapers. Eight years later, the number had increased to twenty-seven. And the next decade saw even that number doubled. Edinburgh was becoming the great center of periodical literature, with no less than ten periodicals being published there in 1792. The country seemed suddenly filled with poets, philosophers, journalists, and writers on political and economic subjects. Byron, Burns, and Scott were but three of the new and potent figures who were soon to make Scotland and its people better understood and respected by native and Englishman alike.

Postscript
and
Acknowledgments

To JOURNALISTS everywhere, and to most of the literate adults in and about New York, the *Herald Tribune* is noted for its splendid format, its excellent news-coverage, its superb book section, and its intelligent conservatism. In origin it stems from the *Tribune* which Horace Greeley founded in 1841. In the 101 years of its existence it has had only three editors: Horace Greeley (1841-1872); Whitelaw Reid (1872-1913) and Ogden M. Reid (1913-   ).

The *New York Herald,* founded in 1835 by James Gordon Bennett, Senior, remained in the hands of his family until two years after the death of his son, James Gordon Bennett, Junior, in 1918.

Frank A. Munsey purchased the *Herald* and the *Telegram* (founded by James Gordon Bennett, Junior) from the Bennett estate for four million dollars in January, 1920.

The *Herald* was merged with the *Sun* which Munsey had acquired at an earlier date. The *Telegram* was sold to the Scripps-Howard chain in 1926, which shortly thereafter acquired Pulitzer's *World* and merged the two into the *World-Telegram.*

The elder Bennett's will provided that the name *"New York Herald"* should always stand, so when the merger with the *Sun* took place, it was the *Sun's* name which disappeared from the masthead.

In March, 1924, Munsey sold the *Herald* to Mrs. Whitelaw Reid for five million dollars. It was then consolidated with the *Tribune,* and thus the *Herald's* name was incorporated with that of its long-time rival. The shades of the respective founders of these two sheets—bitterest of enemies in life—must have smiled at the irony of the situation. Their newspaper creations were the greatest rivals in American newspaper history. Now these were united in life, even as James Gordon Bennett and Horace Greeley were united in death. But stranger still was the fact that the *Herald-Tribune* bore little or no resemblance to either the *Herald* or the *Tribune* of its founders. Gone was the imper-

419

tinence, the flippancy, the hair-raising sensationalism of Bennett's *Herald*. Gone, too, was the "Cause journalism" of Greeley, fighting for Abolitionism, Agrarianism, Socialism, Trade Unionism, Vegetarianism, and all the other Isms.

My interest in the rise and development of American journalism began a good many years ago. But it was not until I began the research work on Albert Brisbane in preparation of my biography of Arthur Brisbane that I delved deeply into the lives of the great newspapermen of the 1830's and 1840's.

The more I probed, the more firmly I became convinced that James Gordon Bennett, the founder of the *New York Herald,* was the greatest single generator of journalistic progress in this country, if not in the world.

Of this most potent figure there were but two biographies extant: that of Isaac Pray, published in 1855, and that of Don C. Seitz, published in 1928.

Isaac Pray was a contemporary of James Gordon Bennett. His admiration for Bennett was unqualified. Although Pray's work contains excellent factual material, it was published sixteen years before Bennett's career ended. Due not only to its personal bias, but also to the time in which it was written, it lacks a correct evaluation of Bennett's place in the field of American journalism.

The sketchy character of Seitz's work gives a very incomplete picture of the man who founded the *Herald*.

James Gordon Bennett lived in a period which, excepting the current one, was perhaps the most vital in American history. It was during his time, and with his help, that the traditions of the newspapers of today were forged.

It is my belief that a more complete presentation, and a new evaluation of James Gordon Bennett and his activities, will help both layman and newsman to understand and appreciate better the fundamental character of one of the most vital institutions in our society—The American Newspaper.

To comprehend the social, religious, political, and economic forces which shaped Bennett's character and environment, I have had to undergo a self-imposed seminar on Scotch history. The results are embodied in "Scotland in the Napoleonic Era," which is published as an appendix to the book, but which was originally intended as its opening chapter.

While a great many books were consulted in the preparation of the manuscript, the bulk of the material was gained from a careful combing of old newspaper files of the *New York Herald,* its immediate predecessors, and its contemporaries.

Help and suggestions were received from a great many friends during the time that this book was in preparation; and to each and all I express my deep appreciation. Many thanks are also due to the staff of the New York University School of Journalism for their generous assistance; as well as to the New York Public Library; the Los Angeles Public Library; the Huntington Library; and the Library of Congress. And to my publishers I must express my gratitude for the manner in which they have borne with me while the manuscript was in preparation.

Finally, my thanks are due to publishers and others for special permission to quote from several books as follows:

To Harcourt, Brace and Company, Inc., for permission to quote a passage from Carl Sandburg's *Abraham Lincoln: The Prairie Years,* and for permission to quote a selection from Vernon L. Parrington's *Main Currents in American Thought;*

To Alfred A. Knopf, Inc., for permission to use a passage from Herbert Asbury's *The Gangs of New York,* and for permission to use several quotations from Isaac Goldberg's *Major Noah, American-Jewish Pioneer;*

To Little, Brown & Company, for permission to use two excerpts from William A. Croffut's *An American Procession;*

And to Oswald Garrison Villard for permission to use quotations from the *Memoirs of Henry Villard.*

Bibliography

Part 1 and Appendix:
Beer, Max: A History of British Socialism, Vol. 1, London, 1919.
—— Social Struggles and Thought, Boston, 1925.
Bellesheim, A.: History of the Catholic Church in Scotland, Edinburgh, 1887.
Bogart and Thompson: Readings in Economic History of the United States, New York, 1924.
Boswell, James: Life of Samuel Johnson, New York, 1932.
Bristed, John: America and Her Resources, London, 1818.
Buckle, Henry Thomas: History of Civilization in England, Vol. 1, New York, 1895.
Burke, Edmund: Reflections, London, 1891.
Burns, Robert: Complete Poetical Works, New York, 1900.
Byron, Lord George: Poems and Dramas, New York, 1894.
Carlyle, Thomas: The French Revolution, London, 1902.
The Catholic Encyclopaedia, New York, 1940.
Cheney, Edward P.: Short History of England, New York, 1920.
Cobbett, William: Tour in Scotland, London, 1833.
Cockburn, Lord: Memoirs of His Times, Edinburgh, 1875.
—— Life of Jeffrey, Edinburgh, 1852.
Craik, H.: A Century of Scottish History, 1745-1845, Edinburgh, 1901.
Cunningham, J.: Church History of Scotland, 2 vols., Edinburgh, 1859.
Cunningham, W.: The Growth of English Industry and Commerce, Vol. 3, Cambridge, England, 1925.
The Dictionary of National Biography, London, 1887.
Ensor, George: An Inquiry Concerning the Population of Nations, London, 1818.
Franklin, Benjamin: Autobiography of Benjamin Franklin, Edinburgh, 1818.
Gibbons, H. de B.: Industry in England, New York, 1912.
Graham, H. Grey: Scottish Men of Letters in the Eighteenth Century, London, 1901.
—— Social Life in Scotland in the Eighteenth Century, London, 1906.

Graham, Walter: English Literary Periodicals, New York, 1930.

Grant, James: History of the Burgh and Parish Schools of Scotland, Glasgow, 1876.

Green, J. R.: A Short History of the English People, New York, 1898.

Hammond, J. L. and Barbara: The Village Laborer, 1760-1832, London, 1919.

—— The Skilled Laborer, 1760-1832, London, 1920.

—— The Town Laborer, 1760-1832, London, 1920.

Hayes, Carleton J. H.: A Political and Social History of Modern Europe, New York, 1930.

Heron, R.: Observations Made in a Journey Through the Western Counties of Scotland in the Autumn of 1792, Perth, 1799.

Hume, David: Treatise on Human Nature, London, 1824.

Mathieson, W. L.: The Awakening of Scotland, 1747-1797, Glasgow, 1910.

Meikle, Henry W.: Scotland and the French Revolution, Glasgow, 1912.

Morley, J. Burke: A Historical Study, London, 1867.

Paine, Thomas: The Writings of Thomas Paine, New York, 1938.

Pray, Isaac C.: Memoirs of James Gordon Bennett, New York, 1855.

Rae, J.: Life of Adam Smith, London, 1895.

Ramsey, Dean: Reminiscences of Scottish Life and Character, Edinburgh, 1911.

Reid, Thomas: Inquiry into the Human Mind, Edinburgh, 1800.

Rogers, Charles: Social Life in Scotland, 3 vols., Edinburgh, 1884.

Schevill, Ferdinand: A History of Europe from the Reformation to Our Own Day, New York, 1925.

Scott, Sir Walter: Waverly, New York, 1894.

—— Complete Poetical Works, New York, 1894.

Smith, Adam: Wealth of Nations, Glasgow, 1776.

Watt, Francis: The Book of Edinburgh Anecdote, New York, 1913.

Parts II, III, IV, and V:

Adams, John Quincy: The Lives of James Madison and James Monroe, Buffalo, 1850.

—— Diary of John Quincy Adams: 1794-1845, Philadelphia, 1875.

Andrews, G. H.: Sketches of Men of Progress, New York, 1871.

Anonymous: Life of James Gordon Bennett, New York, 1844 (Pamphlet).

Asbury, Herbert: The Gangs of New York, New York, 1928.

Atkins, John B.: The Life of Sir William Howard Russell, the First Special Correspondent, 2 vols., London, 1911.

Bassett, John Spencer: Life of Andrew Jackson, New York, 1916.

Beard, Charles: American Government and Politics, New York, 1928.

—— Economic Origins of Jeffersonian Democracy, New York, 1918.

Beard, Charles and Mary: Rise of American Civilization, New York, 1933.

Benton, Thomas H.: Thirty Years' View, 2 vols., New York, 1858.

Bigelow, John: William Cullen Bryant, Boston, 1897.

Blaney, H. R.: Old Boston, Boston, 1896.

Bleyer, Willard G.: The Profession of Journalism, Boston, 1918.

—— Main Currents in the History of American Journalism, Boston, 1927.

Bogart, E. L., and Thompson, Charles M.: Readings in the Economic History of the United States, New York, 1924.

Bourne, H. R. F.: English Newspapers, 2 vols., London, 1887.

Brooks, Van Wyck, The Flowering of New England, New York, 1936.

Browne, James Henri: The Great Metropolis: A Mirror of New York, Hartford, 1869.

Bryan, Wilhelmus B.: A History of the National Capital, 2 vols., New York, 1916.

Buckingham, Joseph T.: Specimens of Newspaper Literature, 2 vols., Boston, 1850.

Bullard, Lauriston: Famous War Correspondents, Boston, 1914.

Bungay, George W.: Off-hand Takings, New York, 1854.

Burgess, John W.: The Middle Period: 1817-1858, New York, 1897.

Carlson, Oliver: Brisbane: A Candid Biography, New York, 1937.

Clemens, Samuel L.: Mark Twain's Autobiography, New York, 1924.

Cobbett, William: Porcupine's Works, 12 vols., London, 1801.

Coleman, Albert E.: New and Authentic History of the Herald of the Bennetts, Editor & Publisher, Vols. 56-58, 1924-25.

Congdon, Charles T.: Reminiscences of a Journalist, Boston, 1880.

Crawford, Mary C.: Romantic Days in Old Boston, Boston, 1910.

—— Old Boston Days and Ways, Boston, 1909.

Croffut, William A.: An American Procession, Boston, 1932.

Davis, Elmer: History of the New York Times, 2 vols., New York, 1921.

Davis, Jefferson: The Rise and Fall of the Confederate Government, 2 vols., New York, 1881.

Dawson, Henry B.: The Federalist, 2 vols., New York, 1863.

De Toqueville, Alexis: Democracy in America, New York, 1900.

Dictionary of American Biography.

Dodd, William Edward: Jefferson Davis, Philadelphia, 1907.

Ely, Margaret: Some Great American Newspaper Editors, New York, 1916.

Fahrney, Ralph Ray: Horace Greeley and the Tribune in the Civil War, Cedar Rapids, 1936.

Faulkner, Harold Underwood: American Economic History, New York, 1924.

Fields, Mrs. James T.: Memories of a Hostess, New York, 1922.

Finley, Ruth E.: The Lady of Godey's: Sarah Josepha Hale, Philadelphia, 1931.

Forster, John: Life of Charles Dickens, Philadelphia, 1920.

Gramling, Oliver: AP—The Story of News, New York, 1940.

Greeley, Horace: Recollections of a Busy Life, New York, 1868.

Hart, Albert Bushnell: Formation of the Union; 1750-1829, New York, 1926.

Headley, J. T.: The Great Riots of New York, New York, 1873.

Herndon, William H., and Week, Jessie W.: Abraham Lincoln: The True Story of a Great Life, New York, 1892.

Hudson, Frederic: Journalism in the United States, New York, 1873.

Hughes, Rev. Dr.: A Letter on Moral Causes That Have Produced the Evil Spirit of the Times, New York, 1844 (Pamphlet).

Hunt, Gaillard: Life in America One Hundred Years Ago, New York, 1914.

Huse, Charles P.: Financial History of Boston, 1822-1909, Boston, 1916.

James, Marquis: The Life of Andrew Jackson, Indianapolis, 1937.

Jefferson, Thomas: Writings of Thomas Jefferson, P. L. Ford ed., Vol. IX.

Koren, John: Boston: 1822-1922, Boston, 1923.

Lee, James Melvin: History of American Journalism, Boston, 1917.

Leach, Margaret: Reveille in Washington, New York, 1941.

Maverick, Augustus: Henry J. Raymond and the New York Press, Hartford, Conn., 1870.

Minnigerode, Meade: The Fabulous Forties, New York, 1924.

Mitchell, Edward P.: Memoirs of an Editor, New York, 1924.

Moore, Albert B.: Conscription and Conflict in the Confederacy, New York, 1924.

Myers, Gustavus: History of Great American Fortunes, New York, 1937.

—— History of Tammany Hall, New York, 1917.

McMasters, John Bach: History of the People of the United States from the Revolution to the Civil War, 8 vols., New York, 1883-1913.

Nevins, Allan: The Evening Post: A Century of Journalism, New York, 1922.

—— American Press Opinion, Boston, 1928.

O'Brien, Frank M.: The Story of the Sun, New York, 1918.

Payne, George H.: History of Journalism in the United States, New York, 1920.

Parrington, Vernon L.: Main Currents in American Thought, 3 vols., New York, 1930.

Parton, James: Life of Horace Greeley, New York, 1854.

—— Famous Americans of Recent Times, Boston, 1867.

—— Men of Progress, New York, 1870.

Pendleton, John: Newspaper Reporting in Olden Times and Today, London, 1890.

Pray, Isaac C.: Memoirs of a Journalist, New York, 1855.

Redpath, James: The Public Life of Captain John Brown, Boston, 1860.

Reid, Whitelaw: Horace Greeley, New York, 1879.

Richardson, Lyon N.: A History of Early American Magazines, New York, 1931.

Sandburg, Carl: Abraham Lincoln: The War Years, 4 vols., New York, 1939.

Scott, James R. A.: The Influence of the Press, London, 1913.

Seitz, Don C.: Life of Horace Greeley, Indianapolis, 1926.

—— The James Gordon Bennetts, Indianapolis, 1928.

Shepard, Edward M.: Martin Van Buren, Boston, 1900.

Stanley, Sir Henry Morton: How I Found Livingstone, Boston, 1872.

—— Autobiography of Sir Henry Morton Stanley, Boston, 1937.

Stephens, Alexander H.: A Constitutional View of the Late War Between the States, Vols. 1 and 2, Philadelphia, 1868.

Stone, Candace: Dana and the Sun, New York, 1938.

Thiving, Annie H.: Crooked and Narrow Streets of Boston, Boston, 1920.

Thomas, Isaiah: History of Printing in America, 2 vols., Albany, 1874.

Villard, Henry: Memoirs of Henry Villard, Journalist and Editor, 2 vols., Boston, 1904.

Villard, Oswald Garrison: Some Newspapers and Newspaper Men, New York, 1923.

Warren, Robert Penn: John Brown, New York, 1929.

Webb, J. W.: Reminiscences of General Samuel B. Webb, New York, 1882.

Weed, Thurlow: Life of Thurlow Weed, 2 vols., Boston, 1883.

Welles, Gideon: Diary of Gideon Welles, Boston, 1909.

—— Horace Greeley, New York, 1879.

Werner, M. R.: Barnum, New York, 1926.

Wilson, Henry: History of the Rise and Fall of the Slave Power in America, 3 vols., New York, 1874-77.

Wilson, James H.: The Life of Charles A. Dana, New York, 1907.

Wilson, Woodrow: A History of the American People, 5 vols., New York, 1902.

—— Division and Reunion: 1829-1889, New York, 1921.

Young, John Russell: Men and Memories, New York, 1907.

Periodicals and Newspapers:

PERIODICALS

Eclectic Magazine, 1845-51.

Godey's Lady's Book, 1850-54.

Graham's Magazine, 1840-55.
Harper's Weekly Magazine, 1857-66.
Ladies Repository, 1860-61.
North American Review, April, 1866.

NEWSPAPERS

Charleston Courier, 1823.
New York Courier, 1826-28.
New York Courier and Enquirer, 1829-42.
New York Daily Tribune, 1841-65.
New York Enquirer, 1827-28.
New York Evening Post, 1836-65.
New York Herald, 1835-65.
New York Sun, 1833-48.
New York Times, 1851-65.
New York World, 1860-65.

Index